School Rumble

13

Jin Kobayashi

TRANSLATED AND ADAPTED BY
William Flanagan

LETTERED BY
HudsonYards

BALLANTINE BOOKS ● NEW YORK

A Del Rey Manga/Kodansha Trade Paperback Original

School Rumble volume 13 copyright © 2006 by Jin Kobayashi
English translation copyright © 2009 by Jin Kobayashi

Published in the United States by Del Rey Books, an imprint of The Random House Publishing Group, a division of Random House, Inc., New York.

DEL REY is a registered trademark and the Del Rey colophon is a trademark of Random House, Inc.

Publication rights arranged through Kodansha Ltd.

First published in Japan in 2006 by Kodansha Ltd., Tokyo

ISBN 978-0-345-50564-4

Printed in the United States of America

www.delreymanga.com

9 8 7 6 5 4 3 2 1

Translator and adapter: William Flanagan
Lettering: HudsonYards
Cover Design: David Stevenson

Honorifics Explained

Throughout the Del Rey Manga books, you will find Japanese honorifics left intact in the translations. For those not familiar with how the Japanese use honorifics and, more important, how they differ from American honorifics, we present this brief overview.

Politeness has always been a critical facet of Japanese culture. Ever since the feudal era, when Japan was a highly stratified society, use of honorifics—which can be defined as polite speech that indicates relationship or status—has played an essential role in the Japanese language. When addressing someone in Japanese, an honorific usually takes the form of a suffix attached to one's name (example: "Asuna-san"), is used as a title at the end of one's name, or appears in place of the name itself (example: "Negi-sensei," or simply "Sensei!").

Honorifics can be expressions of respect or endearment. In the context of manga and anime, honorifics give insight into the nature of the relationship between characters. Many English translations leave out these important honorifics and therefore distort the feel of the original Japanese. Because Japanese honorifics contain nuances that English honorifics lack, it is our policy at Del Rey not to translate them. Here, instead, is a guide to some of the honorifics you may encounter in Del Rey Manga.

-san: This is the most common honorific and is equivalent to Mr., Miss, Ms., or Mrs. It is the all-purpose honorific and can be used in any situation where politeness is required.

-sama: This is one level higher than "-san" and is used to confer great respect.

-dono: This comes from the word "tono," which means "lord." It is an even higher level than "-sama" and confers utmost respect.

-kun: This suffix is used at the end of boys' names to express familiarity or endearment. It is also sometimes used by men among friends, or when addressing someone younger or of a lower station.

-*chan*: This is used to express endearment, mostly toward girls. It is also used for little boys, pets, and even among lovers. It gives a sense of childish cuteness.

Bozu: This is an informal way to refer to a boy, similar to the English terms "kid" and "squirt."

Sempai/Senpai: This title suggests that the addressee is one's senior in a group or organization. It is most often used in a school setting, where underclassmen refer to their upperclassmen as "sempai." It can also be used in the workplace, such as when a newer employee addresses an employee who has seniority in the company.

Kohai: This is the opposite of "sempai" and is used toward underclassmen in school or newcomers in the workplace. It connotes that the addressee is of a lower station.

Sensei: Literally meaning "one who has come before," this title is used for teachers, doctors, or masters of any profession or art.

Onee-san/Onii-san: Normally older siblings are not called by name but rather by the title of older sister (*Onee-san*) or older brother (*Onii-san*). Depending on the relationship, "-chan" or "-sama" can also be used instead of "-san." However, this honorific can also be used with someone unrelated when the relationship resembles that of siblings.

Obaa-san/Ojii-san: Japanese grandparents are called by their titles rather than by name. Grandmothers are called "Obaa-san" (or "Obaa-sama" to imply added respect and distance, or "Obaa-chan" for more intimacy). Likewise grandfathers are called "Ojii-san," "Ojii-sama," or "Ojii-chan."

-*[blank]*: This is usually forgotten in these lists, but it is perhaps the most significant difference between Japanese and English. The lack of honorific means that the speaker has permission to address the person in a very intimate way. Usually, only family, spouses, or very close friends have this kind of permission. Known as *yobisute*, it can be gratifying when someone who has earned the intimacy starts to call one by one's name without an honorific. But when that intimacy hasn't been earned, it can be very insulting.

Cultural Note

To preserve some of the humor found in *School Rumble*, we have elected to keep Japanese names in their original Japanese order—that is to say, with the family name first, followed by the personal name. So when you hear the name Tsukamoto Tenma, Tenma is just one member of the Tsukamoto family.

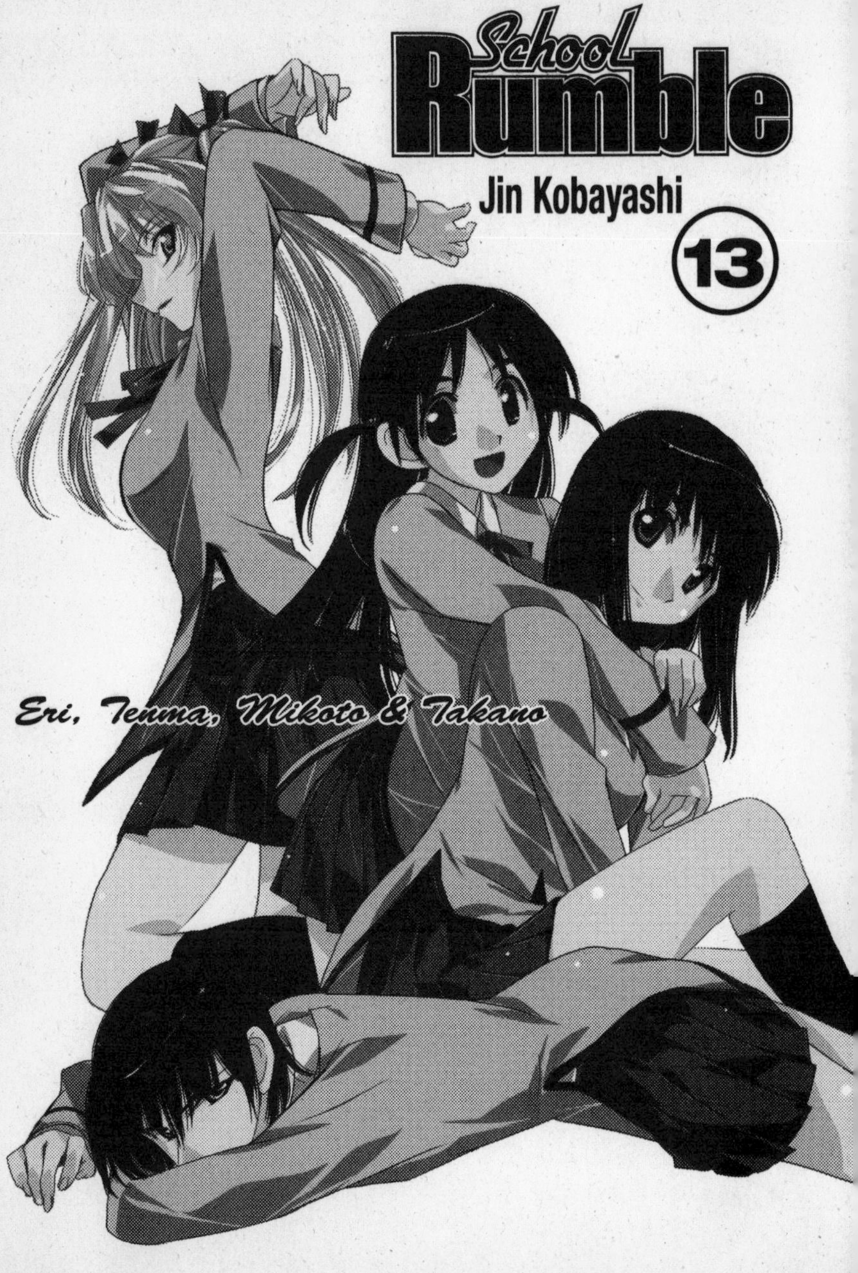
School Rumble
Jin Kobayashi
13
Eri, Tenma, Mikoto & Takano

Contents

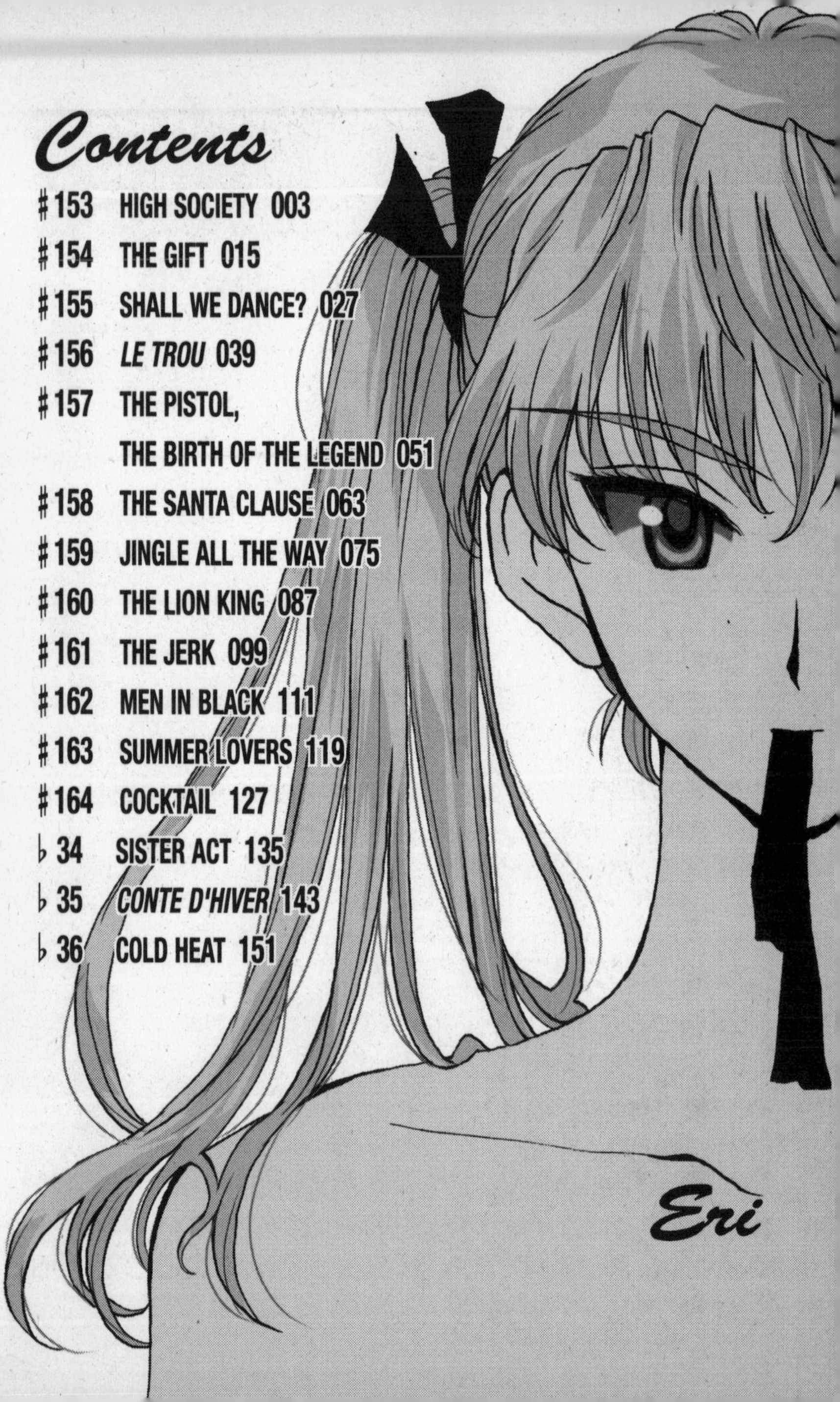

Eri

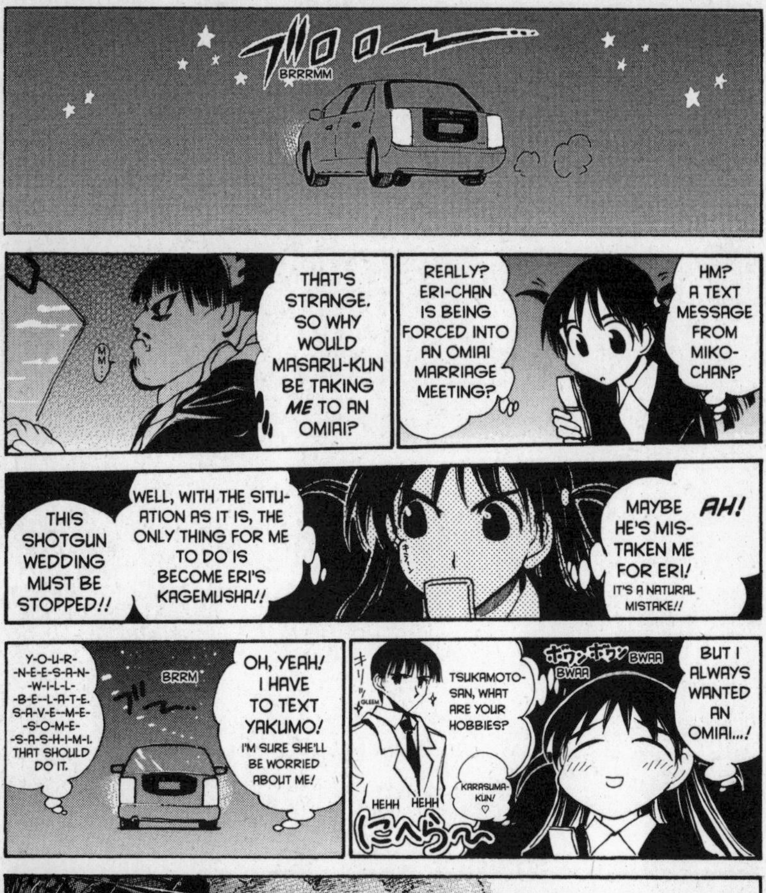
BRRRMM
HM? A TEXT MESSAGE FROM MIKO-CHAN?
REALLY? ERI-CHAN IS BEING FORCED INTO AN OMIAI MARRIAGE MEETING?
MM...
THAT'S STRANGE. SO WHY WOULD MASARU-KUN BE TAKING *ME* TO AN OMIAI?
AH!
MAYBE HE'S MISTAKEN ME FOR ERI! IT'S A NATURAL MISTAKE!!
WELL, WITH THE SITUATION AS IT IS, THE ONLY THING FOR ME TO DO IS BECOME ERI'S KAGEMUSHA!!
THIS SHOTGUN WEDDING MUST BE STOPPED!!
BUT I ALWAYS WANTED AN OMIAI...!
BWAA BWAA
TSUKAMOTO-SAN, WHAT ARE YOUR HOBBIES?
GLEEM
KARASUMA-KUN! ♡
HEHH HEHH
OH, YEAH! I HAVE TO TEXT YAKUMO! I'M SURE SHE'LL BE WORRIED ABOUT ME!
BRRM
Y-O-U-R-N-E-E-S-A-N-W-I-L-L-B-E--L-A-T-E. S-A-V-E--M-E-S-O-M-E-S-A-S-H-I-M-I. THAT SHOULD DO IT.

#153 HIGH SOCIETY

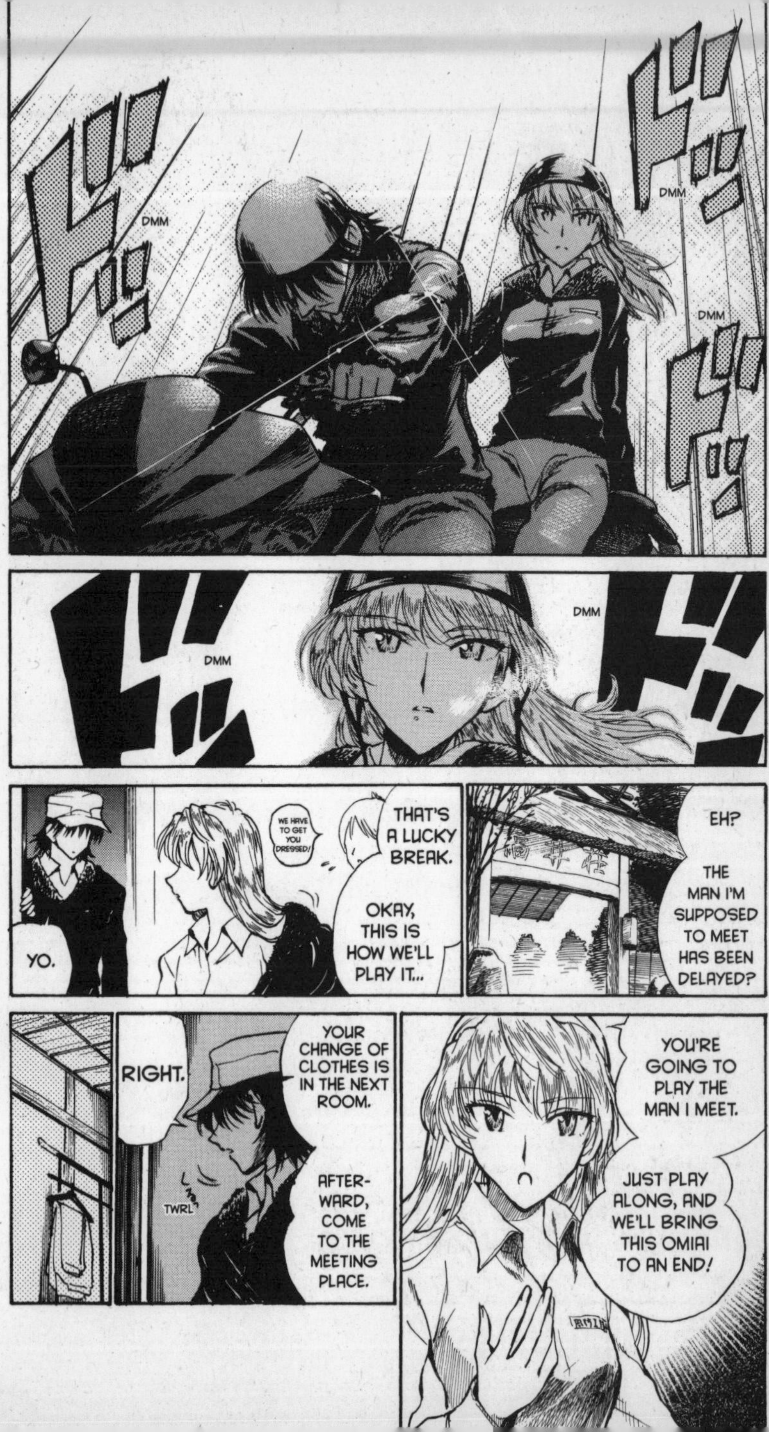
DMM
DMM
DMM
DMM
DMM
EH?
THE MAN I'M SUPPOSED TO MEET HAS BEEN DELAYED?
THAT'S A LUCKY BREAK.
OKAY, THIS IS HOW WE'LL PLAY IT...
WE HAVE TO GET YOU DRESSED!
YO.
YOU'RE GOING TO PLAY THE MAN I MEET.
JUST PLAY ALONG, AND WE'LL BRING THIS OMIAI TO AN END!
YOUR CHANGE OF CLOTHES IS IN THE NEXT ROOM.
RIGHT.
AFTER-WARD, COME TO THE MEETING PLACE.
TWRL
Having Spent the Night Together, Sawachika and Mr. Worker Arrive.

The Kagemusha Has Also Arrived.

STILL...

...I'M IN HER DEBT FOR TENMA'S BIRTHDAY. THIS SHOULD MAKE US EVEN.

TMP
スタ
スタ
TMP

I'M WAY TOO NICE A GUY.

OH, MAN!

ズ000 SST

JUST LIKE HER. SHE ISN'T HERE YET...

松乃間
PINE MATSU
ROOM NO MA

..... SO THIS IS THE PLACE...

LEMME... LET ME INTRO-DUCE MYSELF. I AM SAWA-CHIKA ERI!!!

GLEEM

MY, HOW LONG I'VE WAITED.

VERY NICE TO MEET YOU.

I HAVE COME BEARING OUR MARRIAGE CONTRACT.

NOW LET IT BEGIN!

BISHINNG

GWMM

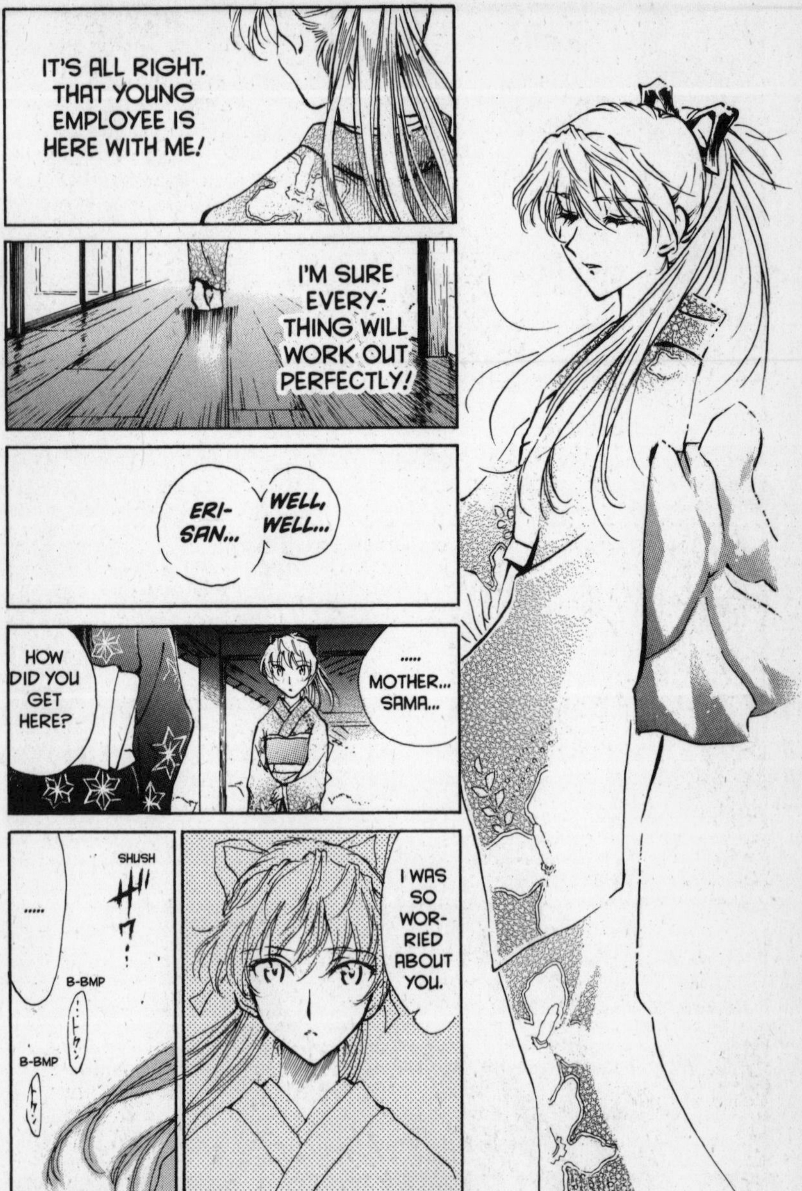
IT'S ALL RIGHT. THAT YOUNG EMPLOYEE IS HERE WITH ME!
I'M SURE EVERY-THING WILL WORK OUT PERFECTLY!
WELL, WELL...
ERI-SAN...
..... MOTHER... SAMA...
HOW DID YOU GET HERE?
I WAS SO WOR-RIED ABOUT YOU.
SHUSH
.....
B-BMP
B-BMP

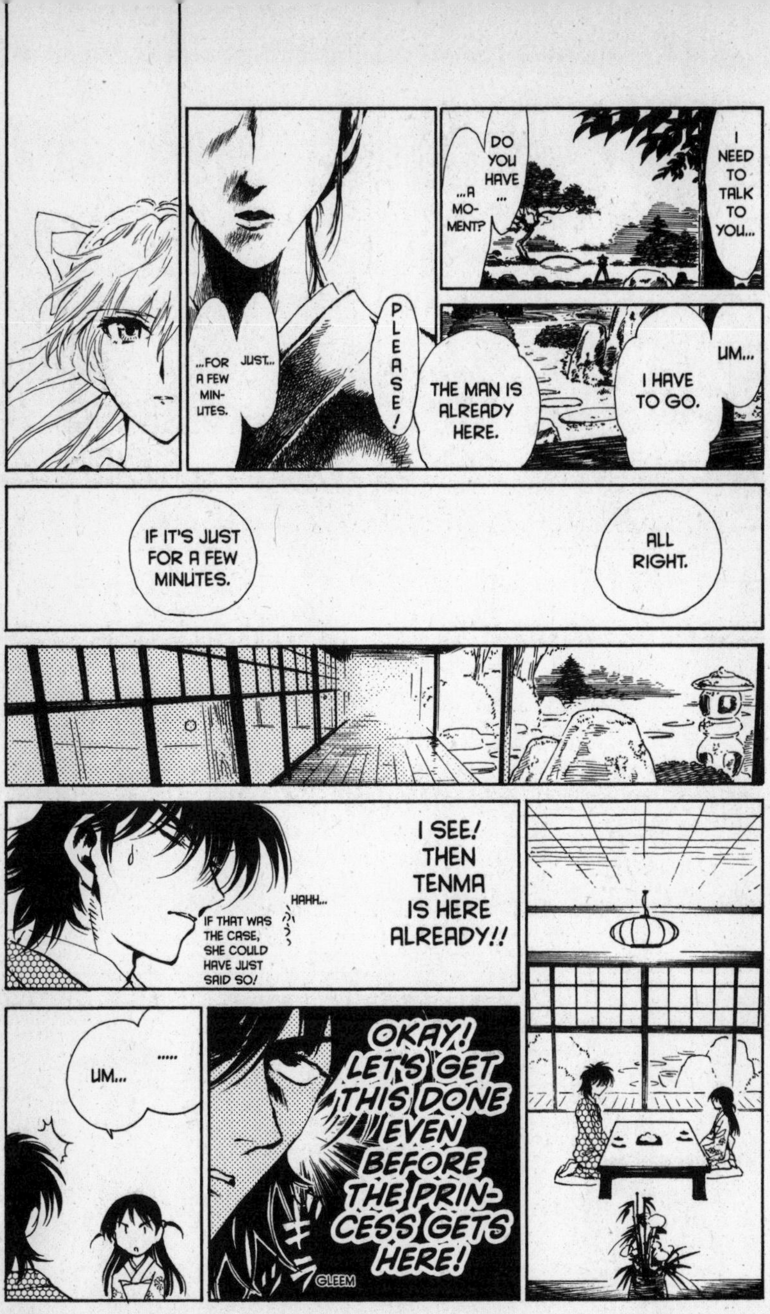
I NEED TO TALK TO YOU...
DO YOU HAVE ...
...A MOMENT?
UM...
I HAVE TO GO.
THE MAN IS ALREADY HERE.
PLEASE!
JUST...
...FOR A FEW MINUTES.
ALL RIGHT.
IF IT'S JUST FOR A FEW MINUTES.
I SEE! THEN TENMA IS HERE ALREADY!!
HAHH...
IF THAT WAS THE CASE, SHE COULD HAVE JUST SAID SO!
OKAY! LET'S GET THIS DONE EVEN BEFORE THE PRIN-CESS GETS HERE!
GLEEM
.....
UM...

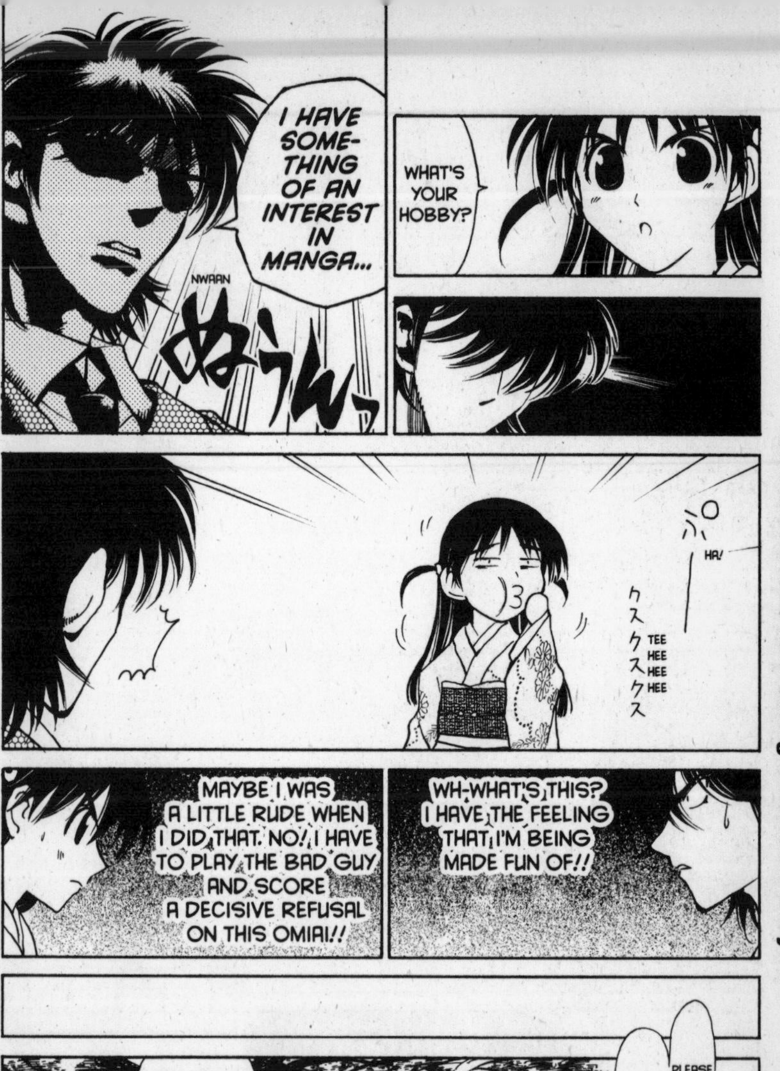
WHAT'S YOUR HOBBY?
I HAVE SOMETHING OF AN INTEREST IN MANGA...
NWAAN
ぬうんっ
ぷ
HA!
クスクスクス
TEE HEE HEE HEE
WH-WHAT'S THIS? I HAVE THE FEELING THAT I'M BEING MADE FUN OF!!
MAYBE I WAS A LITTLE RUDE WHEN I DID THAT. NO! I HAVE TO PLAY THE BAD GUY AND SCORE A DECISIVE REFUSAL ON THIS OMIAI!!
PLEASE FORGIVE ME.
I KNOW HOW IT MUST BE...
...SUCH A BOTHER FOR YOU.
IT'S ALL RIGHT, MOTHER-SAMA.
I KNOW IT ISN'T YOUR FAULT.

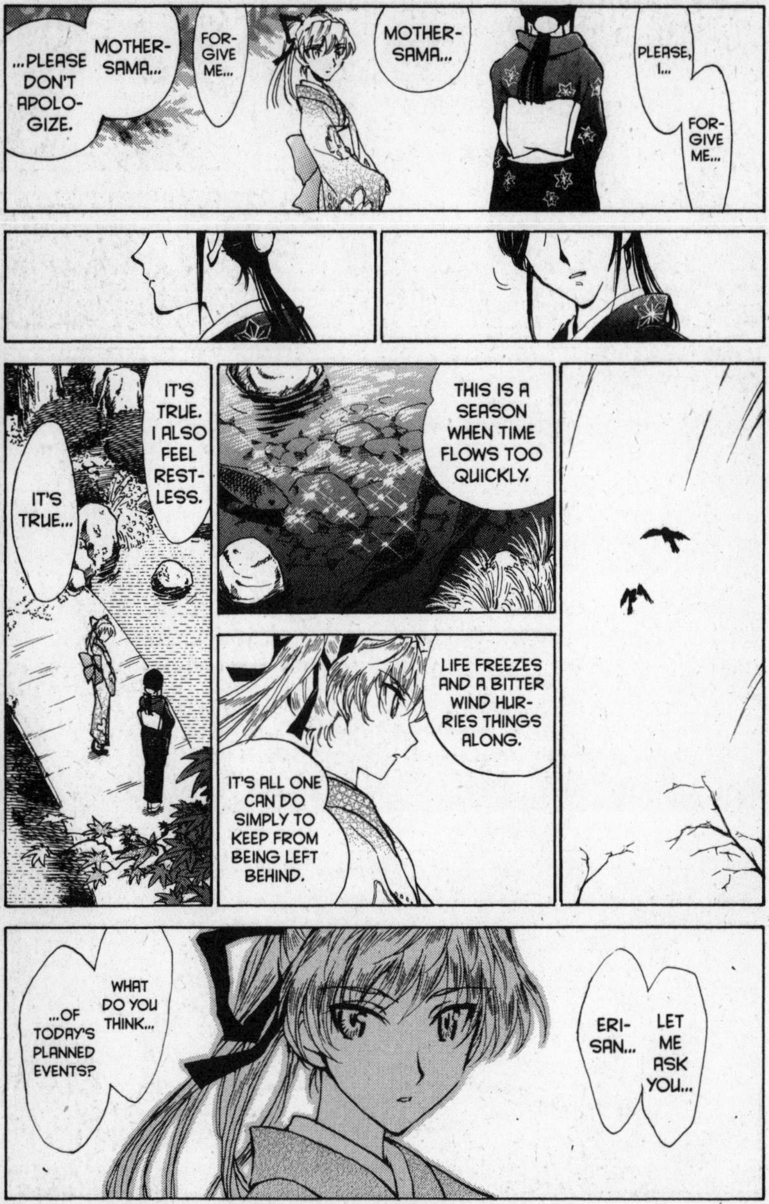
PLEASE, I...
FORGIVE ME...
MOTHER-SAMA...
FORGIVE ME...
MOTHER-SAMA...
...PLEASE DON'T APOLOGIZE.
THIS IS A SEASON WHEN TIME FLOWS TOO QUICKLY.
LIFE FREEZES AND A BITTER WIND HURRIES THINGS ALONG.
IT'S ALL ONE CAN DO SIMPLY TO KEEP FROM BEING LEFT BEHIND.
IT'S TRUE. I ALSO FEEL RESTLESS.
IT'S TRUE...
ERI-SAN...
LET ME ASK YOU...
WHAT DO YOU THINK...
...OF TODAY'S PLANNED EVENTS?

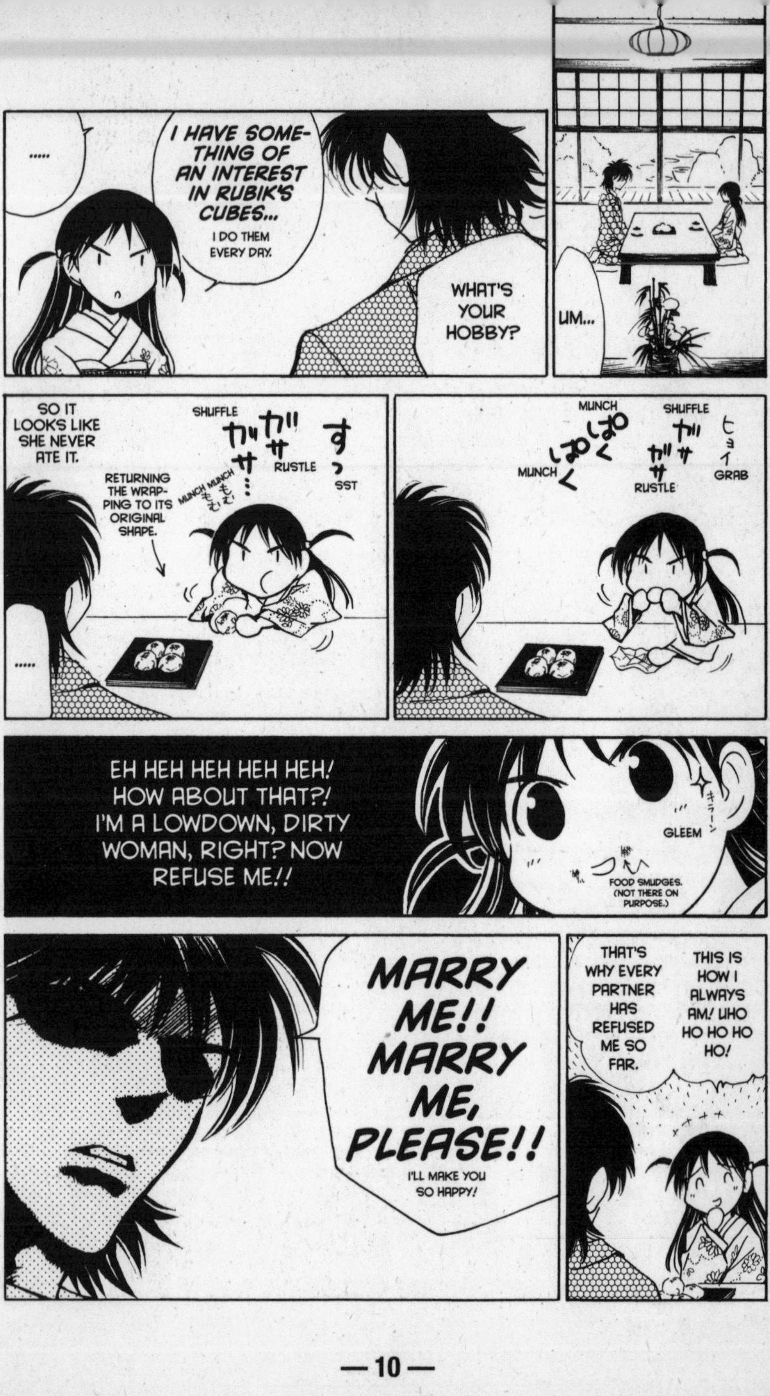
UM...
WHAT'S YOUR HOBBY?
I HAVE SOMETHING OF AN INTEREST IN RUBIK'S CUBES...
I DO THEM EVERY DAY.
......
ヒョイ
GRAB
ガサガサ
SHUFFLE
RUSTLE
ぱくぱく
MUNCH
MUNCH
すっ
SST
ガサガサ...
SHUFFLE
RUSTLE
MUNCH MUNCH
もむもむ
RETURNING THE WRAPPING TO ITS ORIGINAL SHAPE.
SO IT LOOKS LIKE SHE NEVER ATE IT.
......
キラーン
GLEEM
FOOD SMUDGES. (NOT THERE ON PURPOSE.)
EH HEH HEH HEH HEH! HOW ABOUT THAT?! I'M A LOWDOWN, DIRTY WOMAN, RIGHT? NOW REFUSE ME!!
THIS IS HOW I ALWAYS AM! UHO HO HO HO HO!
THAT'S WHY EVERY PARTNER HAS REFUSED ME SO FAR.
MARRY ME!! MARRY ME, PLEASE!!
I'LL MAKE YOU SO HAPPY!

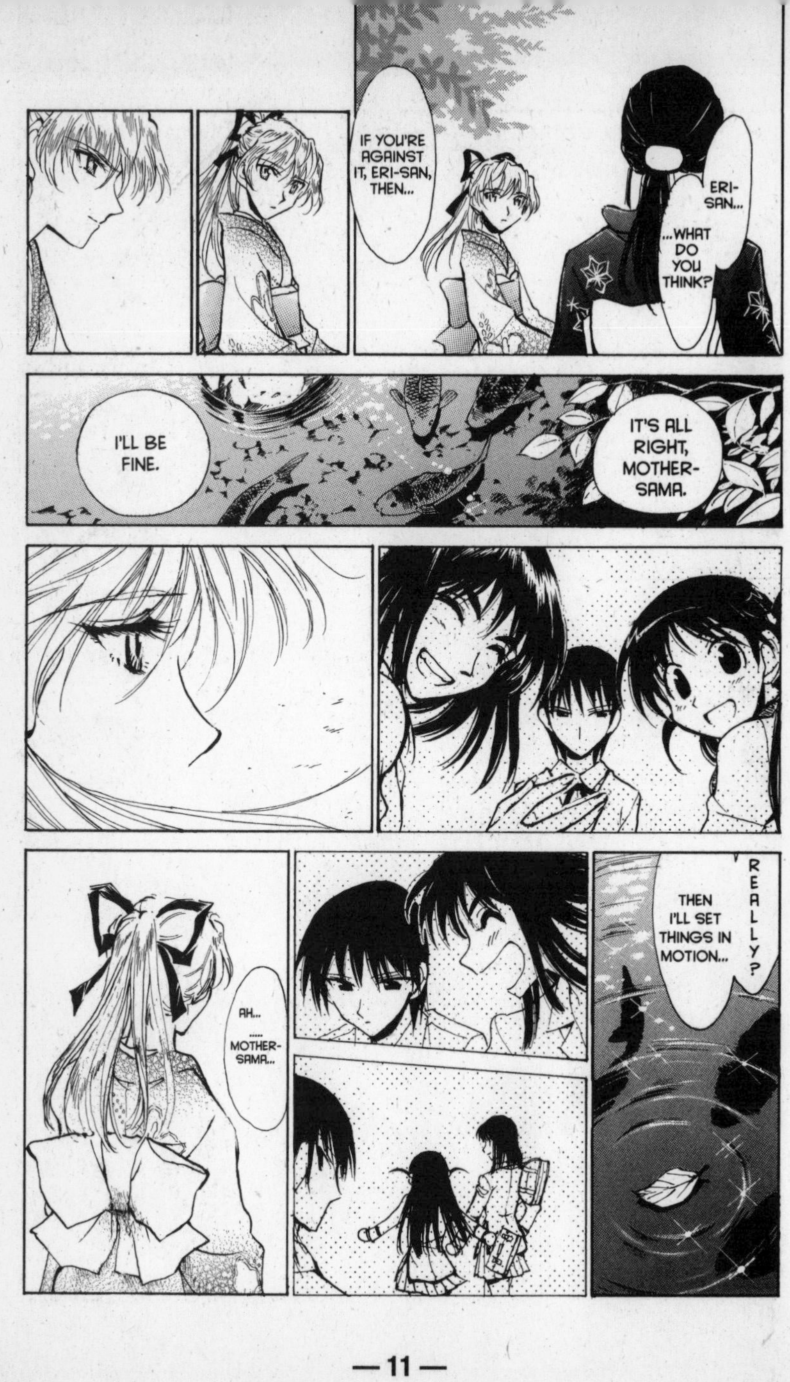
ERI-SAN...
...WHAT DO YOU THINK?
IF YOU'RE AGAINST IT, ERI-SAN, THEN...
IT'S ALL RIGHT, MOTHER-SAMA.
I'LL BE FINE.
REALLY?
THEN I'LL SET THINGS IN MOTION...
AH... ...... MOTHER-SAMA...

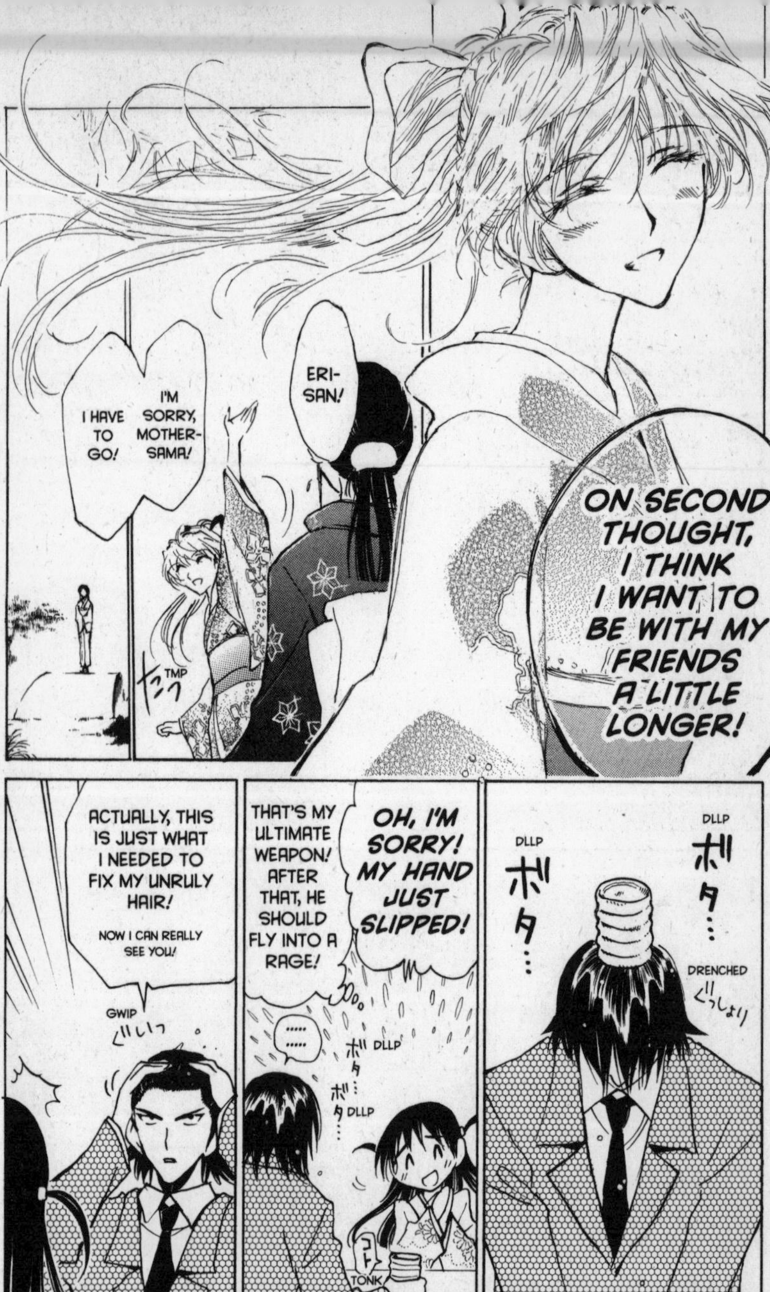
ON SECOND THOUGHT, I THINK I WANT TO BE WITH MY FRIENDS A LITTLE LONGER!
ERI-SAN!
I'M SORRY, MOTHER-SAMA!
I HAVE TO GO!
TMP
DLLP
ボタ…
DLLP
ボタ…
DRENCHED
ぐっしょり
OH, I'M SORRY! MY HAND JUST SLIPPED!
THAT'S MY ULTIMATE WEAPON! AFTER THAT, HE SHOULD FLY INTO A RAGE!
......
......
DLLP
DLLP
TONK
ACTUALLY, THIS IS JUST WHAT I NEEDED TO FIX MY UNRULY HAIR!
NOW I CAN REALLY SEE YOU!
GWIP
ぐいっ

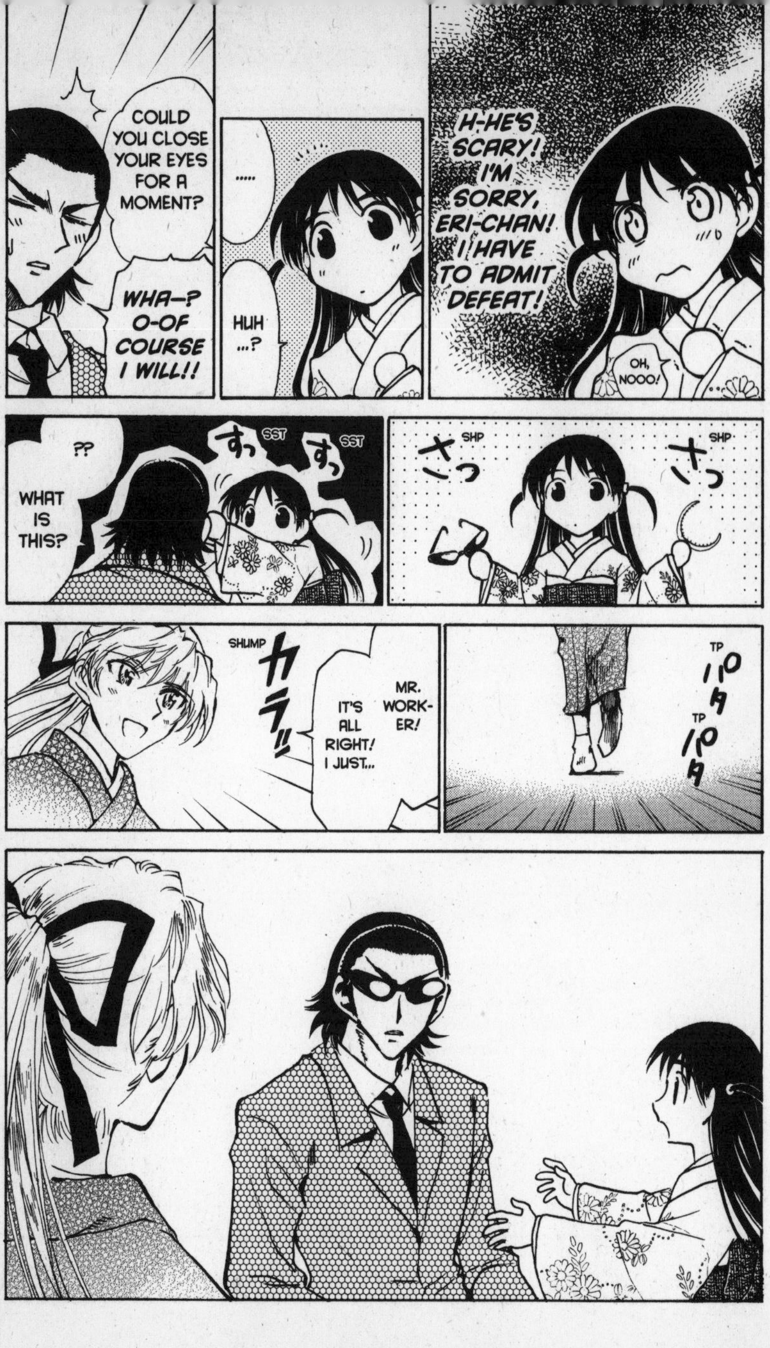
H-HE'S SCARY! I'M SORRY, ERI-CHAN! I HAVE TO ADMIT DEFEAT!
OH, NOOO!
......
HUH ...?
COULD YOU CLOSE YOUR EYES FOR A MOMENT?
WHA—? O-OF COURSE I WILL!!
SHP
SHP
SST
SST
??
WHAT IS THIS?
TP
TP
MR. WORKER!
IT'S ALL RIGHT! I JUST...
SHUMP

It's All Right. I Found the Problem and Stomped It Out.

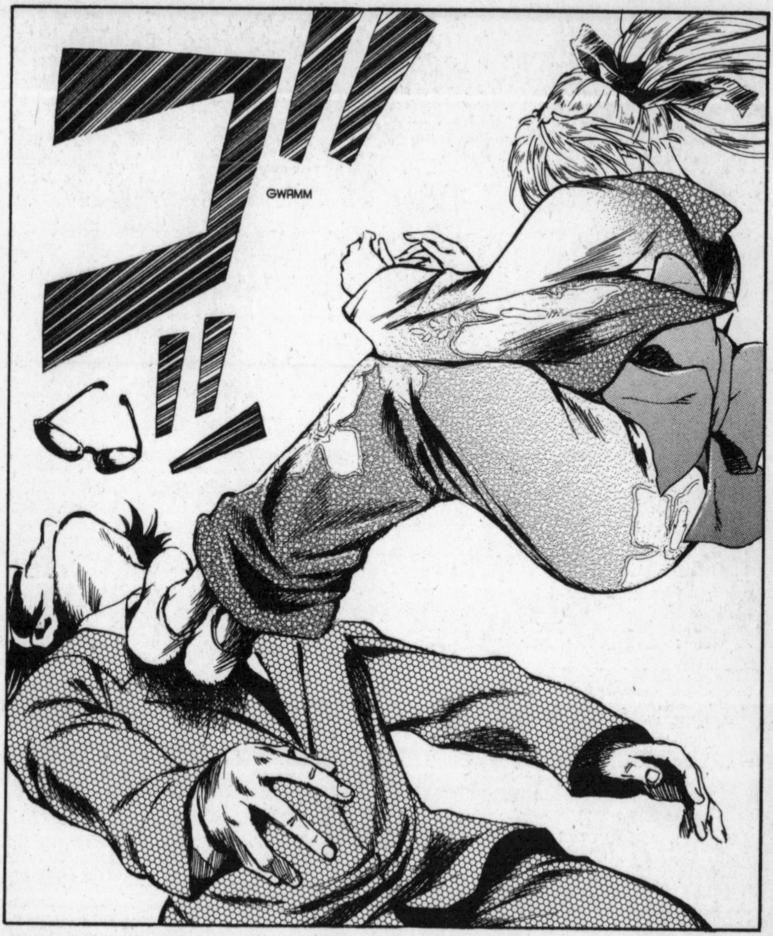
GWAMM

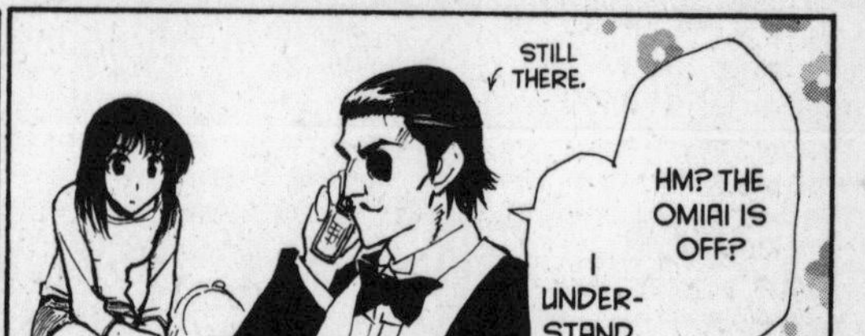
HM? THE OMIAI IS OFF?
I UNDER-STAND.
STILL THERE.

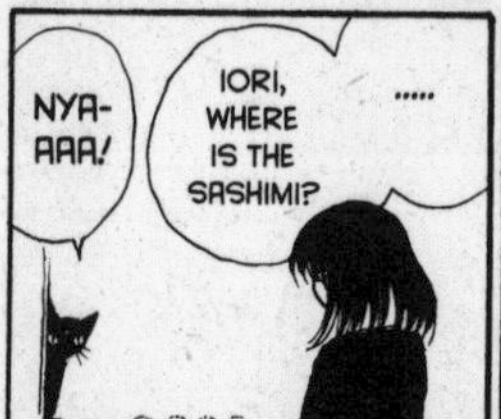
.....
IORI, WHERE IS THE SASHIMI?
NYA-AAA!

153·········Fin

#154 THE GIFT

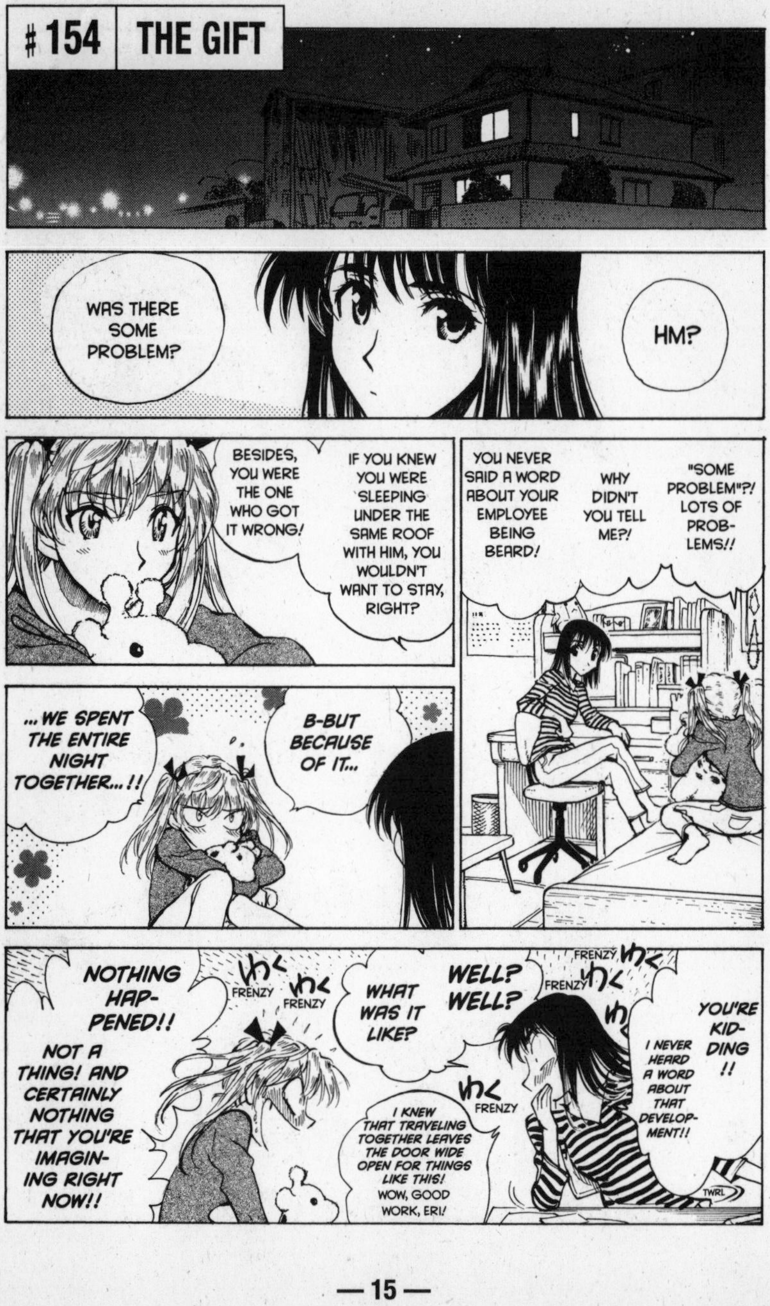

HM?
WAS THERE SOME PROBLEM?
"SOME PROBLEM"?! LOTS OF PROB-LEMS!!
WHY DIDN'T YOU TELL ME?!
YOU NEVER SAID A WORD ABOUT YOUR EMPLOYEE BEING BEARD!
IF YOU KNEW YOU WERE SLEEPING UNDER THE SAME ROOF WITH HIM, YOU WOULDN'T WANT TO STAY, RIGHT?
BESIDES, YOU WERE THE ONE WHO GOT IT WRONG!
B-BUT BECAUSE OF IT...
...WE SPENT THE ENTIRE NIGHT TOGETHER...!!
YOU'RE KID-DING !!
I NEVER HEARD A WORD ABOUT THAT DEVELOP-MENT!!
わく FRENZY わく FRENZY わく
WELL? WELL?
TWRL
わく FRENZY
WHAT WAS IT LIKE?
I KNEW THAT TRAVELING TOGETHER LEAVES THE DOOR WIDE OPEN FOR THINGS LIKE THIS!
WOW, GOOD WORK, ERI!
わく FRENZY わく FRENZY
NOTHING HAP-PENED!!
NOT A THING! AND CERTAINLY NOTHING THAT YOU'RE IMAGIN-ING RIGHT NOW!!

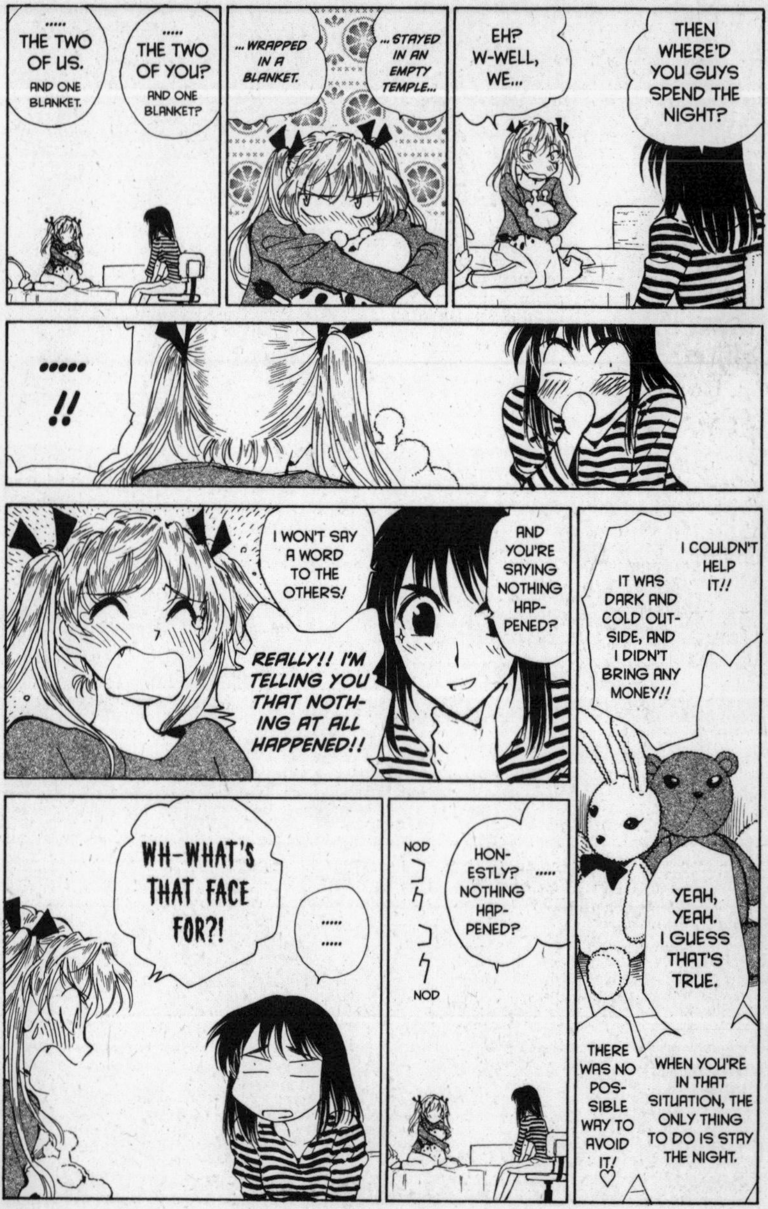
THEN WHERE'D YOU GUYS SPEND THE NIGHT?
EH? W-WELL, WE...
...STAYED IN AN EMPTY TEMPLE...
...WRAPPED IN A BLANKET.
..... THE TWO OF YOU? AND ONE BLANKET?
..... THE TWO OF US. AND ONE BLANKET.
..... !!
I COULDN'T HELP IT!!
IT WAS DARK AND COLD OUT-SIDE, AND I DIDN'T BRING ANY MONEY!!
YEAH, YEAH. I GUESS THAT'S TRUE.
WHEN YOU'RE IN THAT SITUATION, THE ONLY THING TO DO IS STAY THE NIGHT.
THERE WAS NO POS-SIBLE WAY TO AVOID IT! ♡
AND YOU'RE SAYING NOTHING HAP-PENED?
I WON'T SAY A WORD TO THE OTHERS!
REALLY!! I'M TELLING YOU THAT NOTH-ING AT ALL HAPPENED!!
HON-ESTLY? NOTHING HAP-PENED?
.....
NOD コク コク NOD
....
WH-WHAT'S THAT FACE FOR?!

Sawachika Eri: Caught in the Current of Events Even After Returning to Mikoto's.

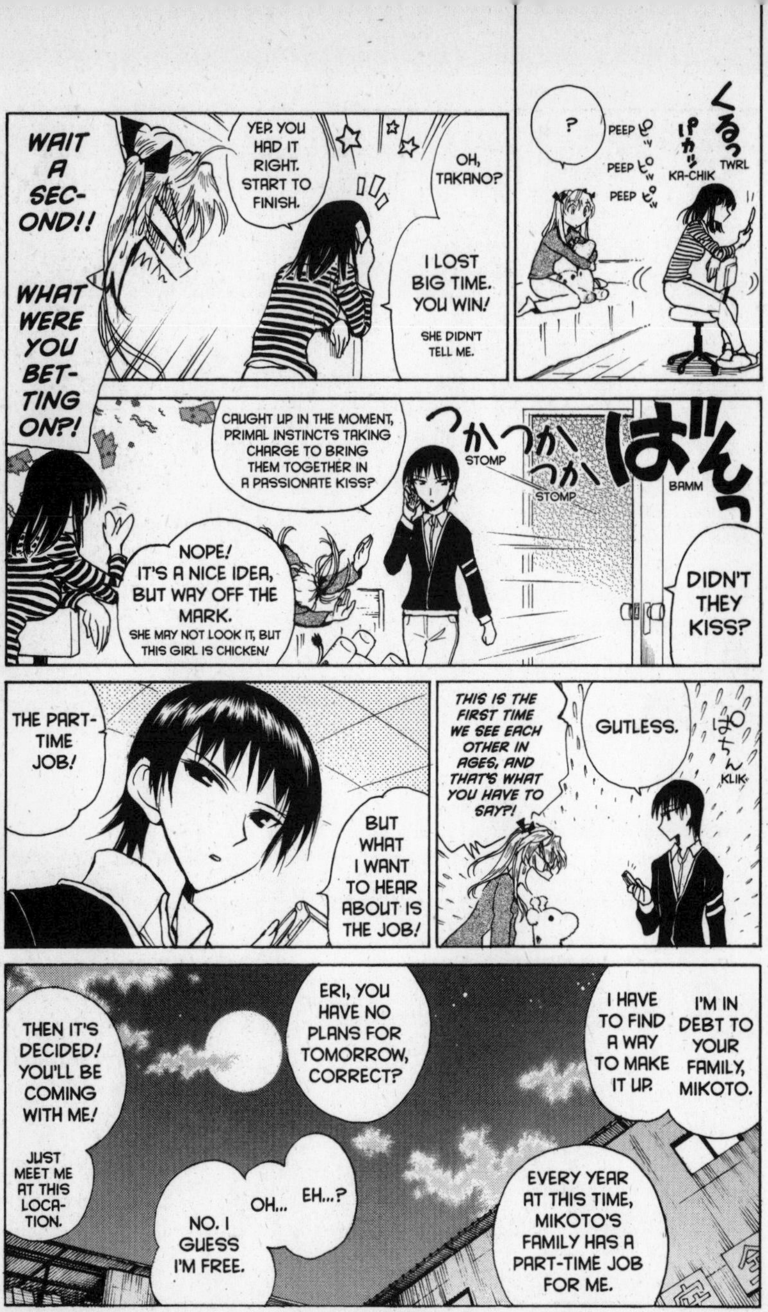
?
ピッ PEEP
ピッ PEEP
ピッ PEEP
くるっ TWRL
ぱカッ KA-CHIK
OH, TAKANO?
YEP. YOU HAD IT RIGHT. START TO FINISH.
I LOST BIG TIME. YOU WIN!
SHE DIDN'T TELL ME.
WAIT A SEC-OND!!
WHAT WERE YOU BET-TING ON?!
DIDN'T THEY KISS?
ばーんっ BAMM
つかつかつか STOMP STOMP
CAUGHT UP IN THE MOMENT, PRIMAL INSTINCTS TAKING CHARGE TO BRING THEM TOGETHER IN A PASSIONATE KISS?
NOPE! IT'S A NICE IDEA, BUT WAY OFF THE MARK.
SHE MAY NOT LOOK IT, BUT THIS GIRL IS CHICKEN!
ぱちん KLIK
GUTLESS.
THIS IS THE FIRST TIME WE SEE EACH OTHER IN AGES, AND THAT'S WHAT YOU HAVE TO SAY?!
BUT WHAT I WANT TO HEAR ABOUT IS THE JOB!
THE PART-TIME JOB!
I'M IN DEBT TO YOUR FAMILY, MIKOTO.
I HAVE TO FIND A WAY TO MAKE IT UP.
EVERY YEAR AT THIS TIME, MIKOTO'S FAMILY HAS A PART-TIME JOB FOR ME.
ERI, YOU HAVE NO PLANS FOR TOMORROW, CORRECT?
EH...?
OH...
NO. I GUESS I'M FREE.
THEN IT'S DECIDED! YOU'LL BE COMING WITH ME!
JUST MEET ME AT THIS LOCA-TION.

The Odds: 1 (Akira) to 10 (Mikoto).

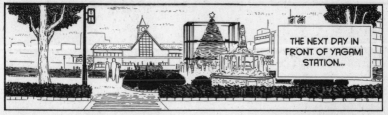

THE NEXT DAY IN FRONT OF YAGAMI STATION...

WHAT AM I SUPPOSED TO DO? I'M GETTING NERVOUS.

COME TO THINK OF IT, THIS IS MY FIRST PART-TIME JOB EVER.

OH, NO! AKIRA ISN'T EVEN HERE...

THANK YOU ALL FOR AGREEING TO TAKE THIS JOB. WE'RE ABOUT TO BEGIN.

HON-ESTLY! GETTING INVITED TO A JOB BY AKIRA IS ENOUGH TO MAKE A GIRL NERVOUS!

Sawachika Eri: Doesn't Need a Job.

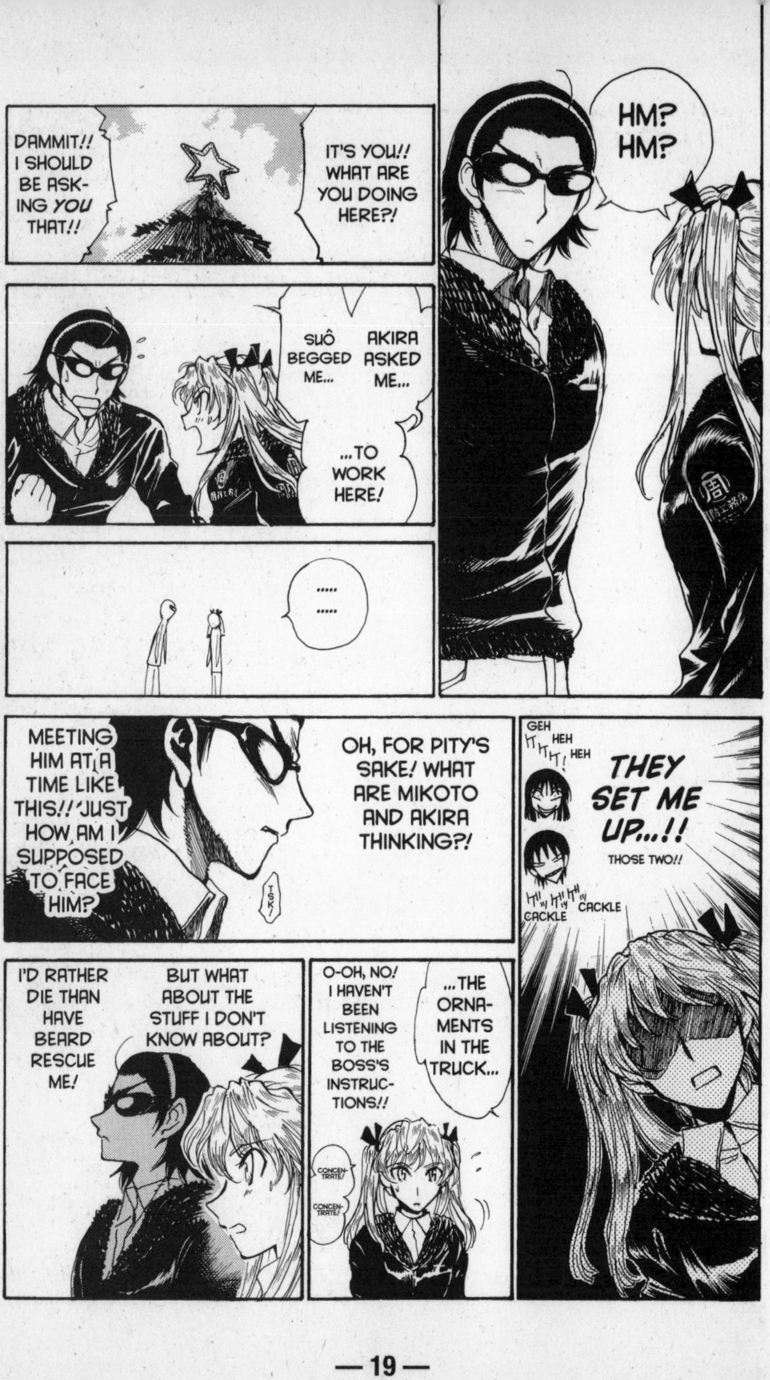
HM? HM?
IT'S YOU!! WHAT ARE YOU DOING HERE?!
DAMMIT!! I SHOULD BE ASK-ING *YOU* THAT!!
AKIRA ASKED ME...
SUÔ BEGGED ME...
...TO WORK HERE!
.....
.....
GEH HEH HEH
THEY SET ME UP...!!
THOSE TWO!!
CACKLE CACKLE
OH, FOR PITY'S SAKE! WHAT ARE MIKOTO AND AKIRA THINKING?!
TSK!
MEETING HIM AT A TIME LIKE THIS!! JUST HOW AM I SUPPOSED TO FACE HIM?
...THE ORNA-MENTS IN THE TRUCK...
O-OH, NO! I HAVEN'T BEEN LISTENING TO THE BOSS'S INSTRUC-TIONS!!
CONCEN-TRATE!
CONCEN-TRATE!
BUT WHAT ABOUT THE STUFF I DON'T KNOW ABOUT?
I'D RATHER DIE THAN HAVE BEARD RESCUE ME!

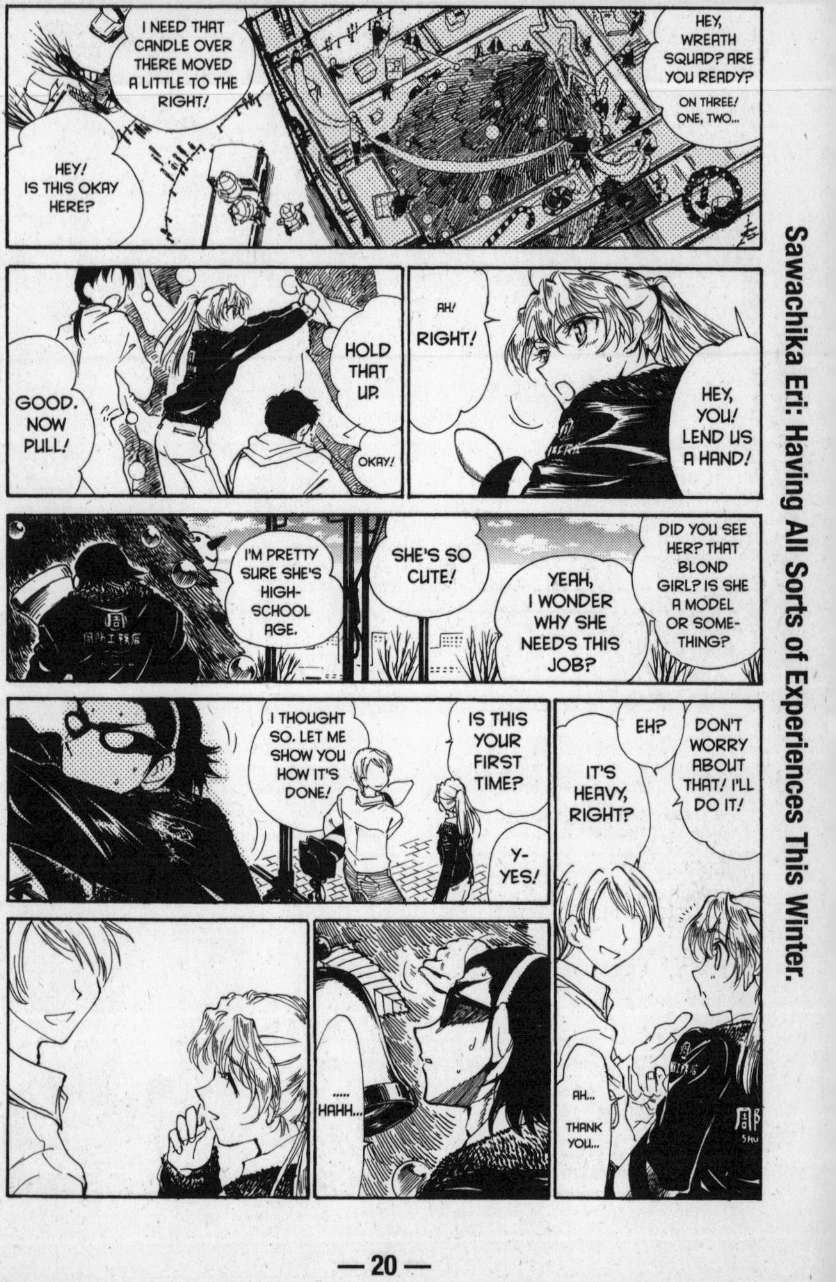
HEY, WREATH SQUAD? ARE YOU READY?
ON THREE! ONE, TWO...
I NEED THAT CANDLE OVER THERE MOVED A LITTLE TO THE RIGHT!
HEY! IS THIS OKAY HERE?
HEY, YOU! LEND US A HAND!
AH!
RIGHT!
HOLD THAT UP.
OKAY!
GOOD. NOW PULL!
DID YOU SEE HER? THAT BLOND GIRL? IS SHE A MODEL OR SOME-THING?
YEAH, I WONDER WHY SHE NEEDS THIS JOB?
SHE'S SO CUTE!
I'M PRETTY SURE SHE'S HIGH-SCHOOL AGE.
DON'T WORRY ABOUT THAT! I'LL DO IT!
EH?
IT'S HEAVY, RIGHT?
AH... THANK YOU...
IS THIS YOUR FIRST TIME?
Y-YES!
I THOUGHT SO. LET ME SHOW YOU HOW IT'S DONE!
..... HAHH...

In a Way, It's a Somewhat Adult Reaction.

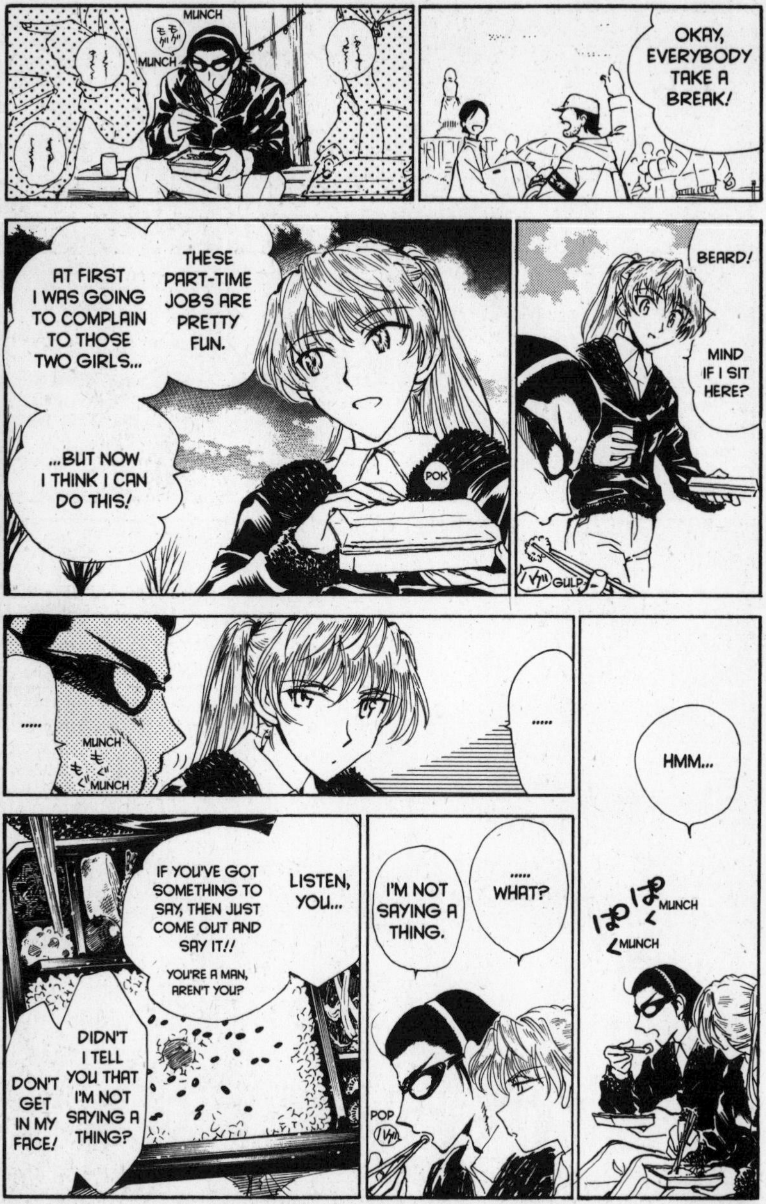

OKAY, EVERYBODY TAKE A BREAK!
MUNCH
MUNCH
BEARD!
MIND IF I SIT HERE?
GULP
THESE PART-TIME JOBS ARE PRETTY FUN.
AT FIRST I WAS GOING TO COMPLAIN TO THOSE TWO GIRLS...
...BUT NOW I THINK I CAN DO THIS!
POK
HMM...
MUNCH
MUNCH
.....
.....
MUNCH
MUNCH
.....
WHAT?
I'M NOT SAYING A THING.
POP
LISTEN, YOU...
IF YOU'VE GOT SOMETHING TO SAY, THEN JUST COME OUT AND SAY IT!!
YOU'RE A MAN, AREN'T YOU?
DIDN'T I TELL YOU THAT I'M NOT SAYING A THING?
DON'T GET IN MY FACE!

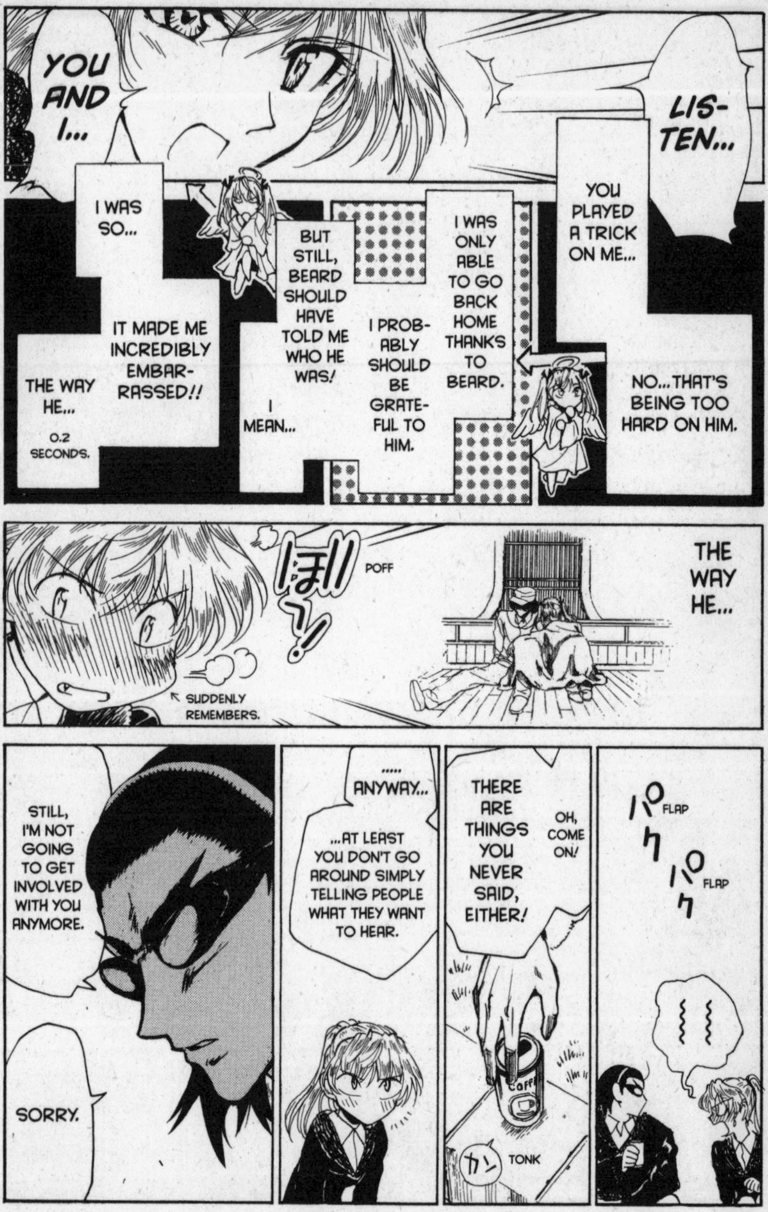
LIS-TEN...
YOU AND I...
YOU PLAYED A TRICK ON ME...
NO...THAT'S BEING TOO HARD ON HIM.
I WAS ONLY ABLE TO GO BACK HOME THANKS TO BEARD.
I PROB-ABLY SHOULD BE GRATE-FUL TO HIM.
BUT STILL, BEARD SHOULD HAVE TOLD ME WHO HE WAS!
I MEAN...
I WAS SO...
IT MADE ME INCREDIBLY EMBAR-RASSED!!
THE WAY HE...
0.2 SECONDS.
THE WAY HE...
POFF
SUDDENLY REMEMBERS.
FLAP
FLAP
THERE ARE THINGS YOU NEVER SAID, EITHER!
OH, COME ON!
TONK
..... ANYWAY...
...AT LEAST YOU DON'T GO AROUND SIMPLY TELLING PEOPLE WHAT THEY WANT TO HEAR.
STILL, I'M NOT GOING TO GET INVOLVED WITH YOU ANYMORE.
SORRY.

Harima Kenji: Finally Learns.

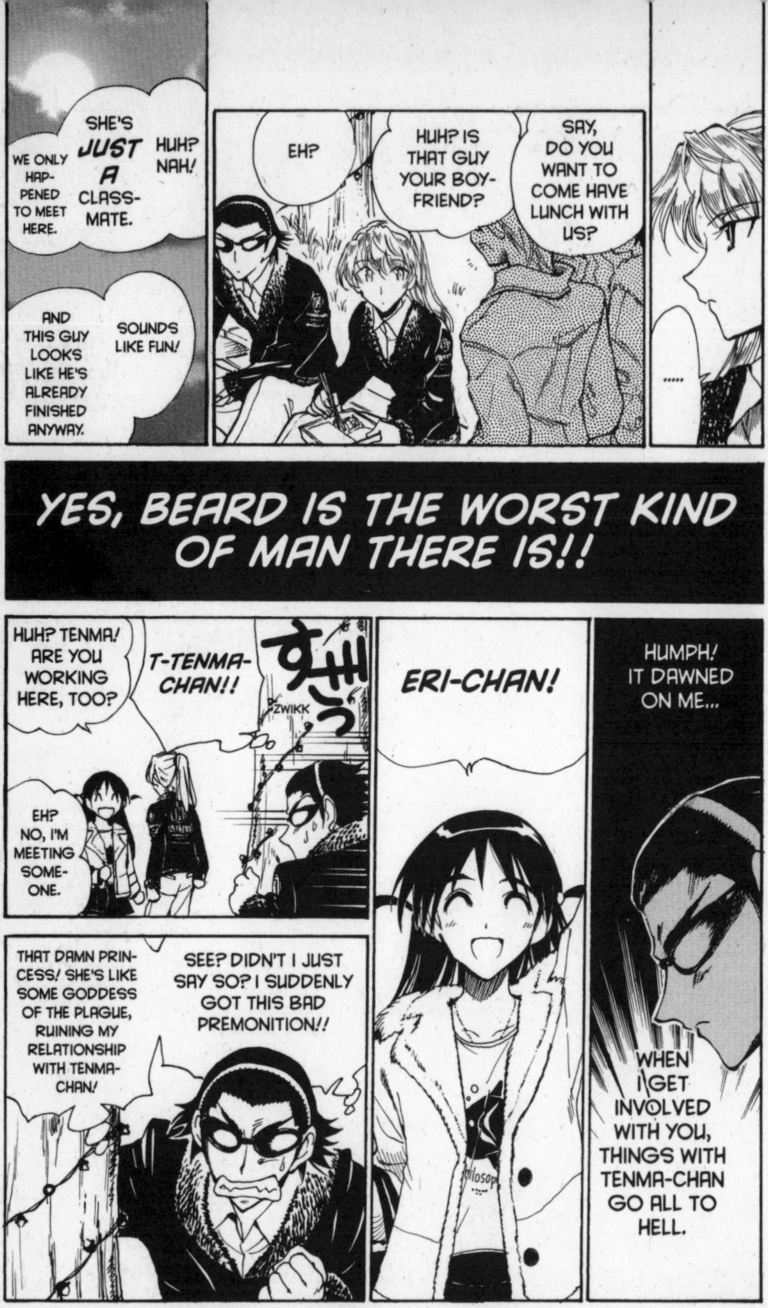
.....
SAY, DO YOU WANT TO COME HAVE LUNCH WITH US?
HUH? IS THAT GUY YOUR BOY-FRIEND?
EH?
HUH? NAH!
SHE'S JUST A CLASS-MATE.
WE ONLY HAP-PENED TO MEET HERE.
SOUNDS LIKE FUN!
AND THIS GUY LOOKS LIKE HE'S ALREADY FINISHED ANYWAY.
YES, BEARD IS THE WORST KIND OF MAN THERE IS!!
HUMPH! IT DAWNED ON ME...
WHEN I GET INVOLVED WITH YOU, THINGS WITH TENMA-CHAN GO ALL TO HELL.
ERI-CHAN!
T-TENMA-CHAN!!
ZWIKK
HUH? TENMA! ARE YOU WORKING HERE, TOO?
EH? NO, I'M MEETING SOME-ONE.
SEE? DIDN'T I JUST SAY SO? I SUDDENLY GOT THIS BAD PREMONITION!!
THAT DAMN PRIN-CESS! SHE'S LIKE SOME GODDESS OF THE PLAGUE, RUINING MY RELATIONSHIP WITH TENMA-CHAN!

Harima Stock: Taking a Tumble.

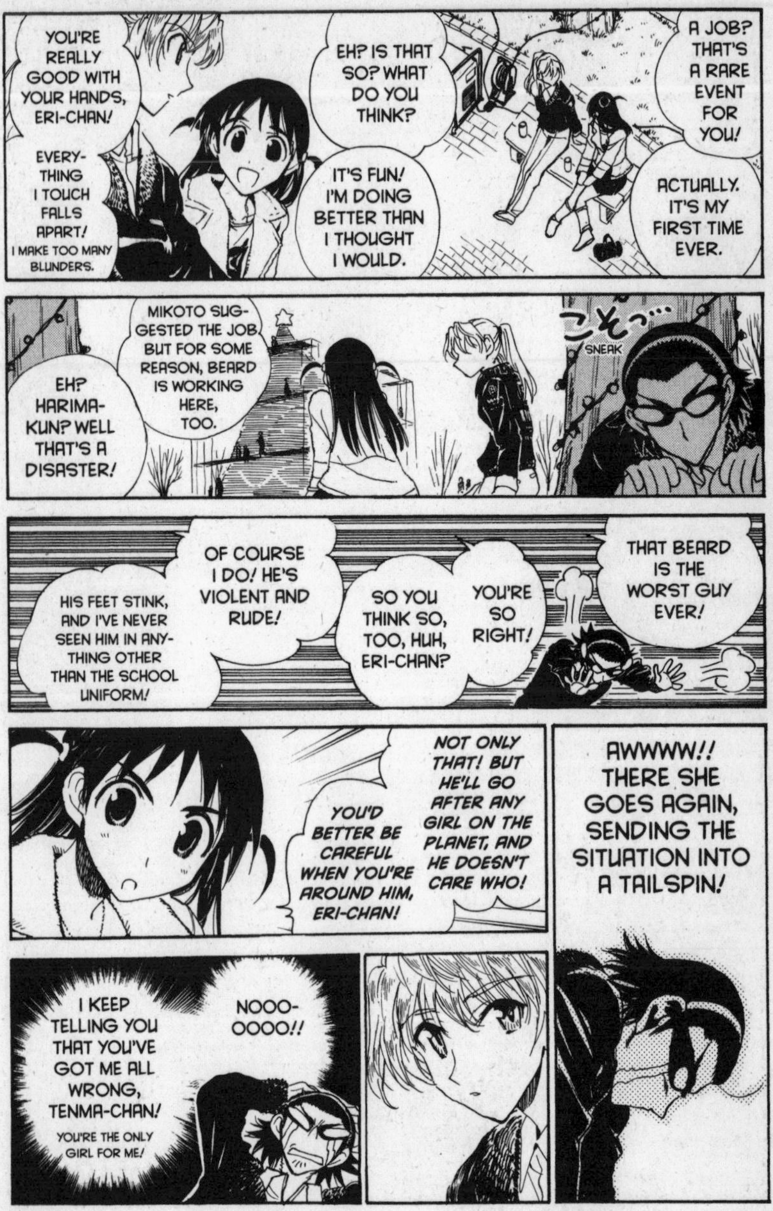

A JOB? THAT'S A RARE EVENT FOR YOU!
ACTUALLY. IT'S MY FIRST TIME EVER.
EH? IS THAT SO? WHAT DO YOU THINK?
IT'S FUN! I'M DOING BETTER THAN I THOUGHT I WOULD.
YOU'RE REALLY GOOD WITH YOUR HANDS, ERI-CHAN!
EVERY-THING I TOUCH FALLS APART!
I MAKE TOO MANY BLUNDERS.
こそっ…
SNEAK
MIKOTO SUG-GESTED THE JOB BUT FOR SOME REASON, BEARD IS WORKING HERE, TOO.
EH? HARIMA-KUN? WELL THAT'S A DISASTER!
THAT BEARD IS THE WORST GUY EVER!
YOU'RE SO RIGHT!
SO YOU THINK SO, TOO, HUH, ERI-CHAN?
OF COURSE I DO! HE'S VIOLENT AND RUDE!
HIS FEET STINK, AND I'VE NEVER SEEN HIM IN ANY-THING OTHER THAN THE SCHOOL UNIFORM!
AWWWW!! THERE SHE GOES AGAIN, SENDING THE SITUATION INTO A TAILSPIN!
NOT ONLY THAT! BUT HE'LL GO AFTER ANY GIRL ON THE PLANET, AND HE DOESN'T CARE WHO!
YOU'D BETTER BE CAREFUL WHEN YOU'RE AROUND HIM, ERI-CHAN!
NOOO-OOOO!!
I KEEP TELLING YOU THAT YOU'VE GOT ME ALL WRONG, TENMA-CHAN!
YOU'RE THE ONLY GIRL FOR ME!

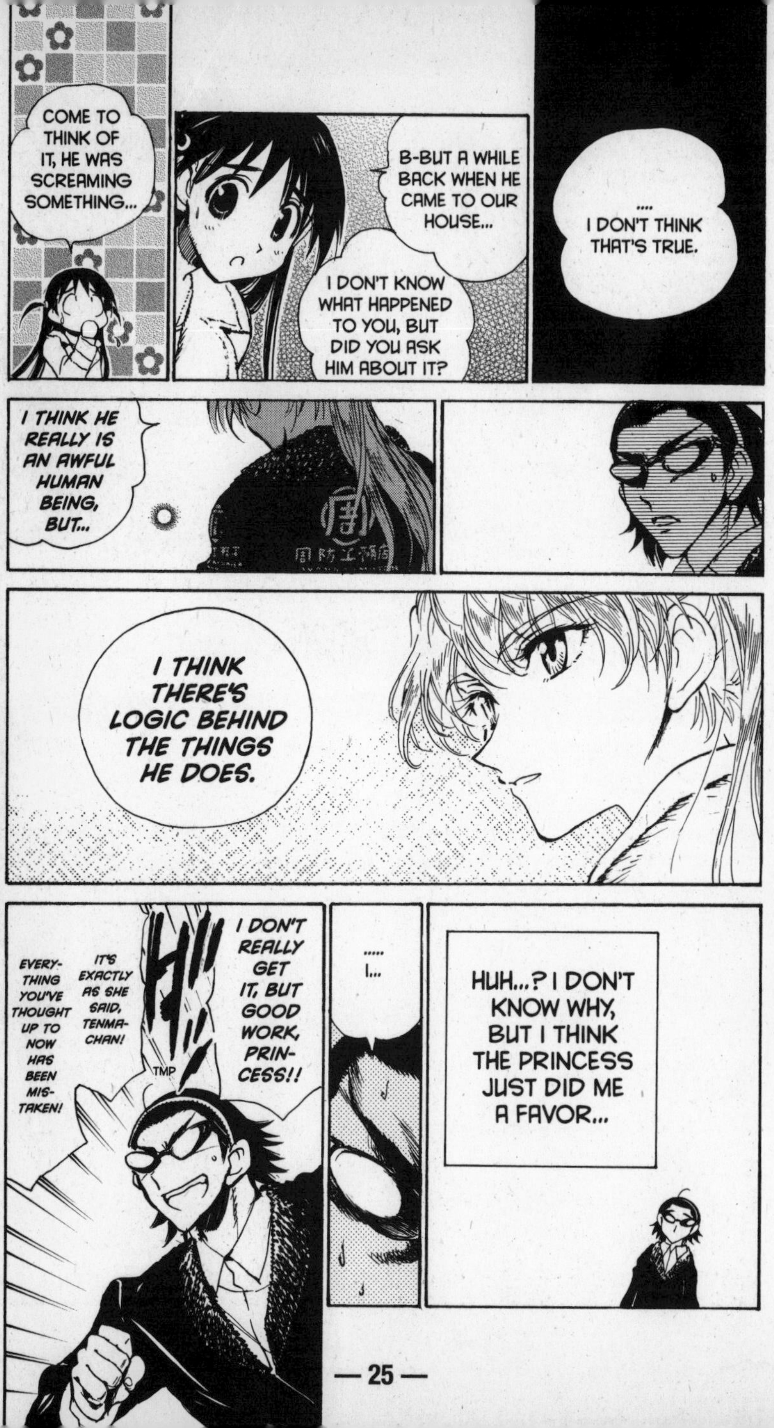
.... I DON'T THINK THAT'S TRUE.
B-BUT A WHILE BACK WHEN HE CAME TO OUR HOUSE...
I DON'T KNOW WHAT HAPPENED TO YOU, BUT DID YOU ASK HIM ABOUT IT?
COME TO THINK OF IT, HE WAS SCREAMING SOMETHING...
I THINK HE REALLY IS AN AWFUL HUMAN BEING, BUT...
I THINK THERE'S LOGIC BEHIND THE THINGS HE DOES.
HUH...? I DON'T KNOW WHY, BUT I THINK THE PRINCESS JUST DID ME A FAVOR...
..... I...
I DON'T REALLY GET IT, BUT GOOD WORK, PRINCESS!!
IT'S EXACTLY AS SHE SAID, TENMA-CHAN!
EVERYTHING YOU'VE THOUGHT UP TO NOW HAS BEEN MISTAKEN!
TMP

A Small Reward for Beard.

グシャッ
GUSHAAM
SORRY TO KEEP YOU WAITING, TENMA.
AKIRA-CHAN! YOU'RE LATE!!
WHEN YOU SAID YOU WERE MEETING SOMEONE, IT WAS AKIRA?!
HOLD ON!!
YOU CHOSE THIS PLACE ON PURPOSE!!
WHAT PURPOSE?

[redacted]

HMM! HAHH!
COMPLETED ALL IN ONE DAY!
UM... PRINCESS?
I DON'T REALLY REMEMBER EVERYTHING, BUT...THANK YOU.
STOP CALLING ME THAT.
WHAT?
FOR WHAT?
.....NO.
NEVER MIND.
WHAT? NOW YOU'VE GOT ME WORRIED!
LIKE I SAID, IT'S NOTHING.
SPILL IT!!

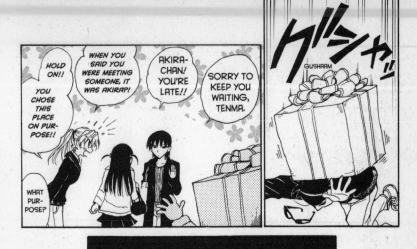

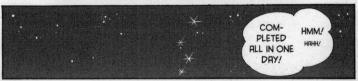

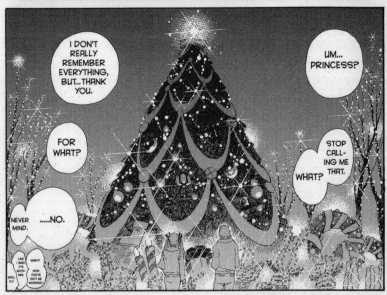

154· · · · · · · · ·Fin

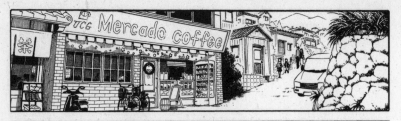

UCC
Mercado coffee
茶
HEY, YOU GUYS! IT'S ALMOST HERE! CHRISTMAS!
IT REALLY COMES ON FAST, HUH? WHAT HAVE I DONE THIS WHOLE YEAR?
MIKOTO, WHAT ARE YOU GOING TO DO?
I ASSUME THAT ASÔ-KUN HAS ALREADY ASKED YOU OUT.
I'M HELPING OUT AT THE DOJO'S CHRISTMAS PARTY.
THEN YOU DON'T MIND IF I ASK ASÔ-KUN OUT?
ENOUGH ABOUT ME! WHAT ABOUT YOU GUYS?
TENMA, YOU'VE PROBABLY ALREADY MADE IT, HUH? THAT CURRY PLATE?
YEAH. I WONDER IF KARASUMA-KUN WILL LIKE IT...?
WHAT WILL YOU BE DOING, AKIRA-CHAN?
WORKING.
AND SO... WHEN ARE YOU GOING TO TELL HIM HOW YOU FEEL, SAWACHIKA?
WH-WHAT KIND OF A QUESTION IS THAT?!
EH?! WHO?! WHO?!
BESIDES, WHY SHOULD I SAY ANYTHING TO THAT APE?!
DAMMIT! THIS MANGA IS NEVER GOING TO GET FINISHED!!
WHAT APE? WHO IS IT, ERI-CHAN?!

155 SHALL WE DANCE?

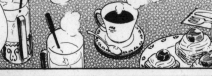

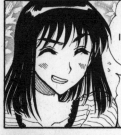

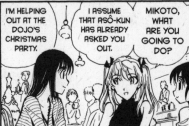

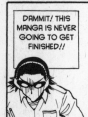

Yoshidayama Squad: Last Meeting of 2005.

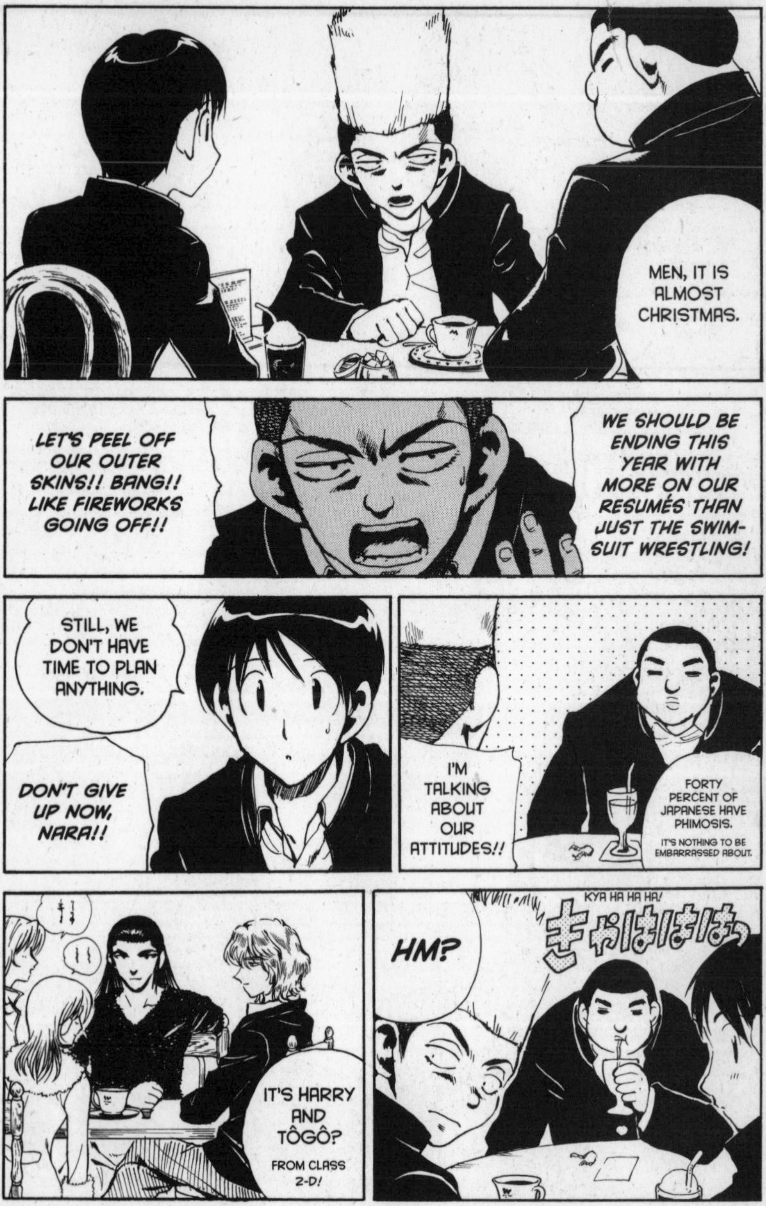
MEN, IT IS ALMOST CHRISTMAS.
WE SHOULD BE ENDING THIS YEAR WITH MORE ON OUR RESUMÉS THAN JUST THE SWIM-SUIT WRESTLING!
LET'S PEEL OFF OUR OUTER SKINS!! BANG!! LIKE FIREWORKS GOING OFF!!
FORTY PERCENT OF JAPANESE HAVE PHIMOSIS.
IT'S NOTHING TO BE EMBARRASSED ABOUT.
I'M TALKING ABOUT OUR ATTITUDES!!
STILL, WE DON'T HAVE TIME TO PLAN ANYTHING.
DON'T GIVE UP NOW, NARA!!
KYA HA HA HA!
きゃはははっ
HM?
IT'S HARRY AND TÔGÔ?
FROM CLASS 2-D!

1216-3050

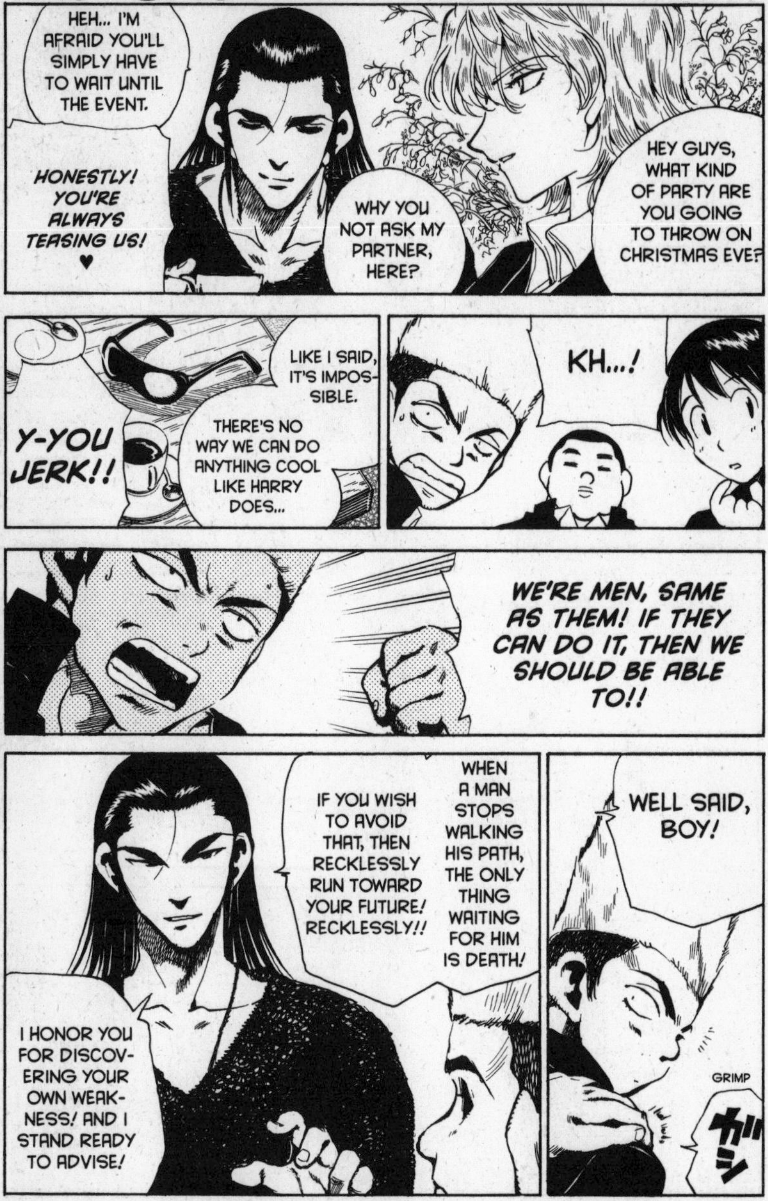
HEY GUYS, WHAT KIND OF PARTY ARE YOU GOING TO THROW ON CHRISTMAS EVE?
WHY YOU NOT ASK MY PARTNER, HERE?
HEH... I'M AFRAID YOU'LL SIMPLY HAVE TO WAIT UNTIL THE EVENT.
HONESTLY! YOU'RE ALWAYS TEASING US! ♥
KH...!
LIKE I SAID, IT'S IMPOSSIBLE.
THERE'S NO WAY WE CAN DO ANYTHING COOL LIKE HARRY DOES...
Y-YOU JERK!!
WE'RE MEN, SAME AS THEM! IF THEY CAN DO IT, THEN WE SHOULD BE ABLE TO!!
WELL SAID, BOY!
GRIMP
WHEN A MAN STOPS WALKING HIS PATH, THE ONLY THING WAITING FOR HIM IS DEATH!
IF YOU WISH TO AVOID THAT, THEN RECKLESSLY RUN TOWARD YOUR FUTURE! RECKLESSLY!!
I HONOR YOU FOR DISCOVERING YOUR OWN WEAKNESS! AND I STAND READY TO ADVISE!

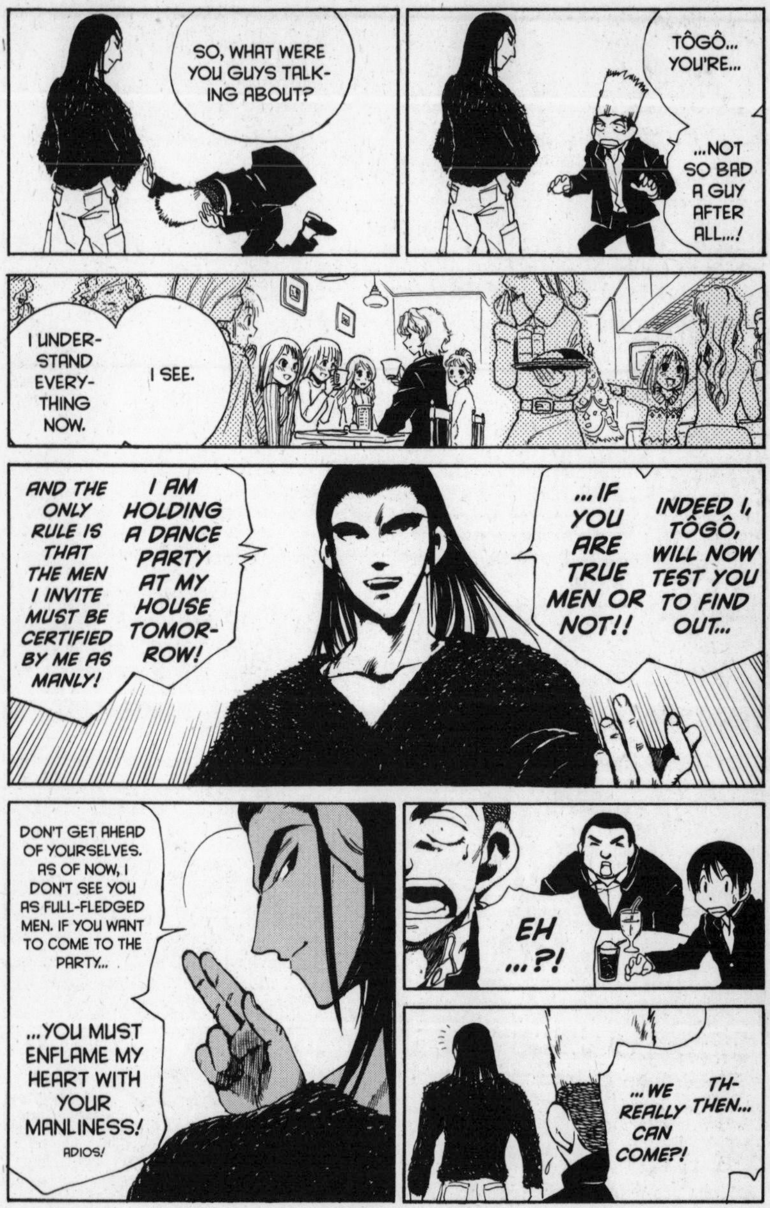
TÔGÔ... YOU'RE...
...NOT SO BAD A GUY AFTER ALL...!
SO, WHAT WERE YOU GUYS TALKING ABOUT?
I SEE.
I UNDERSTAND EVERYTHING NOW.
INDEED I, TÔGÔ, WILL NOW TEST YOU TO FIND OUT...
...IF YOU ARE TRUE MEN OR NOT!!
I AM HOLDING A DANCE PARTY AT MY HOUSE TOMORROW!
AND THE ONLY RULE IS THAT THE MEN I INVITE MUST BE CERTIFIED BY ME AS MANLY!
EH ...?!
TH-THEN...
...WE REALLY CAN COME?!
DON'T GET AHEAD OF YOURSELVES. AS OF NOW, I DON'T SEE YOU AS FULL-FLEDGED MEN. IF YOU WANT TO COME TO THE PARTY...
...YOU MUST ENFLAME MY HEART WITH YOUR MANLINESS!
ADIOS!

Tôgô Masakazu: Overflowing with a Manly Aura.

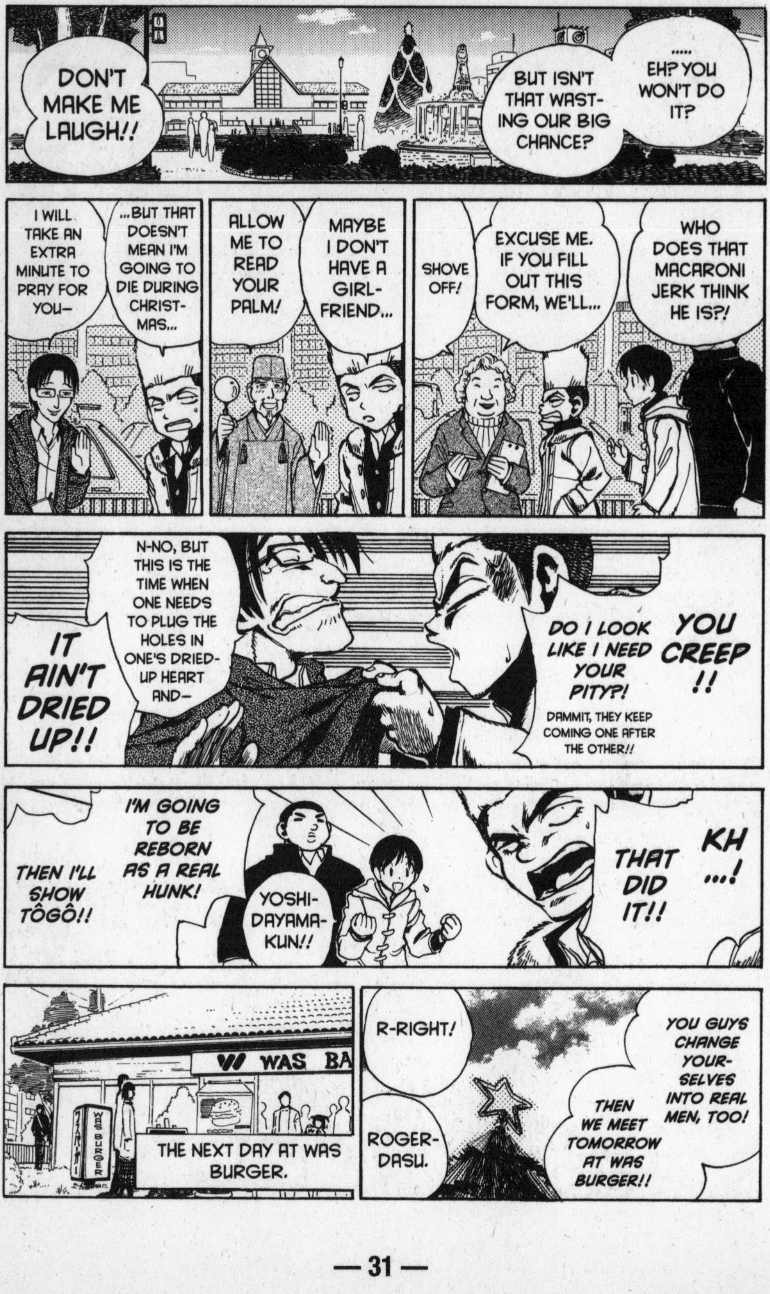

..... EH? YOU WON'T DO IT?
BUT ISN'T THAT WASTING OUR BIG CHANCE?
DON'T MAKE ME LAUGH!!
WHO DOES THAT MACARONI JERK THINK HE IS?!
EXCUSE ME. IF YOU FILL OUT THIS FORM, WE'LL...
SHOVE OFF!
MAYBE I DON'T HAVE A GIRLFRIEND...
ALLOW ME TO READ YOUR PALM!
...BUT THAT DOESN'T MEAN I'M GOING TO DIE DURING CHRISTMAS...
I WILL TAKE AN EXTRA MINUTE TO PRAY FOR YOU—
YOU CREEP!!
DO I LOOK LIKE I NEED YOUR PITY?!
DAMMIT, THEY KEEP COMING ONE AFTER THE OTHER!!
N-NO, BUT THIS IS THE TIME WHEN ONE NEEDS TO PLUG THE HOLES IN ONE'S DRIED-UP HEART AND—
IT AIN'T DRIED UP!!
KH ...!
THAT DID IT!!
I'M GOING TO BE REBORN AS A REAL HUNK!
YOSHIDAYAMA-KUN!!
THEN I'LL SHOW TÔGÔ!!
YOU GUYS CHANGE YOURSELVES INTO REAL MEN, TOO!
THEN WE MEET TOMORROW AT WAS BURGER!!
R-RIGHT!
ROGER-DASU.
WAS BA
WAS BURGER
THE NEXT DAY AT WAS BURGER.

Yoshidayama Jirô: Gives Off a Different Kind of Aura.

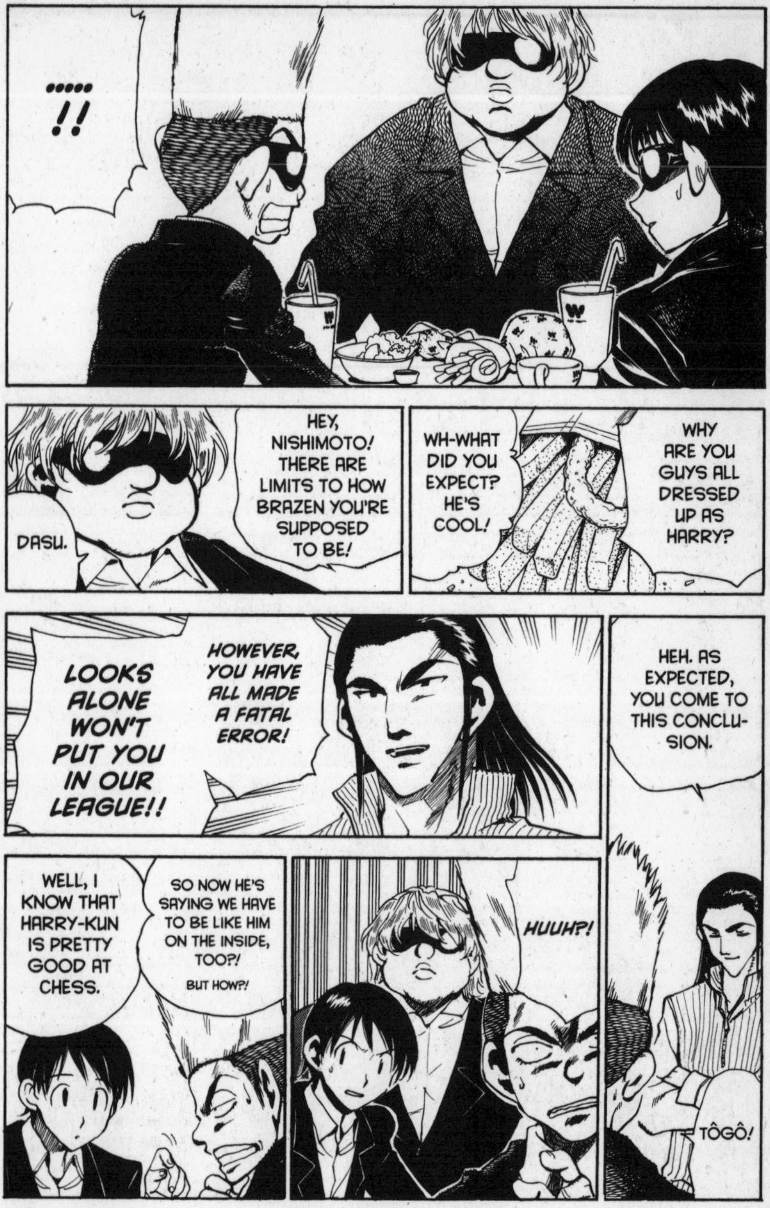
......
!!
WHY ARE YOU GUYS ALL DRESSED UP AS HARRY?
WH-WHAT DID YOU EXPECT? HE'S COOL!
HEY, NISHIMOTO! THERE ARE LIMITS TO HOW BRAZEN YOU'RE SUPPOSED TO BE!
DASU.
HEH. AS EXPECTED, YOU COME TO THIS CONCLUSION.
TÔGÔ!
HOWEVER, YOU HAVE ALL MADE A FATAL ERROR!
LOOKS ALONE WON'T PUT YOU IN OUR LEAGUE!!
HUUH?!
SO NOW HE'S SAYING WE HAVE TO BE LIKE HIM ON THE INSIDE, TOO?!
BUT HOW?!
WELL, I KNOW THAT HARRY-KUN IS PRETTY GOOD AT CHESS.

Harry: Three Votes. Tôgô: None.

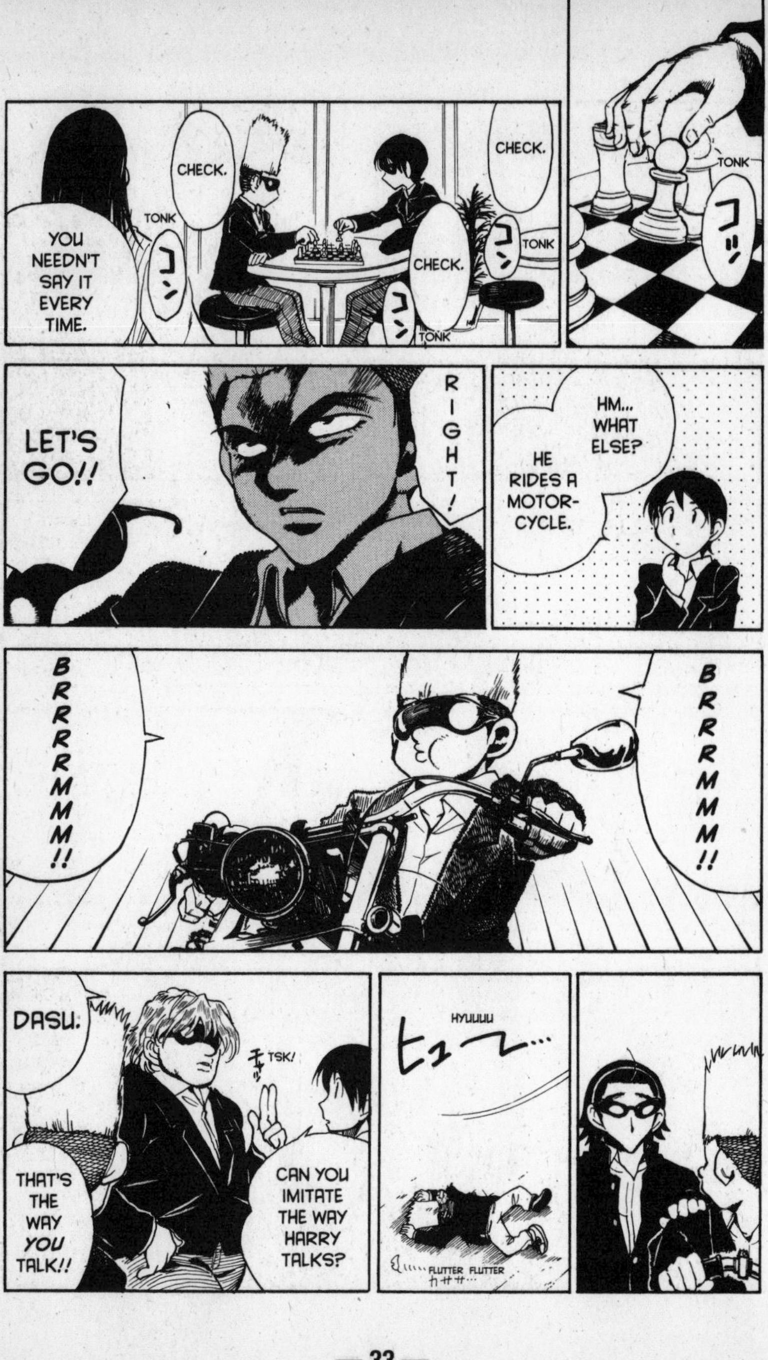
TONK
CHECK.
TONK
CHECK.
TONK
CHECK.
TONK
YOU NEEDN'T SAY IT EVERY TIME.
HM... WHAT ELSE?
HE RIDES A MOTORCYCLE.
RIGHT!
LET'S GO!!
BRRRMMM!!
BRRRMMM!!
HYUUUU
FLUTTER FLUTTER
CAN YOU IMITATE THE WAY HARRY TALKS?
TSK!
DASU.
THAT'S THE WAY YOU TALK!!

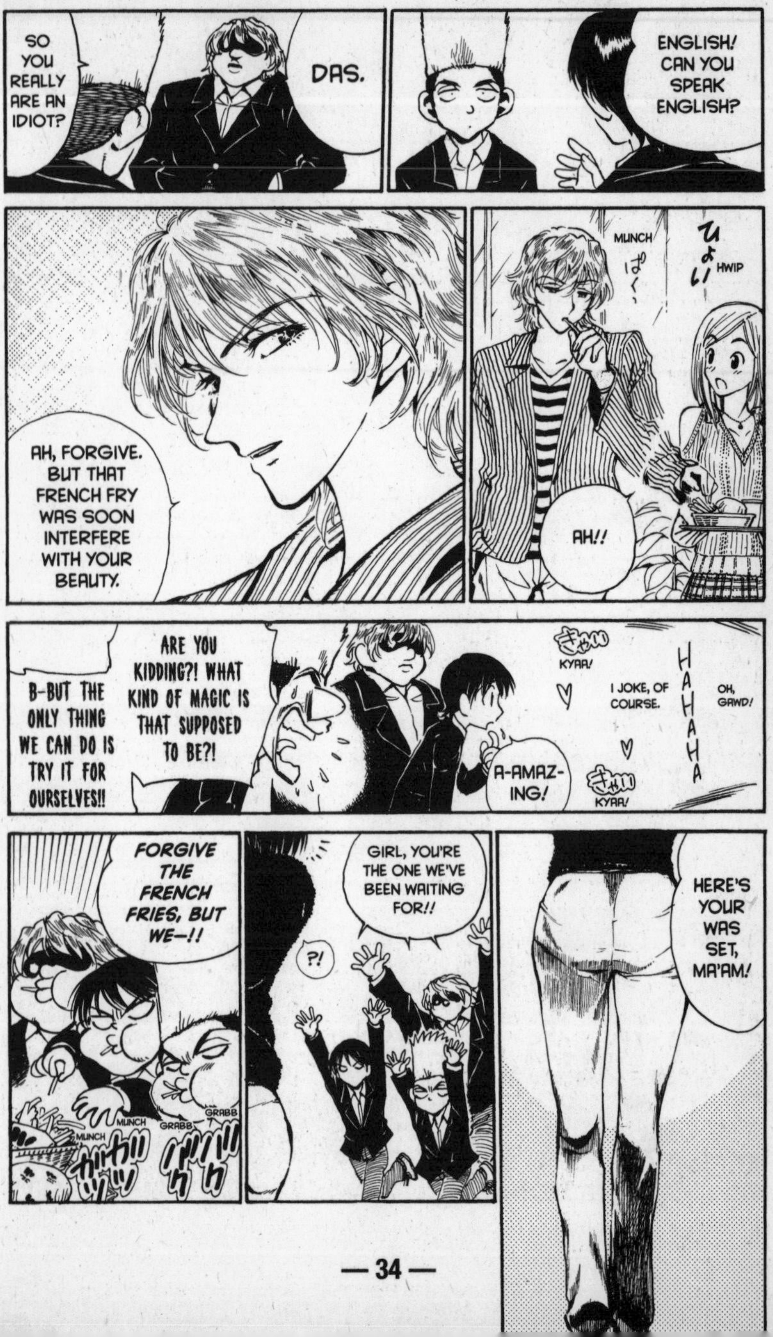
ENGLISH! CAN YOU SPEAK ENGLISH?
DAS.
SO YOU REALLY ARE AN IDIOT?
ひょい
HWIP
MUNCH
ぱく
AH!!
AH, FORGIVE. BUT THAT FRENCH FRY WAS SOON INTERFERE WITH YOUR BEAUTY.
OH, GAWD!
HAHAHA
KYAA!
I JOKE, OF COURSE.
KYAA!
A-AMAZING!
ARE YOU KIDDING?! WHAT KIND OF MAGIC IS THAT SUPPOSED TO BE?!
B-BUT THE ONLY THING WE CAN DO IS TRY IT FOR OURSELVES!!
HERE'S YOUR WAS SET, MA'AM!
GIRL, YOU'RE THE ONE WE'VE BEEN WAITING FOR!!
?!
FORGIVE THE FRENCH FRIES, BUT WE-!!
GRABB
GRABB
MUNCH
MUNCH

Harry: A Wizard of Love.

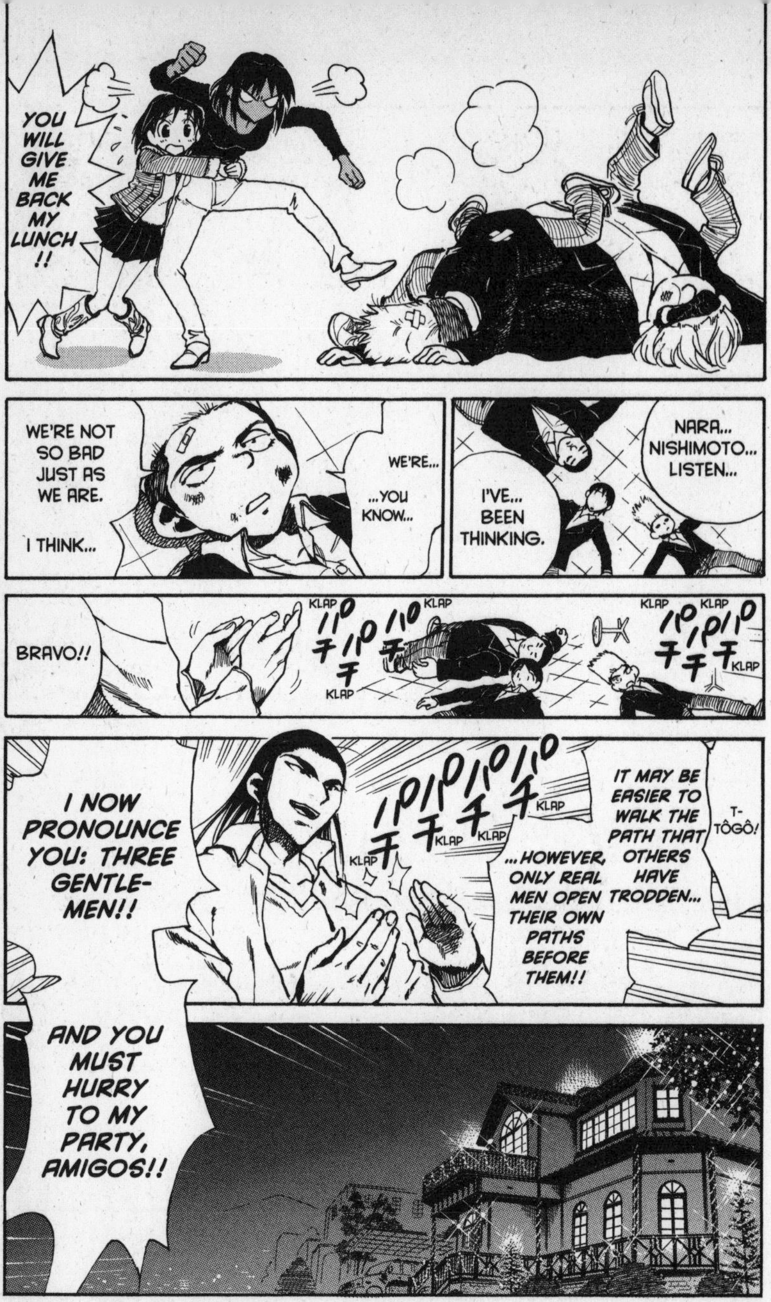
YOU WILL GIVE ME BACK MY LUNCH!!
NARA... NISHIMOTO... LISTEN...
I'VE... BEEN THINKING.
WE'RE...
...YOU KNOW...
WE'RE NOT SO BAD JUST AS WE ARE.
I THINK...
パチパチパチ KLAP KLAP KLAP
パチパチ KLAP KLAP
BRAVO!!
T- TÔGÔ!
IT MAY BE EASIER TO WALK THE PATH THAT OTHERS HAVE TRODDEN...
...HOWEVER, ONLY REAL MEN OPEN THEIR OWN PATHS BEFORE THEM!!
パパパパ チチチチ KLAP KLAP KLAP KLAP
I NOW PRONOUNCE YOU: THREE GENTLEMEN!!
AND YOU MUST HURRY TO MY PARTY, AMIGOS!!

Spread Out Before Them: A Glimpse into Another World.

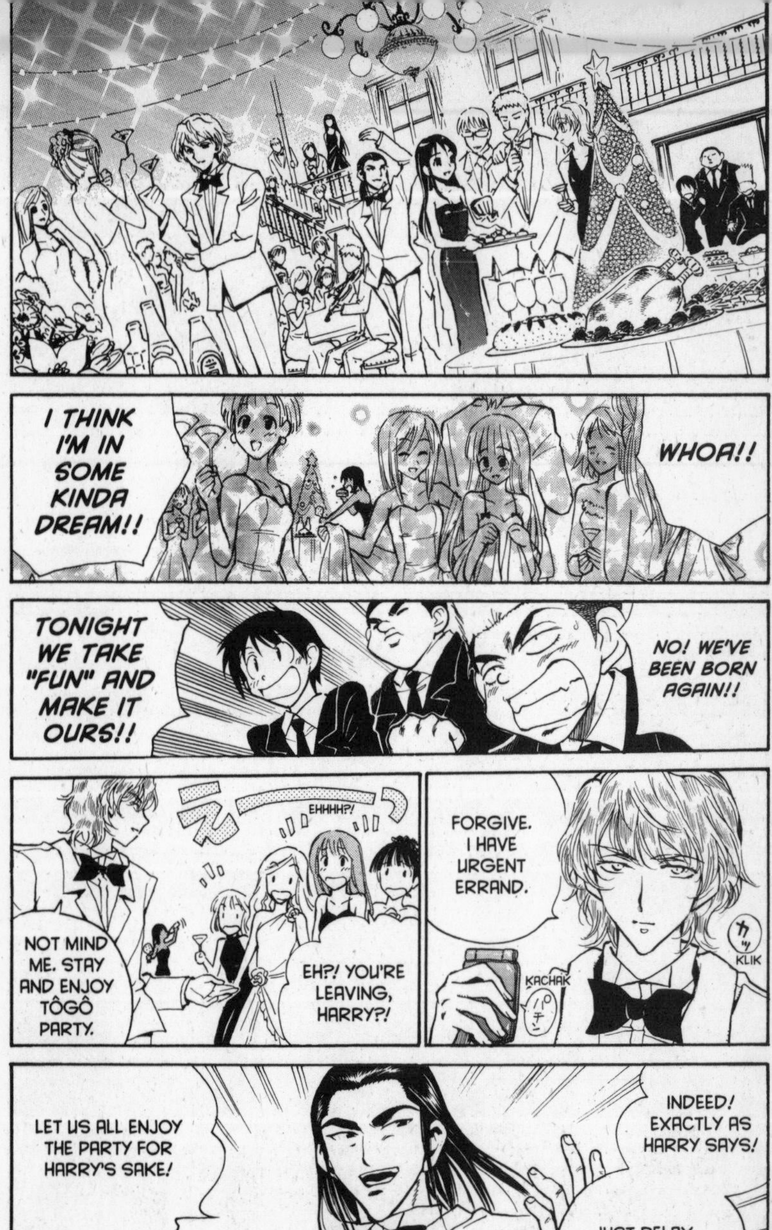
WHOA!!
I THINK I'M IN SOME KINDA DREAM!!
NO! WE'VE BEEN BORN AGAIN!!
TONIGHT WE TAKE "FUN" AND MAKE IT OURS!!
FORGIVE. I HAVE URGENT ERRAND.
KLIK
KACHAK
EHHHH?!
EH?! YOU'RE LEAVING, HARRY?!
NOT MIND ME. STAY AND ENJOY TÔGÔ PARTY.
INDEED! EXACTLY AS HARRY SAYS!
JUST RELAX, MY BAMBINAS!
LET US ALL ENJOY THE PARTY FOR HARRY'S SAKE!

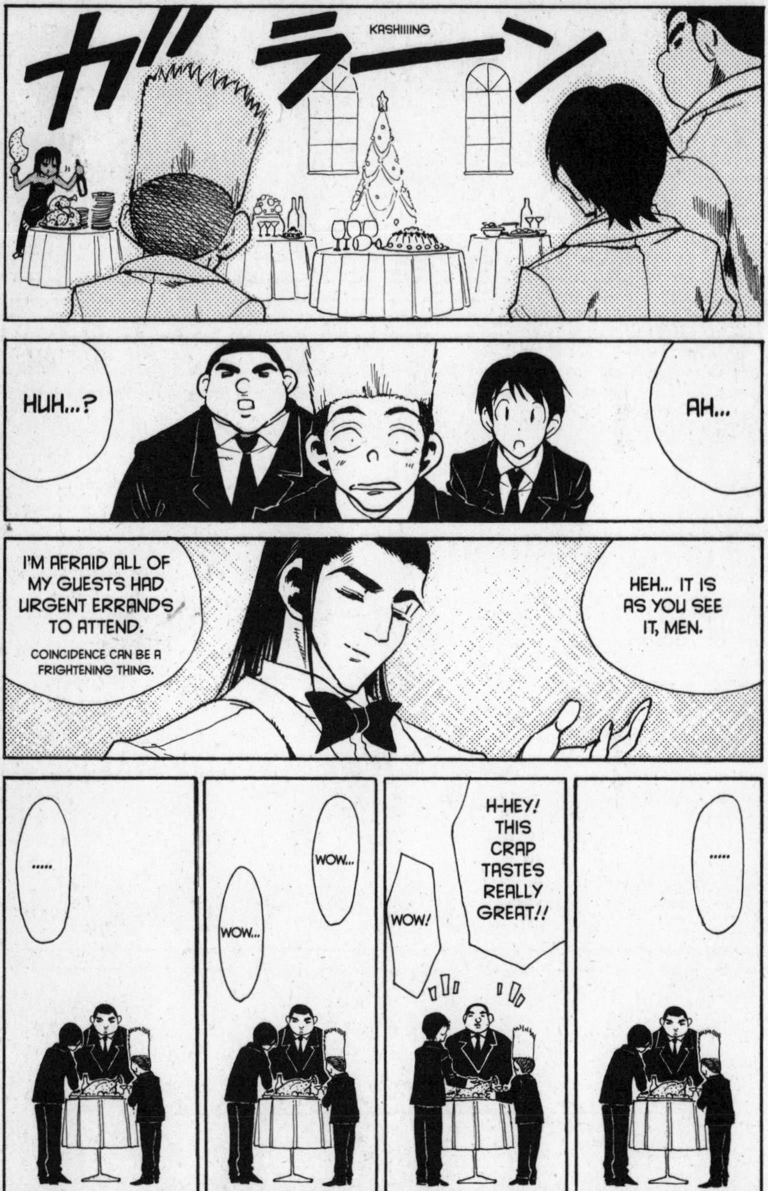
ガラーン
KASHIIIING
AH...
HUH...?
HEH... IT IS AS YOU SEE IT, MEN.
I'M AFRAID ALL OF MY GUESTS HAD URGENT ERRANDS TO ATTEND.
COINCIDENCE CAN BE A FRIGHTENING THING.
......
H-HEY! THIS CRAP TASTES REALLY GREAT!!
WOW!
WOW...
WOW...
......

A Christmas Whiteout.

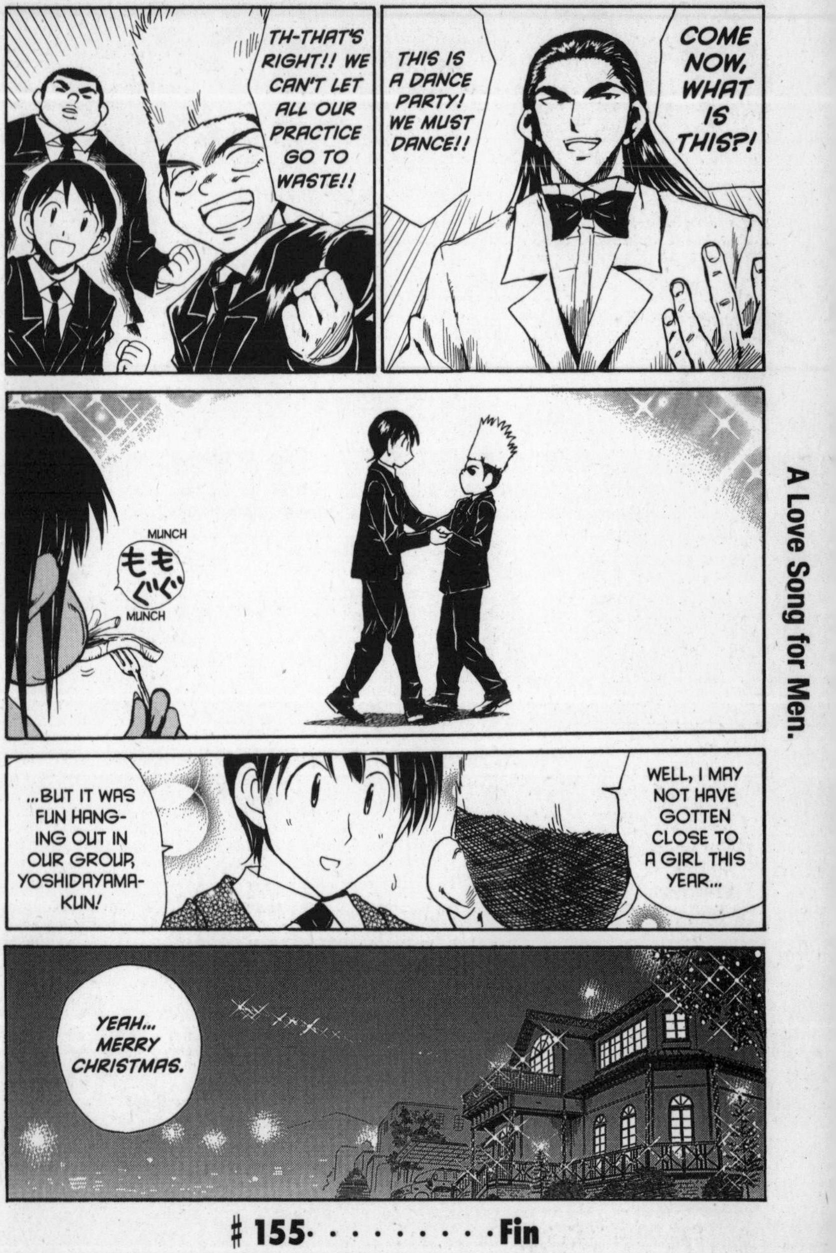
COME NOW, WHAT IS THIS?!
THIS IS A DANCE PARTY! WE MUST DANCE!!
TH-THAT'S RIGHT!! WE CAN'T LET ALL OUR PRACTICE GO TO WASTE!!
MUNCH
もぐもぐ
MUNCH
WELL, I MAY NOT HAVE GOTTEN CLOSE TO A GIRL THIS YEAR...
...BUT IT WAS FUN HANGING OUT IN OUR GROUP, YOSHIDAYAMA-KUN!
YEAH... MERRY CHRISTMAS.

A Love Song for Men.

♯155· · · · · · · · ·Fin

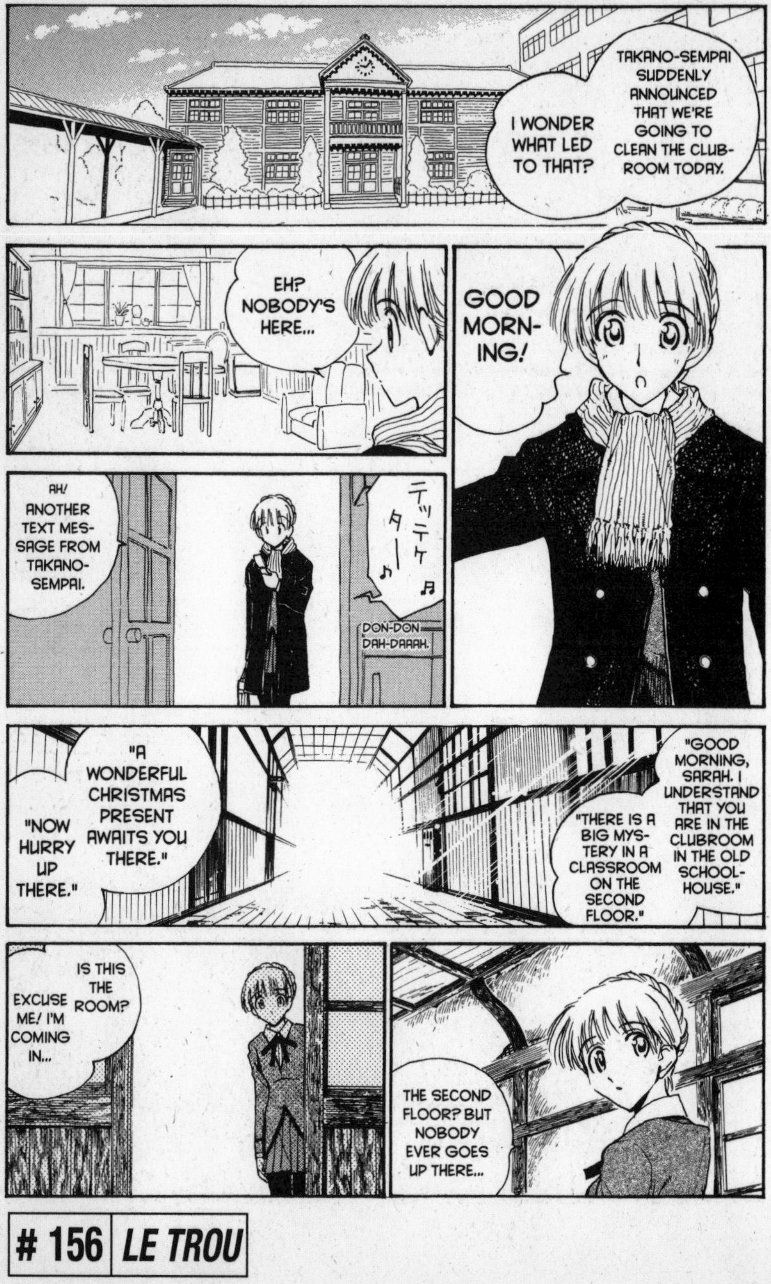
TAKANO-SEMPAI SUDDENLY ANNOUNCED THAT WE'RE GOING TO CLEAN THE CLUB-ROOM TODAY.
I WONDER WHAT LED TO THAT?
GOOD MORNING!
EH? NOBODY'S HERE...
テッテケター♪ ♬
DON-DON DAH-DAAAH.
AH! ANOTHER TEXT MES-SAGE FROM TAKANO-SEMPAI.
"GOOD MORNING, SARAH. I UNDERSTAND THAT YOU ARE IN THE CLUBROOM IN THE OLD SCHOOL-HOUSE."
"THERE IS A BIG MYS-TERY IN A CLASSROOM ON THE SECOND FLOOR."
"A WONDERFUL CHRISTMAS PRESENT AWAITS YOU THERE."
"NOW HURRY UP THERE."
THE SECOND FLOOR? BUT NOBODY EVER GOES UP THERE...
IS THIS THE ROOM?
EXCUSE ME! I'M COMING IN...

156 LE TROU

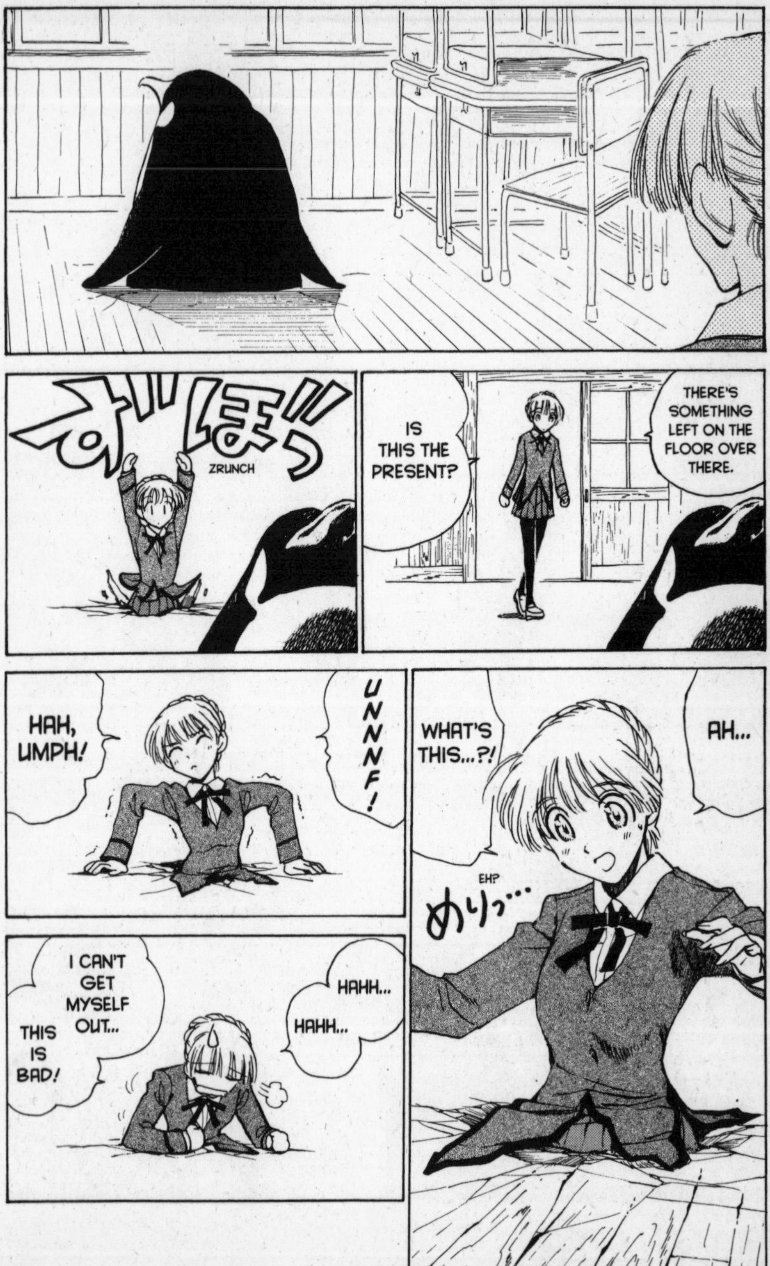
THERE'S SOMETHING LEFT ON THE FLOOR OVER THERE.
IS THIS THE PRESENT?
ずぼっ
ZRUNCH
AH...
WHAT'S THIS...?!
めりっ...
EH?
UNNNF!
HAH, UMPH!
HAHH... HAHH...
I CAN'T GET MYSELF OUT...
THIS IS BAD!

Sarah Adiemus: Member of the Tea Club.

Tsukamoto Yakumo: Also a Tea Club Member.

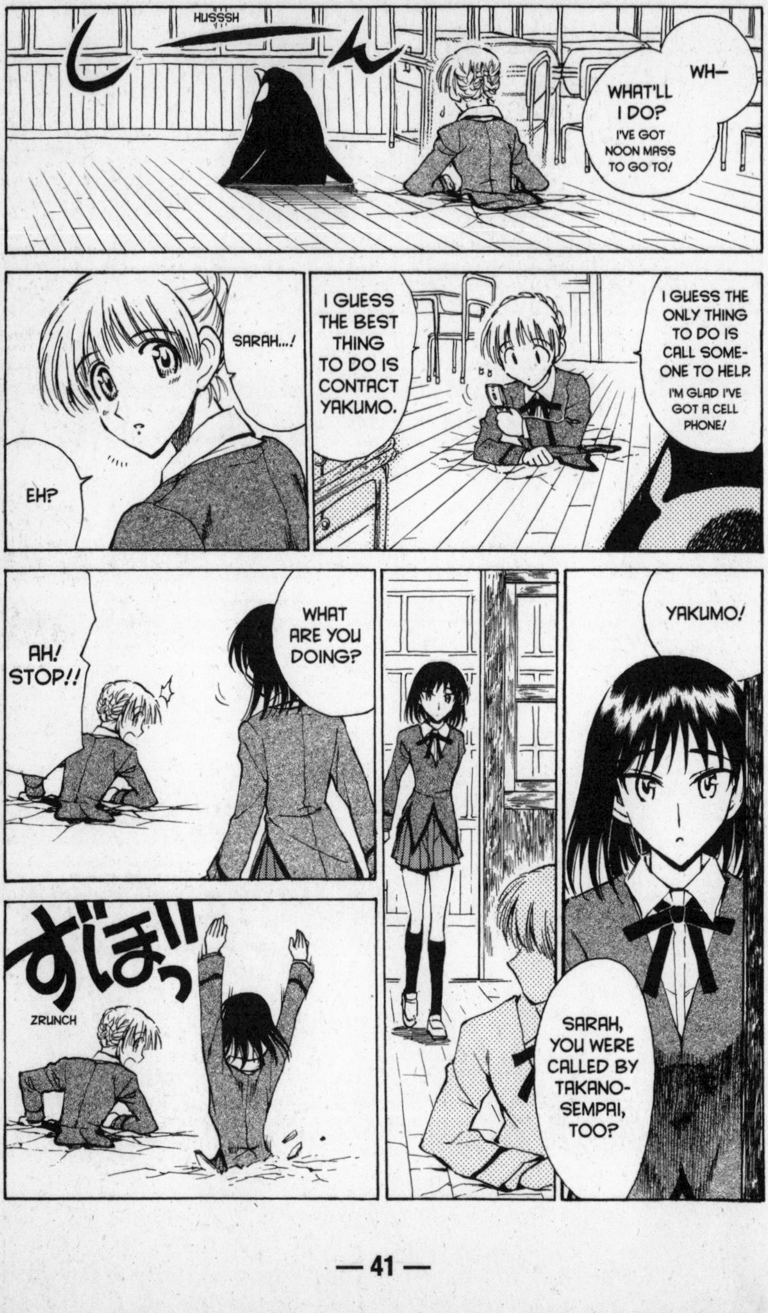
しーん
HUSSSH
WH— WHAT'LL I DO?
I'VE GOT NOON MASS TO GO TO!
I GUESS THE ONLY THING TO DO IS CALL SOME-ONE TO HELP.
I'M GLAD I'VE GOT A CELL PHONE!
I GUESS THE BEST THING TO DO IS CONTACT YAKUMO.
SARAH...!
EH?
YAKUMO!
SARAH, YOU WERE CALLED BY TAKANO-SEMPAI, TOO?
WHAT ARE YOU DOING?
AH! STOP!!
ずぼっ!!
ZRUNCH

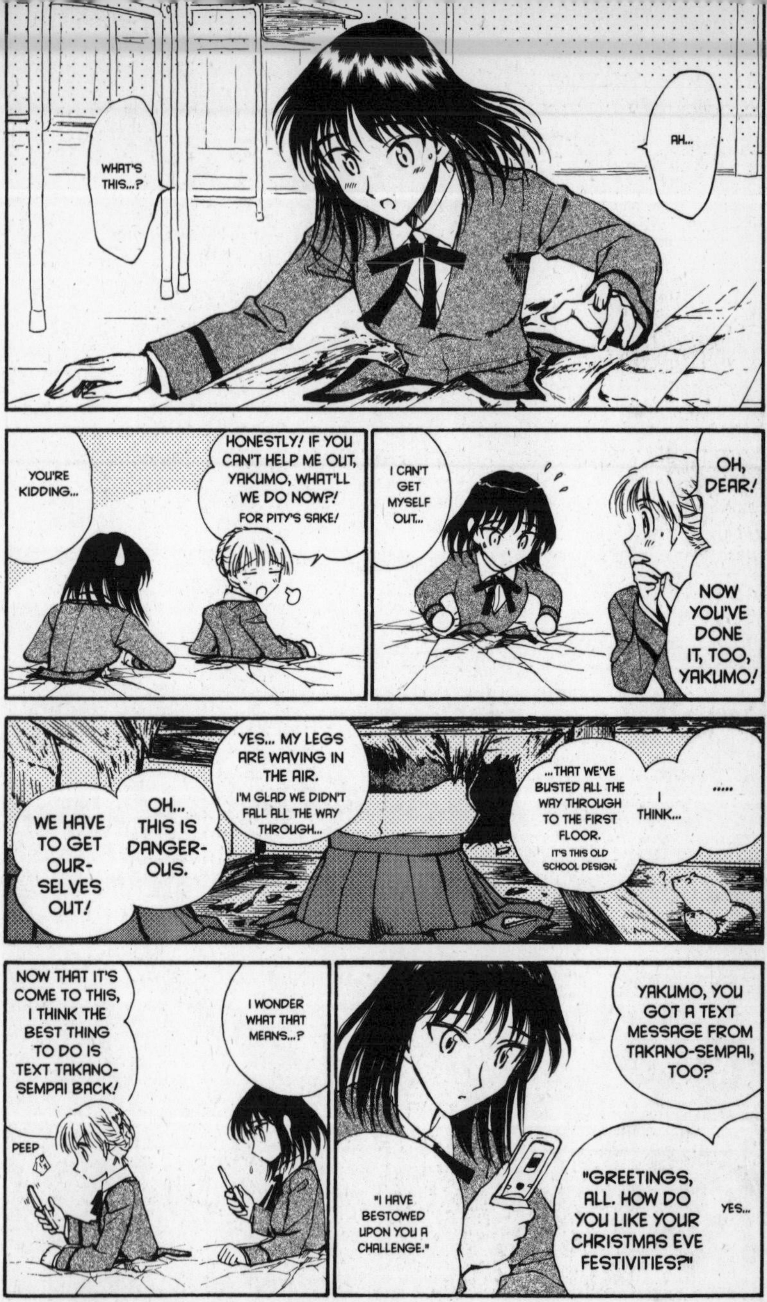
AH...
WHAT'S THIS...?
OH, DEAR!
NOW YOU'VE DONE IT, TOO, YAKUMO!
I CAN'T GET MYSELF OUT...
HONESTLY! IF YOU CAN'T HELP ME OUT, YAKUMO, WHAT'LL WE DO NOW?!
FOR PITY'S SAKE!
YOU'RE KIDDING...
.....
I THINK...
...THAT WE'VE BUSTED ALL THE WAY THROUGH TO THE FIRST FLOOR.
IT'S THIS OLD SCHOOL DESIGN.
YES... MY LEGS ARE WAVING IN THE AIR.
I'M GLAD WE DIDN'T FALL ALL THE WAY THROUGH...
OH... THIS IS DANGEROUS.
WE HAVE TO GET OURSELVES OUT!
YAKUMO, YOU GOT A TEXT MESSAGE FROM TAKANO-SEMPAI, TOO?
YES...
"GREETINGS, ALL. HOW DO YOU LIKE YOUR CHRISTMAS EVE FESTIVITIES?"
"I HAVE BESTOWED UPON YOU A CHALLENGE."
I WONDER WHAT THAT MEANS...?
NOW THAT IT'S COME TO THIS, I THINK THE BEST THING TO DO IS TEXT TAKANO-SEMPAI BACK!
PEEP

Tea Club Room: Old Schoolhouse, First Floor.

Takano Akira: President of the Tea Club. No Matter What It Looks Like.

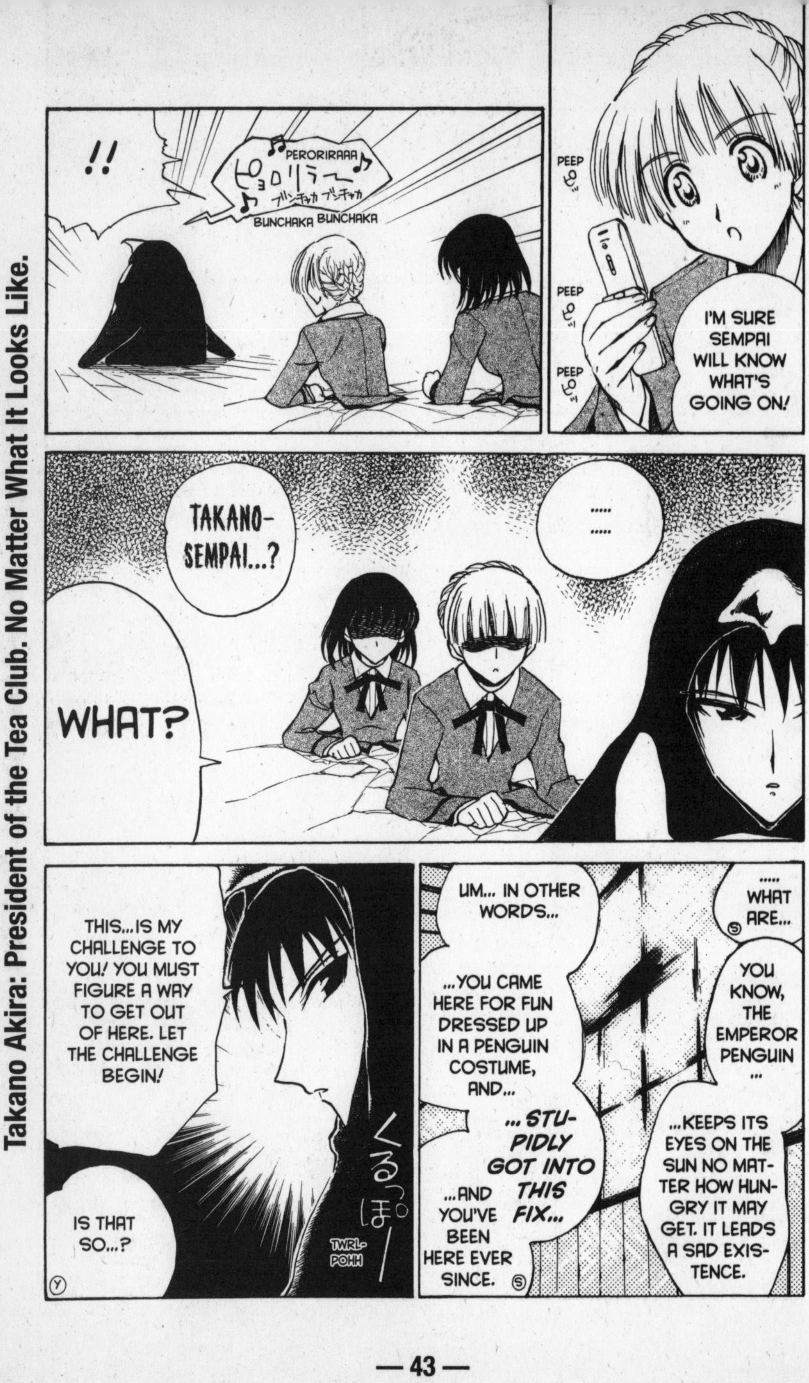
PEEP
ピッ
PEEP
ピッ
PEEP
ピッ
I'M SURE SEMPAI WILL KNOW WHAT'S GOING ON!
!!
PERORIRAAA
ピョロリラ〜
ブンチャカ ブンチャカ
BUNCHAKA BUNCHAKA
....
TAKANO-SEMPAI...?
WHAT?
..... WHAT ARE...
UM... IN OTHER WORDS...
YOU KNOW, THE EMPEROR PENGUIN...
...YOU CAME HERE FOR FUN DRESSED UP IN A PENGUIN COSTUME, AND...
...KEEPS ITS EYES ON THE SUN NO MATTER HOW HUNGRY IT MAY GET. IT LEADS A SAD EXISTENCE.
...STUPIDLY GOT INTO THIS FIX...
...AND YOU'VE BEEN HERE EVER SINCE.
THIS...IS MY CHALLENGE TO YOU! YOU MUST FIGURE A WAY TO GET OUT OF HERE. LET THE CHALLENGE BEGIN!
くるっぽー
TWRL-POHH
IS THAT SO...?

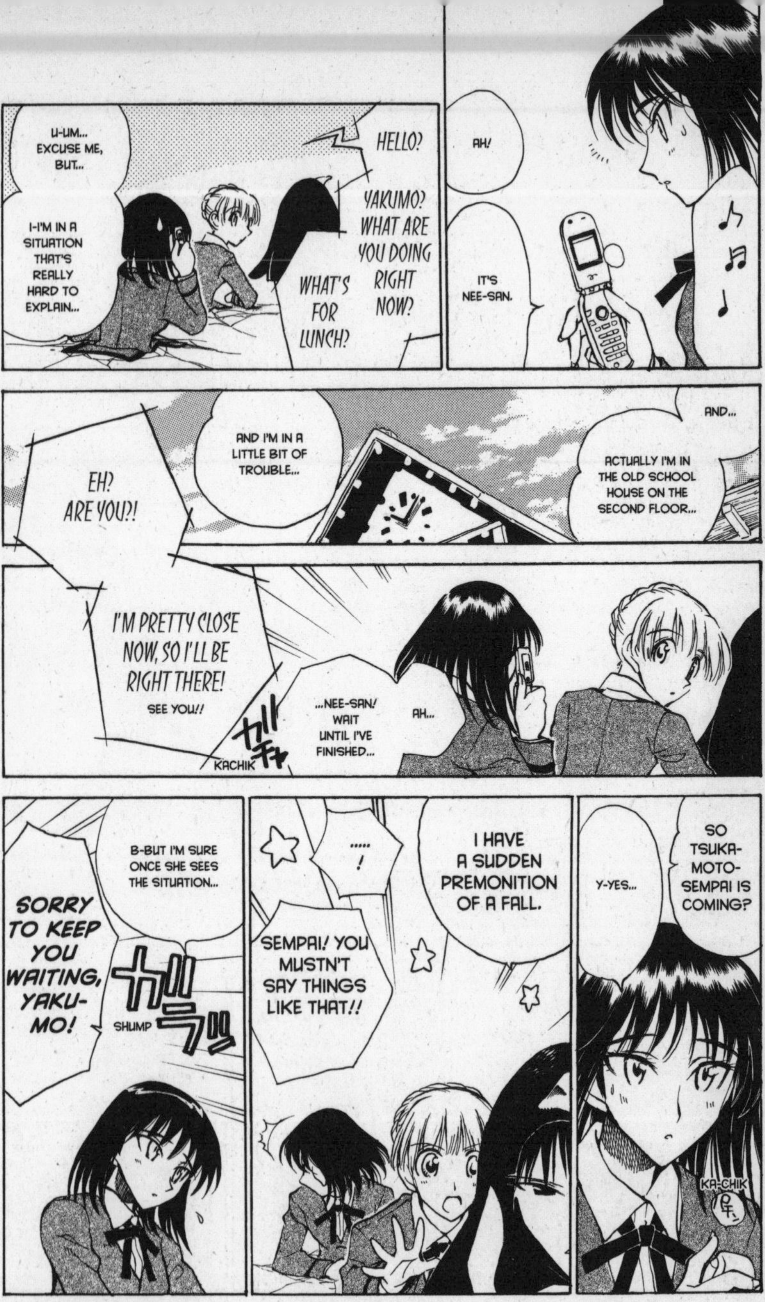
AH!
IT'S NEE-SAN.
HELLO?
YAKUMO? WHAT ARE YOU DOING RIGHT NOW?
WHAT'S FOR LUNCH?
U-UM... EXCUSE ME, BUT...
I-I'M IN A SITUATION THAT'S REALLY HARD TO EXPLAIN...
AND...
ACTUALLY I'M IN THE OLD SCHOOL HOUSE ON THE SECOND FLOOR...
AND I'M IN A LITTLE BIT OF TROUBLE...
EH? ARE YOU?!
AH...
...NEE-SAN! WAIT UNTIL I'VE FINISHED...
I'M PRETTY CLOSE NOW, SO I'LL BE RIGHT THERE!
SEE YOU!!
KACHIK
SO TSUKA-MOTO-SEMPAI IS COMING?
Y-YES...
KA-CHIK
I HAVE A SUDDEN PREMONITION OF A FALL.
......!
SEMPAI! YOU MUSTN'T SAY THINGS LIKE THAT!!
B-BUT I'M SURE ONCE SHE SEES THE SITUATION...
SORRY TO KEEP YOU WAITING, YAKUMO!
SHUMP

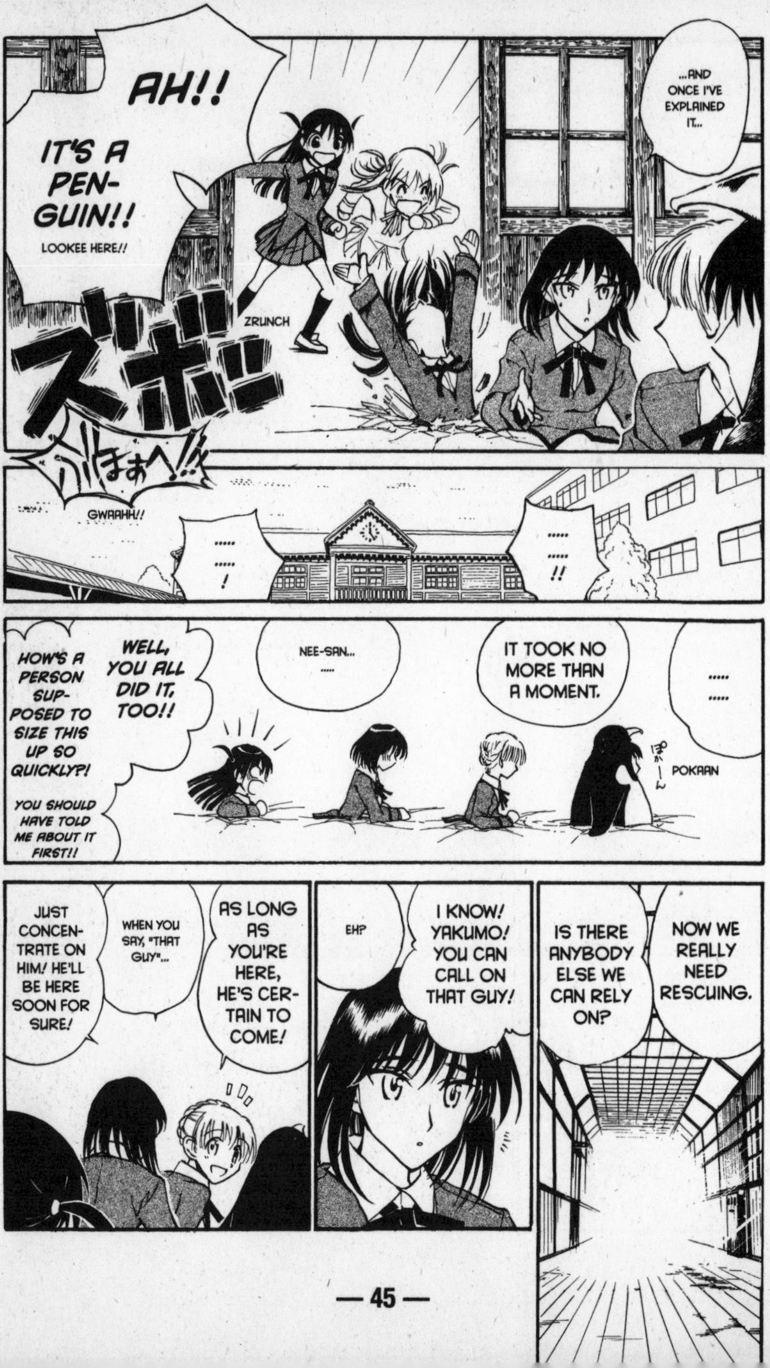
...AND ONCE I'VE EXPLAINED IT...
AH!!
IT'S A PEN-GUIN!!
LOOKEE HERE!!
ZRUNCH
GWAAHH!!
....!!
....!
....
POKAAN
IT TOOK NO MORE THAN A MOMENT.
NEE-SAN... ......
WELL, YOU ALL DID IT, TOO!!
HOW'S A PERSON SUP-POSED TO SIZE THIS UP SO QUICKLY?!
YOU SHOULD HAVE TOLD ME ABOUT IT FIRST!!
NOW WE REALLY NEED RESCUING.
IS THERE ANYBODY ELSE WE CAN RELY ON?
I KNOW! YAKUMO! YOU CAN CALL ON THAT GUY!
EH?
AS LONG AS YOU'RE HERE, HE'S CER-TAIN TO COME!
WHEN YOU SAY, "THAT GUY"...
JUST CONCEN-TRATE ON HIM! HE'LL BE HERE SOON FOR SURE!

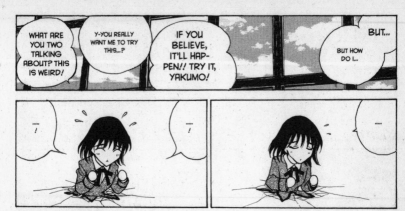

BUT...
BUT HOW DO I...
IF YOU BELIEVE, IT'LL HAP-PEN!! TRY IT, YAKUMO!
Y-YOU REALLY WANT ME TO TRY THIS...?
WHAT ARE YOU TWO TALKING ABOUT? THIS IS WEIRD!
......
......!
......!
...... HE'S NOT COMING.
NO?!
NOW THAT'S ODD!
NO, SARAH. THAT'S NORMAL.
EH?
WHAT'S GOING ON, YAKUMO? DO YOU HAVE PSYCHIC ABILITIES?!
EH...
I HAVE THEM, TOO! I CAN BEND SPOONS!
I'M NOT GOOD AT IT, BUT...
COME TO THINK OF IT, I HEARD HE WAS GET-TING NEW GLASSES.
MAYBE THAT'S THE REASON HE COULDN'T GET HERE, HUH?
HANAI-SEMPAI.
EH?
ぶんぶん ぶんぶん
SHAKE SHAKE SHAKE SHAKE
SO WHAT DO WE DO NOW?
MAYBE WE SHOULD CALL ERI-CHAN AND MIKO-CHAN?
......
ぷしゅううう
PSHHHHHH
EH?
HANAI-SEMPAI...?
ERI IS AT A PARTY.
OF SOME SORT.
MIKOTO IS ON A DATE WITH ASÔ-KUN.
I SEE... WELL, THAT RULES OUT CALLING THEM.

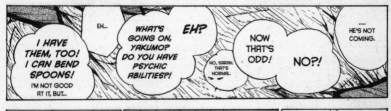

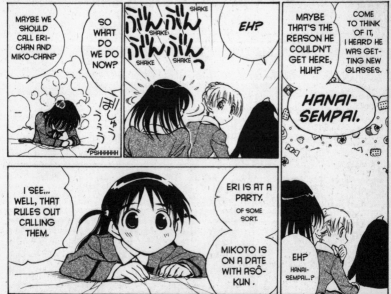

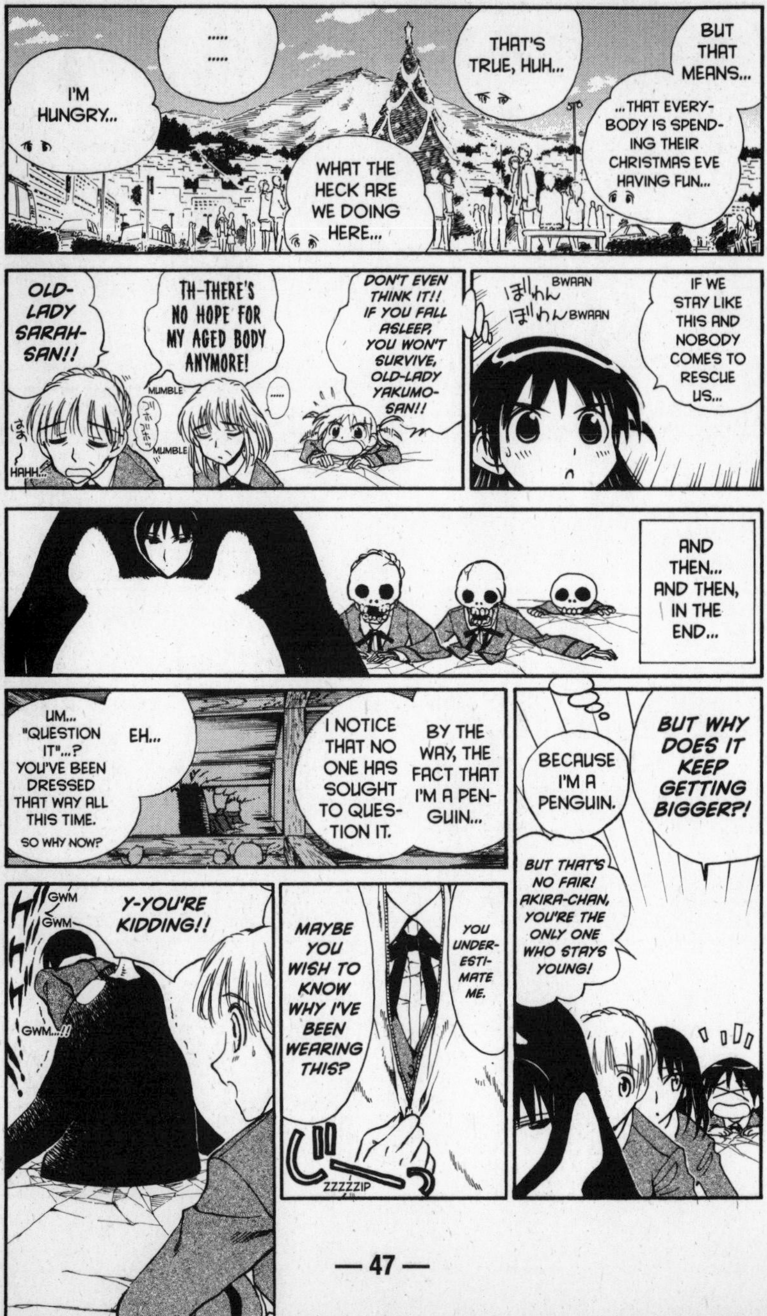
BUT THAT MEANS...
...THAT EVERYBODY IS SPENDING THEIR CHRISTMAS EVE HAVING FUN...
THAT'S TRUE, HUH...
WHAT THE HECK ARE WE DOING HERE...
....
I'M HUNGRY...
IF WE STAY LIKE THIS AND NOBODY COMES TO RESCUE US...
BWAAN
BWAAN
DON'T EVEN THINK IT!! IF YOU FALL ASLEEP, YOU WON'T SURVIVE, OLD-LADY YAKUMO-SAN!!
......
TH-THERE'S NO HOPE FOR MY AGED BODY ANYMORE!
MUMBLE
MUMBLE
OLD-LADY SARAH-SAN!!
HAHH...
AND THEN... AND THEN, IN THE END...
BUT WHY DOES IT KEEP GETTING BIGGER?!
BECAUSE I'M A PENGUIN.
BUT THAT'S NO FAIR! AKIRA-CHAN, YOU'RE THE ONLY ONE WHO STAYS YOUNG!
BY THE WAY, THE FACT THAT I'M A PENGUIN...
I NOTICE THAT NO ONE HAS SOUGHT TO QUESTION IT.
EH...
UM... "QUESTION IT"...? YOU'VE BEEN DRESSED THAT WAY ALL THIS TIME.
SO WHY NOW?
YOU UNDERESTIMATE ME.
MAYBE YOU WISH TO KNOW WHY I'VE BEEN WEARING THIS?
ZZZZZIP
Y-YOU'RE KIDDING!!
GWM
GWM
GWM...!!

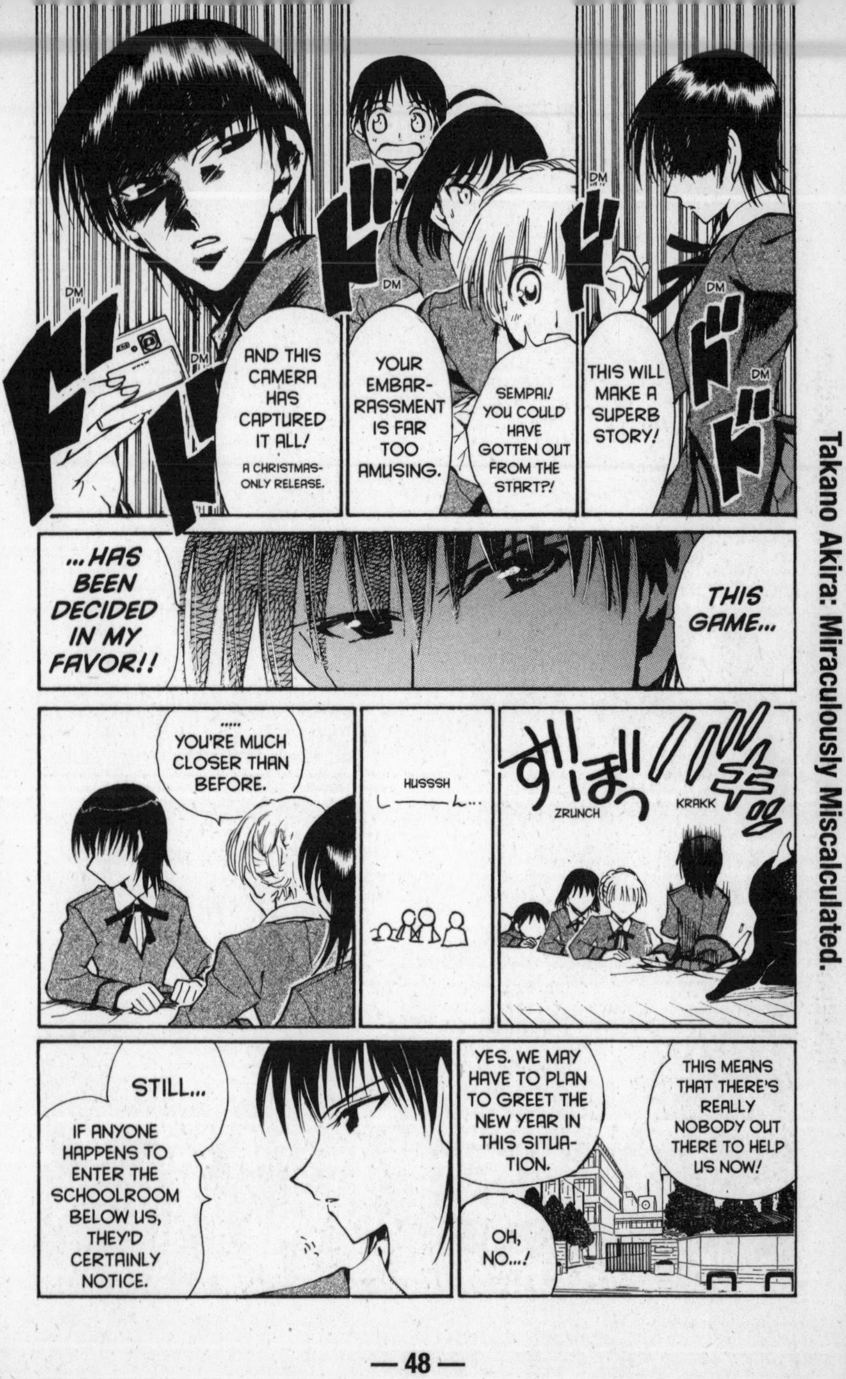
DM
THIS WILL MAKE A SUPERB STORY!
DM
DM
SEMPAI! YOU COULD HAVE GOTTEN OUT FROM THE START?!
DM
YOUR EMBARRASSMENT IS FAR TOO AMUSING.
DM
DM
AND THIS CAMERA HAS CAPTURED IT ALL!
A CHRISTMAS-ONLY RELEASE.
THIS GAME...
...HAS BEEN DECIDED IN MY FAVOR!!
すぽっ
ZRUNCH
バキ
KRAKK
HUSSSH
し——ん...
..... YOU'RE MUCH CLOSER THAN BEFORE.
THIS MEANS THAT THERE'S REALLY NOBODY OUT THERE TO HELP US NOW!
YES. WE MAY HAVE TO PLAN TO GREET THE NEW YEAR IN THIS SITUATION.
OH, NO...!
STILL...
IF ANYONE HAPPENS TO ENTER THE SCHOOLROOM BELOW US, THEY'D CERTAINLY NOTICE.

Takano Akira: Miraculously Miscalculated.

Unexpectedly, a Synopsis of the Winter Vacation Plotline.

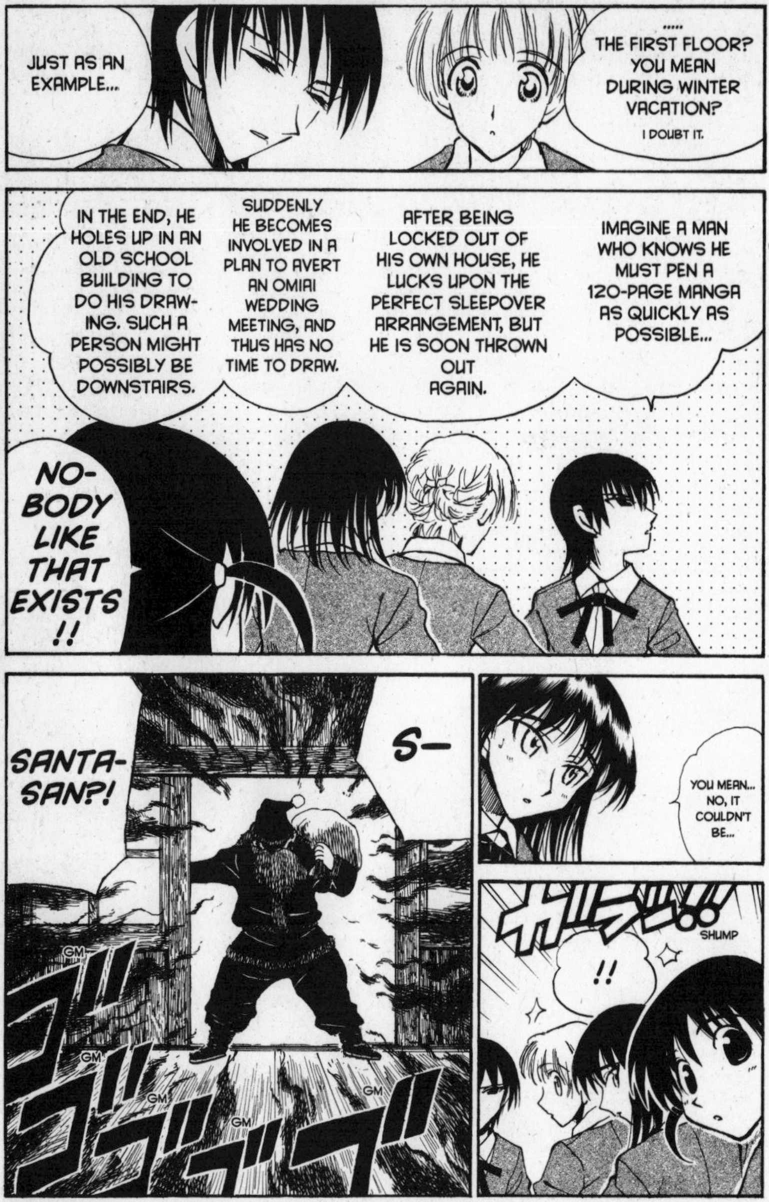

..... THE FIRST FLOOR? YOU MEAN DURING WINTER VACATION?
I DOUBT IT.
JUST AS AN EXAMPLE...
IMAGINE A MAN WHO KNOWS HE MUST PEN A 120-PAGE MANGA AS QUICKLY AS POSSIBLE...
AFTER BEING LOCKED OUT OF HIS OWN HOUSE, HE LUCKS UPON THE PERFECT SLEEPOVER ARRANGEMENT, BUT HE IS SOON THROWN OUT AGAIN.
SUDDENLY HE BECOMES INVOLVED IN A PLAN TO AVERT AN OMIAI WEDDING MEETING, AND THUS HAS NO TIME TO DRAW.
IN THE END, HE HOLES UP IN AN OLD SCHOOL BUILDING TO DO HIS DRAW-ING. SUCH A PERSON MIGHT POSSIBLY BE DOWNSTAIRS.
NO-BODY LIKE THAT EXISTS !!
YOU MEAN... NO, IT COULDN'T BE...
SHUMP
!!
S—
SANTA-SAN?!
GM
GM
GM
GM
GM

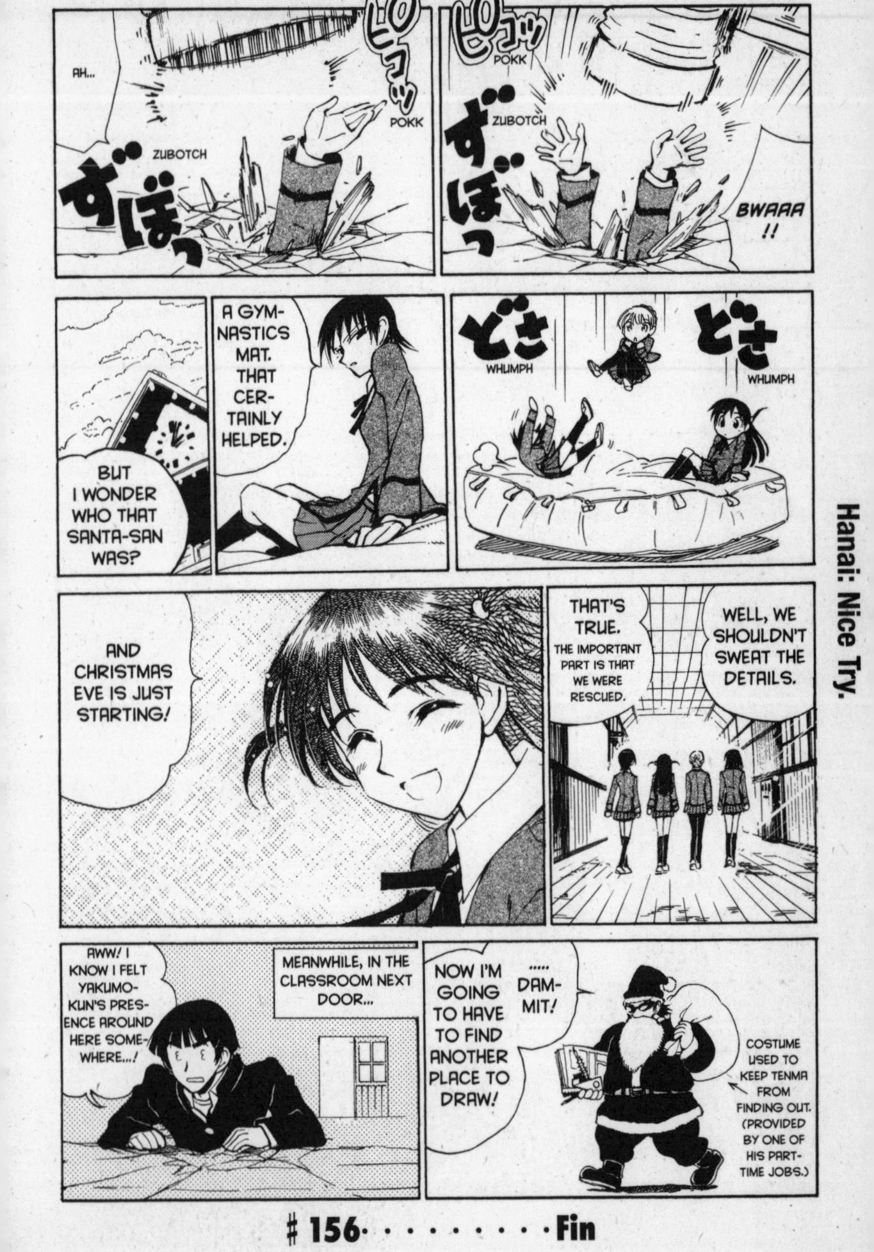
ピコッ
POKK
ずぼっ
ZUBOTCH
BWAAA!!
AH...
ピコッ
POKK
ずぼっ
ZUBOTCH
どさ
WHUMPH
どさ
WHUMPH
A GYMNASTICS MAT. THAT CERTAINLY HELPED.
BUT I WONDER WHO THAT SANTA-SAN WAS?
WELL, WE SHOULDN'T SWEAT THE DETAILS.
THAT'S TRUE. THE IMPORTANT PART IS THAT WE WERE RESCUED.
AND CHRISTMAS EVE IS JUST STARTING!
..... DAMMIT!
NOW I'M GOING TO HAVE TO FIND ANOTHER PLACE TO DRAW!
COSTUME USED TO KEEP TENMA FROM FINDING OUT. (PROVIDED BY ONE OF HIS PART-TIME JOBS.)
MEANWHILE, IN THE CLASSROOM NEXT DOOR...
AWW! I KNOW I FELT YAKUMO-KUN'S PRESENCE AROUND HERE SOMEWHERE...!

Hanai: Nice Try.

156 · · · · · · · · Fin

#157 THE PISTOL, THE BIRTH OF THE LEGEND

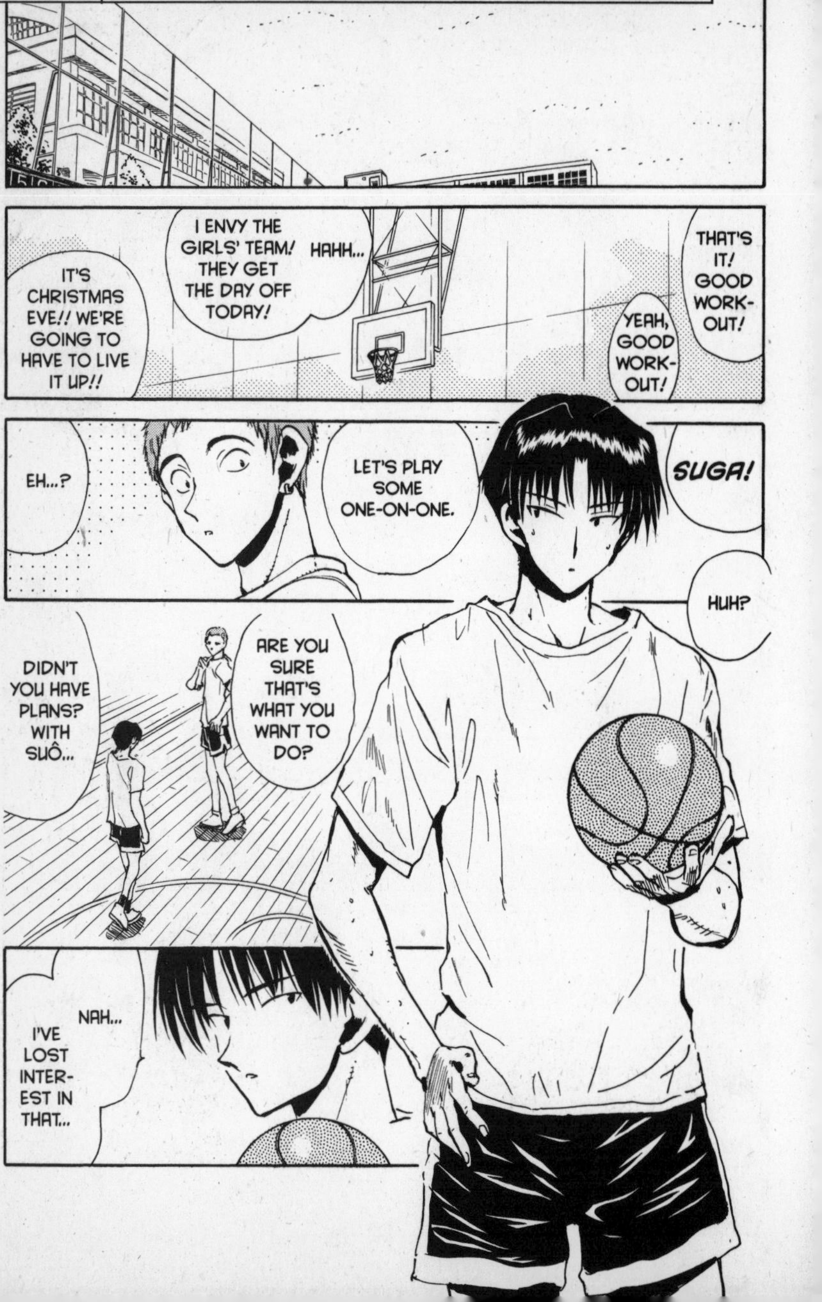
THAT'S IT! GOOD WORK-OUT!
YEAH, GOOD WORK-OUT!
HAHH...
I ENVY THE GIRLS' TEAM! THEY GET THE DAY OFF TODAY!
IT'S CHRISTMAS EVE!! WE'RE GOING TO HAVE TO LIVE IT UP!!
SUGA!
LET'S PLAY SOME ONE-ON-ONE.
EH...?
HUH?
ARE YOU SURE THAT'S WHAT YOU WANT TO DO?
DIDN'T YOU HAVE PLANS? WITH SUÔ...
NAH...
I'VE LOST INTEREST IN THAT...

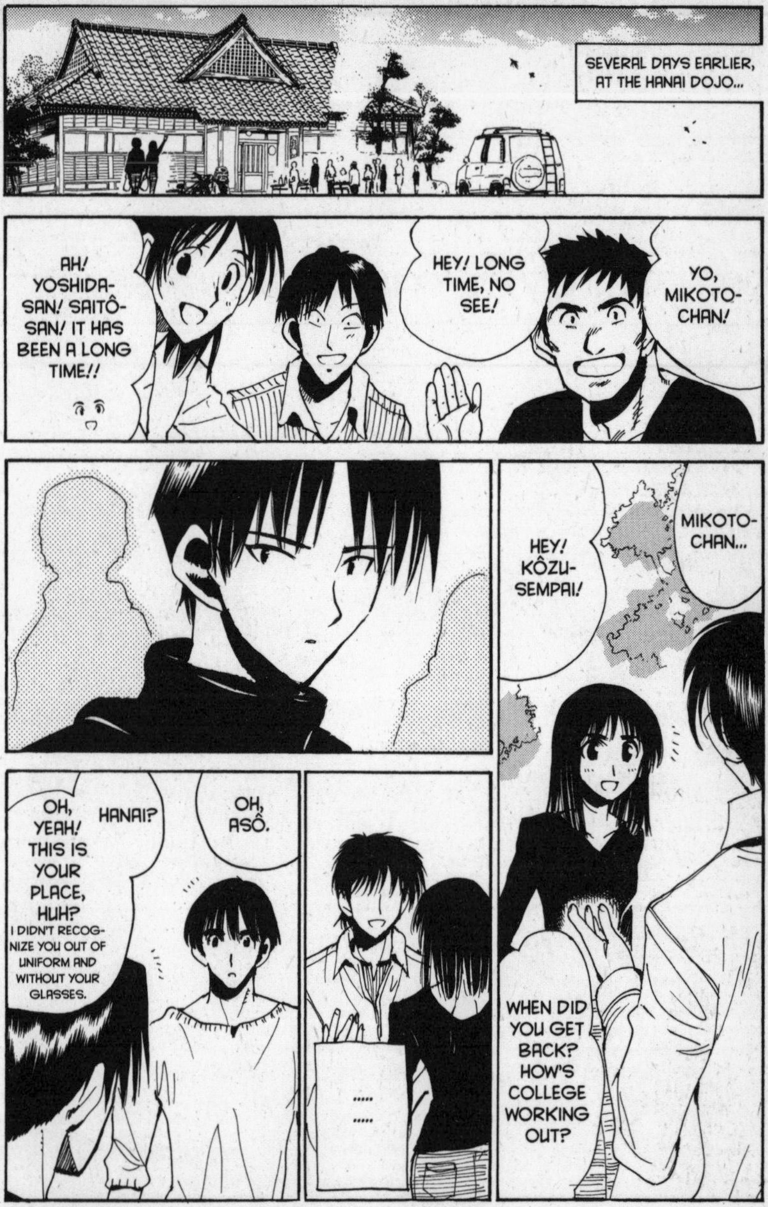
SEVERAL DAYS EARLIER, AT THE HANAI DOJO...
YO, MIKOTO-CHAN!
HEY! LONG TIME, NO SEE!
AH! YOSHIDA-SAN! SAITÔ-SAN! IT HAS BEEN A LONG TIME!!
MIKOTO-CHAN...
HEY! KÔZU-SEMPAI!
WHEN DID YOU GET BACK? HOW'S COLLEGE WORKING OUT?
......
......
OH, ASÔ.
HANAI?
OH, YEAH! THIS IS YOUR PLACE, HUH?
I DIDN'T RECOGNIZE YOU OUT OF UNIFORM AND WITHOUT YOUR GLASSES.

See More About Mikoto and Kôzu in Volume 4.

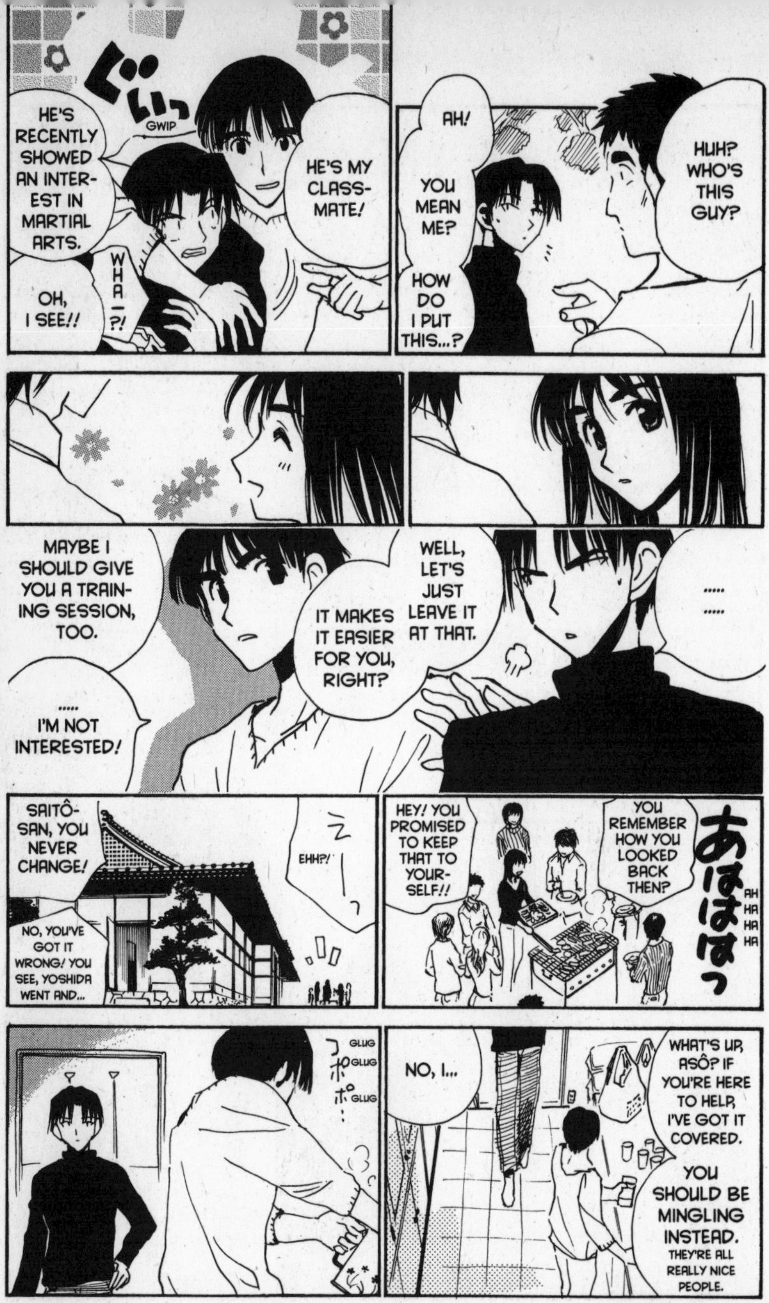
HUH? WHO'S THIS GUY?
AH!
YOU MEAN ME?
HOW DO I PUT THIS...?
HE'S MY CLASSMATE!
ぐいっ GWIP
HE'S RECENTLY SHOWED AN INTEREST IN MARTIAL ARTS.
WHA—?!
OH, I SEE!!
....
WELL, LET'S JUST LEAVE IT AT THAT.
IT MAKES IT EASIER FOR YOU, RIGHT?
MAYBE I SHOULD GIVE YOU A TRAINING SESSION, TOO.
..... I'M NOT INTERESTED!
あははっ AH HA HA HA
YOU REMEMBER HOW YOU LOOKED BACK THEN?
HEY! YOU PROMISED TO KEEP THAT TO YOURSELF!!
え EHH?!
SAITÔ-SAN, YOU NEVER CHANGE!
NO, YOU'VE GOT IT WRONG! YOU SEE, YOSHIDA WENT AND...
WHAT'S UP, ASÔ? IF YOU'RE HERE TO HELP, I'VE GOT IT COVERED.
YOU SHOULD BE MINGLING INSTEAD.
THEY'RE ALL REALLY NICE PEOPLE.
NO, I...
ゴポポ GLUG GLUG GLUG

Hanai: Today Wearing Contacts.

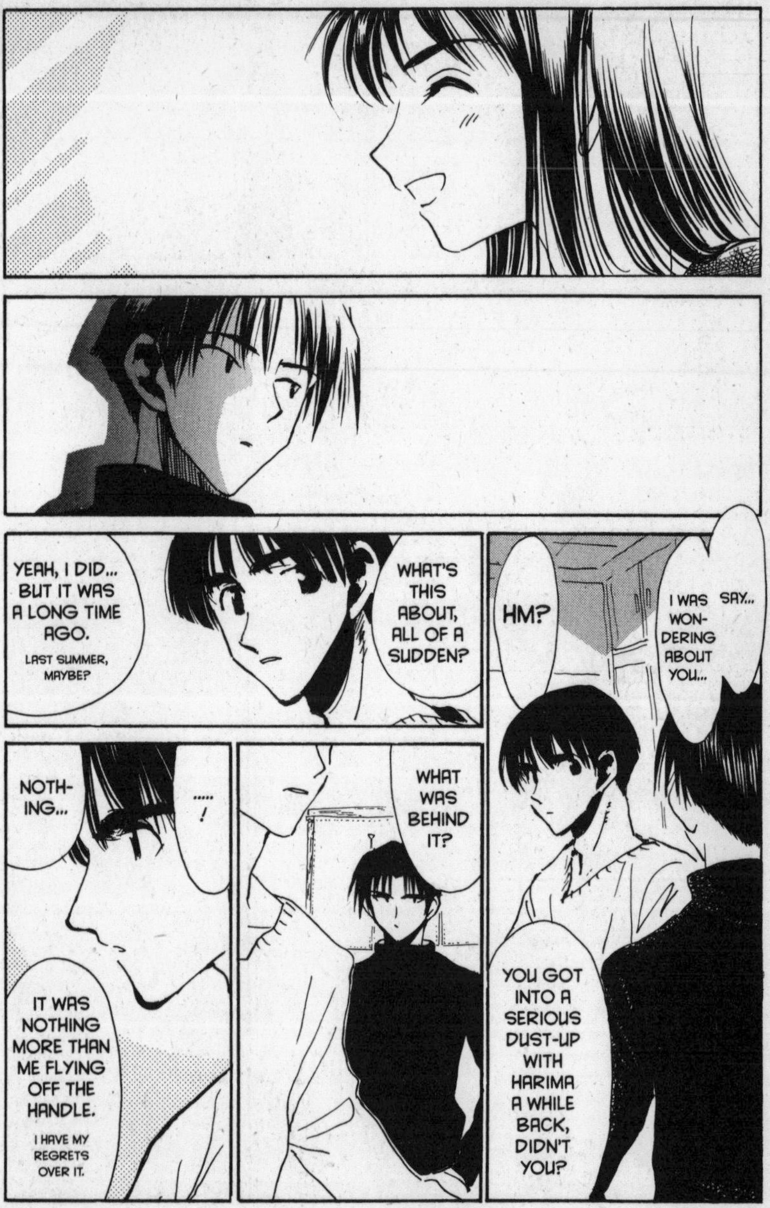
SAY...
I WAS WONDERING ABOUT YOU...
HM?
YOU GOT INTO A SERIOUS DUST-UP WITH HARIMA A WHILE BACK, DIDN'T YOU?
WHAT'S THIS ABOUT, ALL OF A SUDDEN?
YEAH, I DID... BUT IT WAS A LONG TIME AGO.
LAST SUMMER, MAYBE?
WHAT WAS BEHIND IT?
.....!
NOTHING...
IT WAS NOTHING MORE THAN ME FLYING OFF THE HANDLE.
I HAVE MY REGRETS OVER IT.

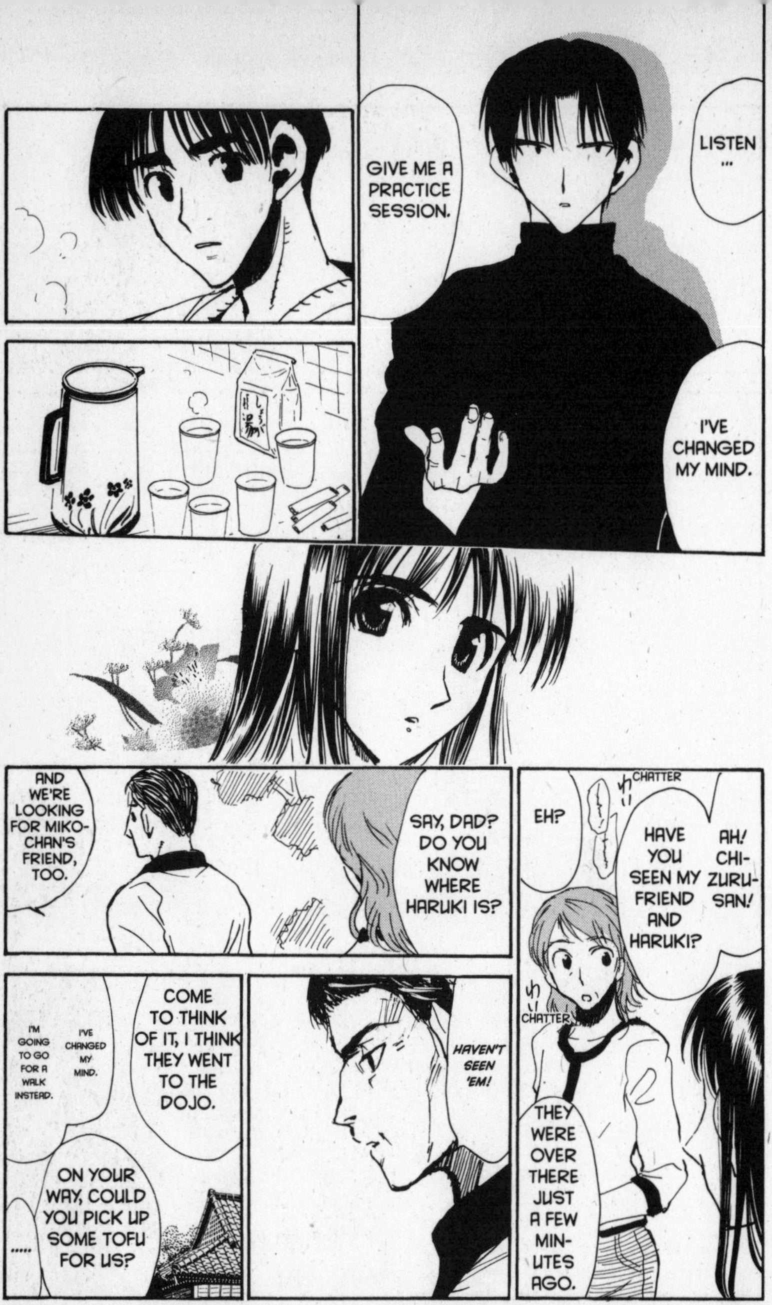
LISTEN ...
GIVE ME A PRACTICE SESSION.
I'VE CHANGED MY MIND.
AH! CHIZURU-SAN!
HAVE YOU SEEN MY FRIEND AND HARUKI?
EH?
CHATTER
CHATTER
THEY WERE OVER THERE JUST A FEW MINUTES AGO.
SAY, DAD? DO YOU KNOW WHERE HARUKI IS?
AND WE'RE LOOKING FOR MIKO-CHAN'S FRIEND, TOO.
HAVEN'T SEEN 'EM!
COME TO THINK OF IT, I THINK THEY WENT TO THE DOJO.
I'VE CHANGED MY MIND.
I'M GOING TO GO FOR A WALK INSTEAD.
ON YOUR WAY, COULD YOU PICK UP SOME TOFU FOR US?
.....

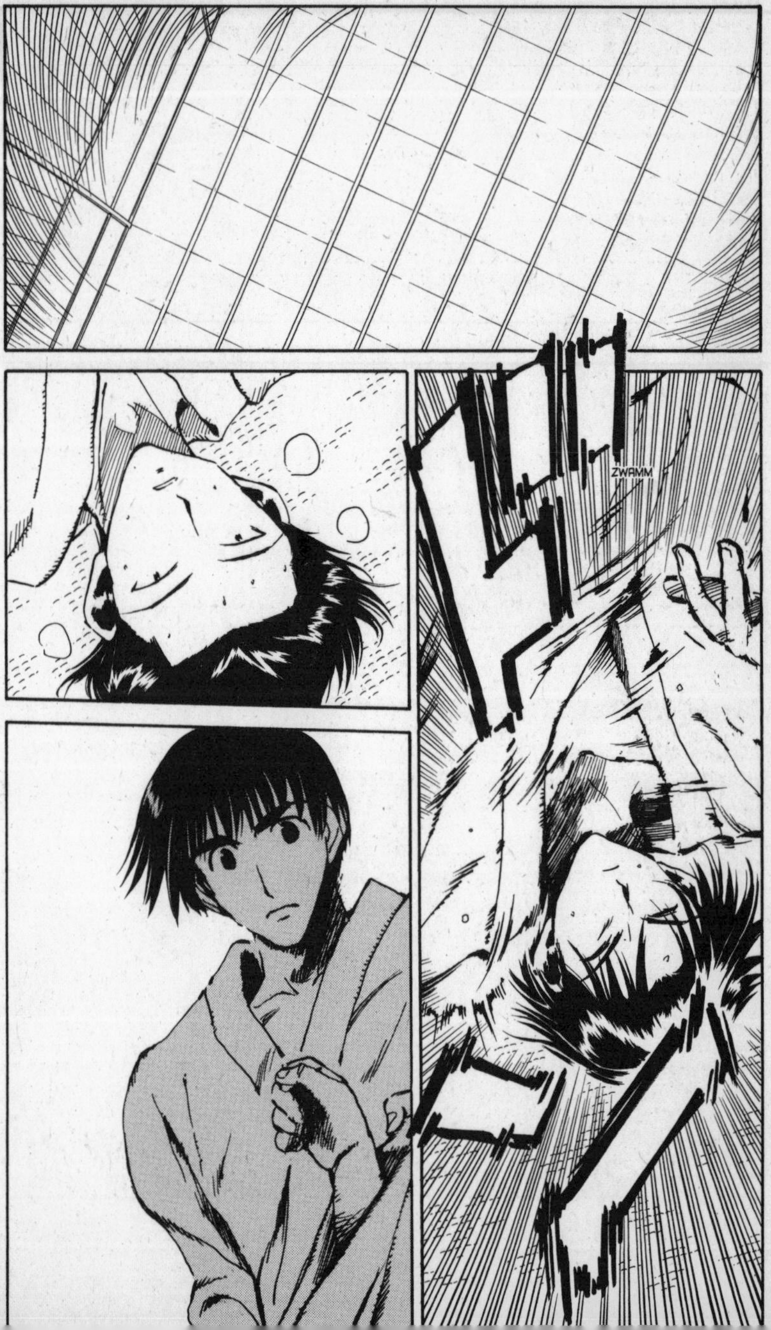
ZWAMM

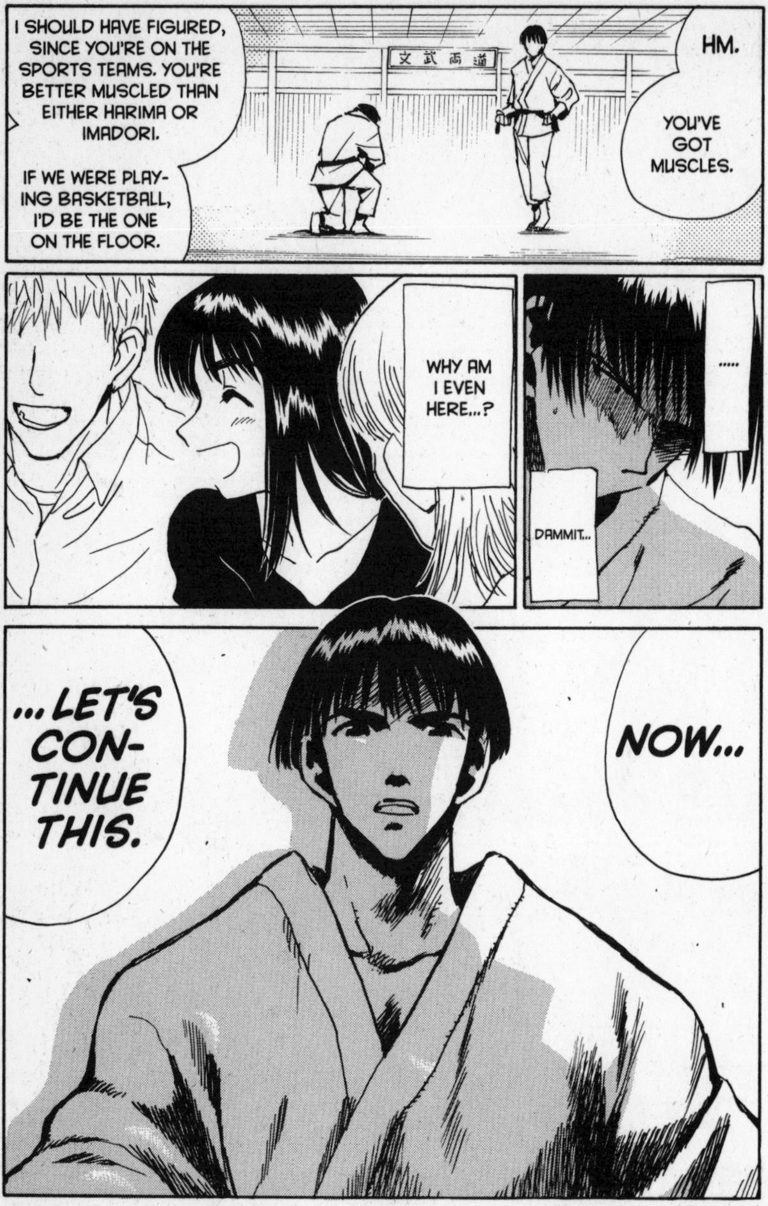
HM.
YOU'VE GOT MUSCLES.
文武両道
I SHOULD HAVE FIGURED, SINCE YOU'RE ON THE SPORTS TEAMS. YOU'RE BETTER MUSCLED THAN EITHER HARIMA OR IMADORI.
IF WE WERE PLAY-ING BASKETBALL, I'D BE THE ONE ON THE FLOOR.
.....
DAMMIT...
WHY AM I EVEN HERE...?
NOW...
...LET'S CON-TINUE THIS.

And the Story Comes Back to the Present Day.

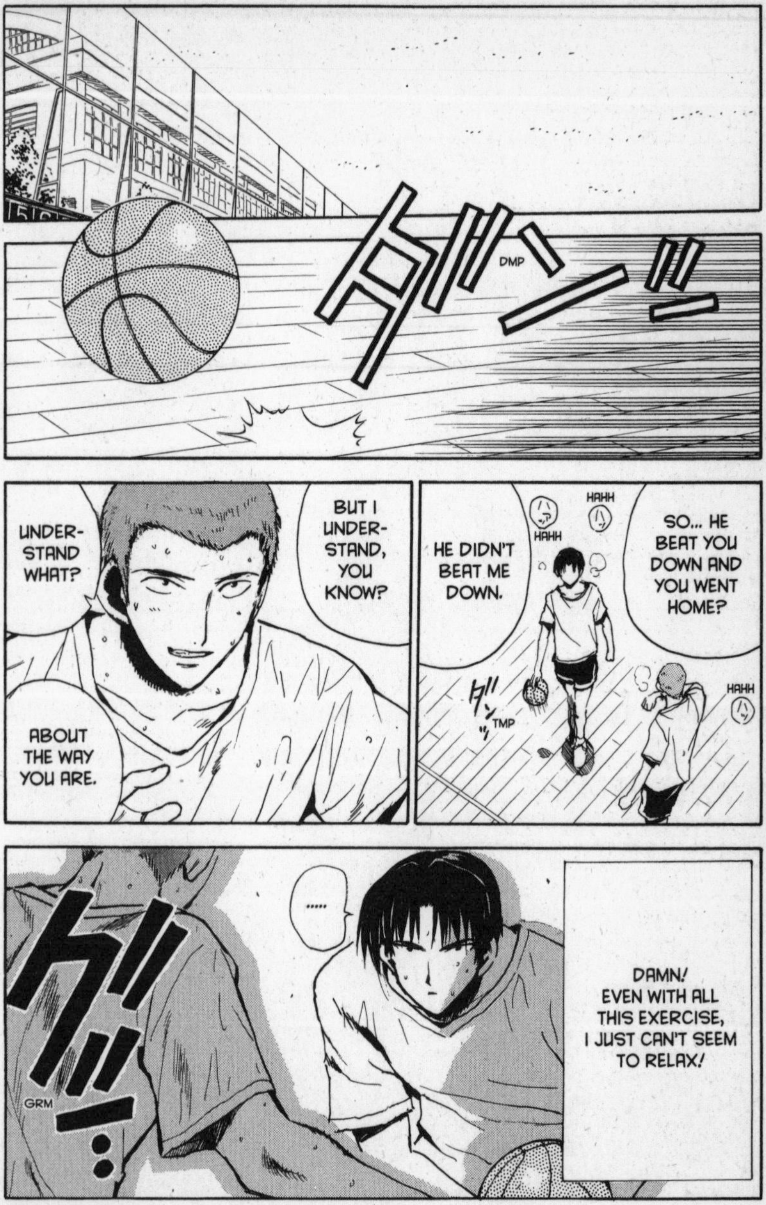
DMP
HAHH
HAHH
SO... HE BEAT YOU DOWN AND YOU WENT HOME?
HE DIDN'T BEAT ME DOWN.
HAHH
TMP
BUT I UNDER-STAND, YOU KNOW?
UNDER-STAND WHAT?
ABOUT THE WAY YOU ARE.
DAMN! EVEN WITH ALL THIS EXERCISE, I JUST CAN'T SEEM TO RELAX!
......
GRM

They're Friends, but There Are Things They Can't Ask.

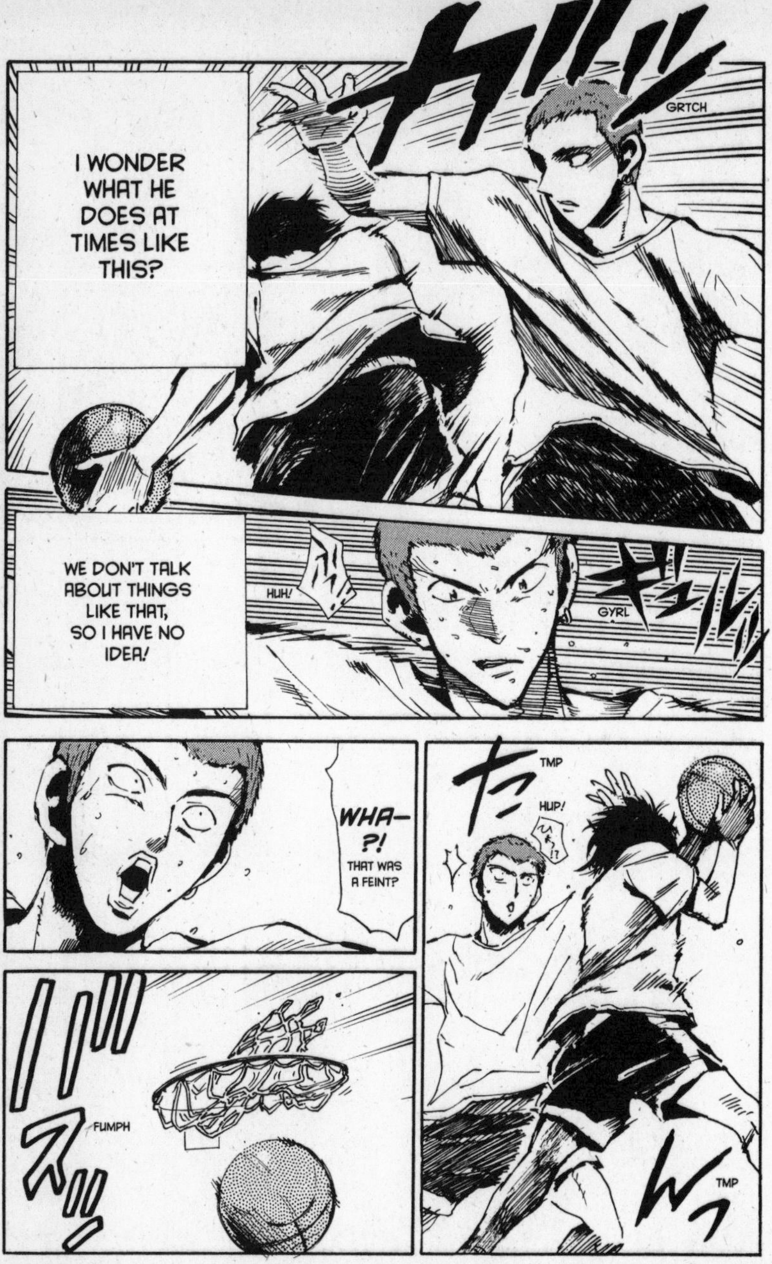
I WONDER WHAT HE DOES AT TIMES LIKE THIS?
GRTCH
WE DON'T TALK ABOUT THINGS LIKE THAT, SO I HAVE NO IDEA!
HUH!
GYRL
TMP
HUP!
TMP
WHA-?!
THAT WAS A FEINT?
FUMPH

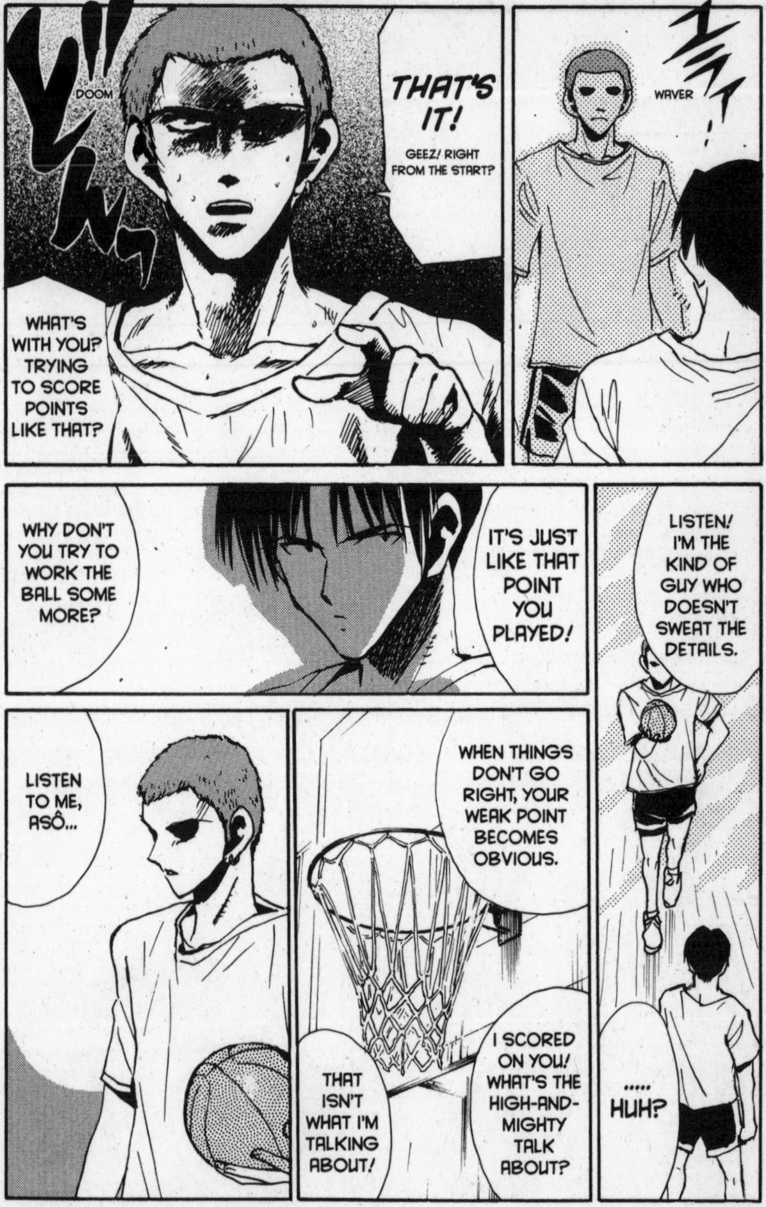
WAVER
THAT'S IT!
GEEZ! RIGHT FROM THE START?
DOOM
WHAT'S WITH YOU? TRYING TO SCORE POINTS LIKE THAT?
LISTEN! I'M THE KIND OF GUY WHO DOESN'T SWEAT THE DETAILS.
...... HUH?
IT'S JUST LIKE THAT POINT YOU PLAYED!
WHY DON'T YOU TRY TO WORK THE BALL SOME MORE?
WHEN THINGS DON'T GO RIGHT, YOUR WEAK POINT BECOMES OBVIOUS.
I SCORED ON YOU! WHAT'S THE HIGH-AND-MIGHTY TALK ABOUT?
THAT ISN'T WHAT I'M TALKING ABOUT!
LISTEN TO ME, ASÔ...

Suga Ryûhei: Asô's Good Friend.

Suga Ryûhei: His Kind of Advice.

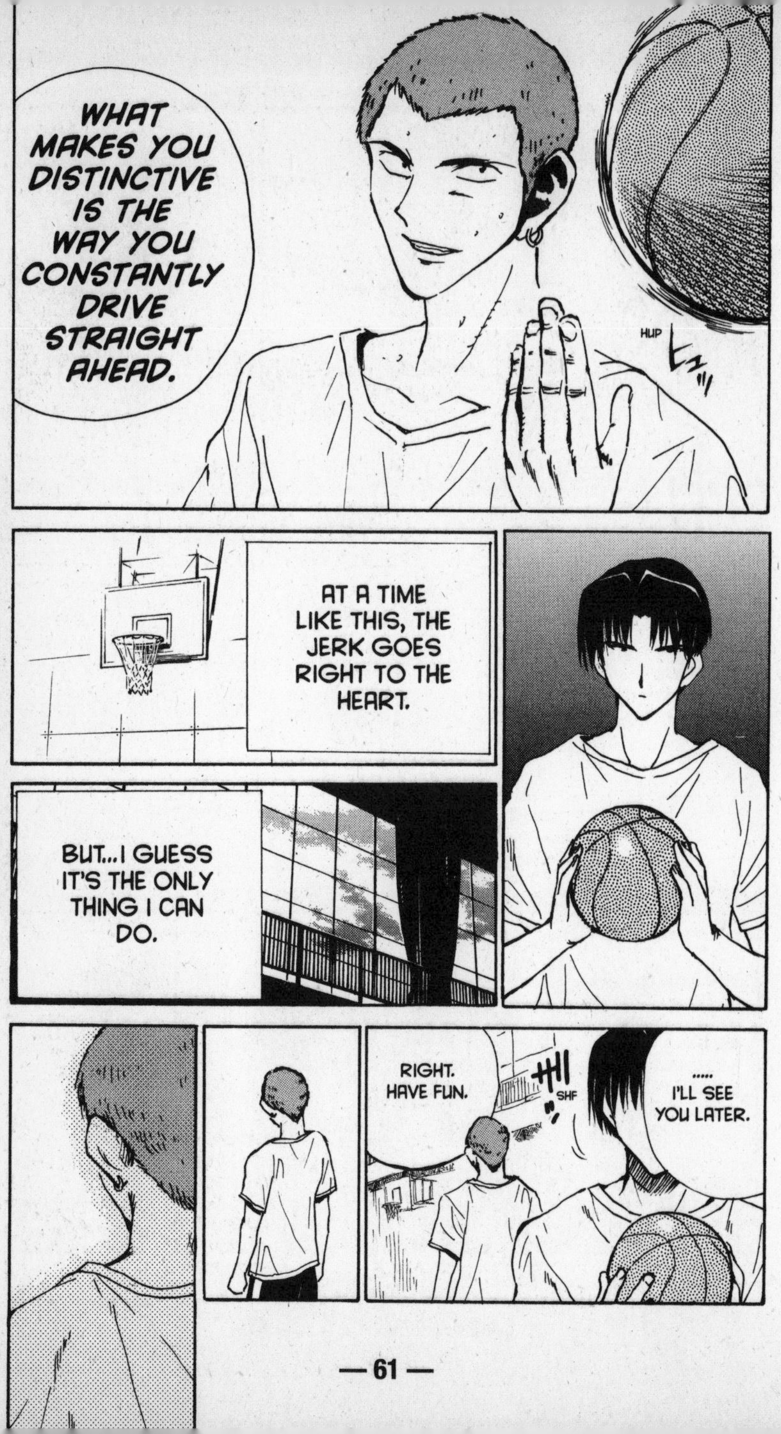
WHAT MAKES YOU DISTINCTIVE IS THE WAY YOU CONSTANTLY DRIVE STRAIGHT AHEAD.
HUP
AT A TIME LIKE THIS, THE JERK GOES RIGHT TO THE HEART.
BUT...I GUESS IT'S THE ONLY THING I CAN DO.
..... I'LL SEE YOU LATER.
SHF
RIGHT. HAVE FUN.

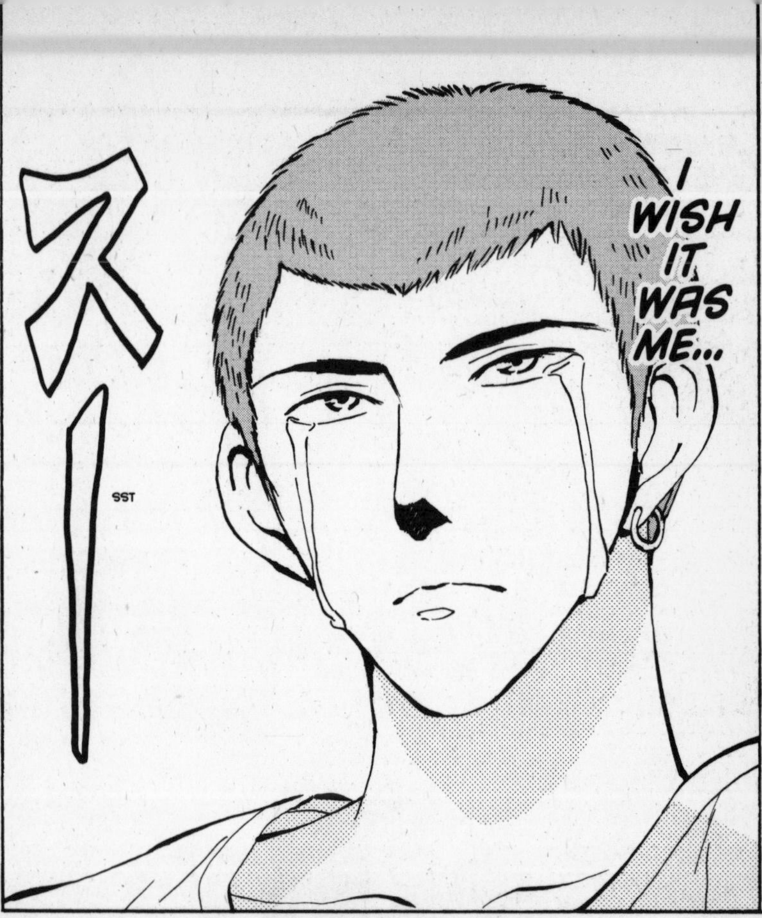
I WISH IT WAS ME...
スー
SST

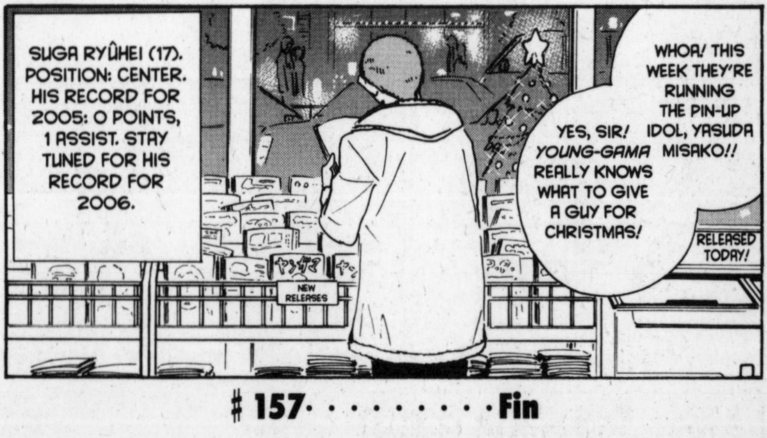
WHOA! THIS WEEK THEY'RE RUNNING THE PIN-UP IDOL, YASUDA MISAKO!!
YES, SIR! *YOUNG-GAMA* REALLY KNOWS WHAT TO GIVE A GUY FOR CHRISTMAS!
RELEASED TODAY!
NEW RELEASES
SUGA RYÛHEI (17). POSITION: CENTER. HIS RECORD FOR 2005: 0 POINTS, 1 ASSIST. STAY TUNED FOR HIS RECORD FOR 2006.

Suga's 2005: The End.

 # 157· · · · · · · · ·Fin

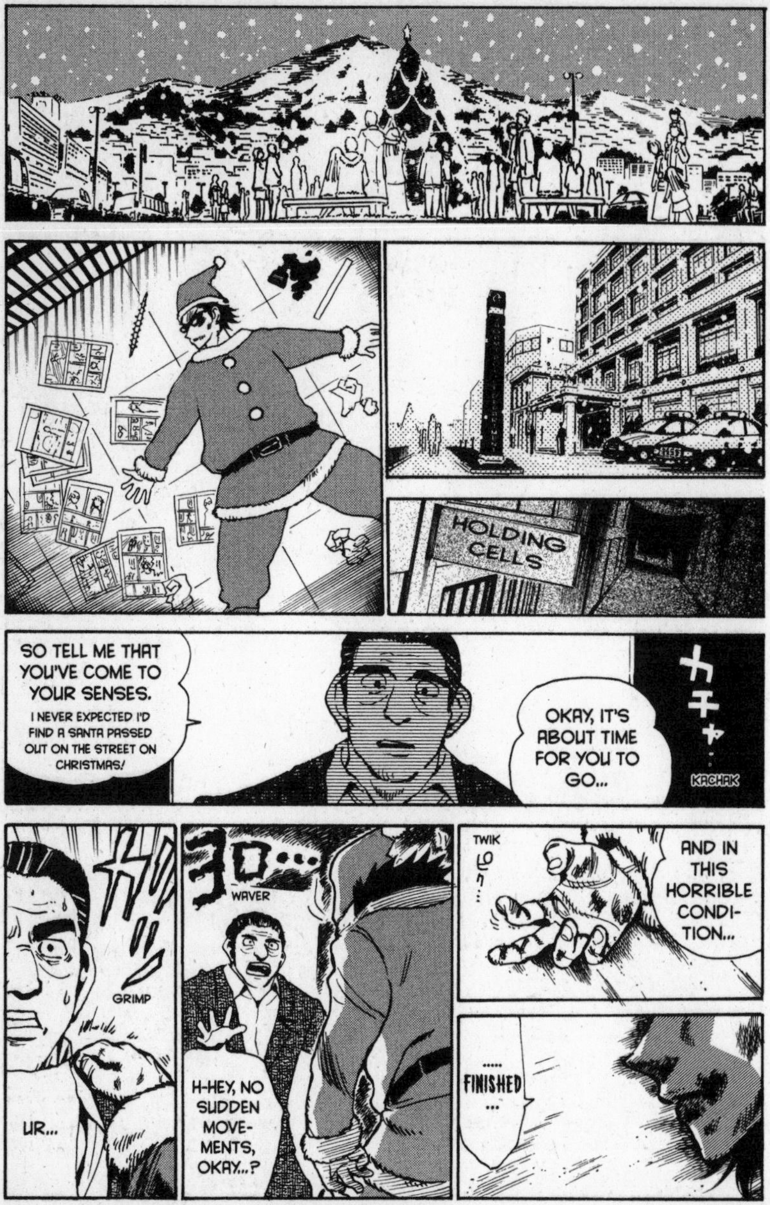
HOLDING CELLS
カチャ
KACHAK
OKAY, IT'S ABOUT TIME FOR YOU TO GO...
SO TELL ME THAT YOU'VE COME TO YOUR SENSES.
I NEVER EXPECTED I'D FIND A SANTA PASSED OUT ON THE STREET ON CHRISTMAS!
TWIK
AND IN THIS HORRIBLE CONDI-TION...
..... FINISHED ...
ヨロ...
WAVER
H-HEY, NO SUDDEN MOVE-MENTS, OKAY...?
GRIMP
UR...

158 THE SANTA CLAUSE

Harima Kenji: Been Through the Battle and Out the Other Side.

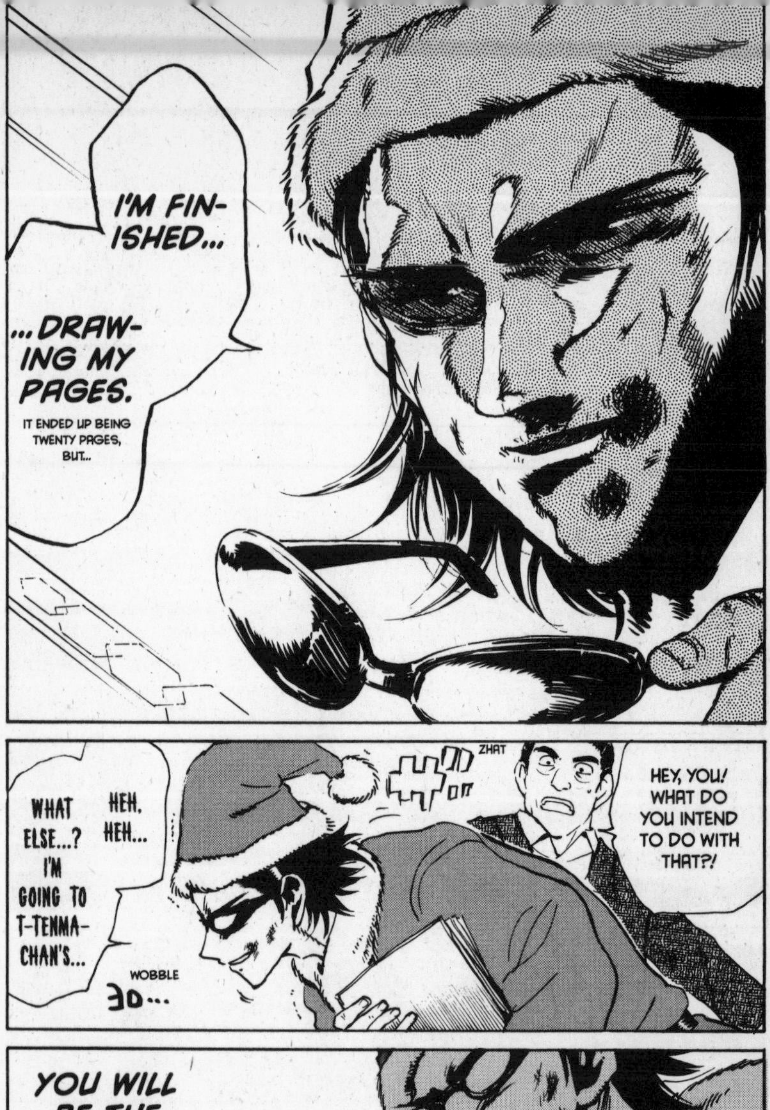
I'M FIN-ISHED...
...DRAWING MY PAGES.
IT ENDED UP BEING TWENTY PAGES, BUT...
HEY, YOU! WHAT DO YOU INTEND TO DO WITH THAT?!
ZHAT
HEH. HEH...
WHAT ELSE...? I'M GOING TO T-TENMA-CHAN'S...
WOBBLE
YOU WILL BE THE FIRST...!!
A LOT HAS HAPPENED...

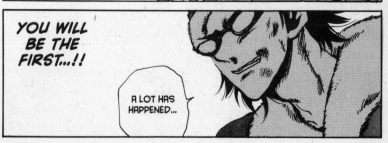

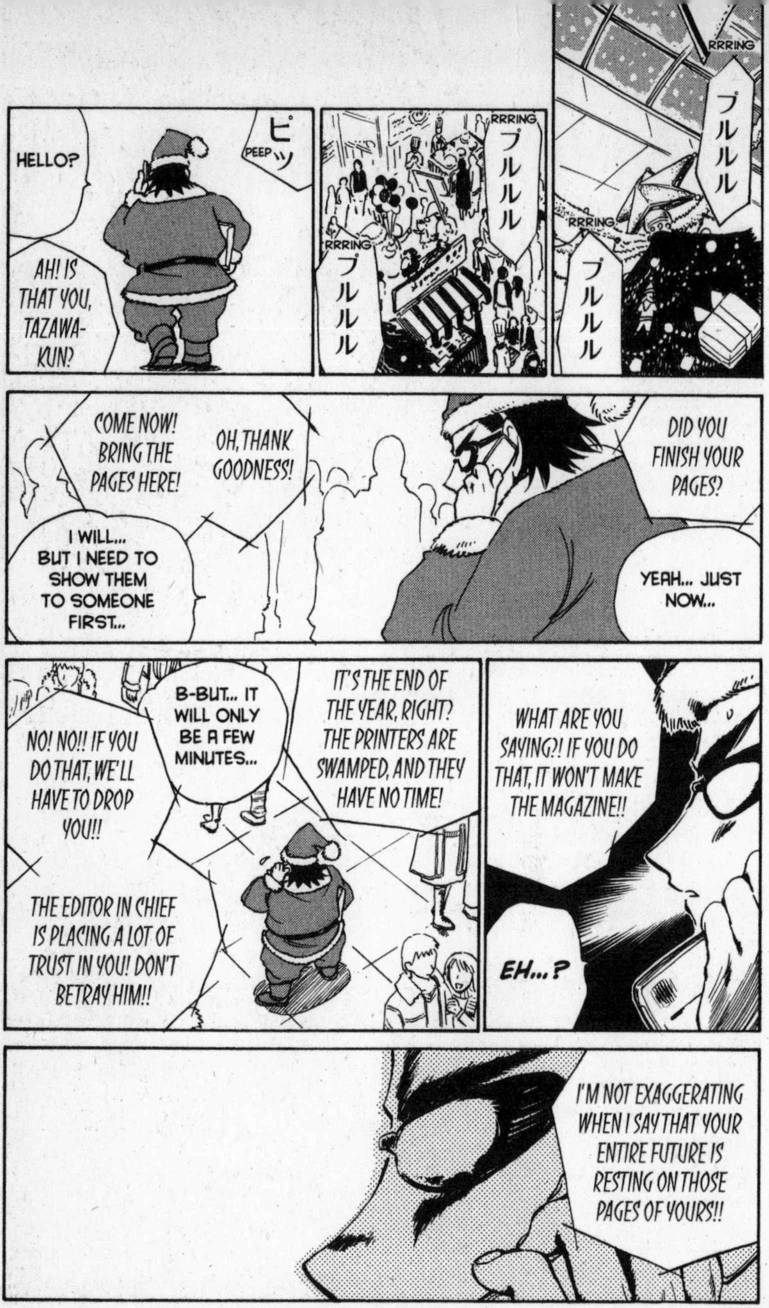
プルルル
RRRING
プルルル
RRRING
プルルル
RRRING
プルルル
RRRING
ピッ
PEEP
HELLO?
AH! IS THAT YOU, TAZAWA-KUN?
DID YOU FINISH YOUR PAGES?
YEAH... JUST NOW...
OH, THANK GOODNESS!
COME NOW! BRING THE PAGES HERE!
I WILL... BUT I NEED TO SHOW THEM TO SOMEONE FIRST...
WHAT ARE YOU SAYING?! IF YOU DO THAT, IT WON'T MAKE THE MAGAZINE!!
EH...?
IT'S THE END OF THE YEAR, RIGHT? THE PRINTERS ARE SWAMPED, AND THEY HAVE NO TIME!
B-BUT... IT WILL ONLY BE A FEW MINUTES...
NO! NO!! IF YOU DO THAT, WE'LL HAVE TO DROP YOU!!
THE EDITOR IN CHIEF IS PLACING A LOT OF TRUST IN YOU! DON'T BETRAY HIM!!
I'M NOT EXAGGERATING WHEN I SAY THAT YOUR ENTIRE FUTURE IS RESTING ON THOSE PAGES OF YOURS!!

On the Phone: *Weekly Jingama* Editor Mitsui Masaaki.

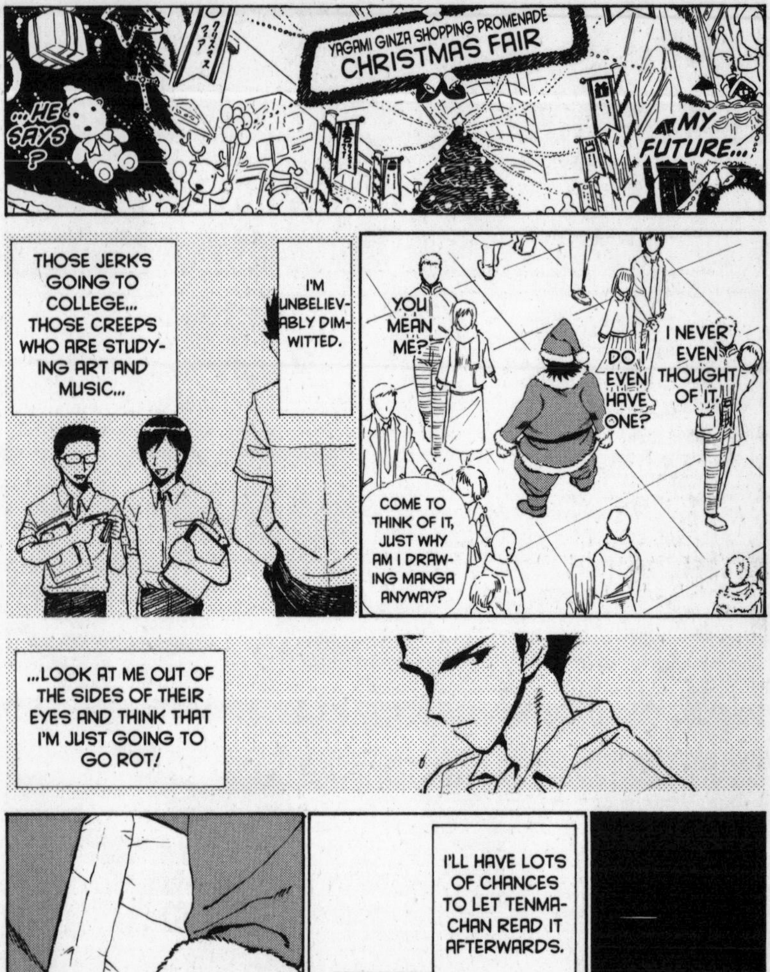
YAGAMI GINZA SHOPPING PROMENADE
CHRISTMAS FAIR
MY FUTURE...
...HE SAYS?
I NEVER EVEN THOUGHT OF IT.
DO I EVEN HAVE ONE?
YOU MEAN ME?
COME TO THINK OF IT, JUST WHY AM I DRAWING MANGA ANYWAY?
I'M UNBELIEVABLY DIM-WITTED.
THOSE JERKS GOING TO COLLEGE... THOSE CREEPS WHO ARE STUDYING ART AND MUSIC...
...LOOK AT ME OUT OF THE SIDES OF THEIR EYES AND THINK THAT I'M JUST GOING TO GO ROT!
I HAVE TO GET THESE PAGES TO THE PUBLISHER!
I'LL HAVE LOTS OF CHANCES TO LET TENMA-CHAN READ IT AFTERWARDS.
IF I WANT TO GRAB MY CHANCE AT A FUTURE, ISN'T THIS THE TIME TO DO IT?
GRIMP

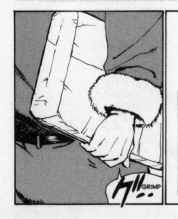

Tsukamoto Tenma: Right Now Making a Present for Karasuma. Just So You Know.

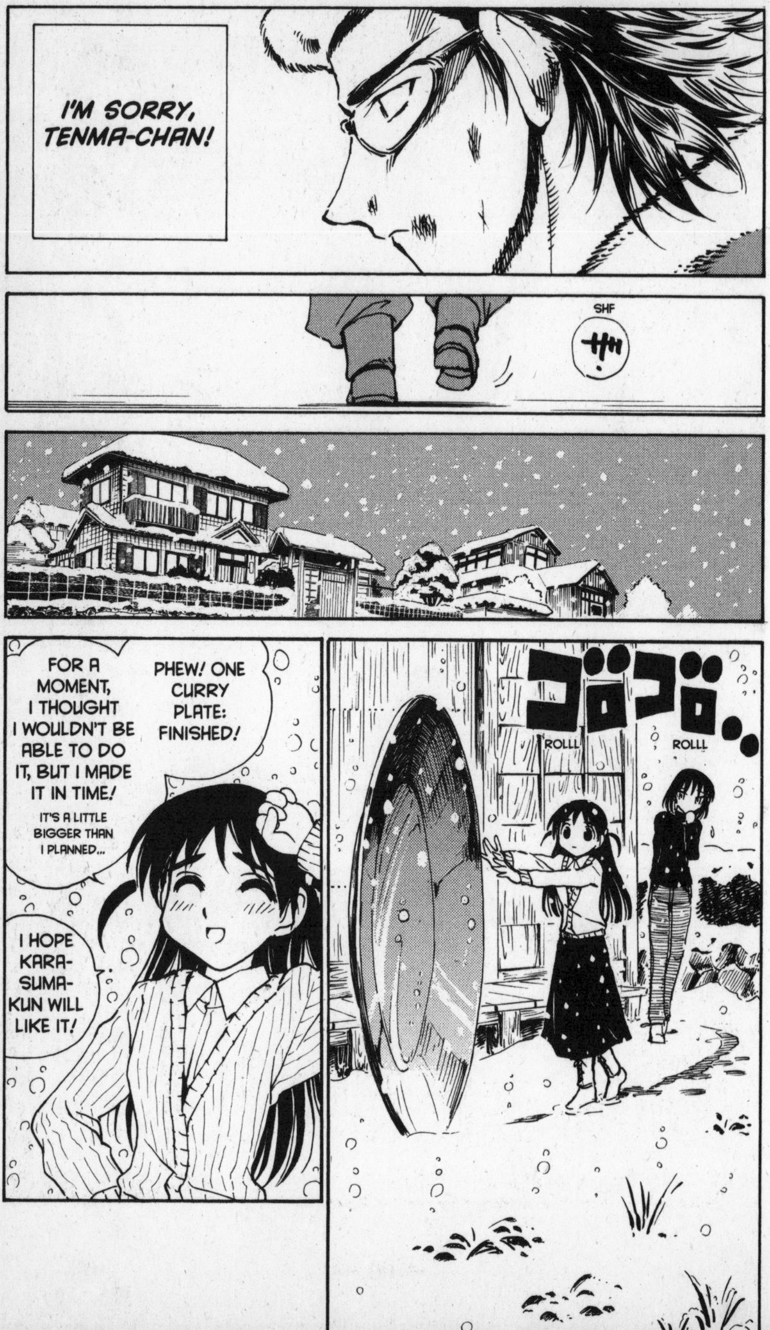
I'M SORRY, TENMA-CHAN!
SHF
ザッ
ゴロゴロ…
ROLLL
ROLLL
PHEW! ONE CURRY PLATE: FINISHED!
FOR A MOMENT, I THOUGHT I WOULDN'T BE ABLE TO DO IT, BUT I MADE IT IN TIME!
IT'S A LITTLE BIGGER THAN I PLANNED...
I HOPE KARA-SUMA-KUN WILL LIKE IT!

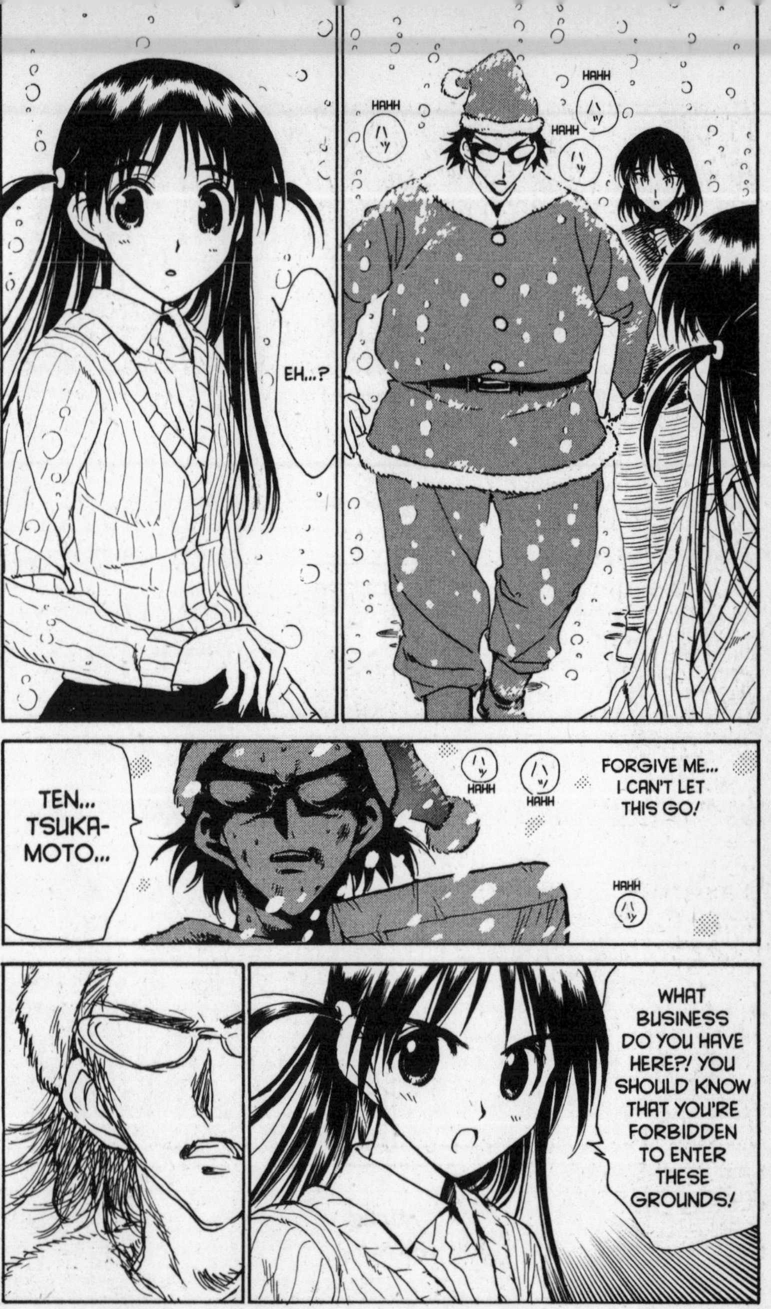
HAHH
ハッ
HAHH
ハッ
HAHH
ハッ
EH...?
FORGIVE ME... I CAN'T LET THIS GO!
ハッ
HAHH
ハッ
HAHH
HAHH
ハッ
TEN... TSUKA-MOTO...
WHAT BUSINESS DO YOU HAVE HERE?! YOU SHOULD KNOW THAT YOU'RE FORBIDDEN TO ENTER THESE GROUNDS!

He Has Not Yet Corrected Her Mistake.

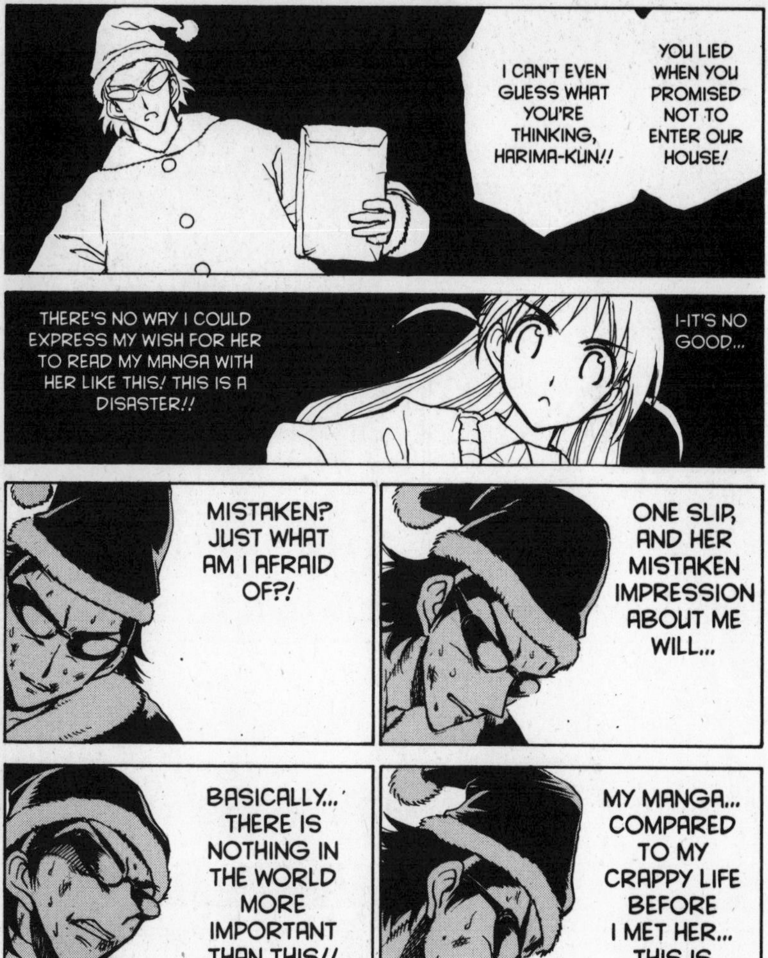
YOU LIED WHEN YOU PROMISED NOT TO ENTER OUR HOUSE!
I CAN'T EVEN GUESS WHAT YOU'RE THINKING, HARIMA-KUN!!
I-IT'S NO GOOD...
THERE'S NO WAY I COULD EXPRESS MY WISH FOR HER TO READ MY MANGA WITH HER LIKE THIS! THIS IS A DISASTER!!
ONE SLIP, AND HER MISTAKEN IMPRESSION ABOUT ME WILL...
MISTAKEN? JUST WHAT AM I AFRAID OF?!
MY MANGA... COMPARED TO MY CRAPPY LIFE BEFORE I MET HER... THIS IS NOTHING!!
BASICALLY... THERE IS NOTHING IN THE WORLD MORE IMPORTANT THAN THIS!!
NOW, KENJI...

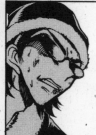

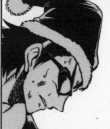

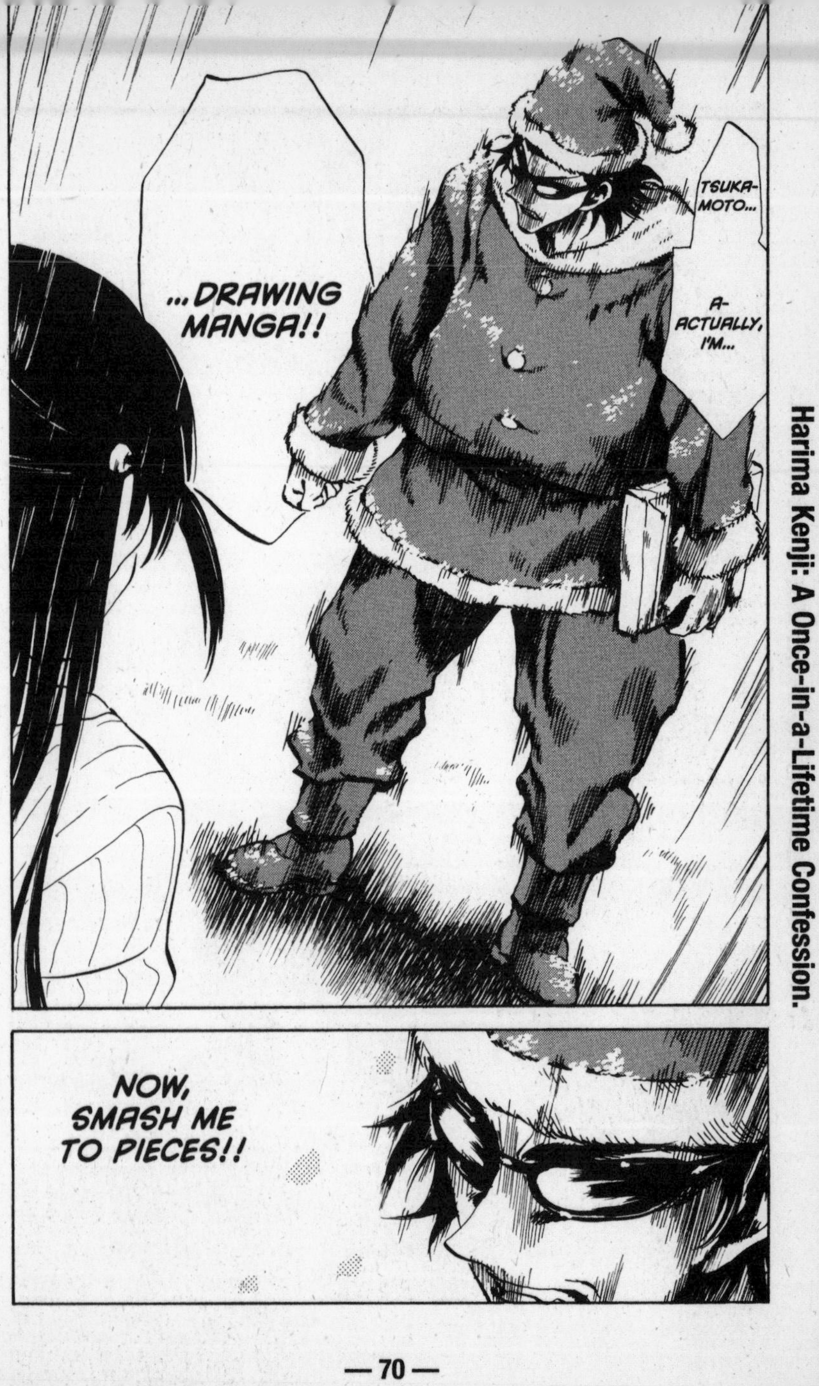
TSUKA-MOTO...
A-ACTUALLY, I'M...
...DRAWING MANGA!!
NOW, SMASH ME TO PIECES!!

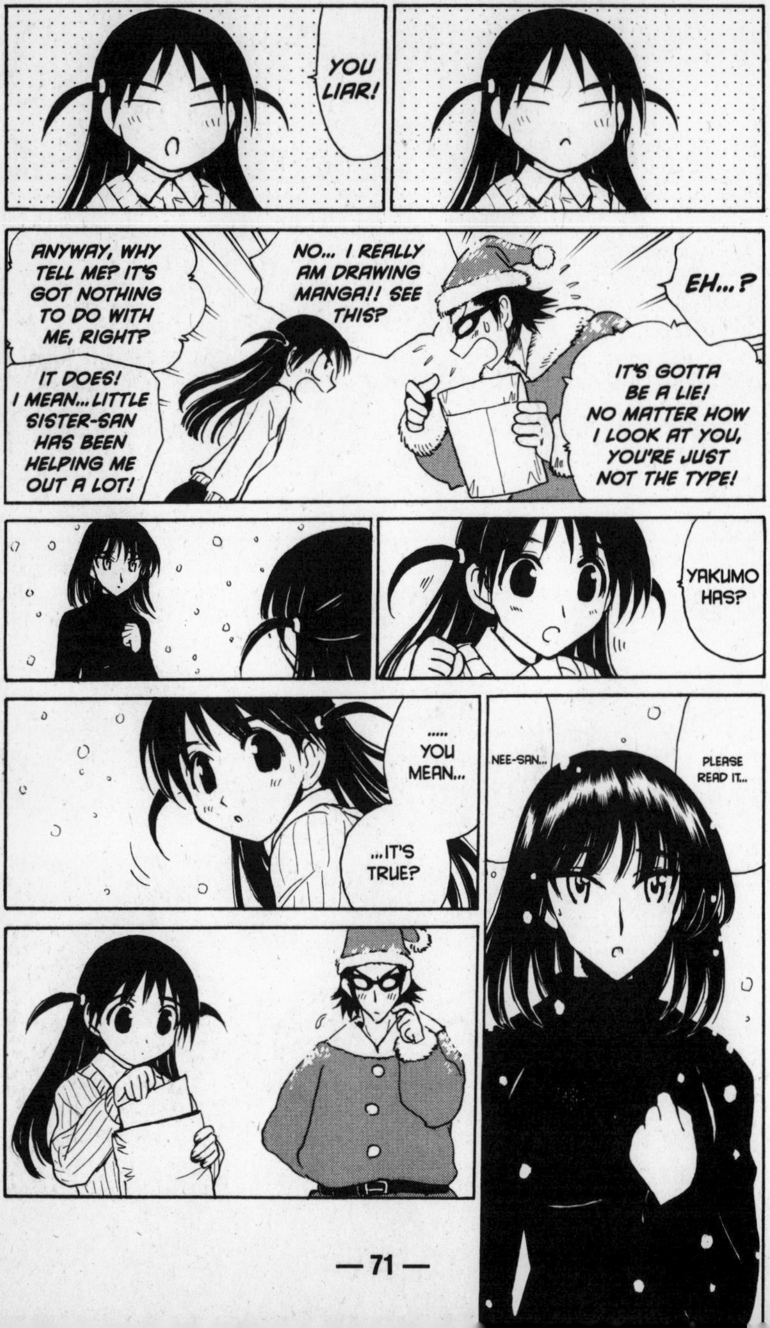
YOU LIAR!
EH...?
IT'S GOTTA BE A LIE! NO MATTER HOW I LOOK AT YOU, YOU'RE JUST NOT THE TYPE!
NO... I REALLY AM DRAWING MANGA!! SEE THIS?
ANYWAY, WHY TELL ME? IT'S GOT NOTHING TO DO WITH ME, RIGHT?
IT DOES! I MEAN... LITTLE SISTER-SAN HAS BEEN HELPING ME OUT A LOT!
YAKUMO HAS?
PLEASE READ IT...
NEE-SAN...
..... YOU MEAN...
...IT'S TRUE?

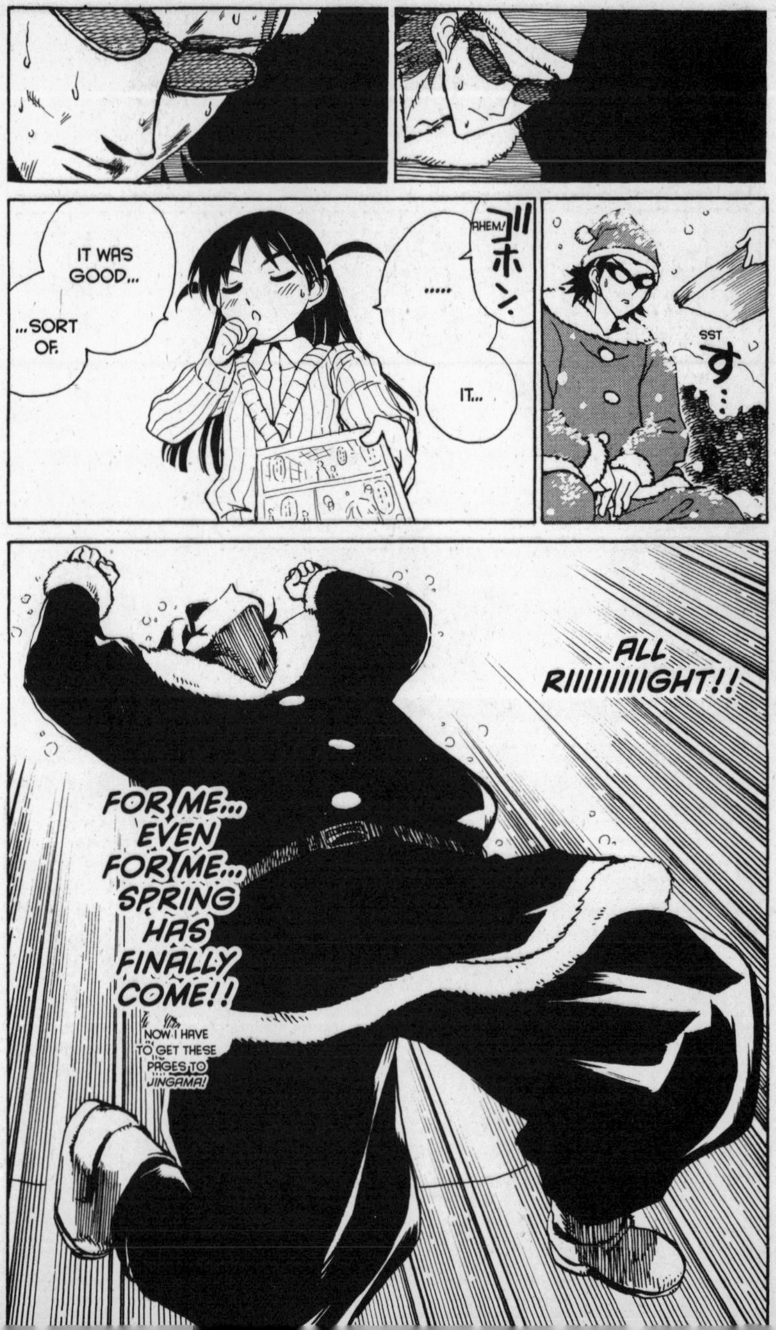
SST
す…
AHEM!
ゴホン。
.....
IT...
IT WAS GOOD...
...SORT OF.
ALL RIIIIIIIIIGHT!!
FOR ME... EVEN FOR ME... SPRING HAS FINALLY COME!!
NOW I HAVE TO GET THESE PAGES TO JINGAMA!

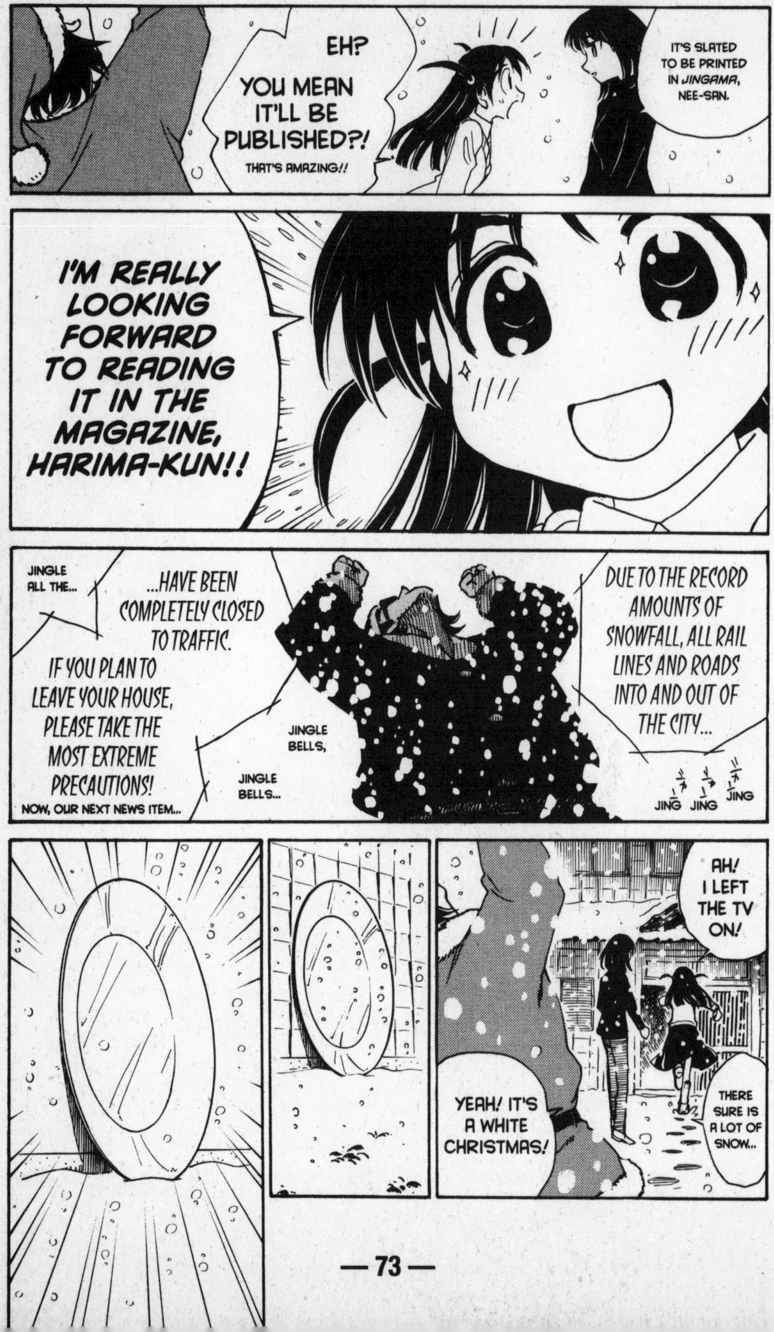
IT'S SLATED TO BE PRINTED IN JINGAMA, NEE-SAN.
EH?
YOU MEAN IT'LL BE PUBLISHED?!
THAT'S AMAZING!!
I'M REALLY LOOKING FORWARD TO READING IT IN THE MAGAZINE, HARIMA-KUN!!
DUE TO THE RECORD AMOUNTS OF SNOWFALL, ALL RAIL LINES AND ROADS INTO AND OUT OF THE CITY...
JING JING JING
...HAVE BEEN COMPLETELY CLOSED TO TRAFFIC.
IF YOU PLAN TO LEAVE YOUR HOUSE, PLEASE TAKE THE MOST EXTREME PRECAUTIONS!
NOW, OUR NEXT NEWS ITEM...
JINGLE BELLS,
JINGLE BELLS...
JINGLE ALL THE...
AH! I LEFT THE TV ON!
THERE SURE IS A LOT OF SNOW...
YEAH! IT'S A WHITE CHRISTMAS!

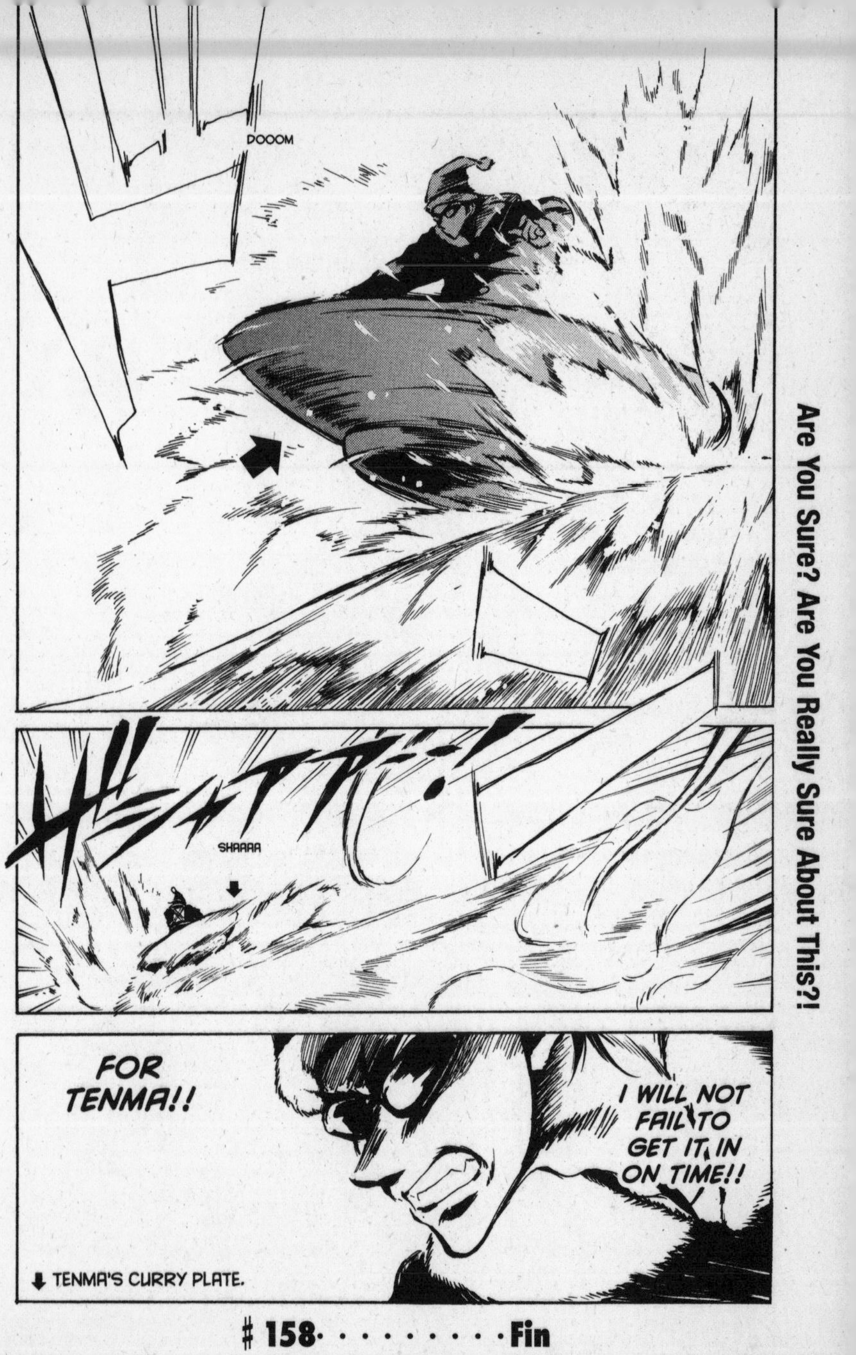
DOOOM
SHAAAA
I WILL NOT FAIL TO GET IT IN ON TIME!!
FOR TENMA!!
⬇ TENMA'S CURRY PLATE.

Are You Sure? Are You Really Sure About This?!

158· · · · · · · · ·Fin

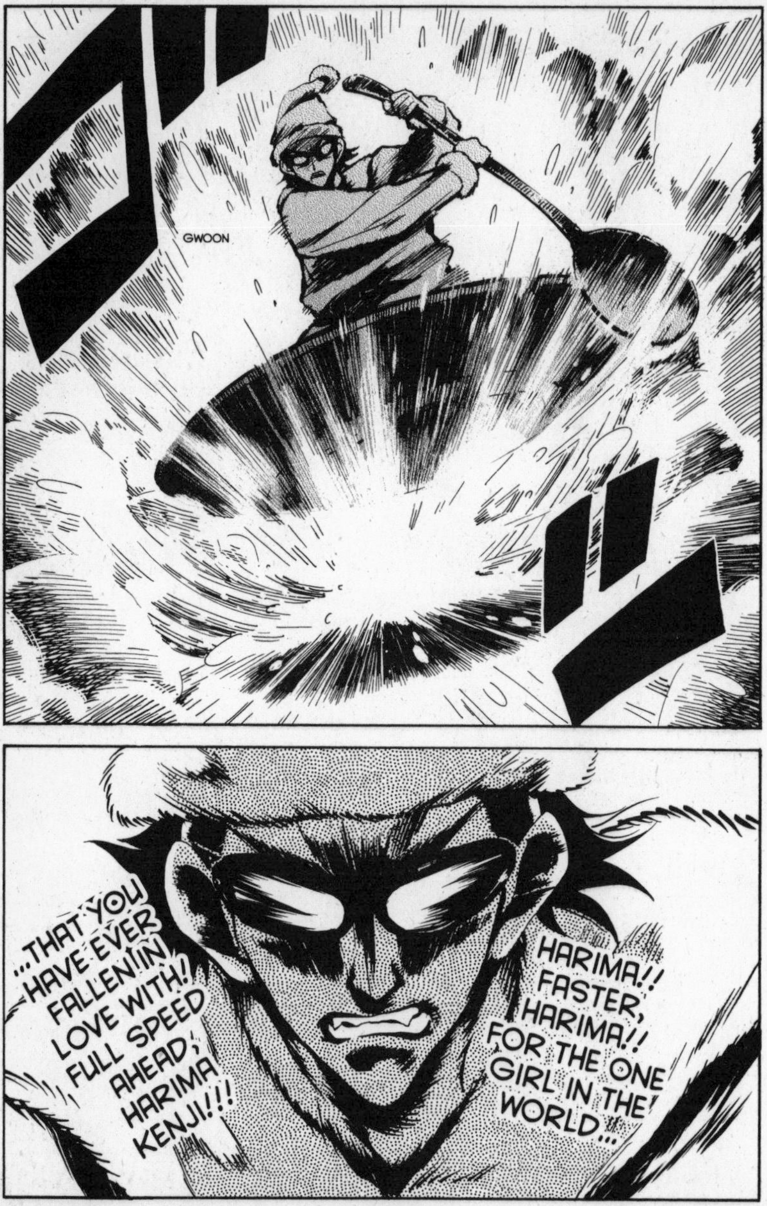
GWOON
HARIMA!! FASTER, HARIMA!! FOR THE ONE GIRL IN THE WORLD...
...THAT YOU HAVE EVER FALLEN IN LOVE WITH! FULL SPEED AHEAD, HARIMA KENJI!!!

#159 JINGLE ALL THE WAY

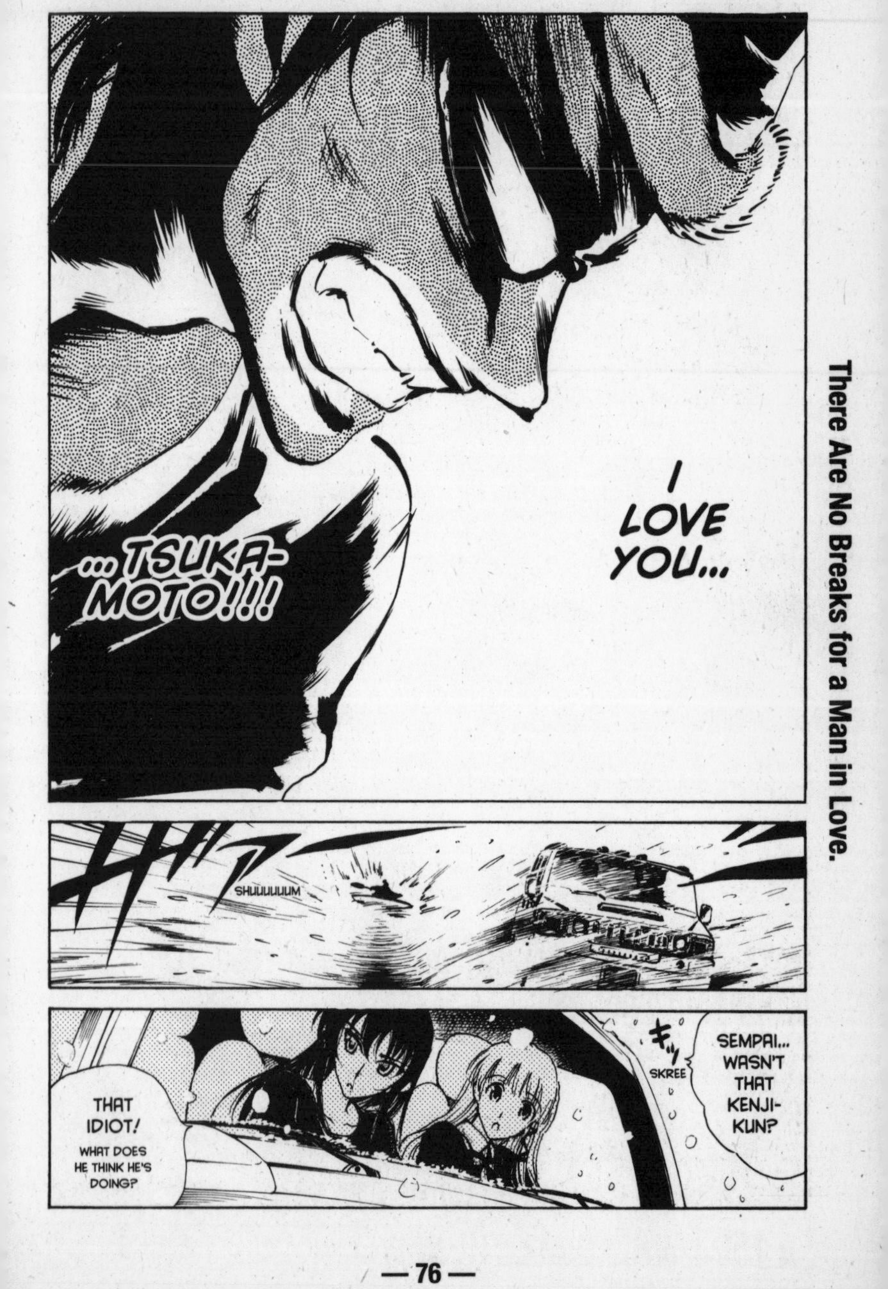
I LOVE YOU...
...TSUKA-MOTO!!!
SHUUUUUUM
SEMPAI... WASN'T THAT KENJI-KUN?
キッ
SKREE
THAT IDIOT!
WHAT DOES HE THINK HE'S DOING?

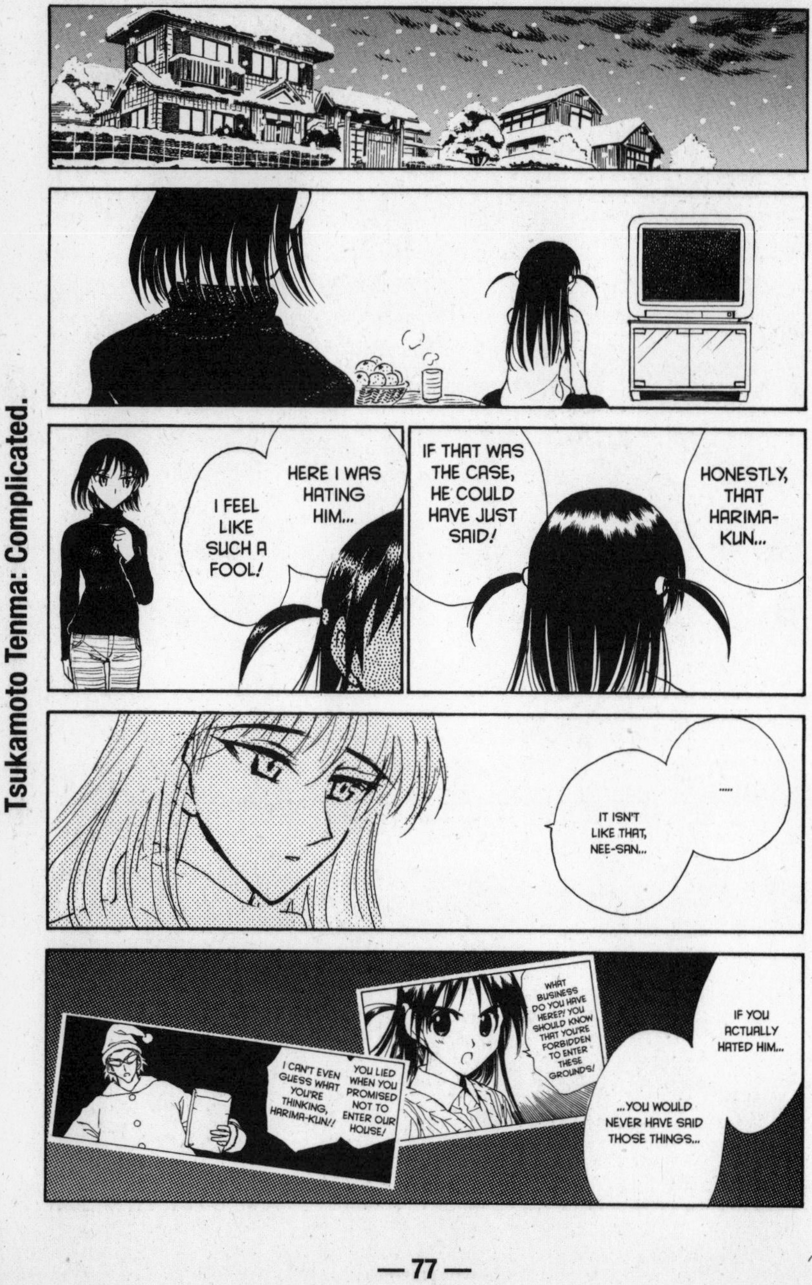
HONESTLY, THAT HARIMA-KUN...
IF THAT WAS THE CASE, HE COULD HAVE JUST SAID!
HERE I WAS HATING HIM...
I FEEL LIKE SUCH A FOOL!
.....
IT ISN'T LIKE THAT, NEE-SAN...
IF YOU ACTUALLY HATED HIM...
...YOU WOULD NEVER HAVE SAID THOSE THINGS...
WHAT BUSINESS DO YOU HAVE HERE?! YOU SHOULD KNOW THAT YOU'RE FORBIDDEN TO ENTER THESE GROUNDS!
YOU LIED WHEN YOU PROMISED NOT TO ENTER OUR HOUSE!
I CAN'T EVEN GUESS WHAT YOU'RE THINKING, HARIMA-KUN!!

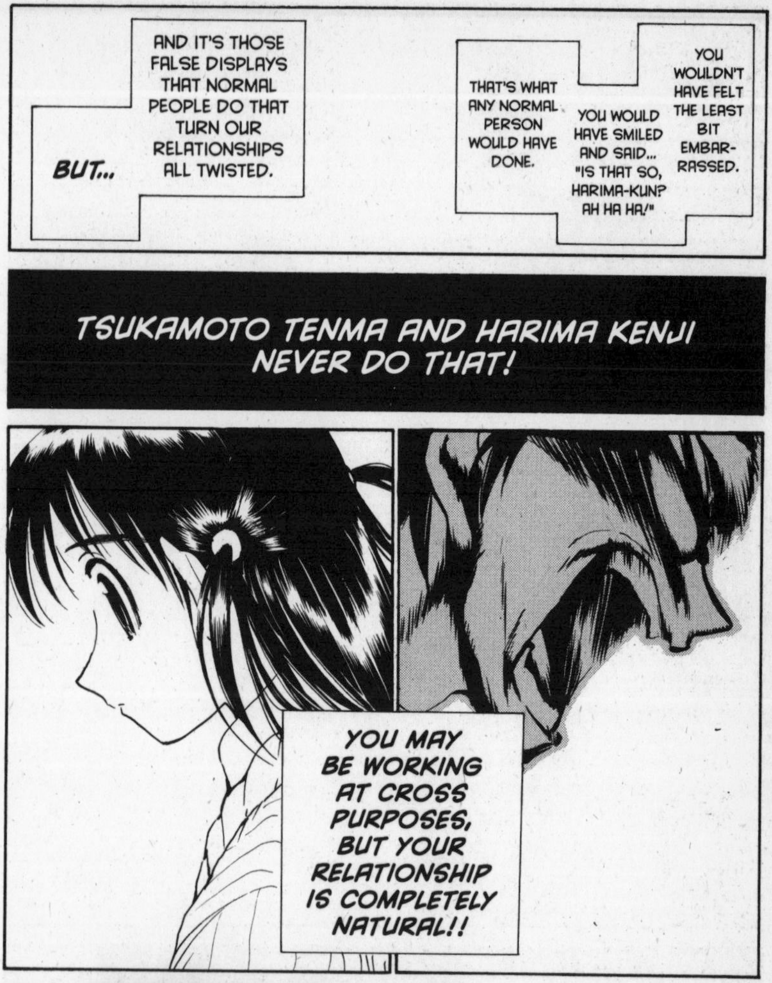
YOU WOULDN'T HAVE FELT THE LEAST BIT EMBARRASSED.
YOU WOULD HAVE SMILED AND SAID... "IS THAT SO, HARIMA-KUN? AH HA HA!"
THAT'S WHAT ANY NORMAL PERSON WOULD HAVE DONE.
AND IT'S THOSE FALSE DISPLAYS THAT NORMAL PEOPLE DO THAT TURN OUR RELATIONSHIPS ALL TWISTED.
BUT...
TSUKAMOTO TENMA AND HARIMA KENJI NEVER DO THAT!
YOU MAY BE WORKING AT CROSS PURPOSES, BUT YOUR RELATIONSHIP IS COMPLETELY NATURAL!!
NEE-SAN...
...IT'S THAT PART OF YOU...
...IS WHAT I'M SURE HARIMA-KUN...

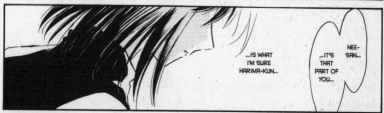

And the Situation Is Complicated, Too.

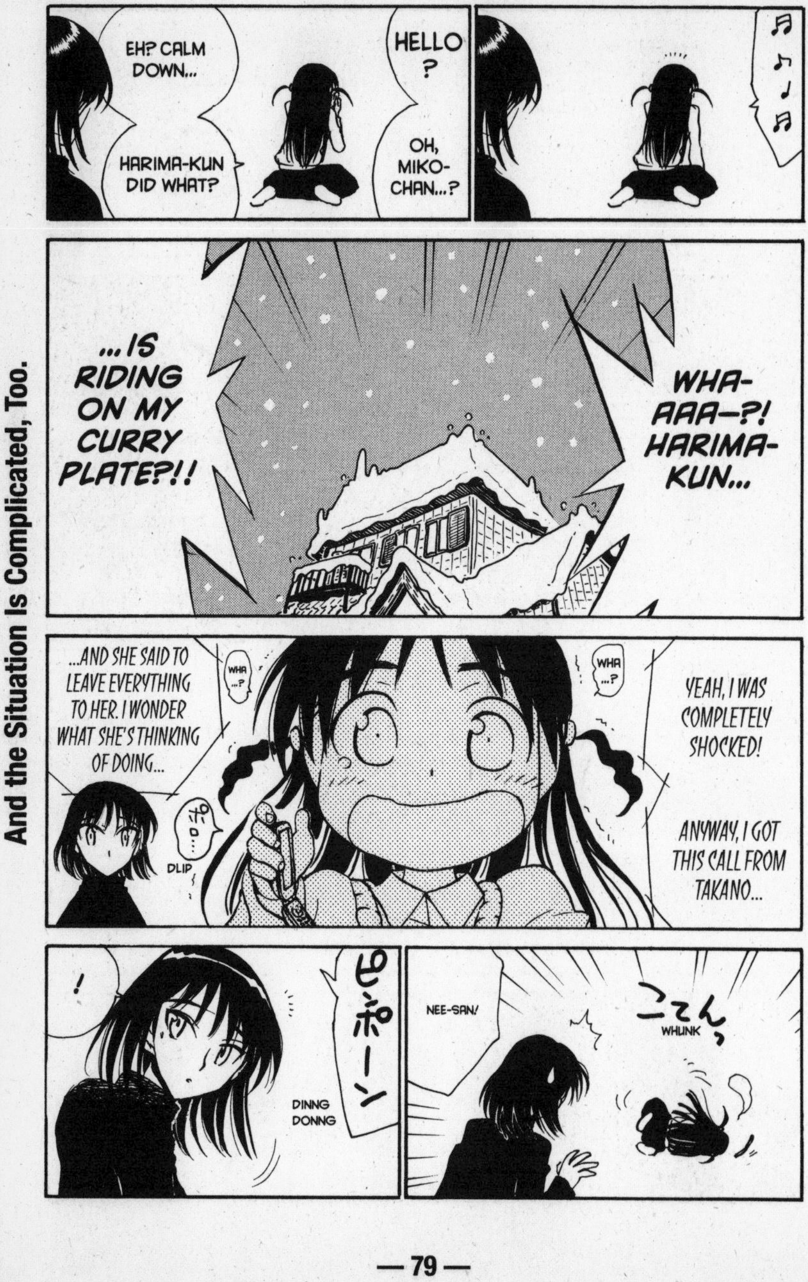
HELLO?
OH, MIKO-CHAN...?
EH? CALM DOWN...
HARIMA-KUN DID WHAT?
WHA-AAA-?! HARIMA-KUN...
...IS RIDING ON MY CURRY PLATE?!!
YEAH, I WAS COMPLETELY SHOCKED!
ANYWAY, I GOT THIS CALL FROM TAKANO...
WHA...?
WHA...?
...AND SHE SAID TO LEAVE EVERYTHING TO HER. I WONDER WHAT SHE'S THINKING OF DOING...
ポロ…
DLIP
こてん
WHUNK
NEE-SAN!
ピンポーン
DINNG DONNG
!

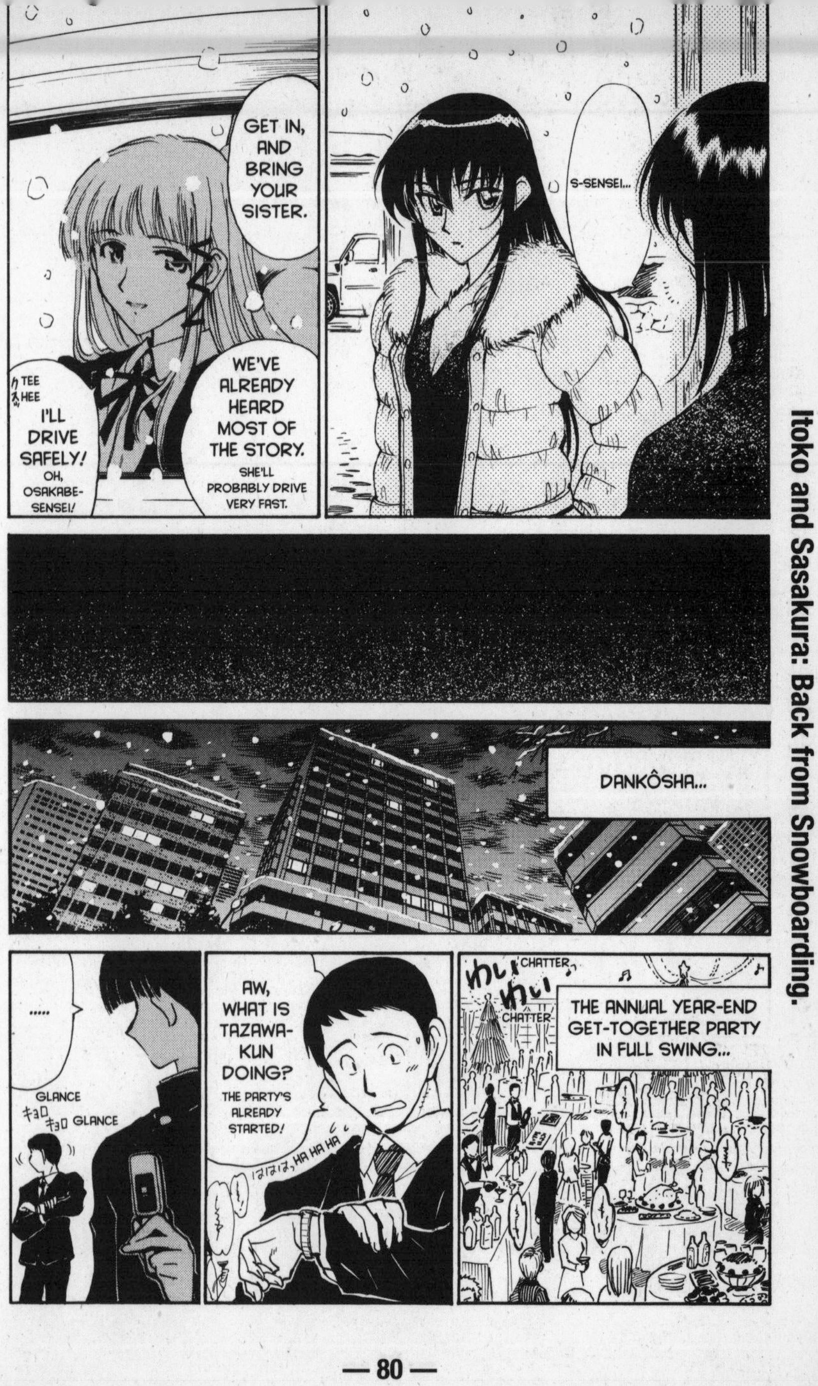
S-SENSEI...
GET IN, AND BRING YOUR SISTER.
WE'VE ALREADY HEARD MOST OF THE STORY.
SHE'LL PROBABLY DRIVE VERY FAST.
TEE HEE
I'LL DRIVE SAFELY!
OH, OSAKABE-SENSEI!
DANKÔSHA...
わいわい
CHATTER
CHATTER
THE ANNUAL YEAR-END GET-TOGETHER PARTY IN FULL SWING...
AW, WHAT IS TAZAWA-KUN DOING?
THE PARTY'S ALREADY STARTED!
ははは, HA HA HA
.....
GLANCE
キョロキョロ GLANCE

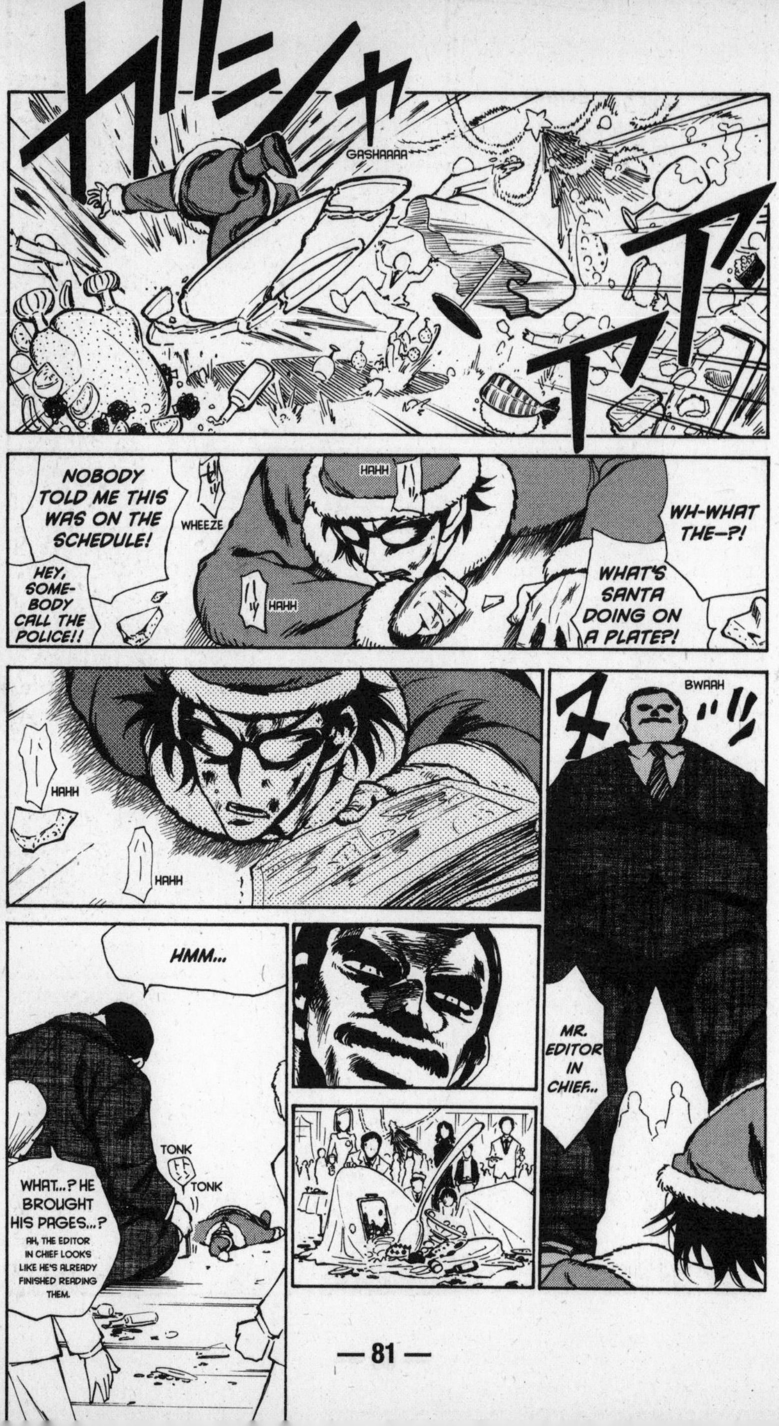
GASHAAAA
WH-WHAT THE-?!
WHAT'S SANTA DOING ON A PLATE?!
HAHH
WHEEZE
NOBODY TOLD ME THIS WAS ON THE SCHEDULE!
HEY, SOMEBODY CALL THE POLICE!!
HAHH
BWAAH
MR. EDITOR IN CHIEF...
HAHH
HAHH
HMM...
TONK
TONK
WHAT...? HE BROUGHT HIS PAGES...?
AH, THE EDITOR IN CHIEF LOOKS LIKE HE'S ALREADY FINISHED READING THEM.

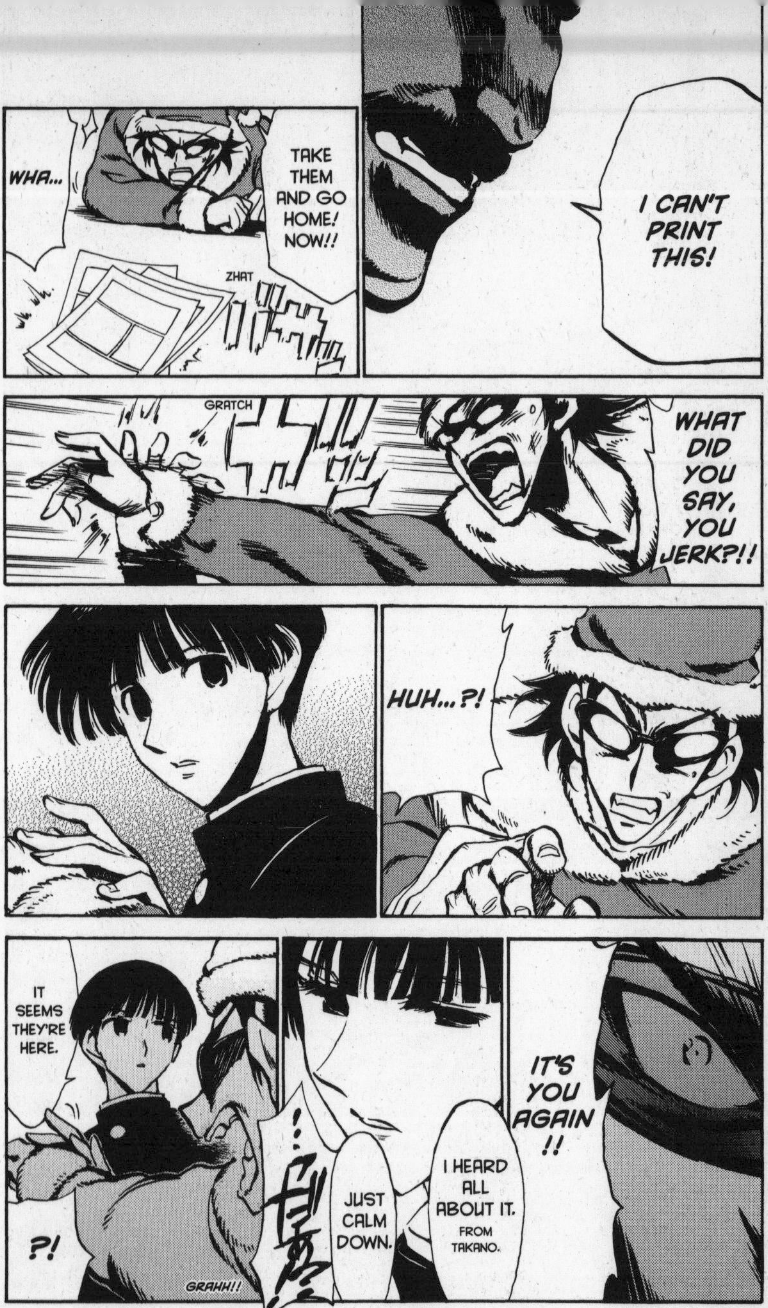
I CAN'T PRINT THIS!
TAKE THEM AND GO HOME! NOW!!
WHA...
ZHAT
WHAT DID YOU SAY, YOU JERK?!!
GRATCH
HUH...?!
IT'S YOU AGAIN!!
I HEARD ALL ABOUT IT.
FROM TAKANO.
JUST CALM DOWN.
IT SEEMS THEY'RE HERE.
?!
GRAHH!!

Karasuma Ôji: Presently Penning a Series for Weekly Jingama. Just So You Know.

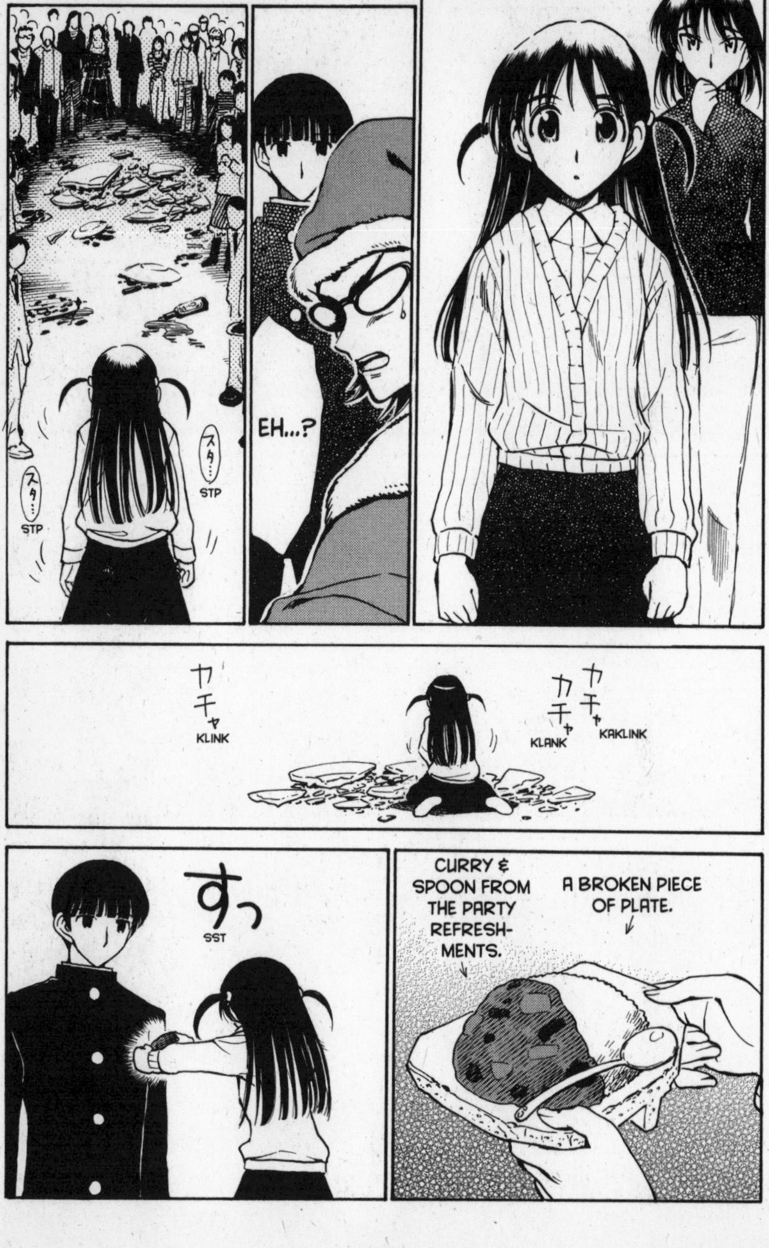
EH...?
スタ…
STP
スタ…
STP
カチャ
KAKLINK
カチャ
KLANK
カチャ
KLINK
A BROKEN PIECE OF PLATE.
CURRY & SPOON FROM THE PARTY REFRESH-MENTS.
すっ
SST

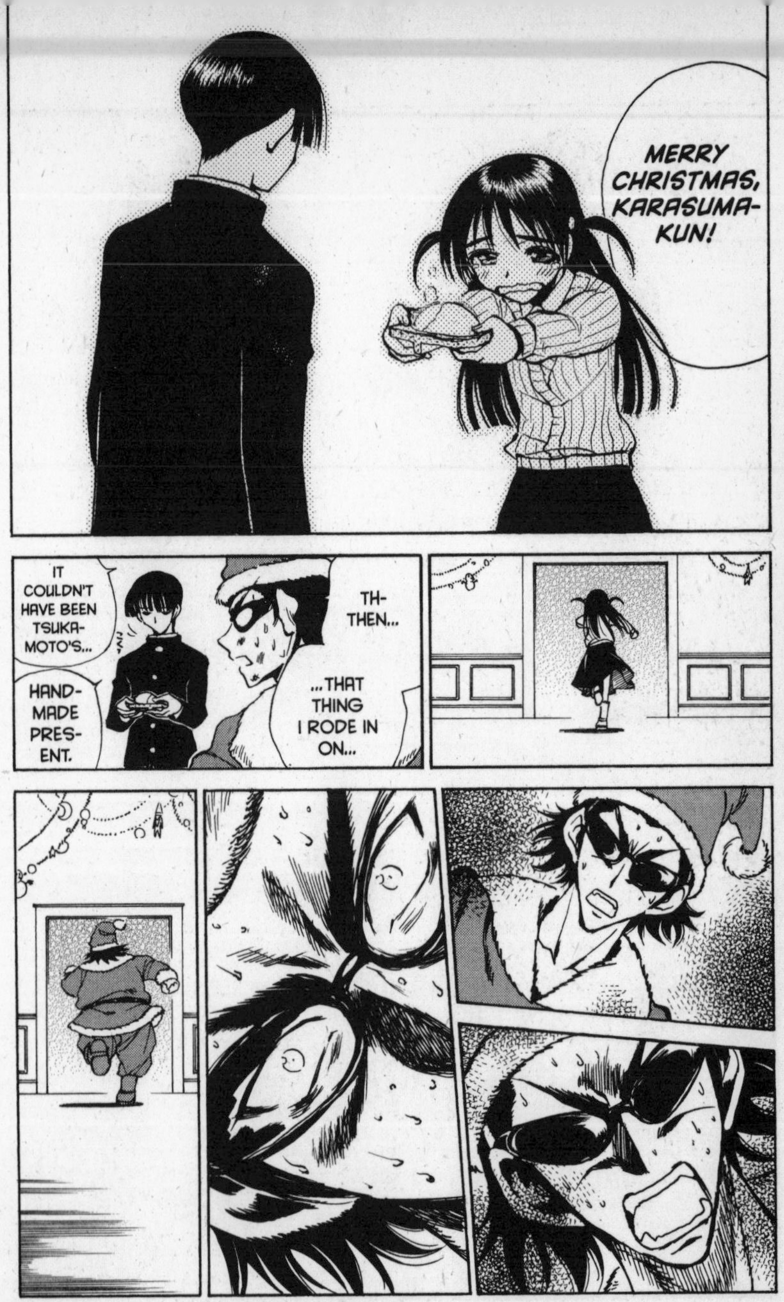
MERRY CHRISTMAS, KARASUMA-KUN!
IT COULDN'T HAVE BEEN TSUKA-MOTO'S...
HAND-MADE PRESENT.
TH- THEN...
...THAT THING I RODE IN ON...

She Was the Reason He Hurried in the First Place.

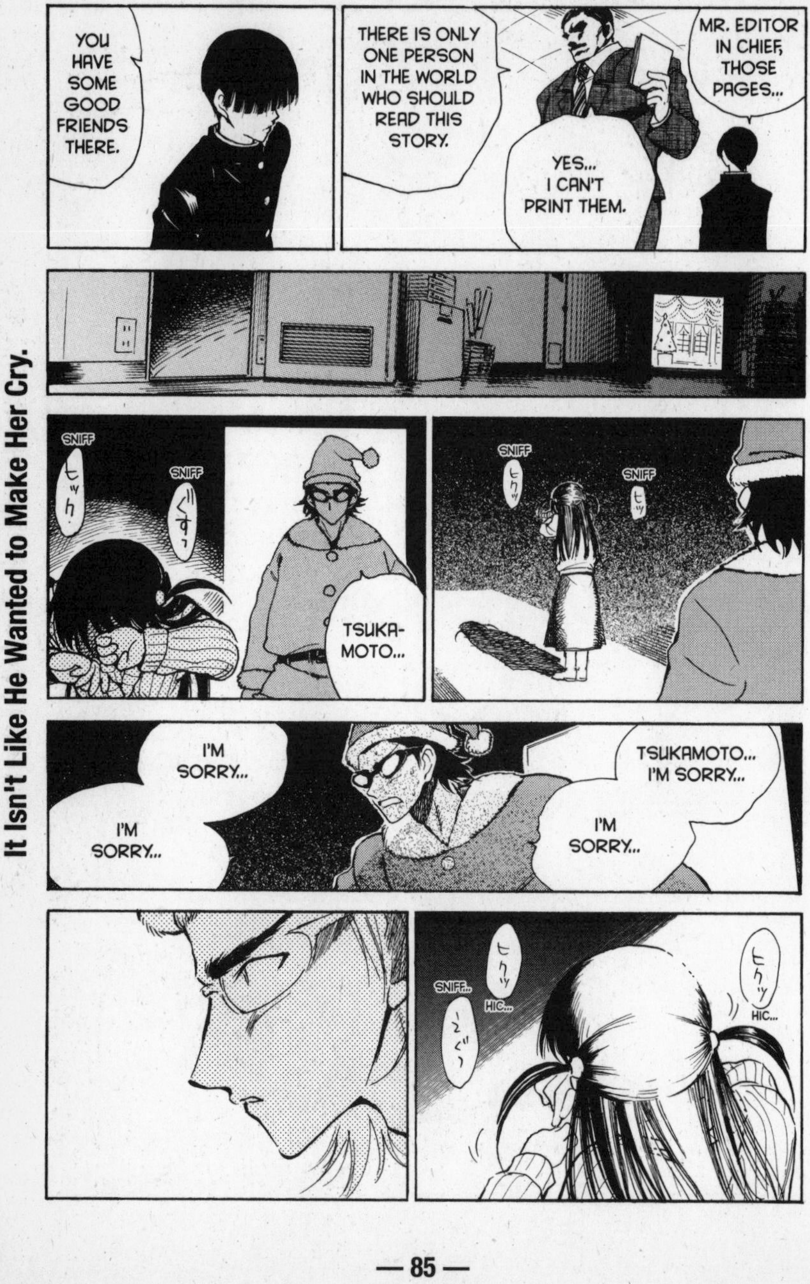
MR. EDITOR IN CHIEF, THOSE PAGES...
YES... I CAN'T PRINT THEM.
THERE IS ONLY ONE PERSON IN THE WORLD WHO SHOULD READ THIS STORY.
YOU HAVE SOME GOOD FRIENDS THERE.
SNIFF
ヒッ
SNIFF
ヒクッ
TSUKA-MOTO...
SNIFF
ぐすっ
SNIFF
ヒック
TSUKAMOTO... I'M SORRY...
I'M SORRY...
I'M SORRY...
I'M SORRY...
ヒクッ
HIC...
ヒクッ
HIC...
SNIFF...
ぐすっ

Well, Anyway, Merry Christmas.

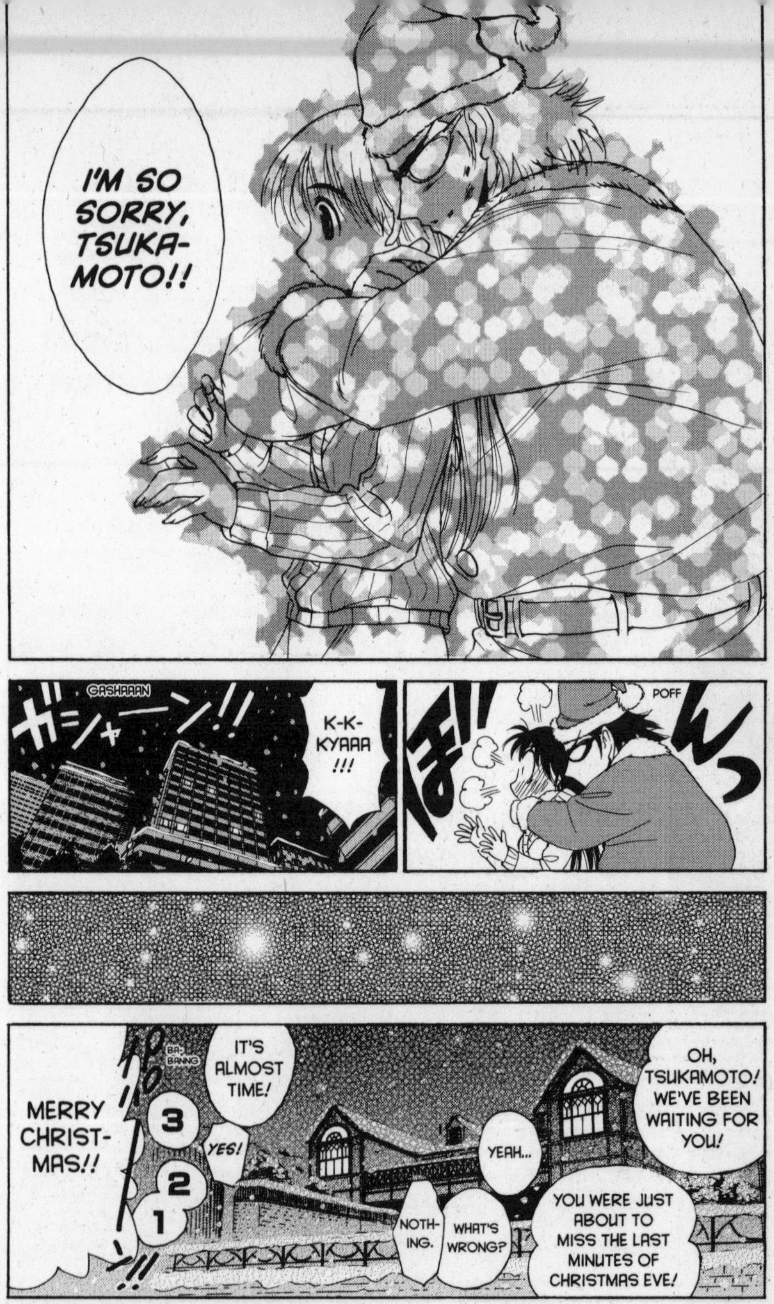
I'M SO SORRY, TSUKAMOTO!!
POFF
ぼ!! んっ
GASHAAAN
ガシャーーン!!
K-K-KYAAA!!!
OH, TSUKAMOTO! WE'VE BEEN WAITING FOR YOU!
YOU WERE JUST ABOUT TO MISS THE LAST MINUTES OF CHRISTMAS EVE!
YEAH...
WHAT'S WRONG?
NOTH-ING.
IT'S ALMOST TIME!
YES!
3
2
1
BA-BANNG
MERRY CHRIST-MAS!!

\# 159· · · · · · · · ·Fin

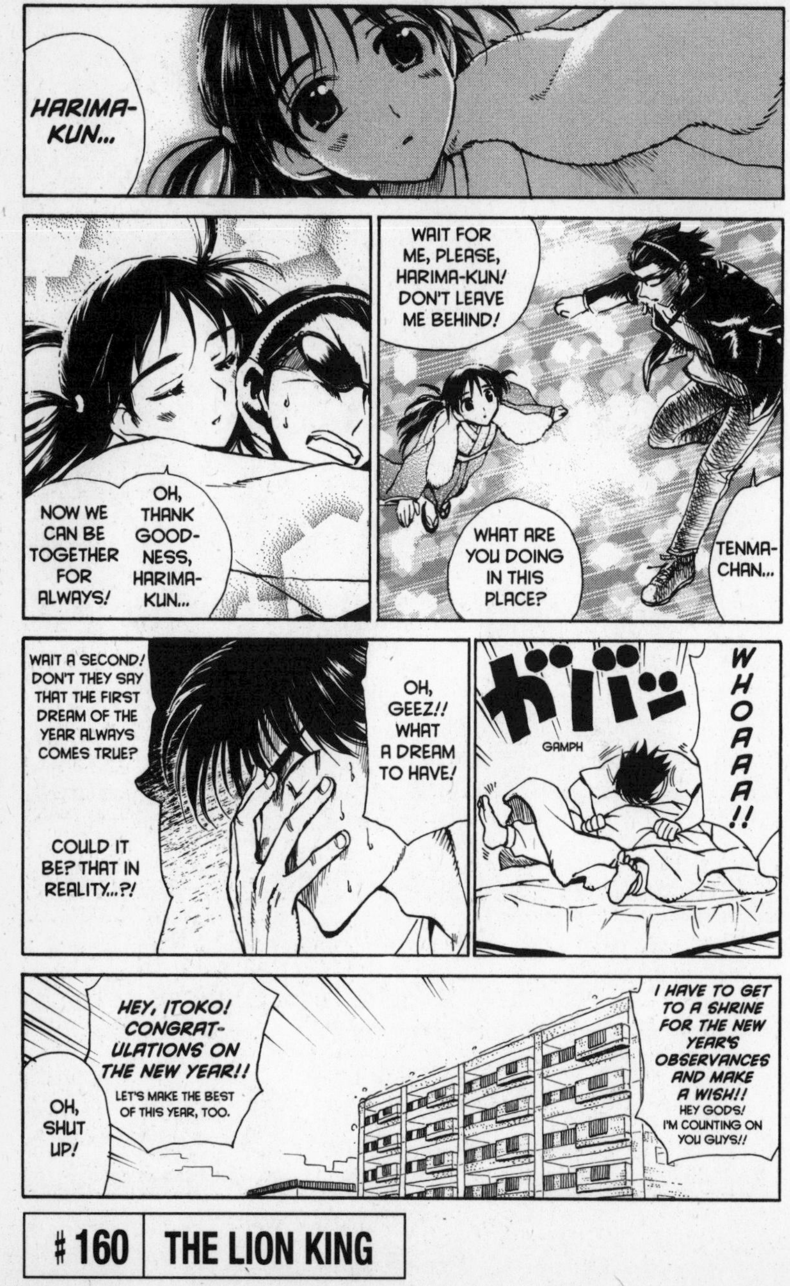
HARIMA-KUN...
WAIT FOR ME, PLEASE, HARIMA-KUN! DON'T LEAVE ME BEHIND!
TENMA-CHAN...
WHAT ARE YOU DOING IN THIS PLACE?
OH, THANK GOODNESS, HARIMA-KUN...
NOW WE CAN BE TOGETHER FOR ALWAYS!
WHOAAAA!!
ガバッ
GAMPH
OH, GEEZ!! WHAT A DREAM TO HAVE!
WAIT A SECOND! DON'T THEY SAY THAT THE FIRST DREAM OF THE YEAR ALWAYS COMES TRUE?
COULD IT BE? THAT IN REALITY...?!
I HAVE TO GET TO A SHRINE FOR THE NEW YEAR'S OBSERVANCES AND MAKE A WISH!!
HEY GODS! I'M COUNTING ON YOU GUYS!!
HEY, ITOKO! CONGRATULATIONS ON THE NEW YEAR!!
LET'S MAKE THE BEST OF THIS YEAR, TOO.
OH, SHUT UP!

#160 THE LION KING

Tsukamoto Tenma: Loves Karasuma Ôji in 2006, Too.

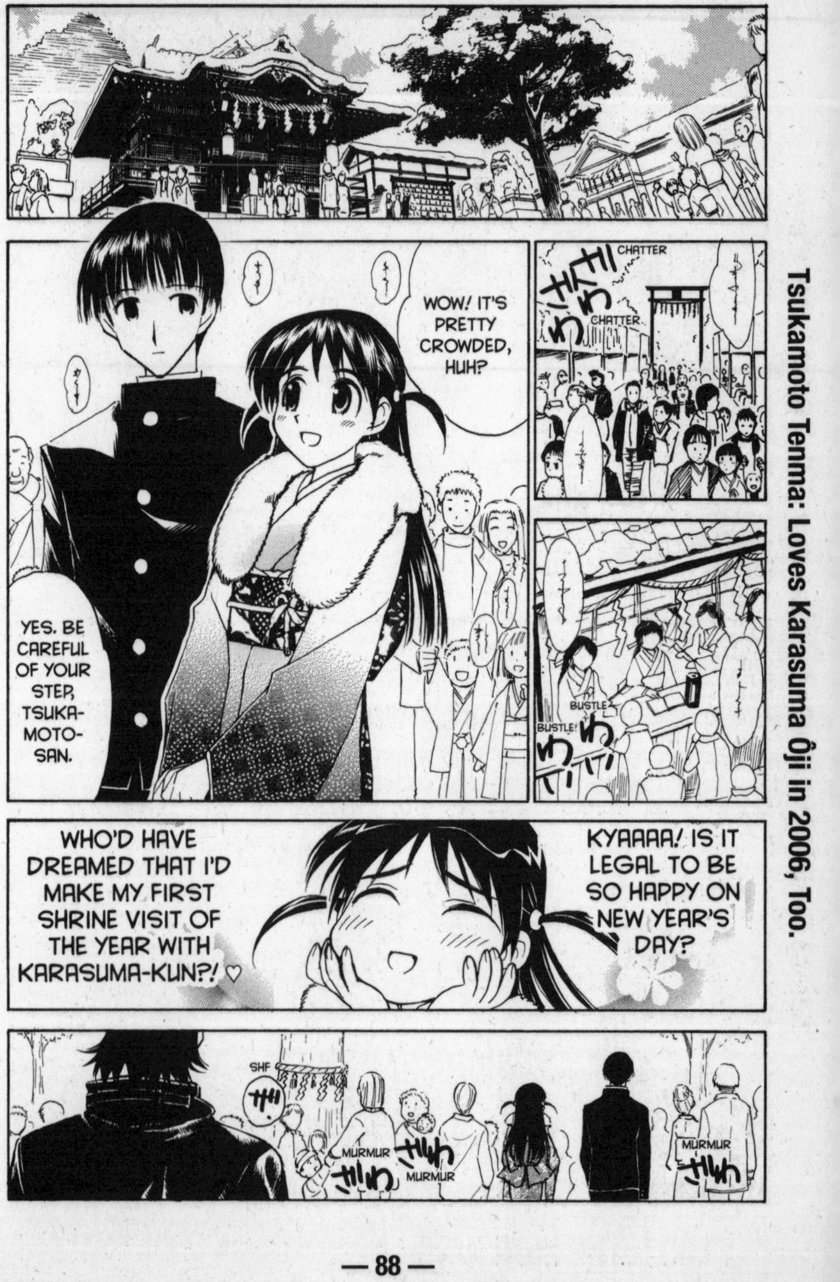
CHATTER
CHATTER
BUSTLE
BUSTLE!
WOW! IT'S PRETTY CROWDED, HUH?
YES. BE CAREFUL OF YOUR STEP, TSUKA-MOTO-SAN.
KYAAAA! IS IT LEGAL TO BE SO HAPPY ON NEW YEAR'S DAY?
WHO'D HAVE DREAMED THAT I'D MAKE MY FIRST SHRINE VISIT OF THE YEAR WITH KARASUMA-KUN?! ♡
MURMUR
MURMUR
MURMUR
SHF

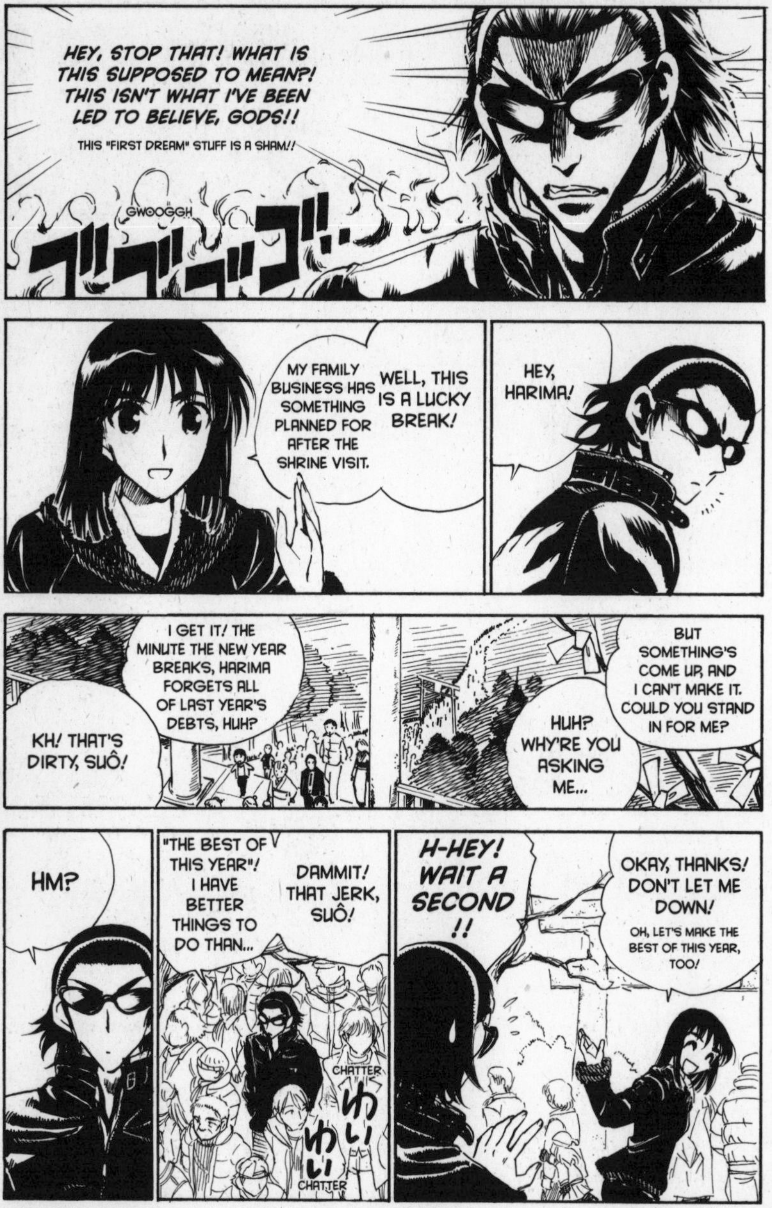
HEY, STOP THAT! WHAT IS THIS SUPPOSED TO MEAN?! THIS ISN'T WHAT I'VE BEEN LED TO BELIEVE, GODS!!
THIS "FIRST DREAM" STUFF IS A SHAM!!
GWOOGGH
HEY, HARIMA!
WELL, THIS IS A LUCKY BREAK!
MY FAMILY BUSINESS HAS SOMETHING PLANNED FOR AFTER THE SHRINE VISIT.
BUT SOMETHING'S COME UP, AND I CAN'T MAKE IT. COULD YOU STAND IN FOR ME?
HUH? WHY'RE YOU ASKING ME...
I GET IT! THE MINUTE THE NEW YEAR BREAKS, HARIMA FORGETS ALL OF LAST YEAR'S DEBTS, HUH?
KH! THAT'S DIRTY, SUÔ!
OKAY, THANKS! DON'T LET ME DOWN!
OH, LET'S MAKE THE BEST OF THIS YEAR, TOO!
H-HEY! WAIT A SECOND!!
DAMMIT! THAT JERK, SUÔ!
"THE BEST OF THIS YEAR"! I HAVE BETTER THINGS TO DO THAN...
CHATTER
CHATTER
HM?

Harima Kenji: Spent the End of Last Year Holing Up at Suô's Place.

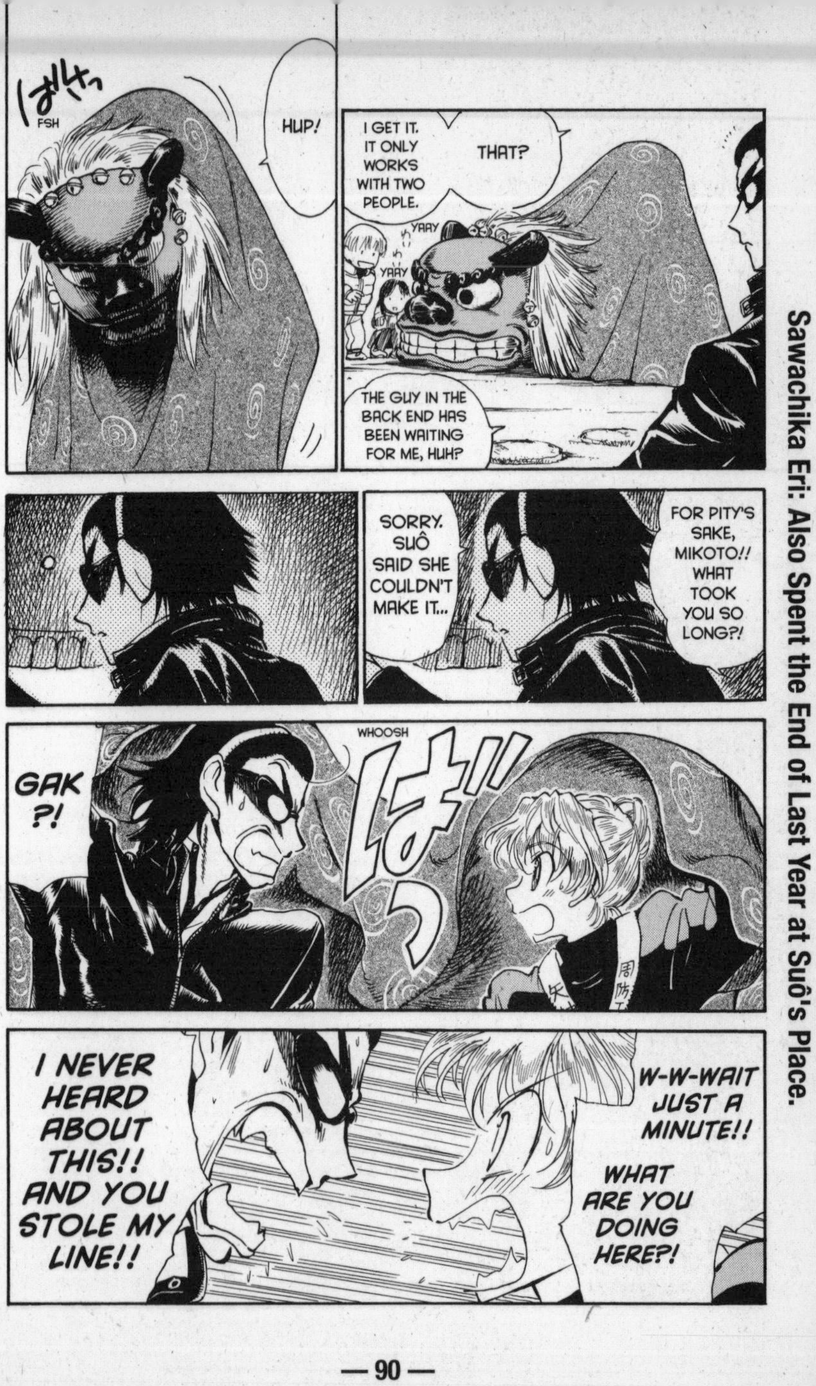
THAT?
I GET IT. IT ONLY WORKS WITH TWO PEOPLE.
YAAY
YAAY
THE GUY IN THE BACK END HAS BEEN WAITING FOR ME, HUH?
HUP!
FSH
FOR PITY'S SAKE, MIKOTO!! WHAT TOOK YOU SO LONG?!
SORRY. SUÔ SAID SHE COULDN'T MAKE IT...
WHOOSH
GAK ?!
W-W-WAIT JUST A MINUTE!!
WHAT ARE YOU DOING HERE?!
I NEVER HEARD ABOUT THIS!! AND YOU STOLE MY LINE!!

Sawachika Eri: Also Spent the End of Last Year at Suô's Place.

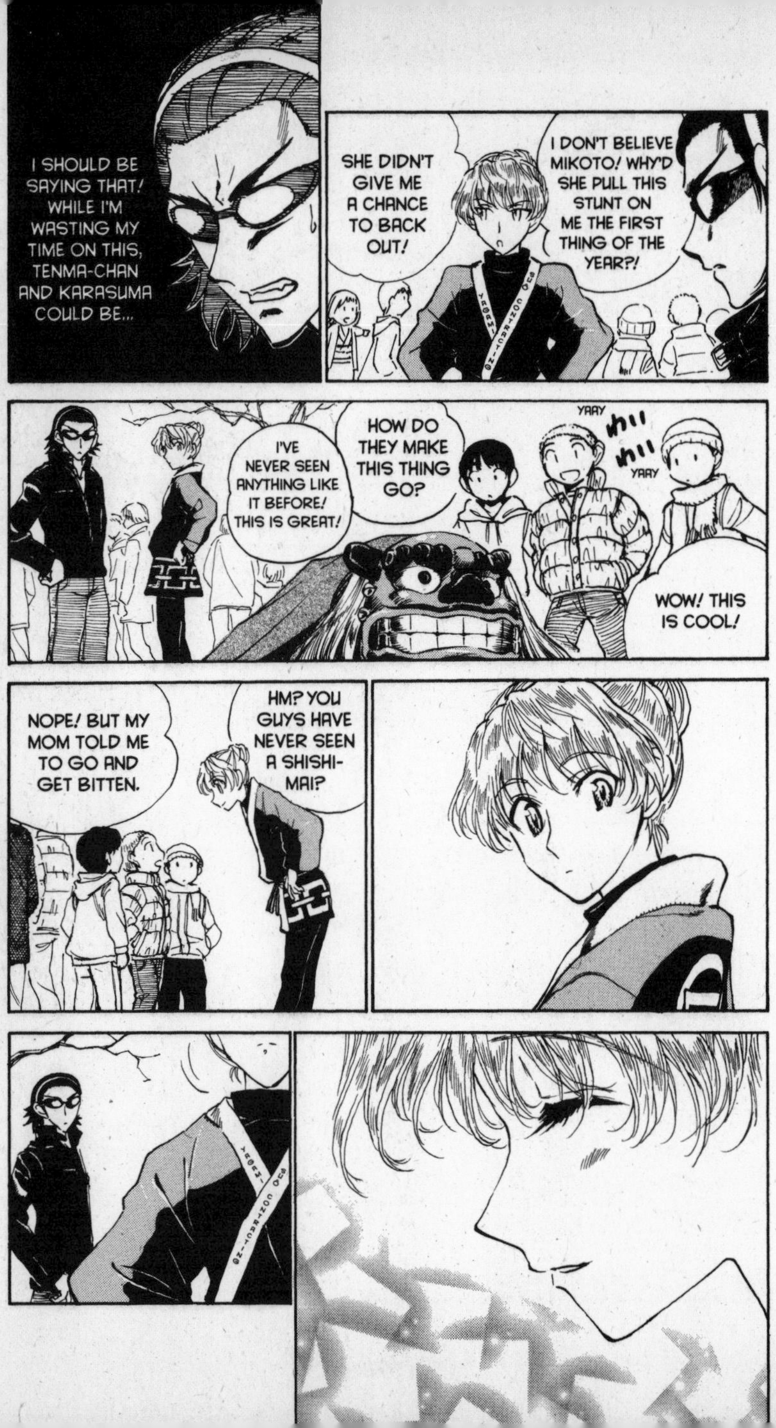
I DON'T BELIEVE MIKOTO! WHY'D SHE PULL THIS STUNT ON ME THE FIRST THING OF THE YEAR?!
SHE DIDN'T GIVE ME A CHANCE TO BACK OUT!
I SHOULD BE SAYING THAT! WHILE I'M WASTING MY TIME ON THIS, TENMA-CHAN AND KARASUMA COULD BE...
YAAY
わい わい
YAAY
HOW DO THEY MAKE THIS THING GO?
I'VE NEVER SEEN ANYTHING LIKE IT BEFORE! THIS IS GREAT!
WOW! THIS IS COOL!
HM? YOU GUYS HAVE NEVER SEEN A SHISHI-MAI?
NOPE! BUT MY MOM TOLD ME TO GO AND GET BITTEN.

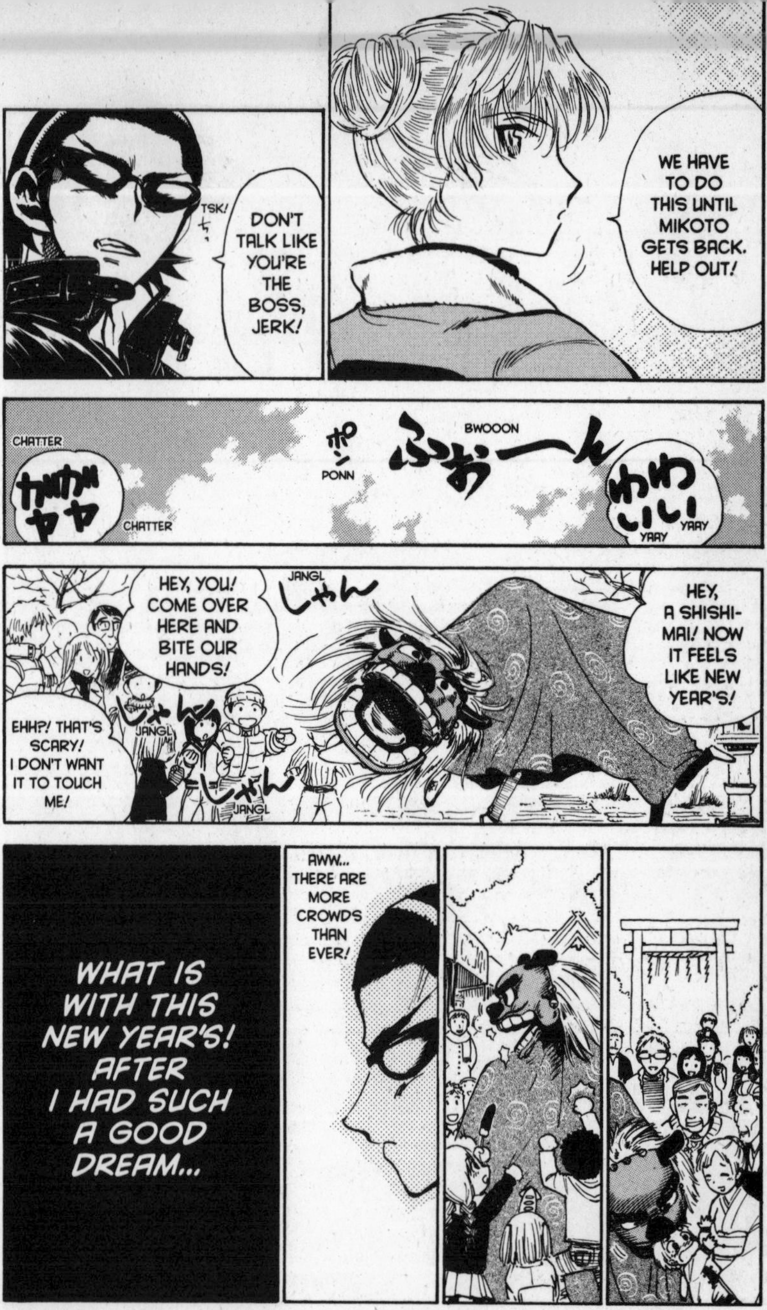
WE HAVE TO DO THIS UNTIL MIKOTO GETS BACK. HELP OUT!
TSK!
ち、
DON'T TALK LIKE YOU'RE THE BOSS, JERK!
わいわい
YAAY YAAY
ふぉーん
BWOOON
ポン
PONN
ガヤガヤ
CHATTER
CHATTER
HEY, A SHISHI-MAI! NOW IT FEELS LIKE NEW YEAR'S!
しゃん
JANGL
HEY, YOU! COME OVER HERE AND BITE OUR HANDS!
しゃん
JANGL
EHH?! THAT'S SCARY! I DON'T WANT IT TO TOUCH ME!
しゃん
JANGL
AWW... THERE ARE MORE CROWDS THAN EVER!
WHAT IS WITH THIS NEW YEAR'S! AFTER I HAD SUCH A GOOD DREAM...

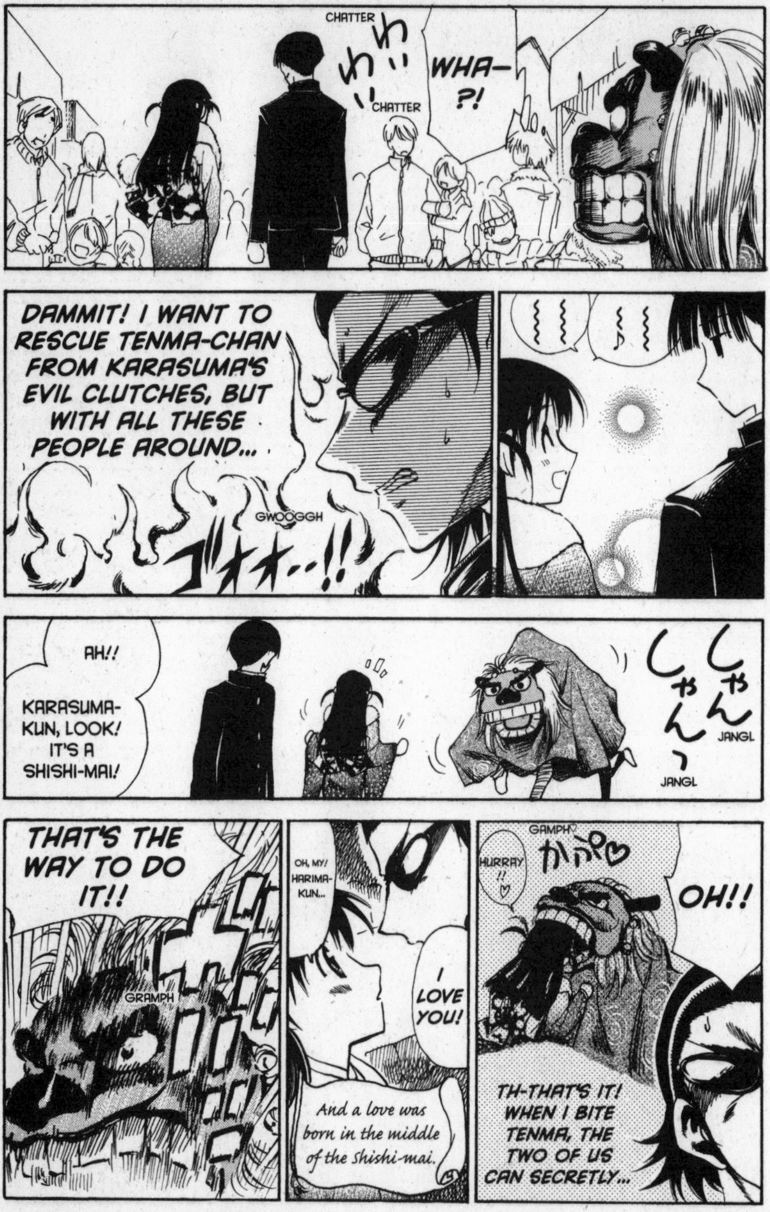
WHA—?!
CHATTER
CHATTER
DAMMIT! I WANT TO RESCUE TENMA-CHAN FROM KARASUMA'S EVIL CLUTCHES, BUT WITH ALL THESE PEOPLE AROUND...
GWOOGGH
しゃん しゃん
JANGL
JANGL
AH!!
KARASUMA-KUN, LOOK! IT'S A SHISHI-MAI!
OH!!
GAMPH♡
HURRAY!! ♡
TH-THAT'S IT! WHEN I BITE TENMA, THE TWO OF US CAN SECRETLY...
OH, MY! HARIMA-KUN...
I LOVE YOU!
And a love was born in the middle of the shishi-mai.
THAT'S THE WAY TO DO IT!!
GRAMPH

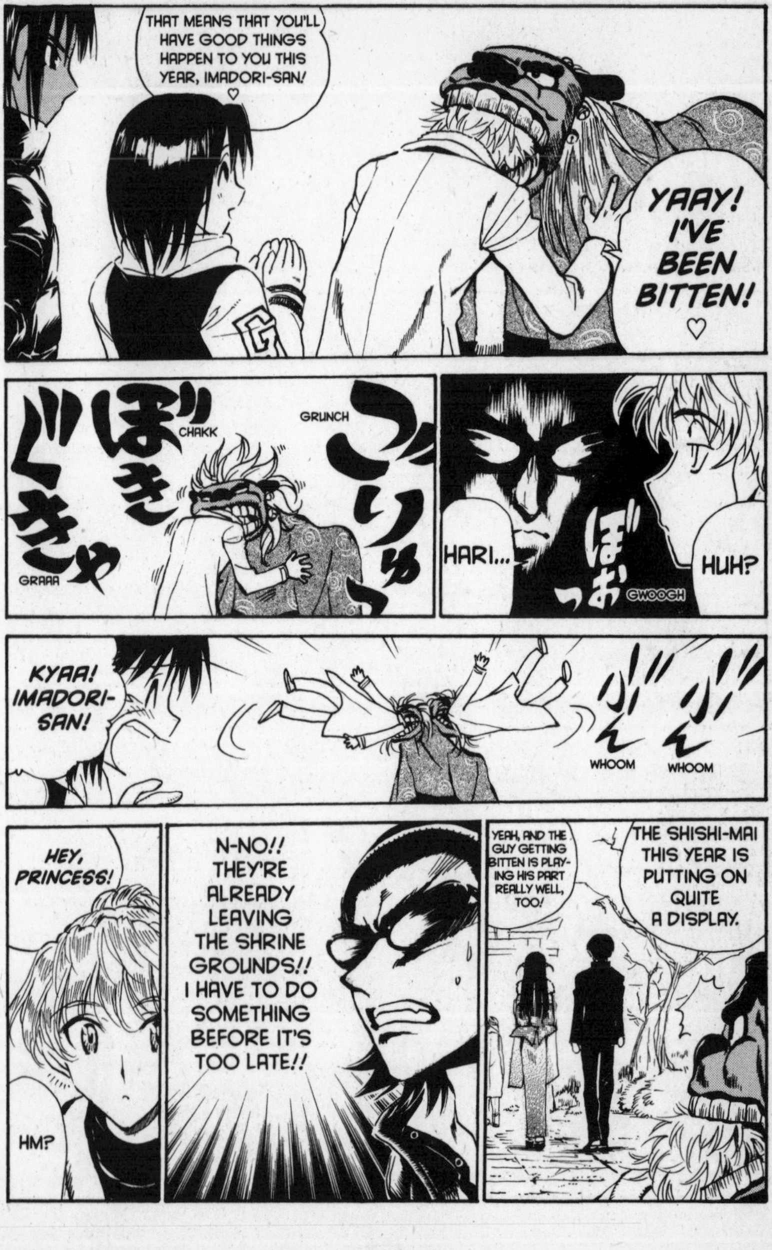
YAAY! I'VE BEEN BITTEN! ♡
THAT MEANS THAT YOU'LL HAVE GOOD THINGS HAPPEN TO YOU THIS YEAR, IMADORI-SAN! ♡
HUH?
GWOOGH
HARI...
GRUNCH
CHAKK
GRAAA
WHOOM
WHOOM
KYAA! IMADORI-SAN!
THE SHISHI-MAI THIS YEAR IS PUTTING ON QUITE A DISPLAY.
YEAH, AND THE GUY GETTING BITTEN IS PLAYING HIS PART REALLY WELL, TOO!
N-NO!! THEY'RE ALREADY LEAVING THE SHRINE GROUNDS!! I HAVE TO DO SOMETHING BEFORE IT'S TOO LATE!!
HEY, PRINCESS!
HM?

The Shishi-mai: Shows a Violent Aspect.

Shishi-mai: A Café Patron....It Seems.

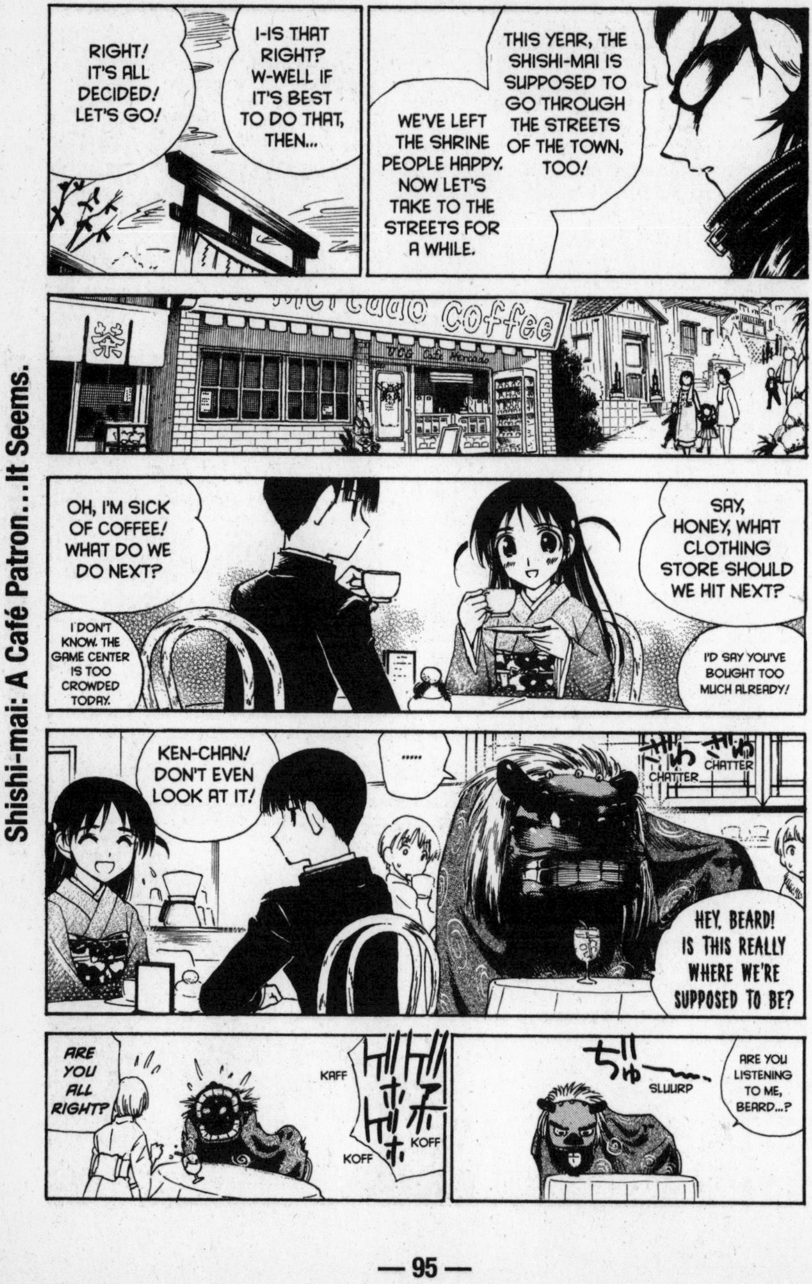
THIS YEAR, THE SHISHI-MAI IS SUPPOSED TO GO THROUGH THE STREETS OF THE TOWN, TOO!
WE'VE LEFT THE SHRINE PEOPLE HAPPY. NOW LET'S TAKE TO THE STREETS FOR A WHILE.
I-IS THAT RIGHT? W-WELL IF IT'S BEST TO DO THAT, THEN...
RIGHT! IT'S ALL DECIDED! LET'S GO!
coffee
SAY, HONEY, WHAT CLOTHING STORE SHOULD WE HIT NEXT?
I'D SAY YOU'VE BOUGHT TOO MUCH ALREADY!
OH, I'M SICK OF COFFEE! WHAT DO WE DO NEXT?
I DON'T KNOW. THE GAME CENTER IS TOO CROWDED TODAY.
CHATTER
CHATTER
HEY, BEARD! IS THIS REALLY WHERE WE'RE SUPPOSED TO BE?
......
KEN-CHAN! DON'T EVEN LOOK AT IT!
SLUURP
ARE YOU LISTENING TO ME, BEARD...?
KAFF
KOFF
KOFF
ARE YOU ALL RIGHT?

Tsukamoto Tenma: Watched the Summer Fireworks from Here.

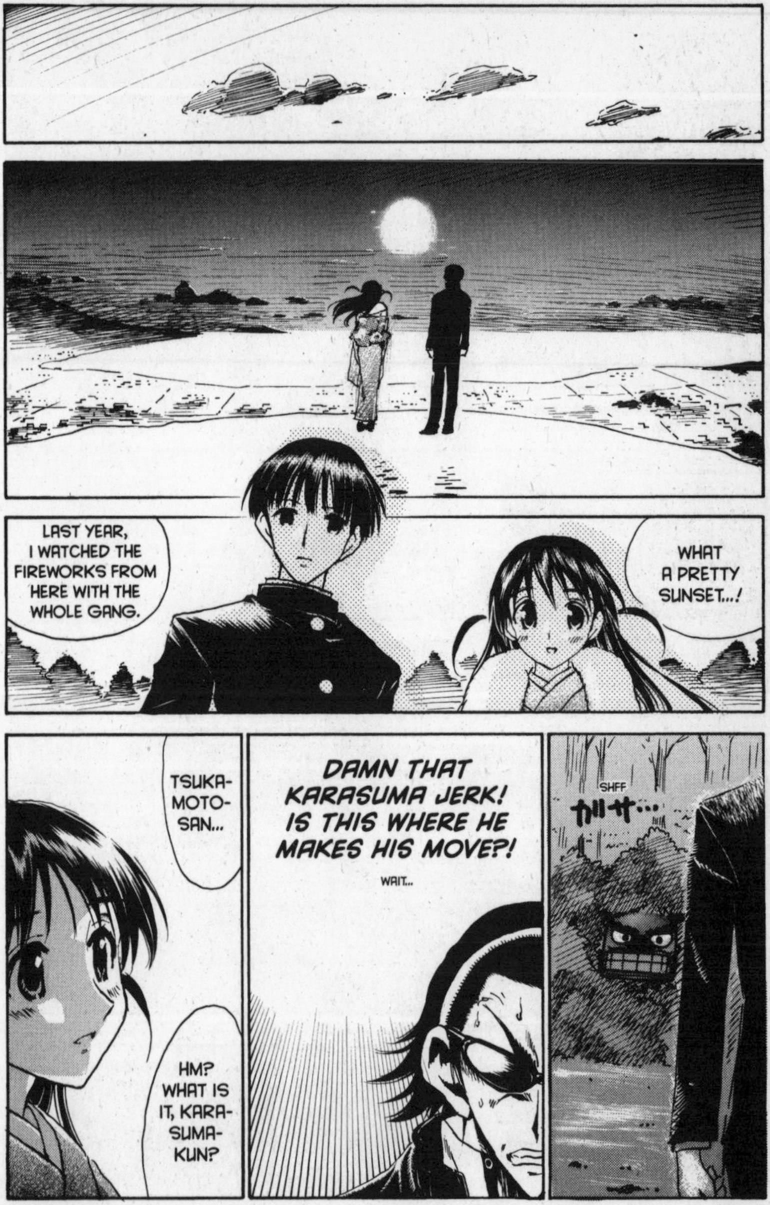
WHAT A PRETTY SUNSET...!
LAST YEAR, I WATCHED THE FIREWORKS FROM HERE WITH THE WHOLE GANG.
SHFF
DAMN THAT KARASUMA JERK! IS THIS WHERE HE MAKES HIS MOVE?!
WAIT...
TSUKA-MOTO-SAN...
HM? WHAT IS IT, KARA-SUMA-KUN?

Harima Kenji: Teeters on the Cliff Again This Year.

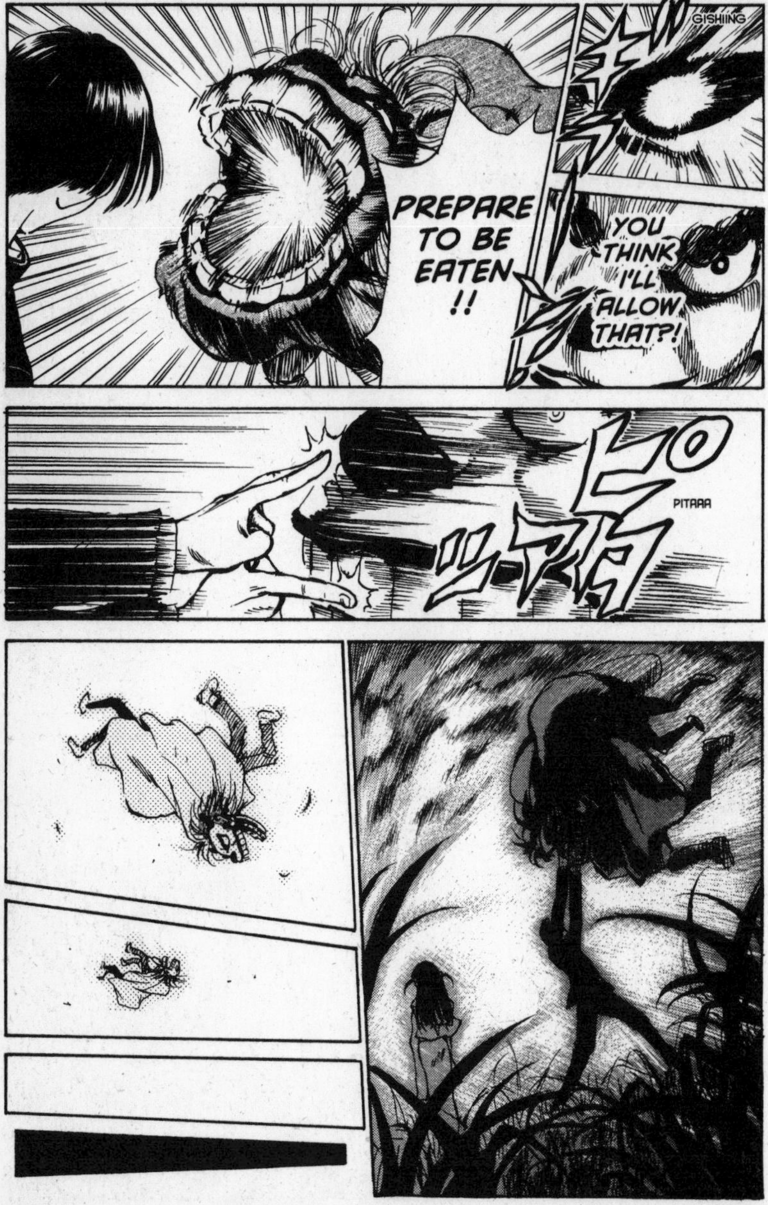
GISHIING
YOU THINK I'LL ALLOW THAT?!
PREPARE TO BE EATEN !!
PITARR

First Dream: Not Very Close to Reality.

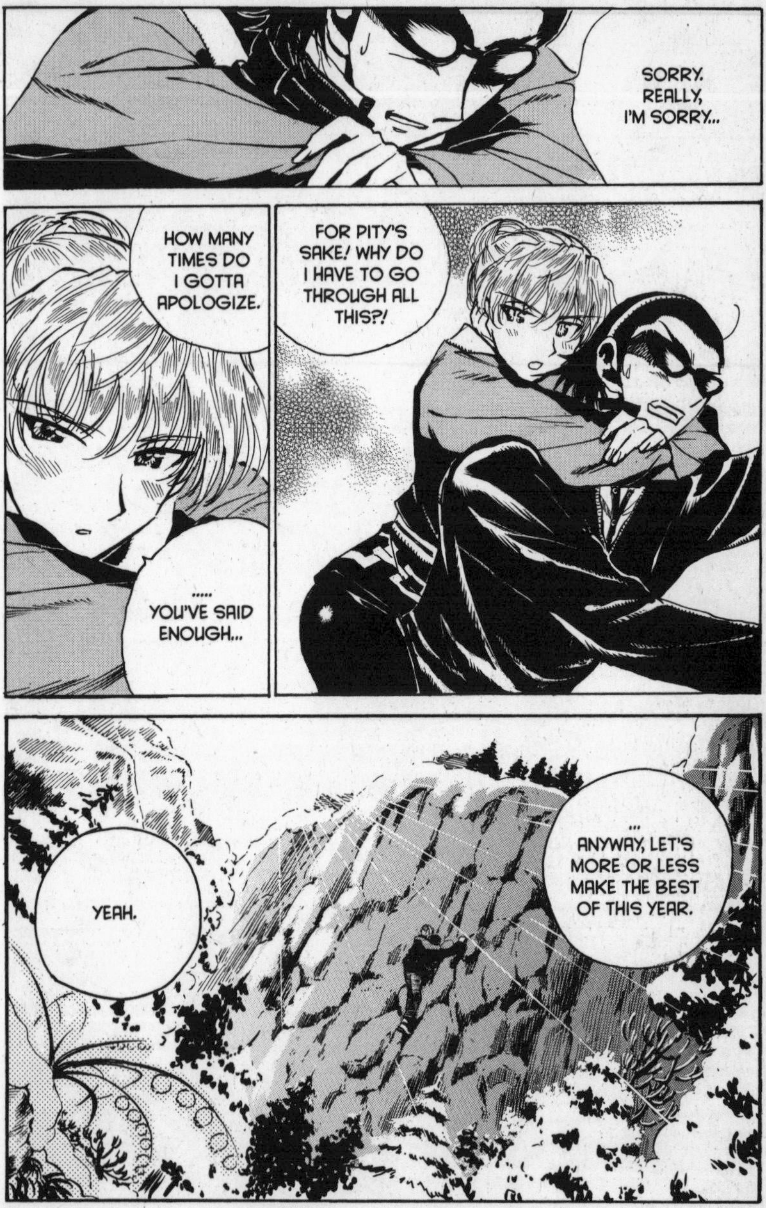
SORRY. REALLY, I'M SORRY...
FOR PITY'S SAKE! WHY DO I HAVE TO GO THROUGH ALL THIS?!
HOW MANY TIMES DO I GOTTA APOLOGIZE.
..... YOU'VE SAID ENOUGH...
... ANYWAY, LET'S MORE OR LESS MAKE THE BEST OF THIS YEAR.
YEAH.

160· · · · · · · ·Fin

161 THE JERK

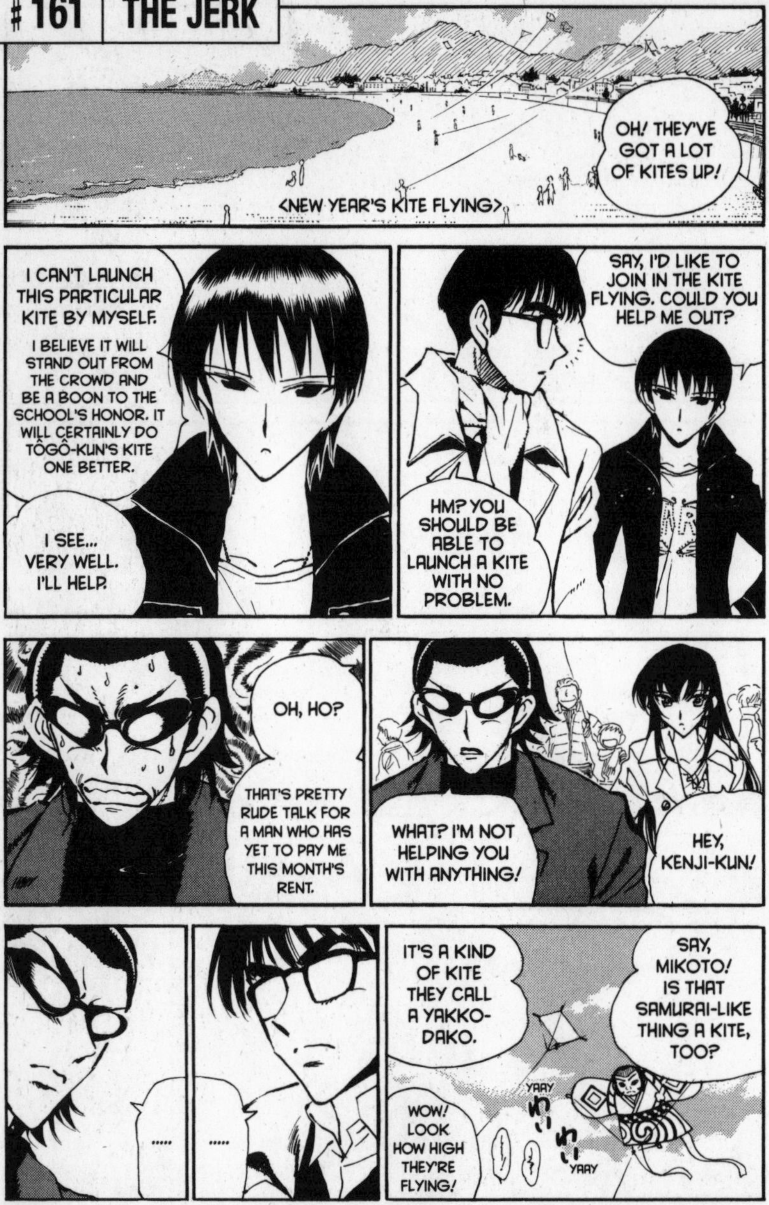

OH! THEY'VE GOT A LOT OF KITES UP!
<NEW YEAR'S KITE FLYING>
SAY, I'D LIKE TO JOIN IN THE KITE FLYING. COULD YOU HELP ME OUT?
HM? YOU SHOULD BE ABLE TO LAUNCH A KITE WITH NO PROBLEM.
I CAN'T LAUNCH THIS PARTICULAR KITE BY MYSELF.
I BELIEVE IT WILL STAND OUT FROM THE CROWD AND BE A BOON TO THE SCHOOL'S HONOR. IT WILL CERTAINLY DO TÔGÔ-KUN'S KITE ONE BETTER.
I SEE... VERY WELL. I'LL HELP.
HEY, KENJI-KUN!
WHAT? I'M NOT HELPING YOU WITH ANYTHING!
OH, HO?
THAT'S PRETTY RUDE TALK FOR A MAN WHO HAS YET TO PAY ME THIS MONTH'S RENT.
SAY, MIKOTO! IS THAT SAMURAI-LIKE THING A KITE, TOO?
IT'S A KIND OF KITE THEY CALL A YAKKO-DAKO.
YAAY
YAAY
WOW! LOOK HOW HIGH THEY'RE FLYING!
.....
.....

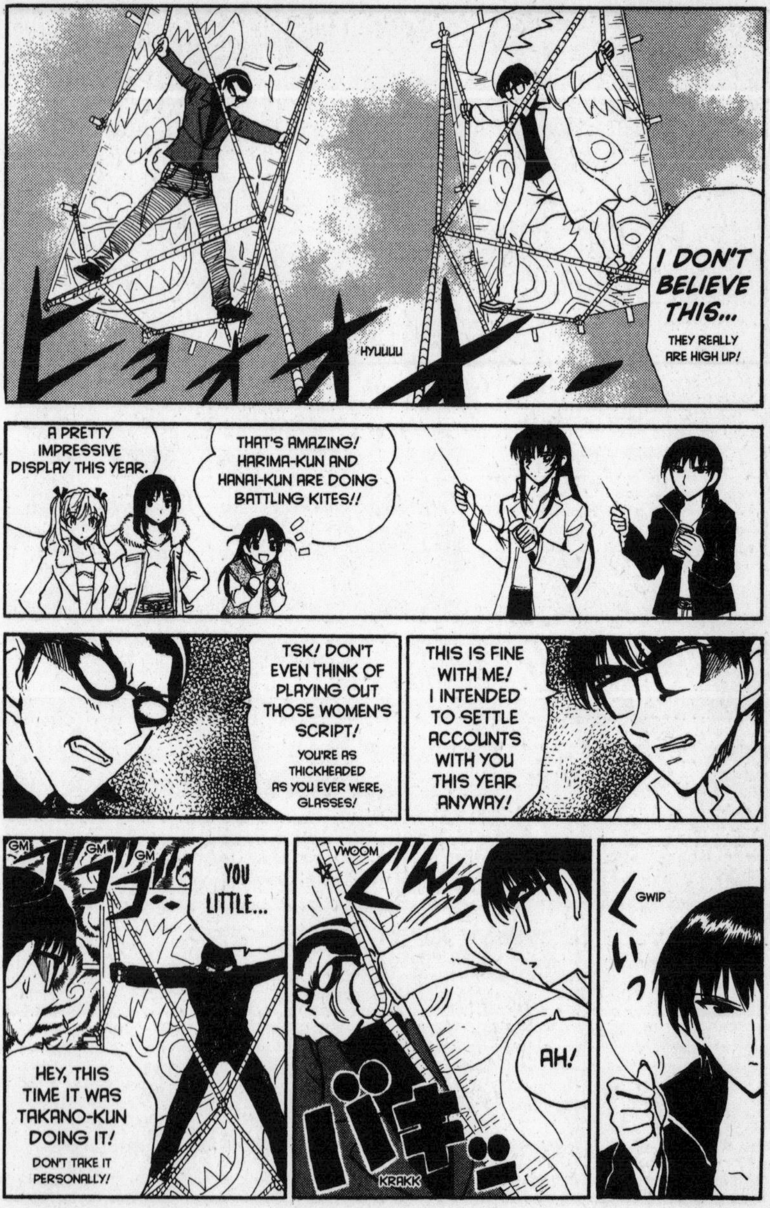
I DON'T BELIEVE THIS...
THEY REALLY ARE HIGH UP!
HYUUUU
THAT'S AMAZING! HARIMA-KUN AND HANAI-KUN ARE DOING BATTLING KITES!!
A PRETTY IMPRESSIVE DISPLAY THIS YEAR.
THIS IS FINE WITH ME! I INTENDED TO SETTLE ACCOUNTS WITH YOU THIS YEAR ANYWAY!
TSK! DON'T EVEN THINK OF PLAYING OUT THOSE WOMEN'S SCRIPT!
YOU'RE AS THICKHEADED AS YOU EVER WERE, GLASSES!
GWIP
VWOOM
AH!
KRAKK
GM
GM
GM
YOU LITTLE...
HEY, THIS TIME IT WAS TAKANO-KUN DOING IT!
DON'T TAKE IT PERSONALLY!

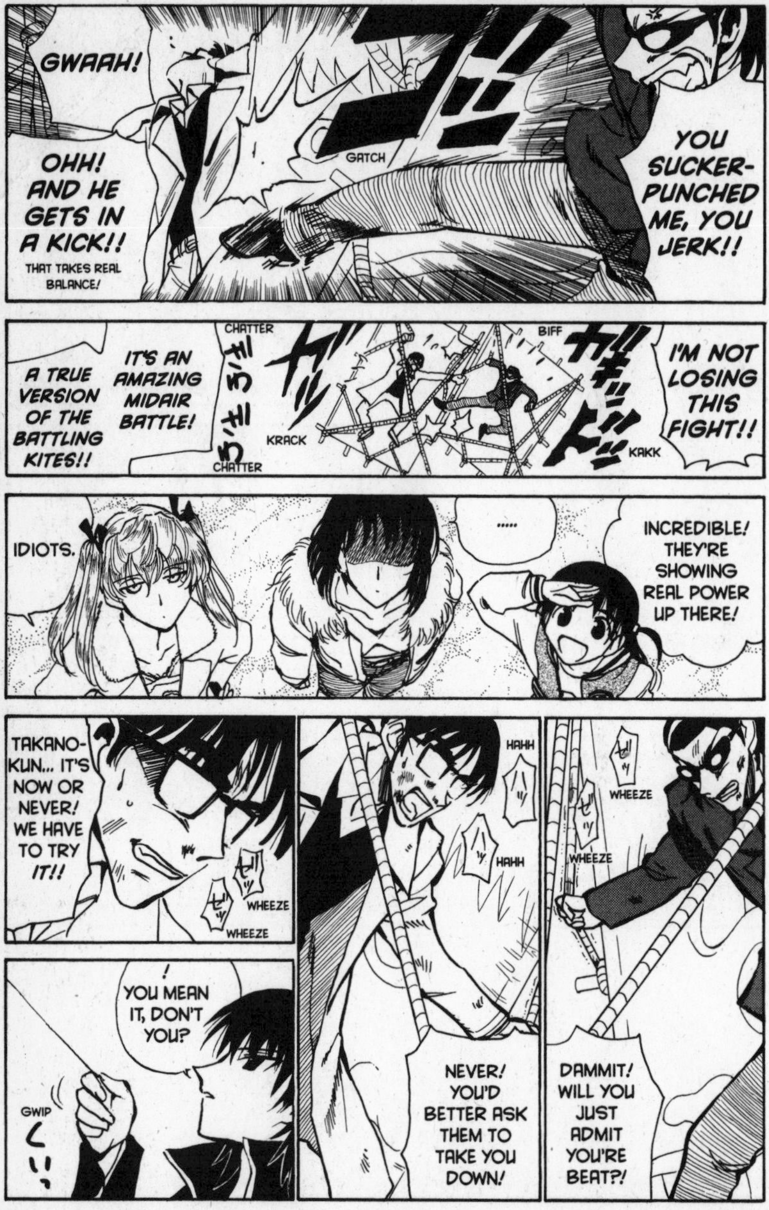
YOU SUCKER-PUNCHED ME, YOU JERK!!
GATCH
GWAAH!
OHH! AND HE GETS IN A KICK!!
THAT TAKES REAL BALANCE!
I'M NOT LOSING THIS FIGHT!!
BIFF
KAKK
CHATTER
KRACK
CHATTER
IT'S AN AMAZING MIDAIR BATTLE!
A TRUE VERSION OF THE BATTLING KITES!!
INCREDIBLE! THEY'RE SHOWING REAL POWER UP THERE!
.....
IDIOTS.
WHEEZE
WHEEZE
DAMMIT! WILL YOU JUST ADMIT YOU'RE BEAT?!
HAHH
HAHH
NEVER! YOU'D BETTER ASK THEM TO TAKE YOU DOWN!
TAKANO-KUN... IT'S NOW OR NEVER! WE HAVE TO TRY IT!!
WHEEZE
WHEEZE
!
YOU MEAN IT, DON'T YOU?
GWIP

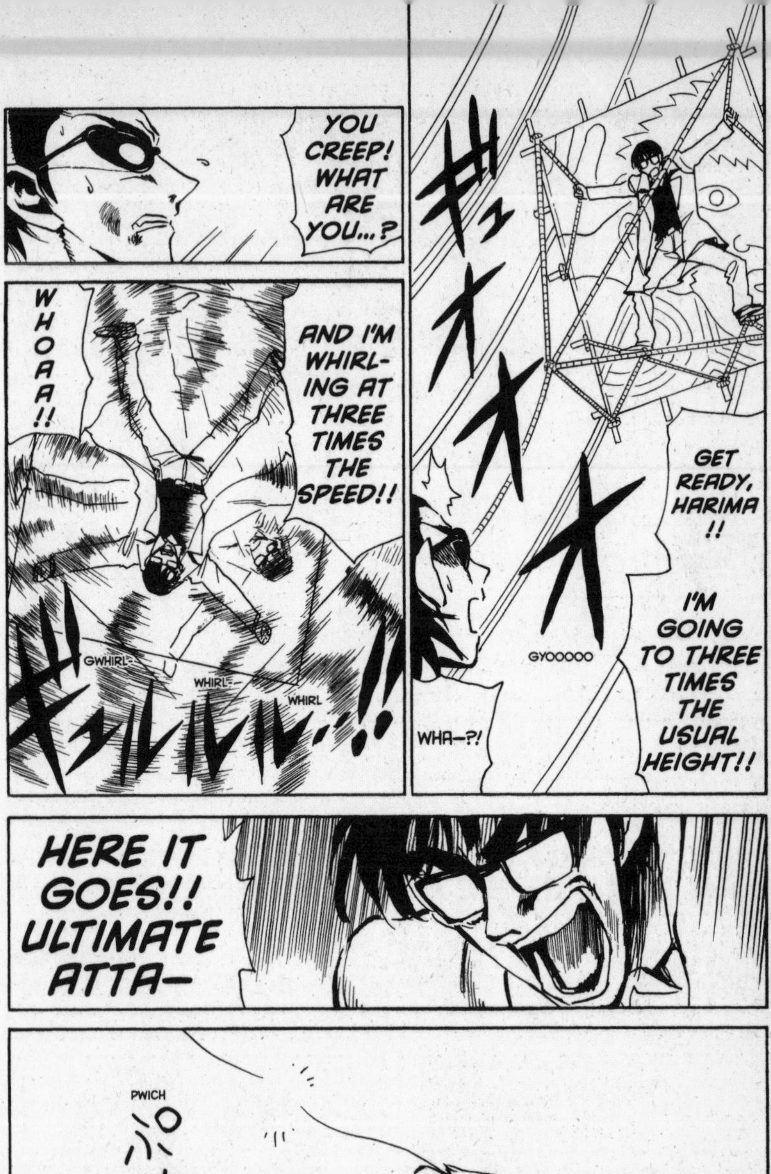
GET READY, HARIMA!!
I'M GOING TO THREE TIMES THE USUAL HEIGHT!!
GYOOOOO
WHA—?!
YOU CREEP! WHAT ARE YOU...?
AND I'M WHIRLING AT THREE TIMES THE SPEED!!
WHOAAA!!
GWHIRL-
WHIRL-
WHIRL
HERE IT GOES!! ULTIMATE ATTA—
PWICH

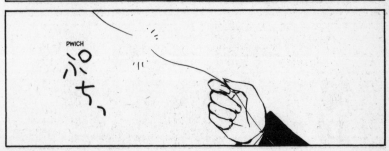

<HUNDRED VERSES COLLECTION>

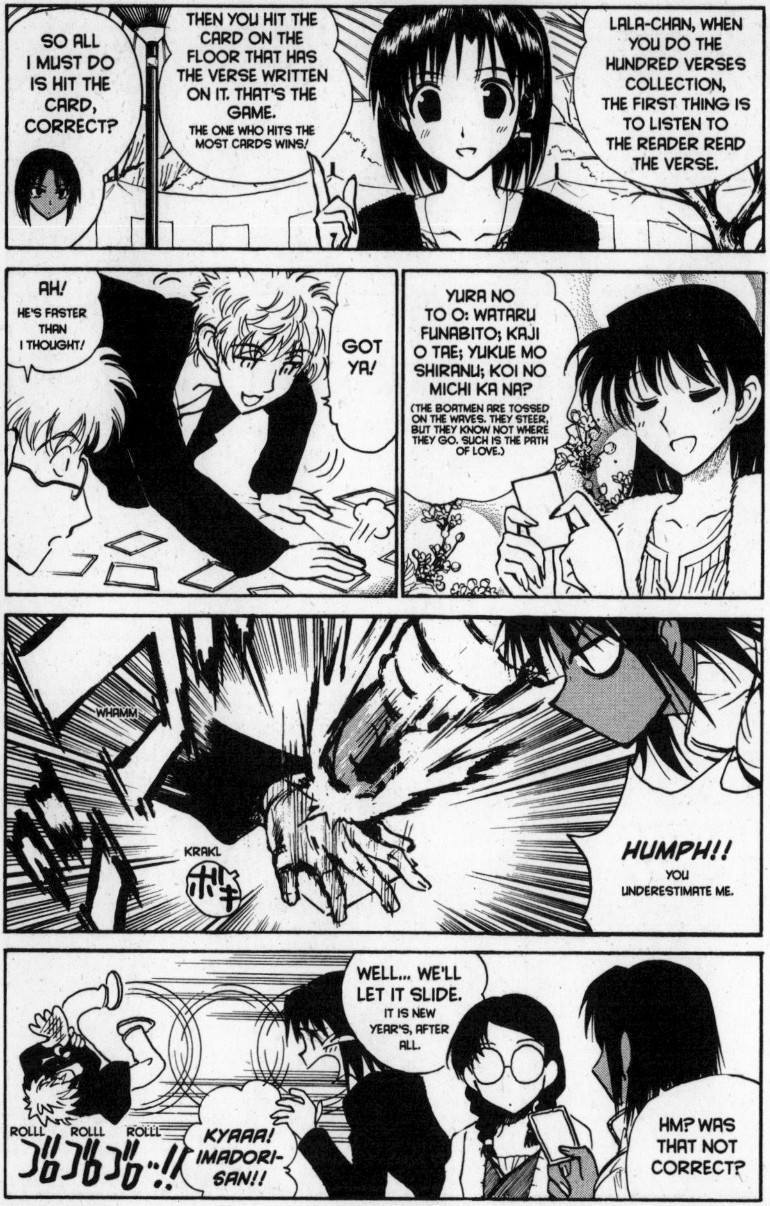
LALA-CHAN, WHEN YOU DO THE HUNDRED VERSES COLLECTION, THE FIRST THING IS TO LISTEN TO THE READER READ THE VERSE.
THEN YOU HIT THE CARD ON THE FLOOR THAT HAS THE VERSE WRITTEN ON IT. THAT'S THE GAME.
THE ONE WHO HITS THE MOST CARDS WINS!
SO ALL I MUST DO IS HIT THE CARD, CORRECT?
YURA NO TO O: WATARU FUNABITO; KAJI O TAE; YUKUE MO SHIRANU; KOI NO MICHI KA NA?
(THE BOATMEN ARE TOSSED ON THE WAVES. THEY STEER, BUT THEY KNOW NOT WHERE THEY GO. SUCH IS THE PATH OF LOVE.)
GOT YA!
AH!
HE'S FASTER THAN I THOUGHT!
HUMPH!!
YOU UNDERESTIMATE ME.
KRAKL
WHAMM
HM? WAS THAT NOT CORRECT?
WELL... WE'LL LET IT SLIDE.
IT IS NEW YEAR'S, AFTER ALL.
KYAAA! IMADORI-SAN!!
ROLLL ROLLL ROLLL

TKO: Lala Wins.

<HAGOITA (BATTLEDORE AND SHUTTLECOCK)>

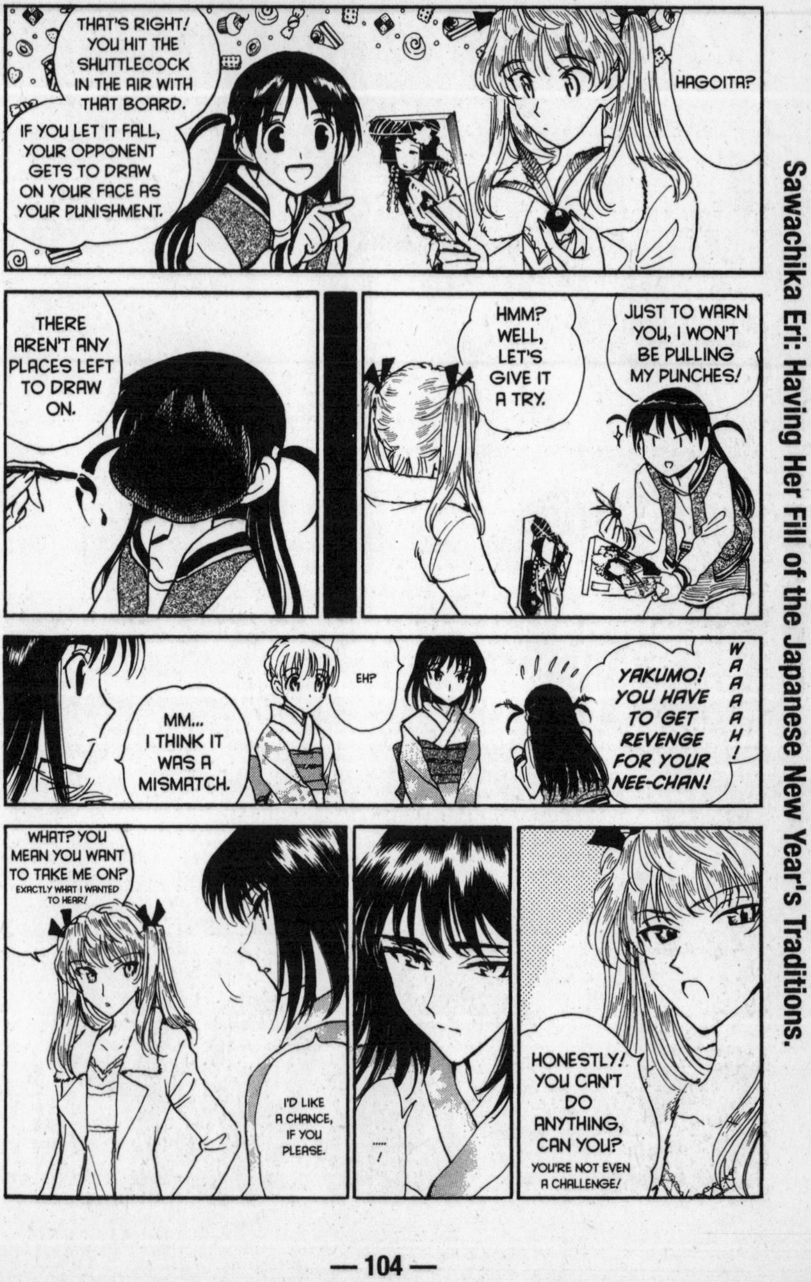
HAGOITA?
THAT'S RIGHT! YOU HIT THE SHUTTLECOCK IN THE AIR WITH THAT BOARD.
IF YOU LET IT FALL, YOUR OPPONENT GETS TO DRAW ON YOUR FACE AS YOUR PUNISHMENT.
JUST TO WARN YOU, I WON'T BE PULLING MY PUNCHES!
HMM? WELL, LET'S GIVE IT A TRY.
THERE AREN'T ANY PLACES LEFT TO DRAW ON.
WAAAAH!
YAKUMO! YOU HAVE TO GET REVENGE FOR YOUR NEE-CHAN!
EH?
MM... I THINK IT WAS A MISMATCH.
HONESTLY! YOU CAN'T DO ANYTHING, CAN YOU?
YOU'RE NOT EVEN A CHALLENGE!
.....!
I'D LIKE A CHANCE, IF YOU PLEASE.
WHAT? YOU MEAN YOU WANT TO TAKE ME ON?
EXACTLY WHAT I WANTED TO HEAR!

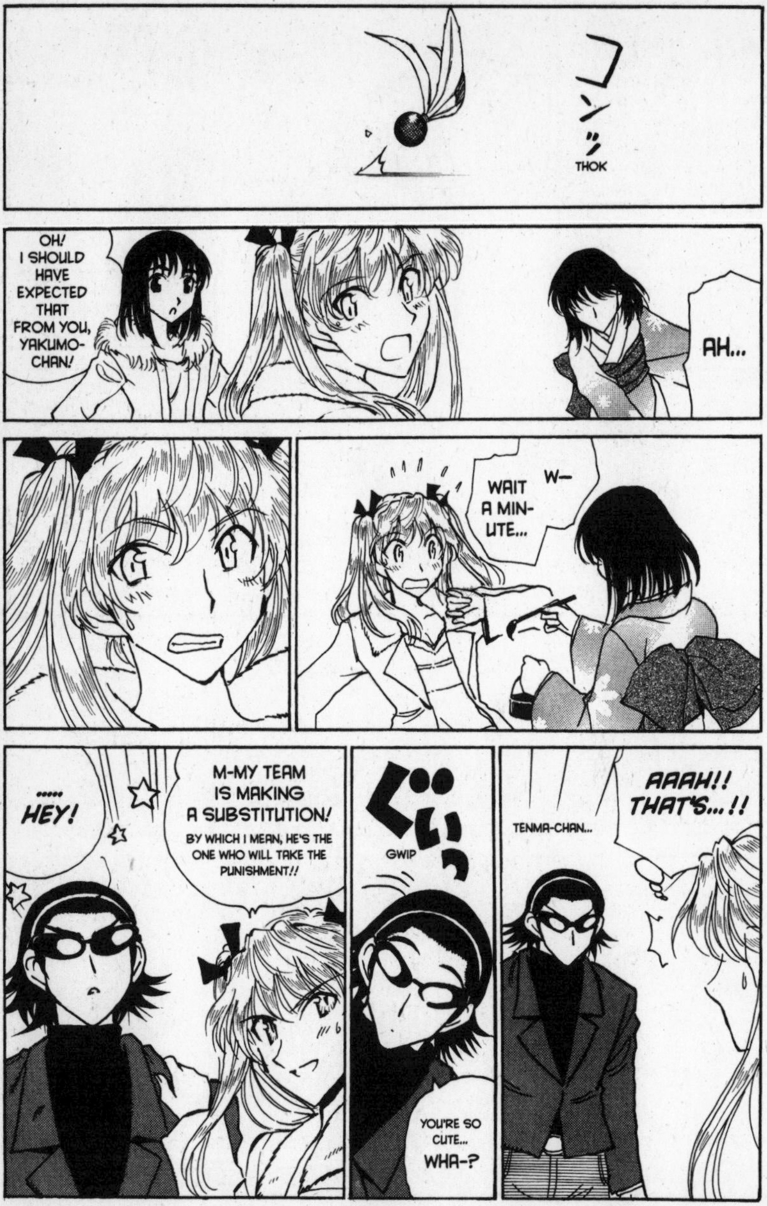
コンッ
THOK
AH...
OH! I SHOULD HAVE EXPECTED THAT FROM YOU, YAKUMO-CHAN!
W—
WAIT A MIN-UTE...
AAAH!! THAT'S...!!
TENMA-CHAN...
ぐいっ
GWIP
YOU'RE SO CUTE...
WHA-?
M-MY TEAM IS MAKING A SUBSTITUTION!
BY WHICH I MEAN, HE'S THE ONE WHO WILL TAKE THE PUNISHMENT!!
...... HEY!

2006: Suddenly Harima's Beard Makes a Reappearance.

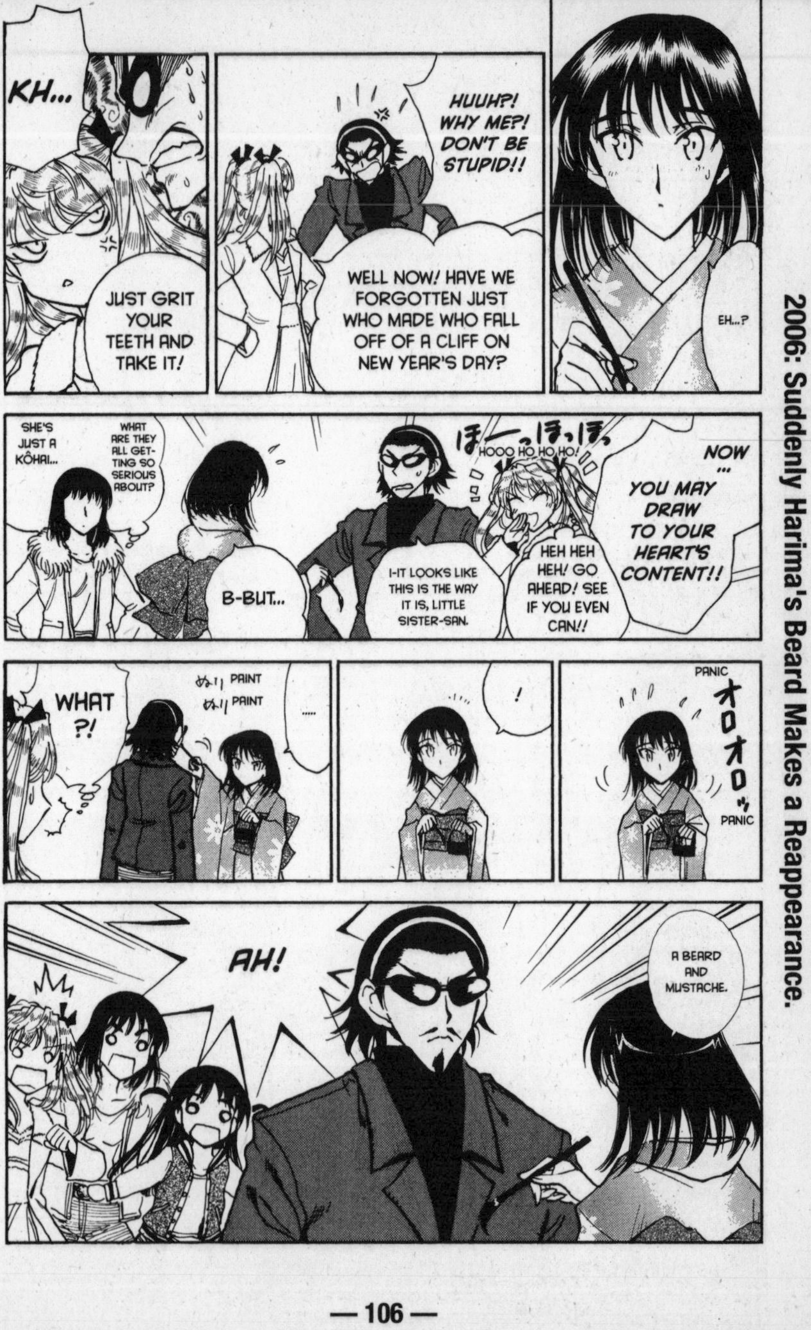
EH...?
HUUH?! WHY ME?! DON'T BE STUPID!!
WELL NOW! HAVE WE FORGOTTEN JUST WHO MADE WHO FALL OFF OF A CLIFF ON NEW YEAR'S DAY?
KH...
JUST GRIT YOUR TEETH AND TAKE IT!
NOW... YOU MAY DRAW TO YOUR HEART'S CONTENT!!
ほーっほっほっ HOOO HO HO HO!
HEH HEH HEH! GO AHEAD! SEE IF YOU EVEN CAN!!
I-IT LOOKS LIKE THIS IS THE WAY IT IS, LITTLE SISTER-SAN.
B-BUT...
WHAT ARE THEY ALL GET-TING SO SERIOUS ABOUT?
SHE'S JUST A KÔHAI...
PANIC オロオロッ PANIC
!
......
ぬり PAINT
ぬり PAINT
WHAT?!
A BEARD AND MUSTACHE.
AH!

<THIRD SEMESTER>

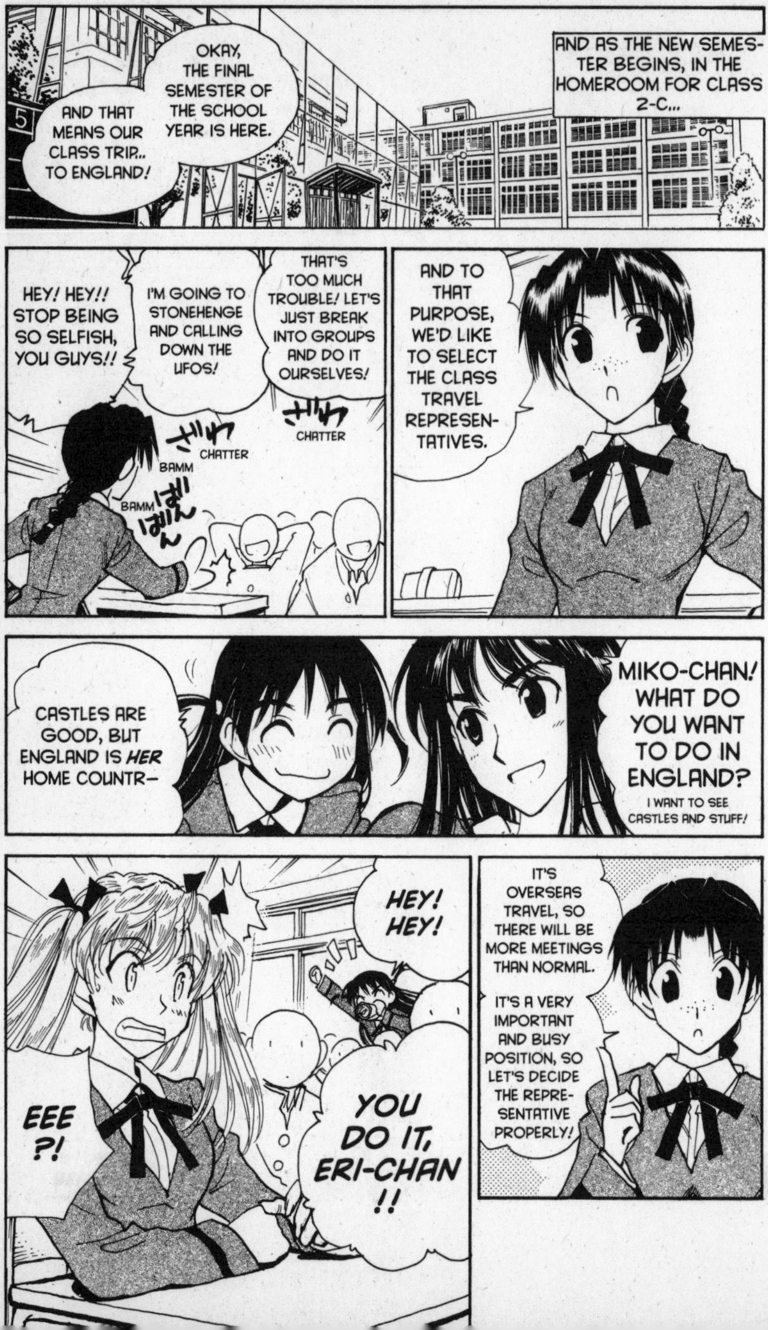
AND AS THE NEW SEMESTER BEGINS, IN THE HOMEROOM FOR CLASS 2-C...
OKAY, THE FINAL SEMESTER OF THE SCHOOL YEAR IS HERE.
AND THAT MEANS OUR CLASS TRIP.. TO ENGLAND!
5
AND TO THAT PURPOSE, WE'D LIKE TO SELECT THE CLASS TRAVEL REPRESENTATIVES.
THAT'S TOO MUCH TROUBLE! LET'S JUST BREAK INTO GROUPS AND DO IT OURSELVES!
ざわ CHATTER
I'M GOING TO STONEHENGE AND CALLING DOWN THE UFOS!
ざわ CHATTER
HEY! HEY!! STOP BEING SO SELFISH, YOU GUYS!!
BAMM
ばん BAMM ばん
MIKO-CHAN! WHAT DO YOU WANT TO DO IN ENGLAND?
I WANT TO SEE CASTLES AND STUFF!
CASTLES ARE GOOD, BUT ENGLAND IS *HER* HOME COUNTR—
IT'S OVERSEAS TRAVEL, SO THERE WILL BE MORE MEETINGS THAN NORMAL.
IT'S A VERY IMPORTANT AND BUSY POSITION, SO LET'S DECIDE THE REPRESENTATIVE PROPERLY!
HEY! HEY!
YOU DO IT, ERI-CHAN!!
EEE?!

Ôtsuka Mai: 2-C Class Representative.

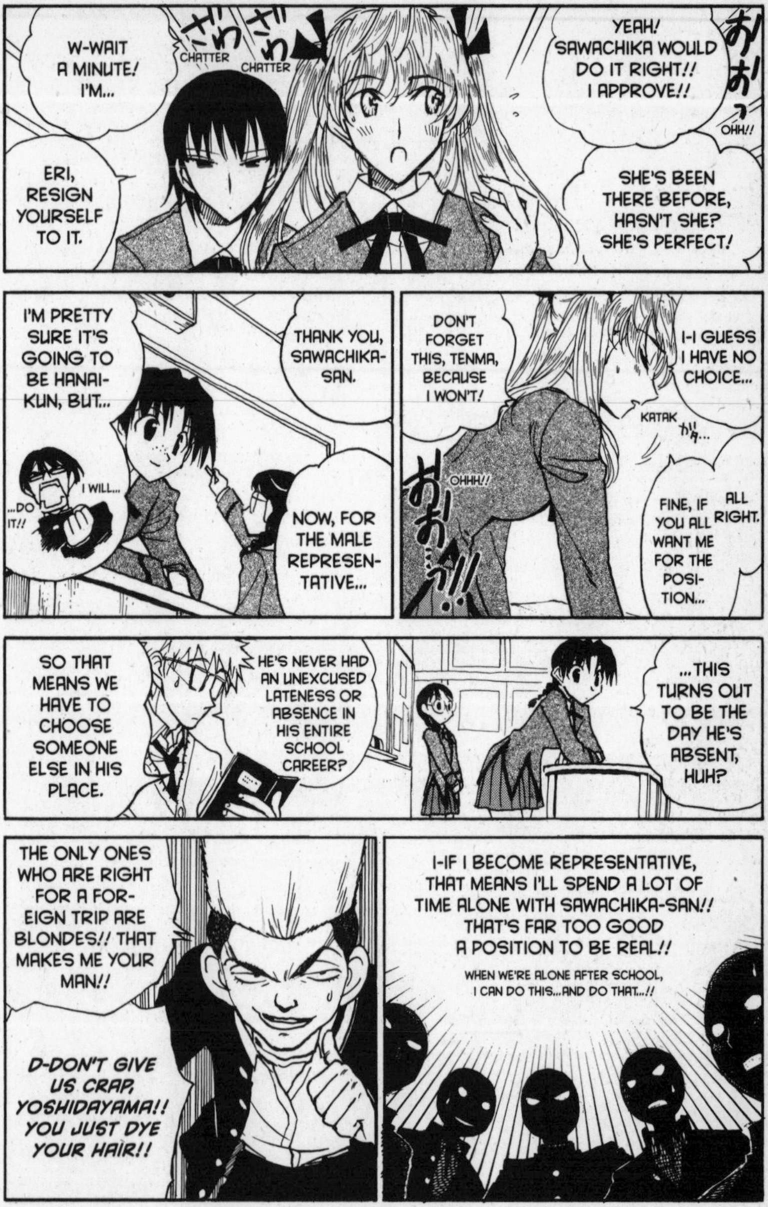
おおっ
OHH!!
YEAH! SAWACHIKA WOULD DO IT RIGHT!! I APPROVE!!
SHE'S BEEN THERE BEFORE, HASN'T SHE? SHE'S PERFECT!
ざわ ざわ
CHATTER CHATTER
W-WAIT A MINUTE! I'M...
ERI, RESIGN YOURSELF TO IT.
I-I GUESS I HAVE NO CHOICE...
DON'T FORGET THIS, TENMA, BECAUSE I WON'T!
KATAK
ALL RIGHT.
FINE, IF YOU ALL WANT ME FOR THE POSITION...
OHHH!!
THANK YOU, SAWACHIKA-SAN.
I'M PRETTY SURE IT'S GOING TO BE HANAI-KUN, BUT...
NOW, FOR THE MALE REPRESENTATIVE...
I WILL...
...DO IT!!
...THIS TURNS OUT TO BE THE DAY HE'S ABSENT, HUH?
HE'S NEVER HAD AN UNEXCUSED LATENESS OR ABSENCE IN HIS ENTIRE SCHOOL CAREER?
SO THAT MEANS WE HAVE TO CHOOSE SOMEONE ELSE IN HIS PLACE.
I-IF I BECOME REPRESENTATIVE, THAT MEANS I'LL SPEND A LOT OF TIME ALONE WITH SAWACHIKA-SAN!! THAT'S FAR TOO GOOD A POSITION TO BE REAL!!
WHEN WE'RE ALONE AFTER SCHOOL, I CAN DO THIS...AND DO THAT...!!
THE ONLY ONES WHO ARE RIGHT FOR A FOREIGN TRIP ARE BLONDES!! THAT MAKES ME YOUR MAN!!
D-DON'T GIVE US CRAP, YOSHIDAYAMA!! YOU JUST DYE YOUR HAIR!!

Sawachika Eri: Lived Abroad Until a Point During Her Junior High Years.

A Fool's Battle Royale in Progress.

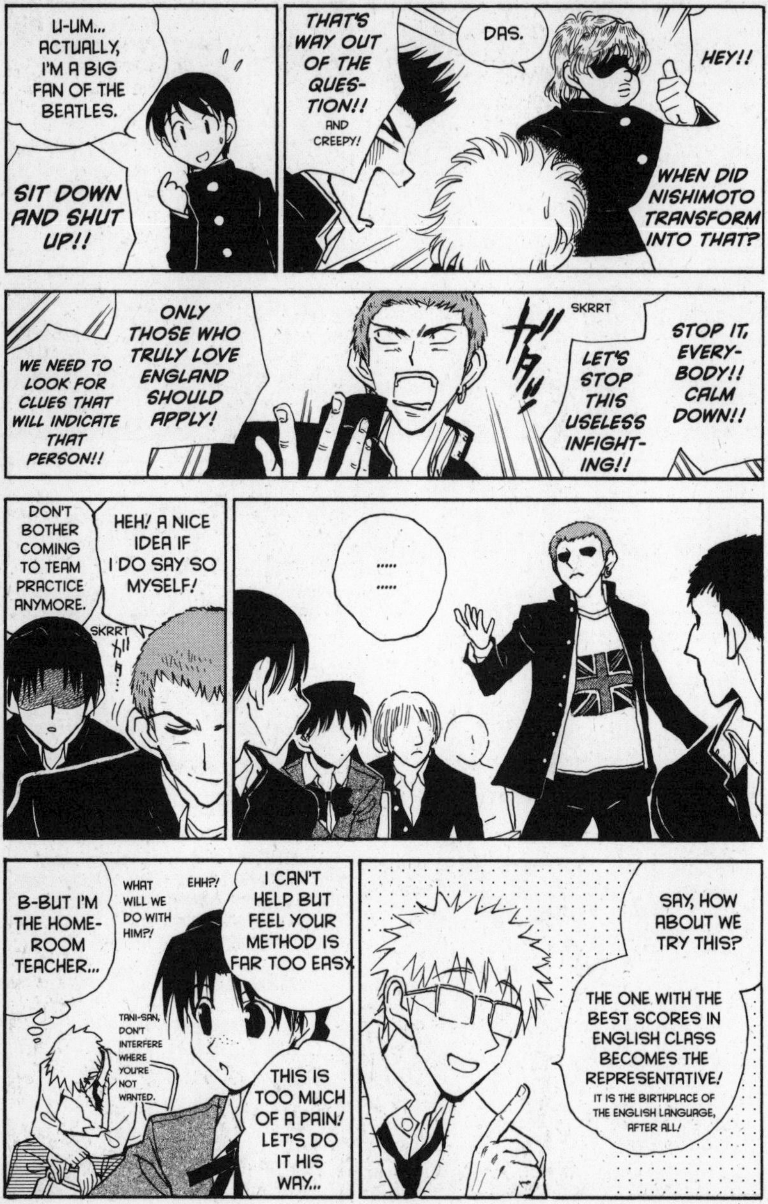
HEY!!
DAS.
THAT'S WAY OUT OF THE QUES-TION!!
AND CREEPY!
WHEN DID NISHIMOTO TRANSFORM INTO THAT?
U-UM... ACTUALLY, I'M A BIG FAN OF THE BEATLES.
SIT DOWN AND SHUT UP!!
STOP IT, EVERY-BODY!! CALM DOWN!!
SKRRT
LET'S STOP THIS USELESS INFIGHT-ING!!
ONLY THOSE WHO TRULY LOVE ENGLAND SHOULD APPLY!
WE NEED TO LOOK FOR CLUES THAT WILL INDICATE THAT PERSON!!
......
......
HEH! A NICE IDEA IF I DO SAY SO MYSELF!
DON'T BOTHER COMING TO TEAM PRACTICE ANYMORE.
SKRRT
SAY, HOW ABOUT WE TRY THIS?
THE ONE WITH THE BEST SCORES IN ENGLISH CLASS BECOMES THE REPRESENTATIVE!
IT IS THE BIRTHPLACE OF THE ENGLISH LANGUAGE, AFTER ALL!
I CAN'T HELP BUT FEEL YOUR METHOD IS FAR TOO EASY
EHH?!
WHAT WILL WE DO WITH HIM?!
THIS IS TOO MUCH OF A PAIN! LET'S DO IT HIS WAY...
TANI-SAN, DON'T INTERFERE WHERE YOU'RE NOT WANTED.
B-BUT I'M THE HOME-ROOM TEACHER...

To Repeat: Harima's Beard Makes Its Return.

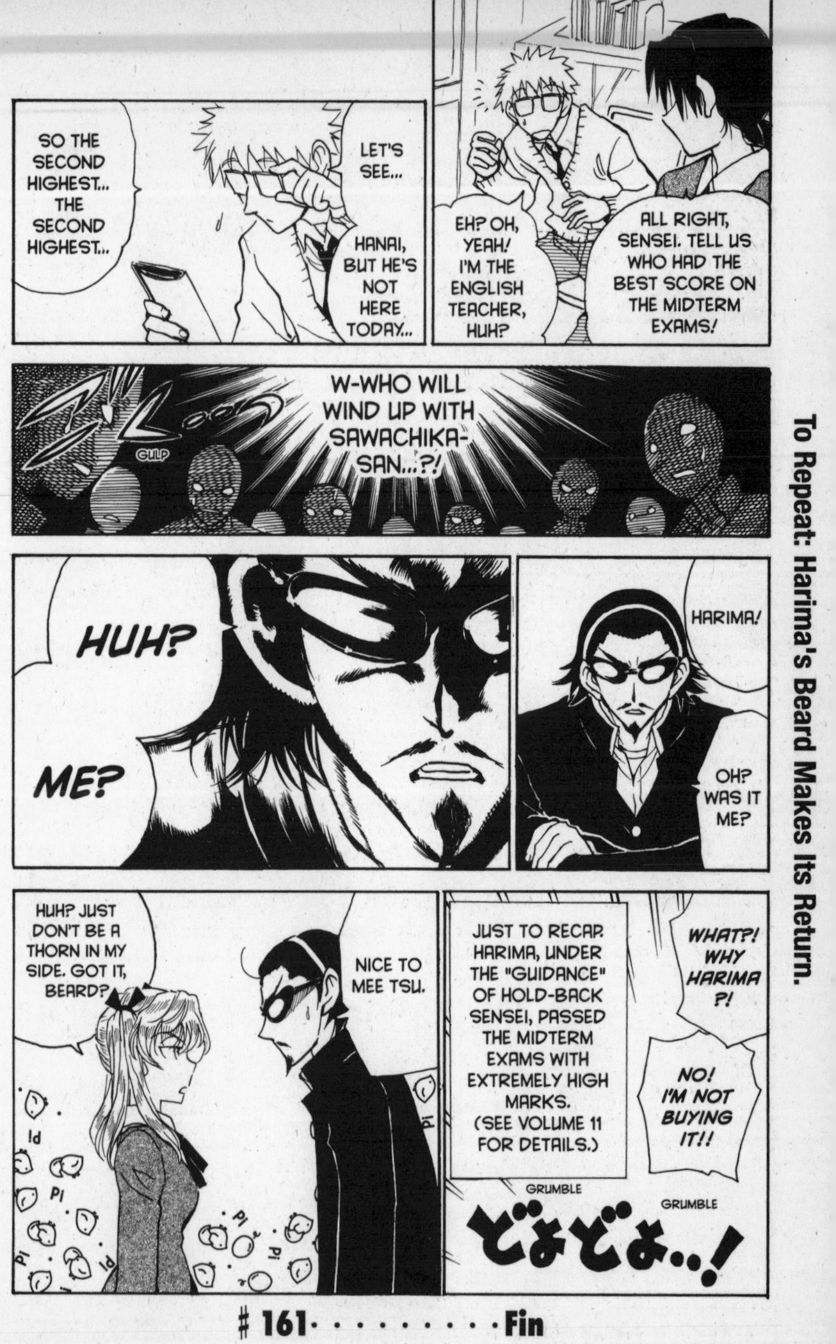
ALL RIGHT, SENSEI. TELL US WHO HAD THE BEST SCORE ON THE MIDTERM EXAMS!
EH? OH, YEAH! I'M THE ENGLISH TEACHER, HUH?
LET'S SEE...
HANAI, BUT HE'S NOT HERE TODAY...
SO THE SECOND HIGHEST... THE SECOND HIGHEST...
W-WHO WILL WIND UP WITH SAWACHIKA-SAN...?!
GULP
HARIMA!
OH? WAS IT ME?
HUH?
ME?
WHAT?! WHY HARIMA?!
NO! I'M NOT BUYING IT!!
JUST TO RECAP. HARIMA, UNDER THE "GUIDANCE" OF HOLD-BACK SENSEI, PASSED THE MIDTERM EXAMS WITH EXTREMELY HIGH MARKS. (SEE VOLUME 11 FOR DETAILS.)
GRUMBLE
GRUMBLE
どよどよ…!
NICE TO MEE TSU.
HUH? JUST DON'T BE A THORN IN MY SIDE. GOT IT, BEARD?
Pi
Pi
Pi
Pi

161· · · · · · · · ·Fin

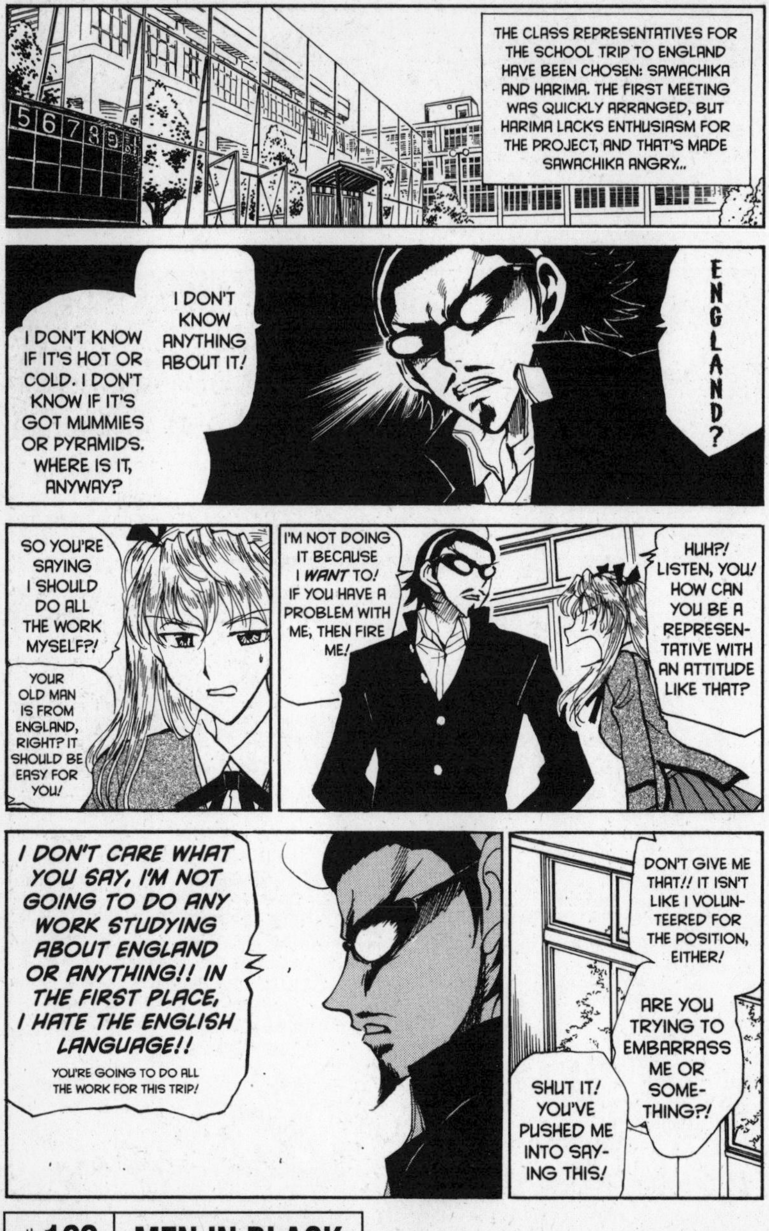
THE CLASS REPRESENTATIVES FOR THE SCHOOL TRIP TO ENGLAND HAVE BEEN CHOSEN: SAWACHIKA AND HARIMA. THE FIRST MEETING WAS QUICKLY ARRANGED, BUT HARIMA LACKS ENTHUSIASM FOR THE PROJECT, AND THAT'S MADE SAWACHIKA ANGRY...
ENGLAND?
I DON'T KNOW ANYTHING ABOUT IT!
I DON'T KNOW IF IT'S HOT OR COLD. I DON'T KNOW IF IT'S GOT MUMMIES OR PYRAMIDS. WHERE IS IT, ANYWAY?
HUH?! LISTEN, YOU! HOW CAN YOU BE A REPRESENTATIVE WITH AN ATTITUDE LIKE THAT?
I'M NOT DOING IT BECAUSE I *WANT* TO! IF YOU HAVE A PROBLEM WITH ME, THEN FIRE ME!
SO YOU'RE SAYING I SHOULD DO ALL THE WORK MYSELF?!
YOUR OLD MAN IS FROM ENGLAND, RIGHT? IT SHOULD BE EASY FOR YOU!
DON'T GIVE ME THAT!! IT ISN'T LIKE I VOLUNTEERED FOR THE POSITION, EITHER!
ARE YOU TRYING TO EMBARRASS ME OR SOMETHING?!
SHUT IT! YOU'VE PUSHED ME INTO SAYING THIS!
I DON'T CARE WHAT YOU SAY, I'M NOT GOING TO DO ANY WORK STUDYING ABOUT ENGLAND OR ANYTHING!! IN THE FIRST PLACE, I HATE THE ENGLISH LANGUAGE!!
YOU'RE GOING TO DO ALL THE WORK FOR THIS TRIP!

#162 MEN IN BLACK

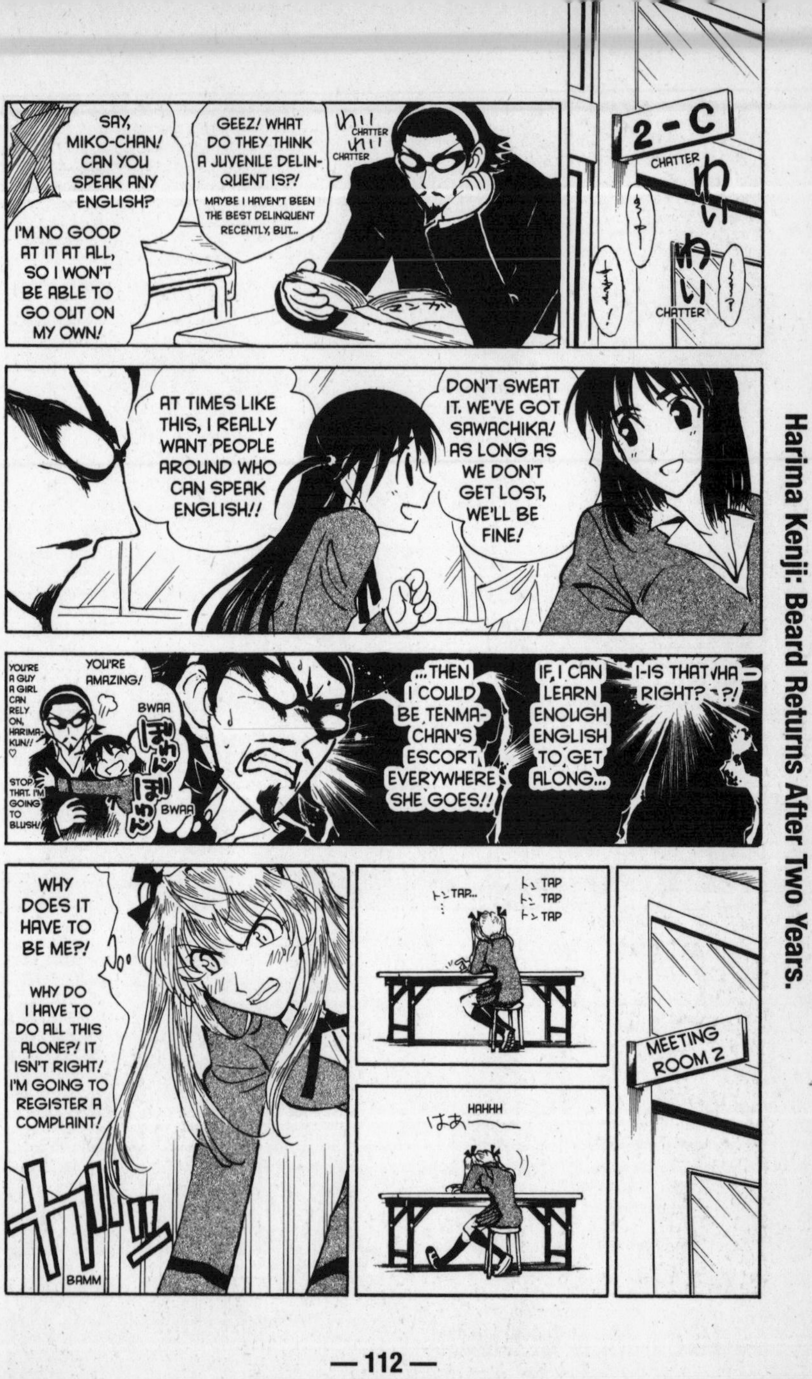
2-C
わいわい
CHATTER
わいわい
CHATTER
わい
CHATTER
わい
CHATTER
GEEZ! WHAT DO THEY THINK A JUVENILE DELINQUENT IS?!
MAYBE I HAVEN'T BEEN THE BEST DELINQUENT RECENTLY, BUT...
SAY, MIKO-CHAN! CAN YOU SPEAK ANY ENGLISH?
I'M NO GOOD AT IT AT ALL, SO I WON'T BE ABLE TO GO OUT ON MY OWN!
DON'T SWEAT IT. WE'VE GOT SAWACHIKA! AS LONG AS WE DON'T GET LOST, WE'LL BE FINE!
AT TIMES LIKE THIS, I REALLY WANT PEOPLE AROUND WHO CAN SPEAK ENGLISH!!
I-IS THAT RIGHT?
WHA--?!
IF I CAN LEARN ENOUGH ENGLISH TO GET ALONG...
...THEN I COULD BE TENMA-CHAN'S ESCORT EVERYWHERE SHE GOES!!
YOU'RE AMAZING!
BWAA
YOU'RE A GUY A GIRL CAN RELY ON, HARIMA-KUN!! ♡
STOP THAT. I'M GOING TO BLUSH!
BWAA
MEETING ROOM 2
トン TAP...
トン TAP
トン TAP
トン TAP
はあー
HAHHH
WHY DOES IT HAVE TO BE ME?!
WHY DO I HAVE TO DO ALL THIS ALONE?! IT ISN'T RIGHT! I'M GOING TO REGISTER A COMPLAINT!
BAMM

Harima Kenji: Beard Returns After Two Years.

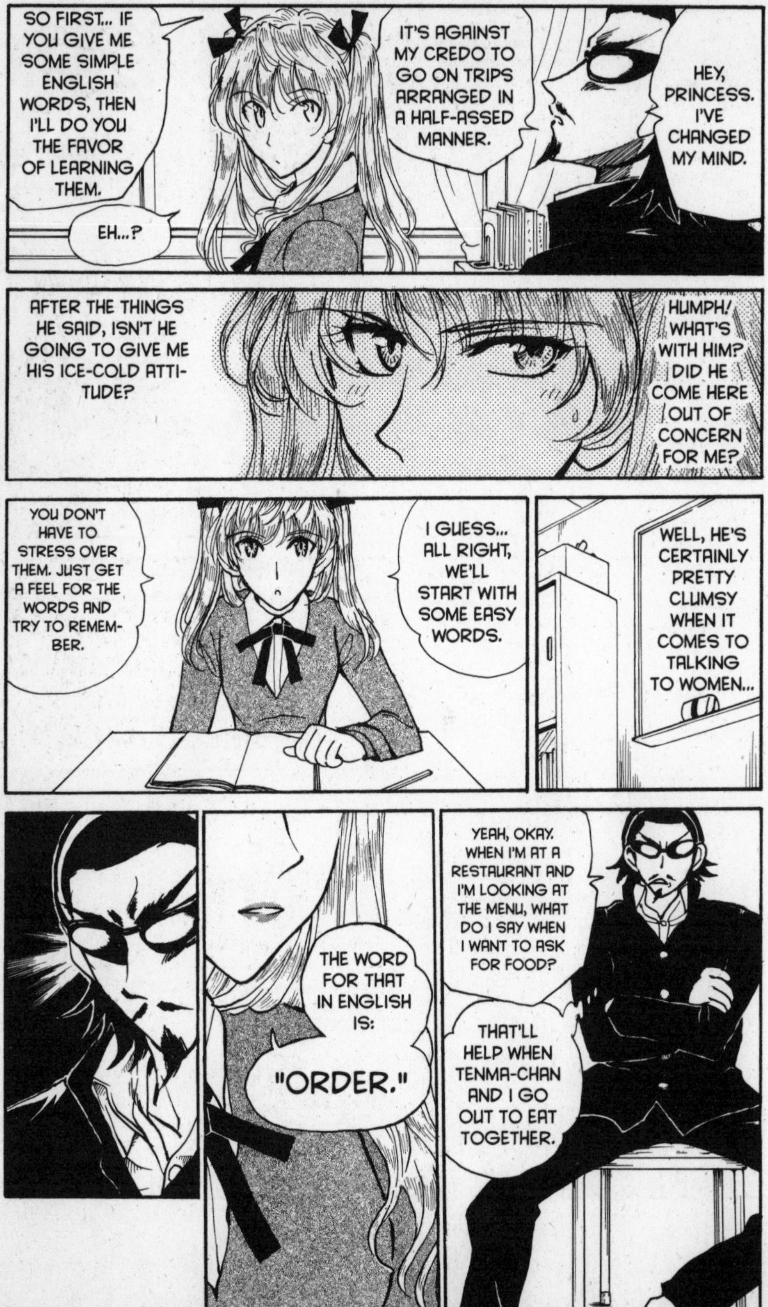
HEY, PRINCESS. I'VE CHANGED MY MIND.
IT'S AGAINST MY CREDO TO GO ON TRIPS ARRANGED IN A HALF-ASSED MANNER.
SO FIRST... IF YOU GIVE ME SOME SIMPLE ENGLISH WORDS, THEN I'LL DO YOU THE FAVOR OF LEARNING THEM.
EH...?
HUMPH! WHAT'S WITH HIM? DID HE COME HERE OUT OF CONCERN FOR ME?
AFTER THE THINGS HE SAID, ISN'T HE GOING TO GIVE ME HIS ICE-COLD ATTI-TUDE?
WELL, HE'S CERTAINLY PRETTY CLUMSY WHEN IT COMES TO TALKING TO WOMEN...
I GUESS... ALL RIGHT, WE'LL START WITH SOME EASY WORDS.
YOU DON'T HAVE TO STRESS OVER THEM. JUST GET A FEEL FOR THE WORDS AND TRY TO REMEM-BER.
YEAH, OKAY. WHEN I'M AT A RESTAURANT AND I'M LOOKING AT THE MENU, WHAT DO I SAY WHEN I WANT TO ASK FOR FOOD?
THAT'LL HELP WHEN TENMA-CHAN AND I GO OUT TO EAT TOGETHER.
THE WORD FOR THAT IN ENGLISH IS:
"ORDER."

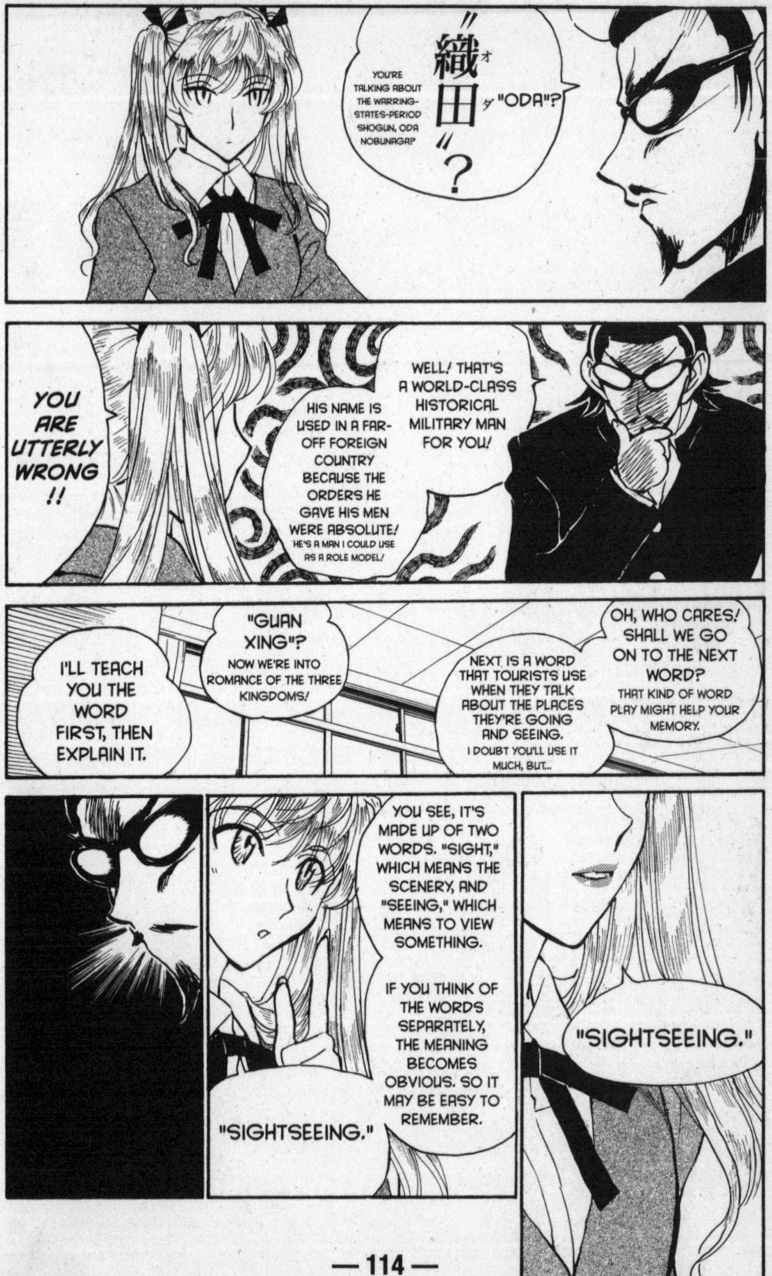
"織田(オダ)"? "ODA"?
YOU'RE TALKING ABOUT THE WARRING-STATES-PERIOD SHOGUN, ODA NOBUNAGA?
WELL! THAT'S A WORLD-CLASS HISTORICAL MILITARY MAN FOR YOU!
HIS NAME IS USED IN A FAR-OFF FOREIGN COUNTRY BECAUSE THE ORDERS HE GAVE HIS MEN WERE ABSOLUTE! HE'S A MAN I COULD USE AS A ROLE MODEL!
YOU ARE UTTERLY WRONG!!
OH, WHO CARES! SHALL WE GO ON TO THE NEXT WORD? THAT KIND OF WORD PLAY MIGHT HELP YOUR MEMORY.
NEXT, IS A WORD THAT TOURISTS USE WHEN THEY TALK ABOUT THE PLACES THEY'RE GOING AND SEEING. I DOUBT YOU'LL USE IT MUCH, BUT...
"GUAN XING"? NOW WE'RE INTO ROMANCE OF THE THREE KINGDOMS!
I'LL TEACH YOU THE WORD FIRST, THEN EXPLAIN IT.
"SIGHTSEEING."
YOU SEE, IT'S MADE UP OF TWO WORDS. "SIGHT," WHICH MEANS THE SCENERY, AND "SEEING," WHICH MEANS TO VIEW SOMETHING.
IF YOU THINK OF THE WORDS SEPARATELY, THE MEANING BECOMES OBVIOUS. SO IT MAY BE EASY TO REMEMBER.
"SIGHTSEEING."

Take That: Take-da.

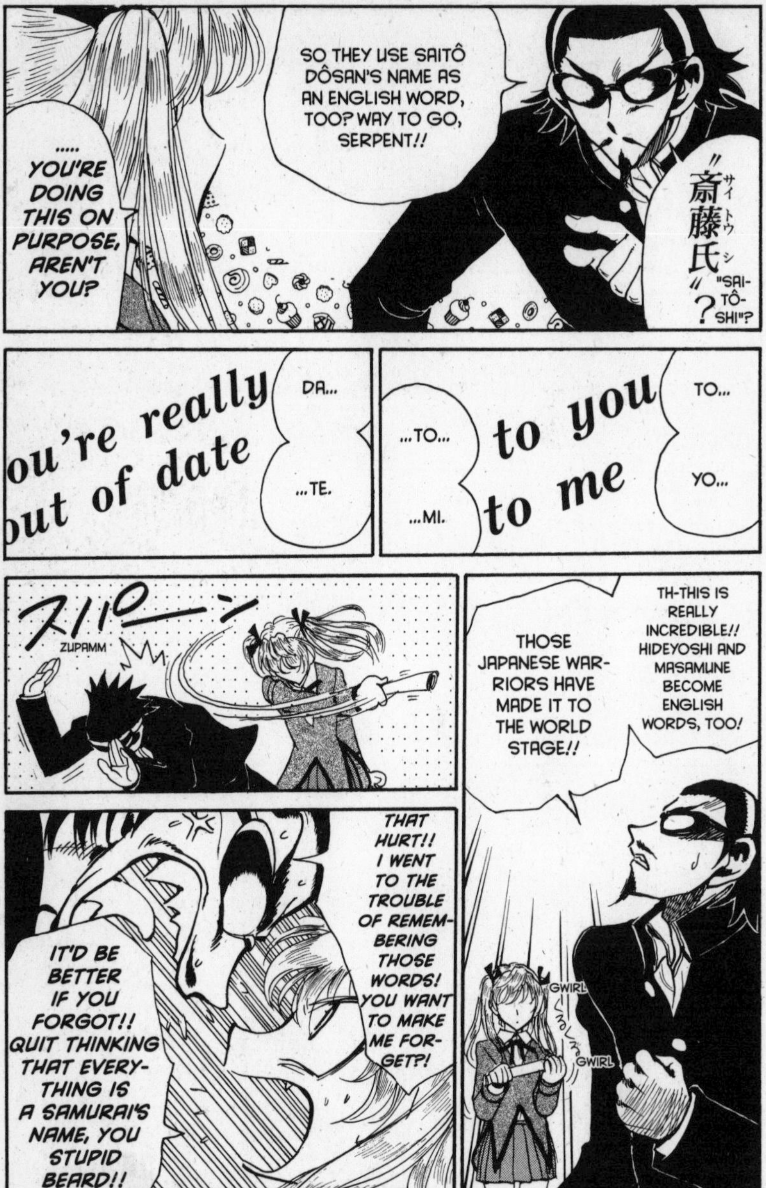
"斎藤氏(サイトウシ)"? "SAI-TÔ-SHI"?
SO THEY USE SAITÔ DÔSAN'S NAME AS AN ENGLISH WORD, TOO? WAY TO GO, SERPENT!!
..... YOU'RE DOING THIS ON PURPOSE, AREN'T YOU?
TO... YO...
to you to me
...TO... ...MI.
DA... ...TE.
ou're really out of date
TH-THIS IS REALLY INCREDIBLE!! HIDEYOSHI AND MASAMUNE BECOME ENGLISH WORDS, TOO!
THOSE JAPANESE WARRIORS HAVE MADE IT TO THE WORLD STAGE!!
GWIRL
GWIRL
ZUPAMM
THAT HURT!! I WENT TO THE TROUBLE OF REMEMBERING THOSE WORDS! YOU WANT TO MAKE ME FORGET?!
IT'D BE BETTER IF YOU FORGOT!! QUIT THINKING THAT EVERYTHING IS A SAMURAI'S NAME, YOU STUPID BEARD!!

Whiskey: Uesugi.

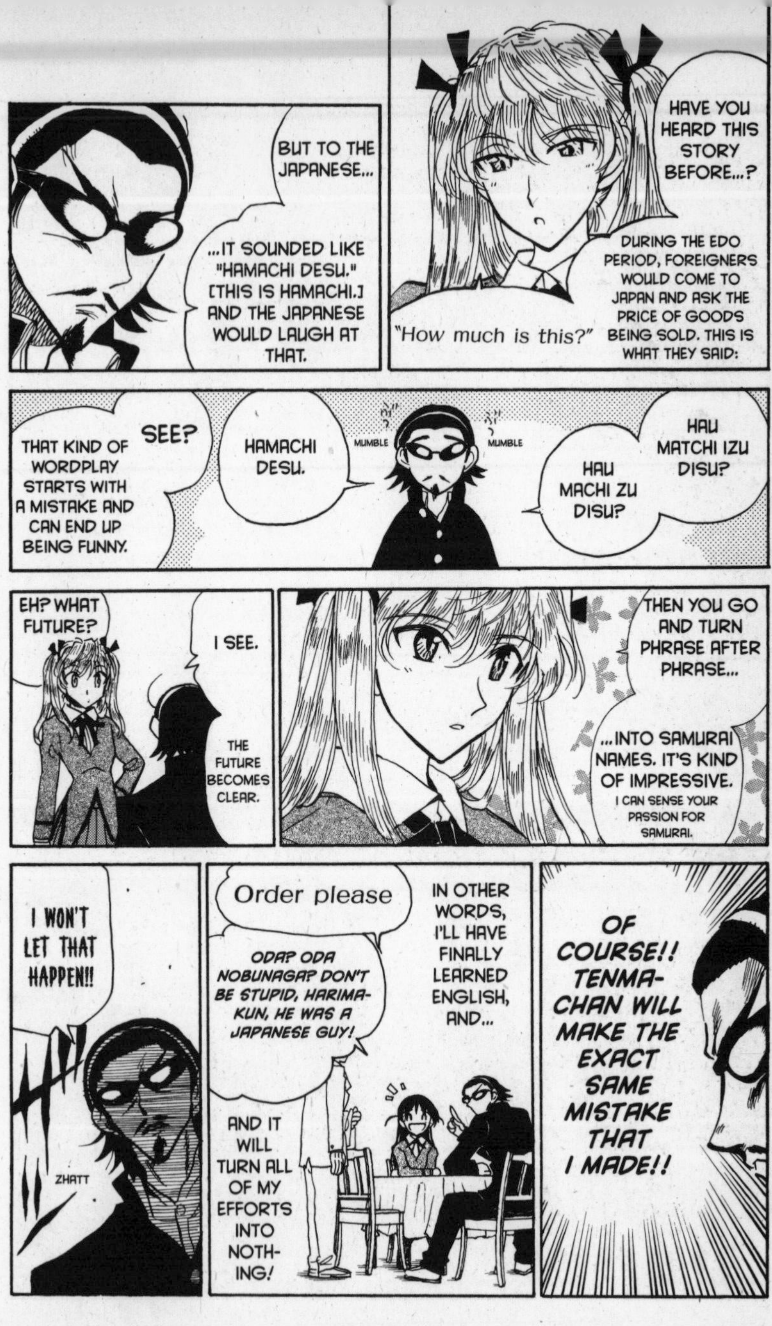
HAVE YOU HEARD THIS STORY BEFORE...?
DURING THE EDO PERIOD, FOREIGNERS WOULD COME TO JAPAN AND ASK THE PRICE OF GOODS BEING SOLD. THIS IS WHAT THEY SAID:
"How much is this?"
BUT TO THE JAPANESE...
...IT SOUNDED LIKE "HAMACHI DESU." [THIS IS HAMACHI.] AND THE JAPANESE WOULD LAUGH AT THAT.
HAU MATCHI IZU DISU?
HAU MACHI ZU DISU?
MUMBLE
MUMBLE
HAMACHI DESU.
SEE?
THAT KIND OF WORDPLAY STARTS WITH A MISTAKE AND CAN END UP BEING FUNNY.
THEN YOU GO AND TURN PHRASE AFTER PHRASE...
...INTO SAMURAI NAMES. IT'S KIND OF IMPRESSIVE.
I CAN SENSE YOUR PASSION FOR SAMURAI.
I SEE.
THE FUTURE BECOMES CLEAR.
EH? WHAT FUTURE?
OF COURSE!! TENMA-CHAN WILL MAKE THE EXACT SAME MISTAKE THAT I MADE!!
IN OTHER WORDS, I'LL HAVE FINALLY LEARNED ENGLISH, AND...
Order please
ODA? ODA NOBUNAGA? DON'T BE STUPID, HARIMA-KUN, HE WAS A JAPANESE GUY!
AND IT WILL TURN ALL OF MY EFFORTS INTO NOTH-ING!
I WON'T LET THAT HAPPEN!!
ZHATT

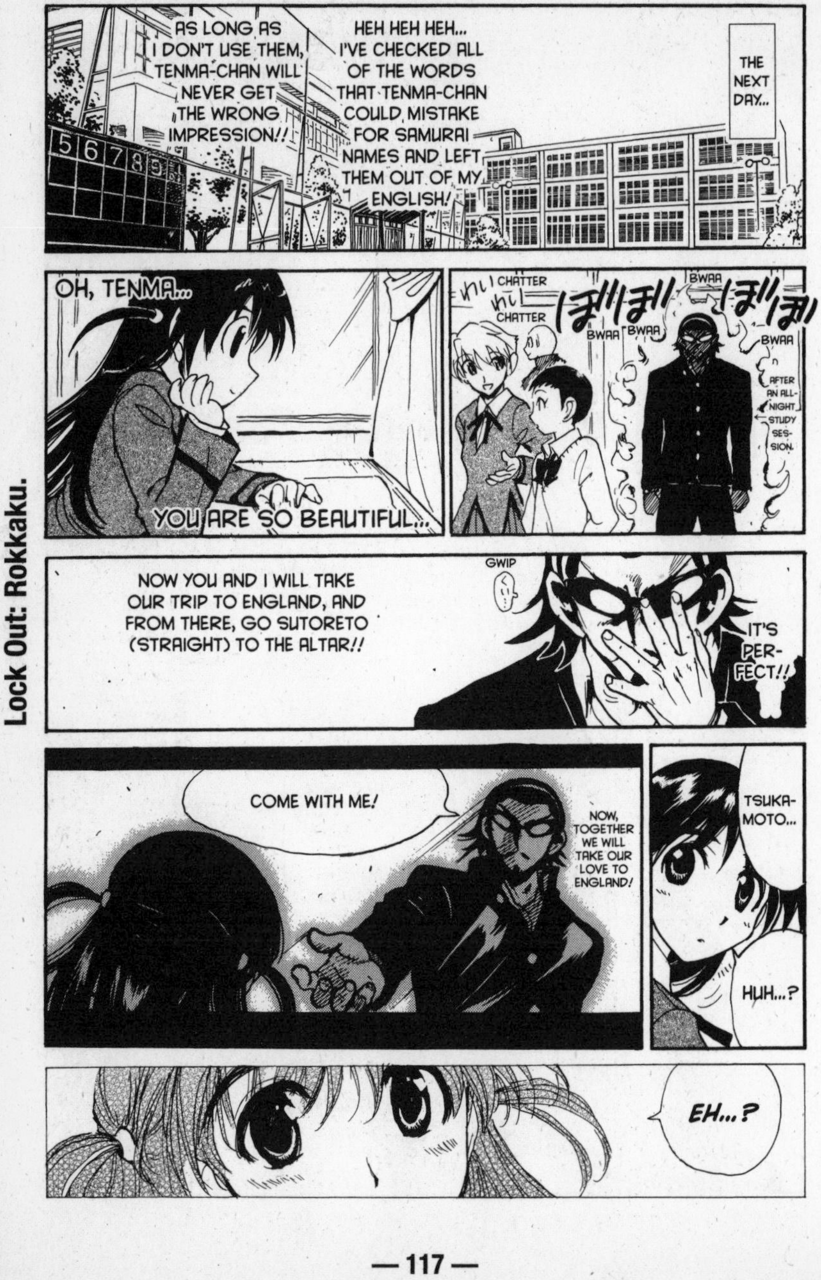
THE NEXT DAY...
HEH HEH HEH... I'VE CHECKED ALL OF THE WORDS THAT TENMA-CHAN COULD MISTAKE FOR SAMURAI NAMES AND LEFT THEM OUT OF MY ENGLISH!
AS LONG AS I DON'T USE THEM, TENMA-CHAN WILL NEVER GET THE WRONG IMPRESSION!!
CHATTER
CHATTER
BWAA
BWAA
BWAA
BWAA
AFTER AN ALL-NIGHT STUDY SESSION.
OH, TENMA...
YOU ARE SO BEAUTIFUL...
GWIP
IT'S PERFECT!!
NOW YOU AND I WILL TAKE OUR TRIP TO ENGLAND, AND FROM THERE, GO SUTORETO (STRAIGHT) TO THE ALTAR!!
TSUKA-MOTO...
HUH...?
NOW, TOGETHER WE WILL TAKE OUR LOVE TO ENGLAND!
COME WITH ME!
EH...?

Lock Out: Rokkaku.

Love You: Yagiyû...Sorry.

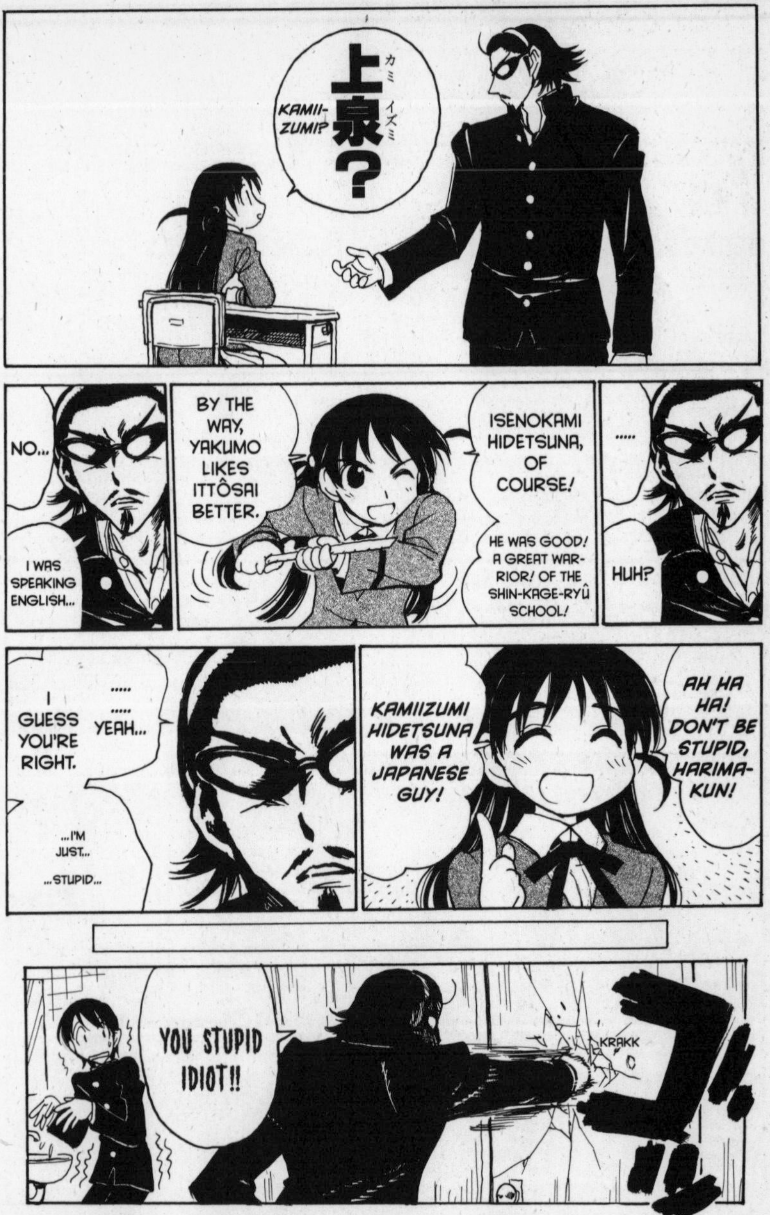
上泉?
カミ イズミ
KAMII-ZUMI?
.....
HUH?
ISENOKAMI HIDETSUNA, OF COURSE!
HE WAS GOOD! A GREAT WAR-RIOR! OF THE SHIN-KAGE-RYÛ SCHOOL!
BY THE WAY, YAKUMO LIKES ITTÔSAI BETTER.
NO...
I WAS SPEAKING ENGLISH...
AH HA HA! DON'T BE STUPID, HARIMA-KUN!
KAMIIZUMI HIDETSUNA WAS A JAPANESE GUY!
.... YEAH...
I GUESS YOU'RE RIGHT.
...I'M JUST...
...STUPID...
YOU STUPID IDIOT!!
KRAKK

162· · · · · · · · ·Fin

#163 SUMMER LOVERS

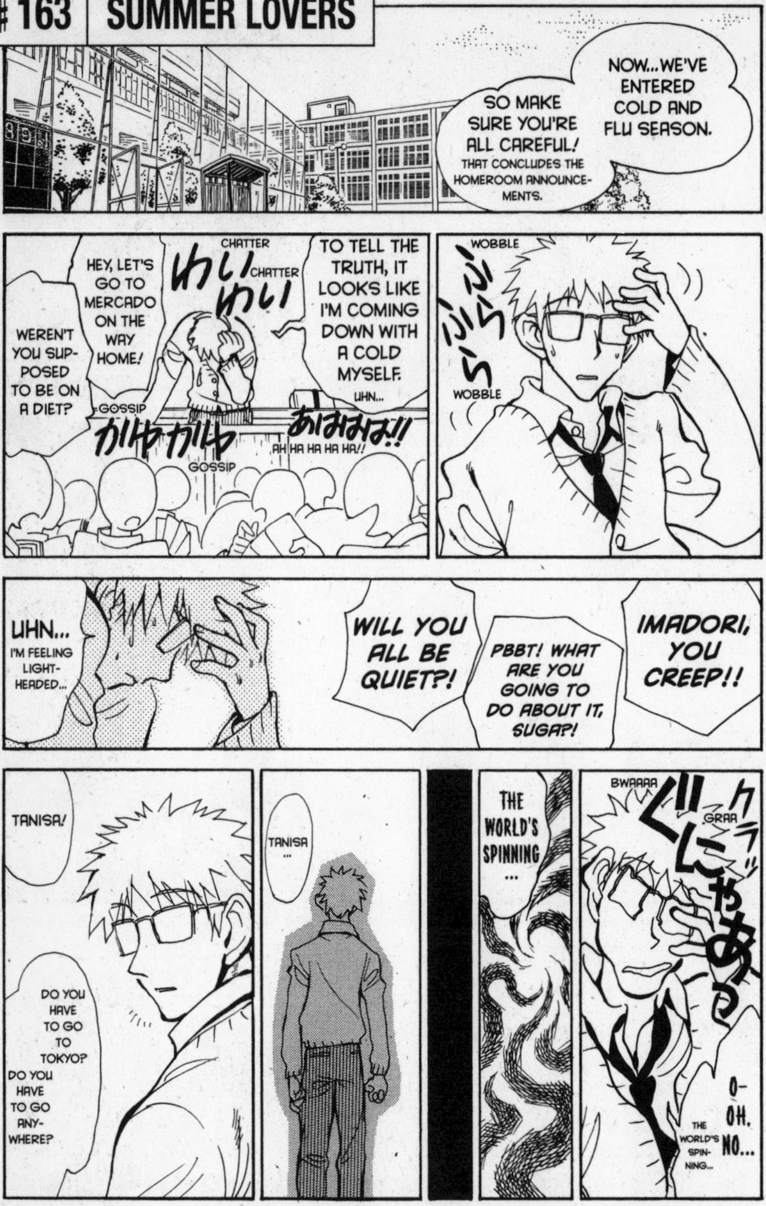
NOW...WE'VE ENTERED COLD AND FLU SEASON.
SO MAKE SURE YOU'RE ALL CAREFUL!
THAT CONCLUDES THE HOMEROOM ANNOUNCEMENTS.
WOBBLE
ふらふら
WOBBLE
TO TELL THE TRUTH, IT LOOKS LIKE I'M COMING DOWN WITH A COLD MYSELF.
UHN...
CHATTER
わいわい
CHATTER
HEY, LET'S GO TO MERCADO ON THE WAY HOME!
WEREN'T YOU SUPPOSED TO BE ON A DIET?
あはははは!!
AH HA HA HA HA!!
GOSSIP
がやがや
GOSSIP
IMADORI, YOU CREEP!!
PBBT! WHAT ARE YOU GOING TO DO ABOUT IT, SUGA?!
WILL YOU ALL BE QUIET?!
UHN...
I'M FEELING LIGHT-HEADED...
BWAAAA
ぐにゃあ
GRAA
クラッ
O-OH. NO...
THE WORLD'S SPINNING...
THE WORLD'S SPINNING...
TANISA...
TANISA!
DO YOU HAVE TO GO TO TOKYO?
DO YOU HAVE TO GO ANYWHERE?

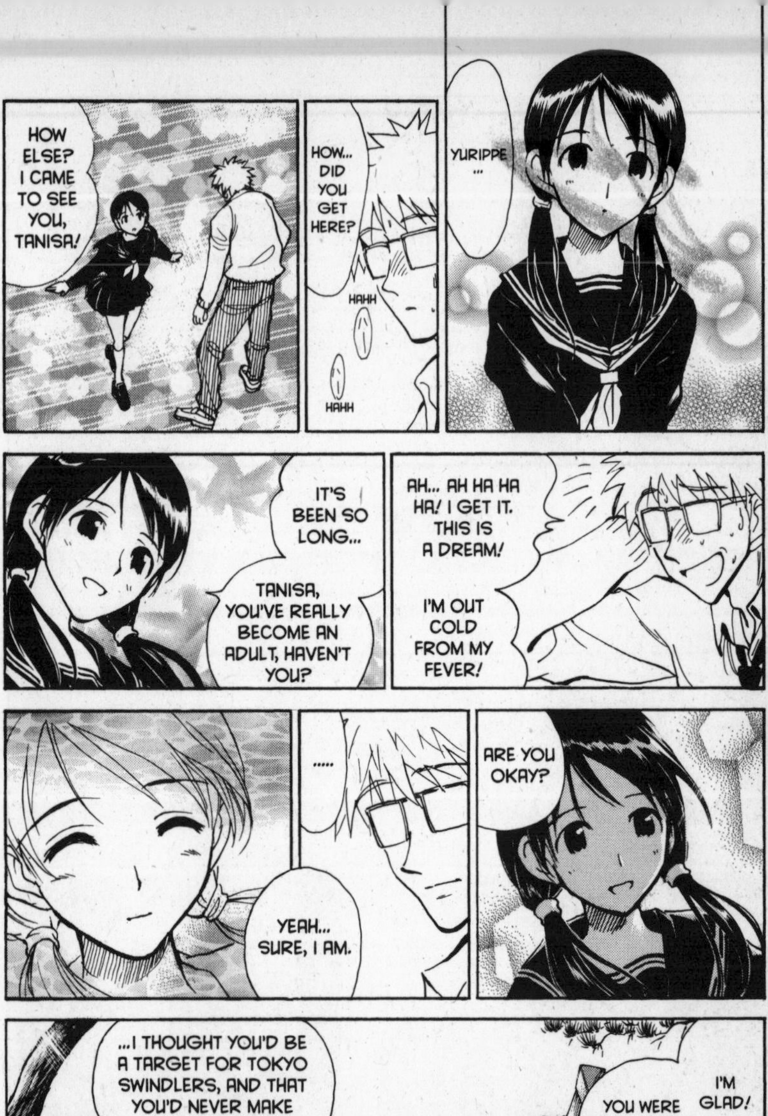
YURIPPE ...
HOW... DID YOU GET HERE?
HAHH
HAHH
HOW ELSE? I CAME TO SEE YOU, TANISA!
AH... AH HA HA HA! I GET IT. THIS IS A DREAM!
I'M OUT COLD FROM MY FEVER!
IT'S BEEN SO LONG...
TANISA, YOU'VE REALLY BECOME AN ADULT, HAVEN'T YOU?
ARE YOU OKAY?
......
YEAH... SURE, I AM.
I'M GLAD!
YOU WERE ALWAYS TIMID AND ASSUMED THE BEST OF PEOPLE...
...I THOUGHT YOU'D BE A TARGET FOR TOKYO SWINDLERS, AND THAT YOU'D NEVER MAKE FRIENDS!
HA HA... THAT ISN'T TRUE! YOU WERE ALWAYS SUCH A WORRIER, YURIPPE!

Tani Hayato: English Teacher. From Aomori.

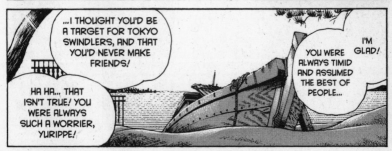

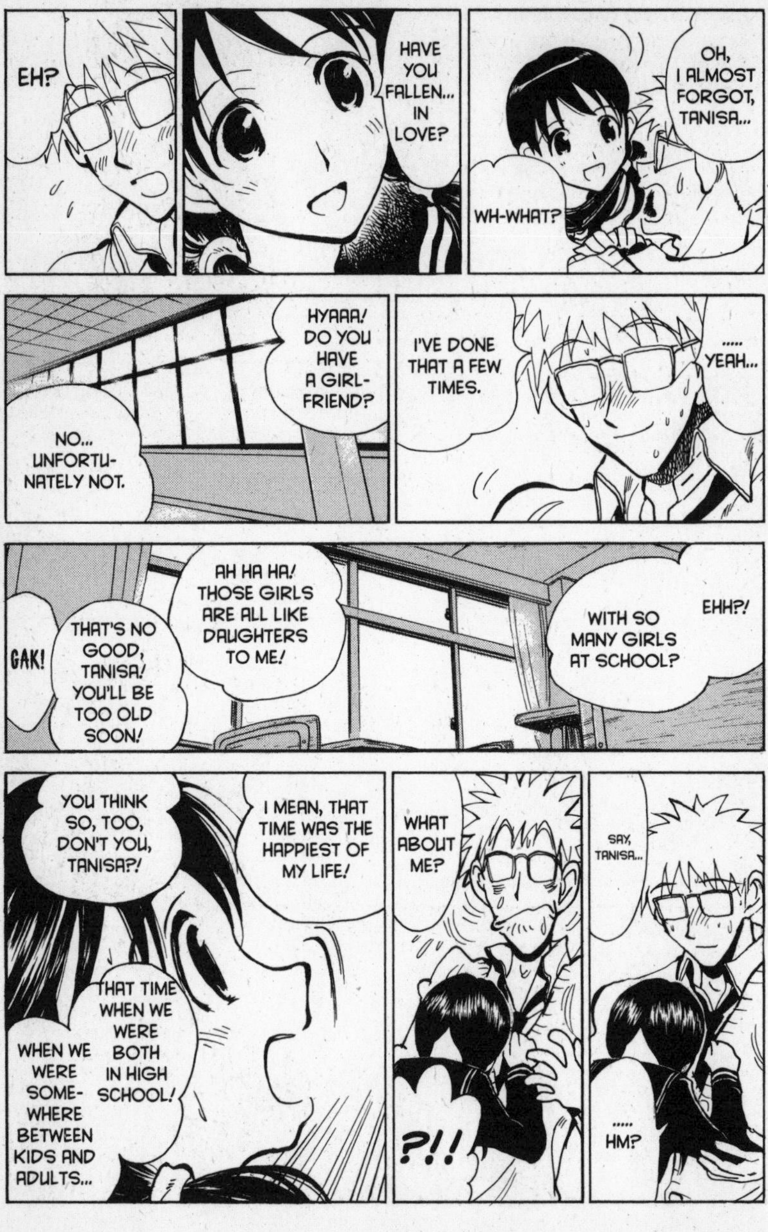
OH, I ALMOST FORGOT, TANISA...
WH-WHAT?
HAVE YOU FALLEN... IN LOVE?
EH?
.....YEAH...
I'VE DONE THAT A FEW TIMES.
HYAAA! DO YOU HAVE A GIRL-FRIEND?
NO... UNFORTU-NATELY NOT.
EHH?!
WITH SO MANY GIRLS AT SCHOOL?
AH HA HA! THOSE GIRLS ARE ALL LIKE DAUGHTERS TO ME!
THAT'S NO GOOD, TANISA! YOU'LL BE TOO OLD SOON!
GAK!
SAY, TANISA...
.....HM?
WHAT ABOUT ME?
?!!
I MEAN, THAT TIME WAS THE HAPPIEST OF MY LIFE!
YOU THINK SO, TOO, DON'T YOU, TANISA?!
THAT TIME WHEN WE WERE BOTH IN HIGH SCHOOL!
WHEN WE WERE SOME-WHERE BETWEEN KIDS AND ADULTS...

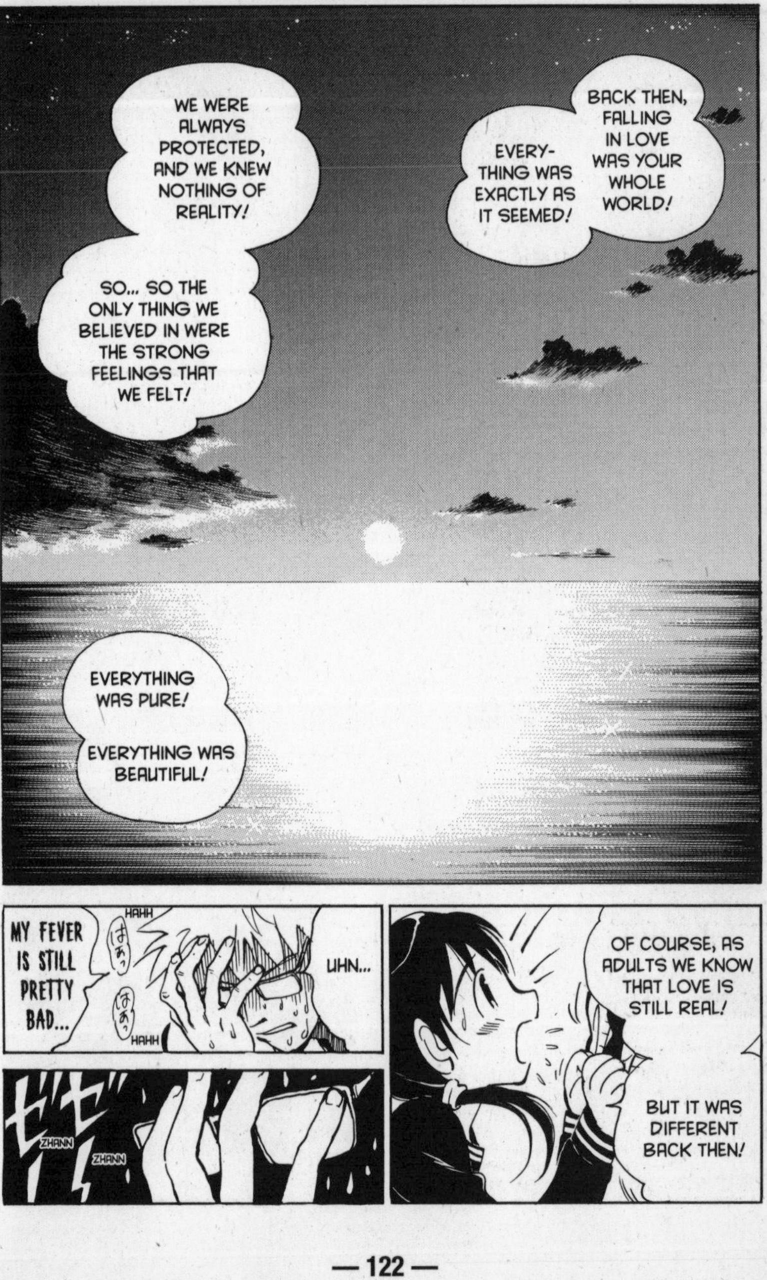
BACK THEN, FALLING IN LOVE WAS YOUR WHOLE WORLD!
EVERY-THING WAS EXACTLY AS IT SEEMED!
WE WERE ALWAYS PROTECTED, AND WE KNEW NOTHING OF REALITY!
SO... SO THE ONLY THING WE BELIEVED IN WERE THE STRONG FEELINGS THAT WE FELT!
EVERYTHING WAS PURE!
EVERYTHING WAS BEAUTIFUL!
OF COURSE, AS ADULTS WE KNOW THAT LOVE IS STILL REAL!
BUT IT WAS DIFFERENT BACK THEN!
UHN...
はあっ
HAHH
はあっ
HAHH
MY FEVER IS STILL PRETTY BAD...
ZHANN
ZHANN

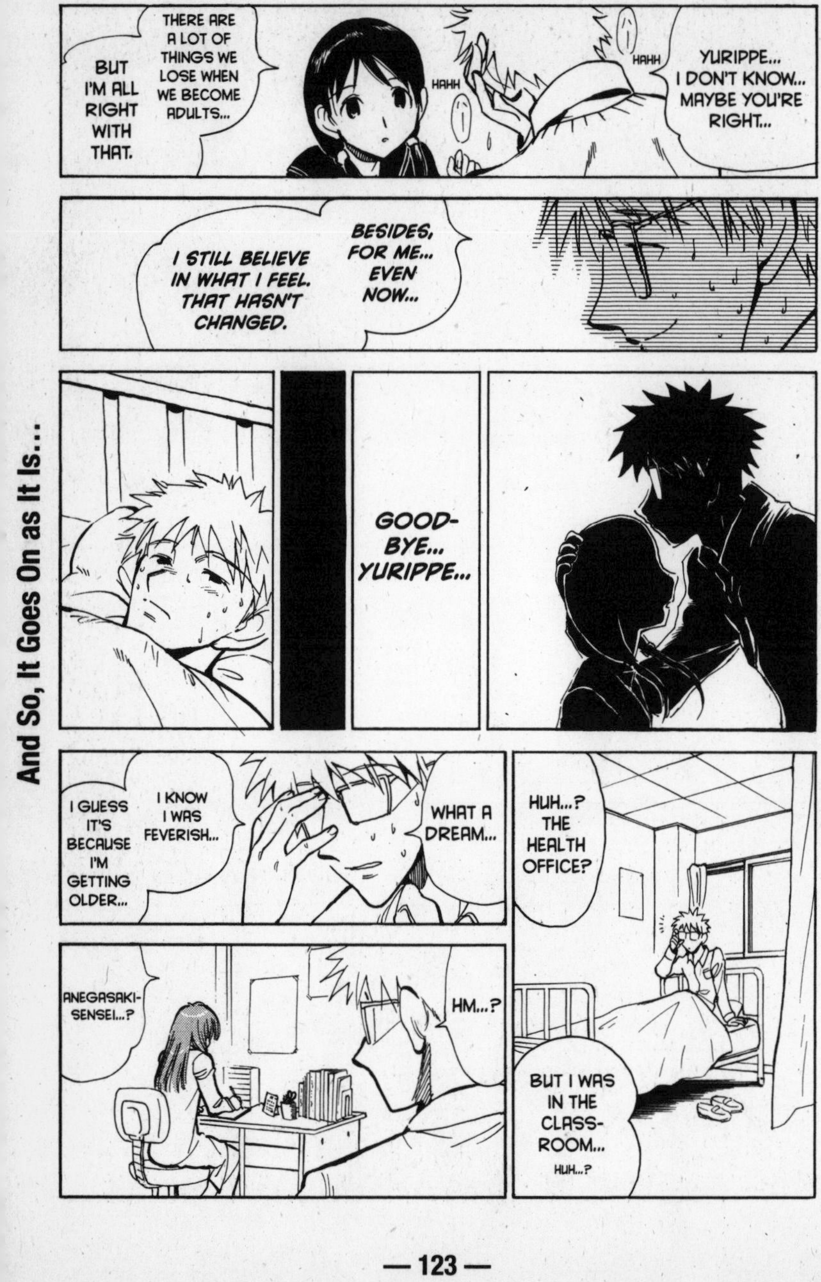
YURIPPE... I DON'T KNOW... MAYBE YOU'RE RIGHT...
HAHH
HAHH
THERE ARE A LOT OF THINGS WE LOSE WHEN WE BECOME ADULTS...
BUT I'M ALL RIGHT WITH THAT.
BESIDES, FOR ME... EVEN NOW...
I STILL BELIEVE IN WHAT I FEEL. THAT HASN'T CHANGED.
GOOD-BYE... YURIPPE...
HUH...? THE HEALTH OFFICE?
BUT I WAS IN THE CLASS-ROOM...
HUH...?
WHAT A DREAM...
I KNOW I WAS FEVERISH...
I GUESS IT'S BECAUSE I'M GETTING OLDER...
HM...?
ANEGASAKI-SENSEI...?

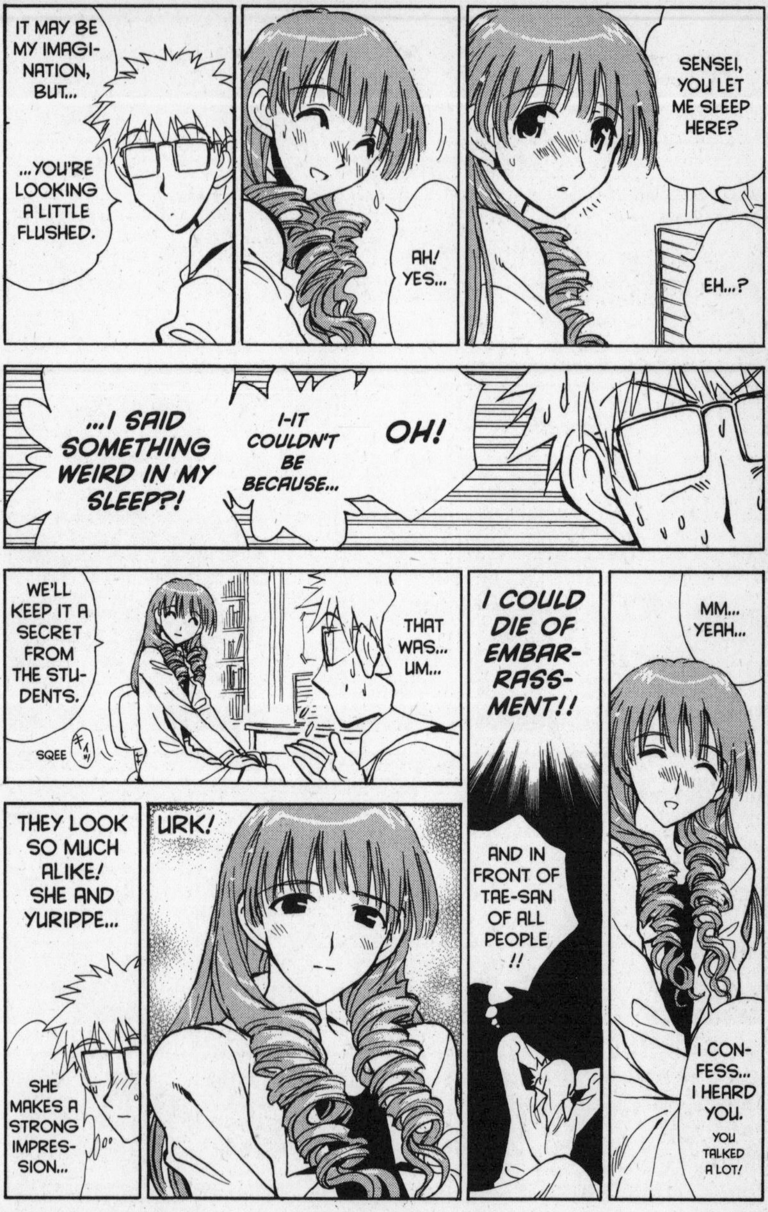
SENSEI, YOU LET ME SLEEP HERE?
EH...?
AH! YES...
IT MAY BE MY IMAGINATION, BUT...
...YOU'RE LOOKING A LITTLE FLUSHED.
OH!
I-IT COULDN'T BE BECAUSE...
...I SAID SOMETHING WEIRD IN MY SLEEP?!
MM... YEAH...
I CONFESS... I HEARD YOU.
YOU TALKED A LOT!
I COULD DIE OF EMBARRASSMENT!!
AND IN FRONT OF TAE-SAN OF ALL PEOPLE!!
THAT WAS... UM...
WE'LL KEEP IT A SECRET FROM THE STUDENTS.
SQEE
URK!
THEY LOOK SO MUCH ALIKE! SHE AND YURIPPE...
SHE MAKES A STRONG IMPRESSION...

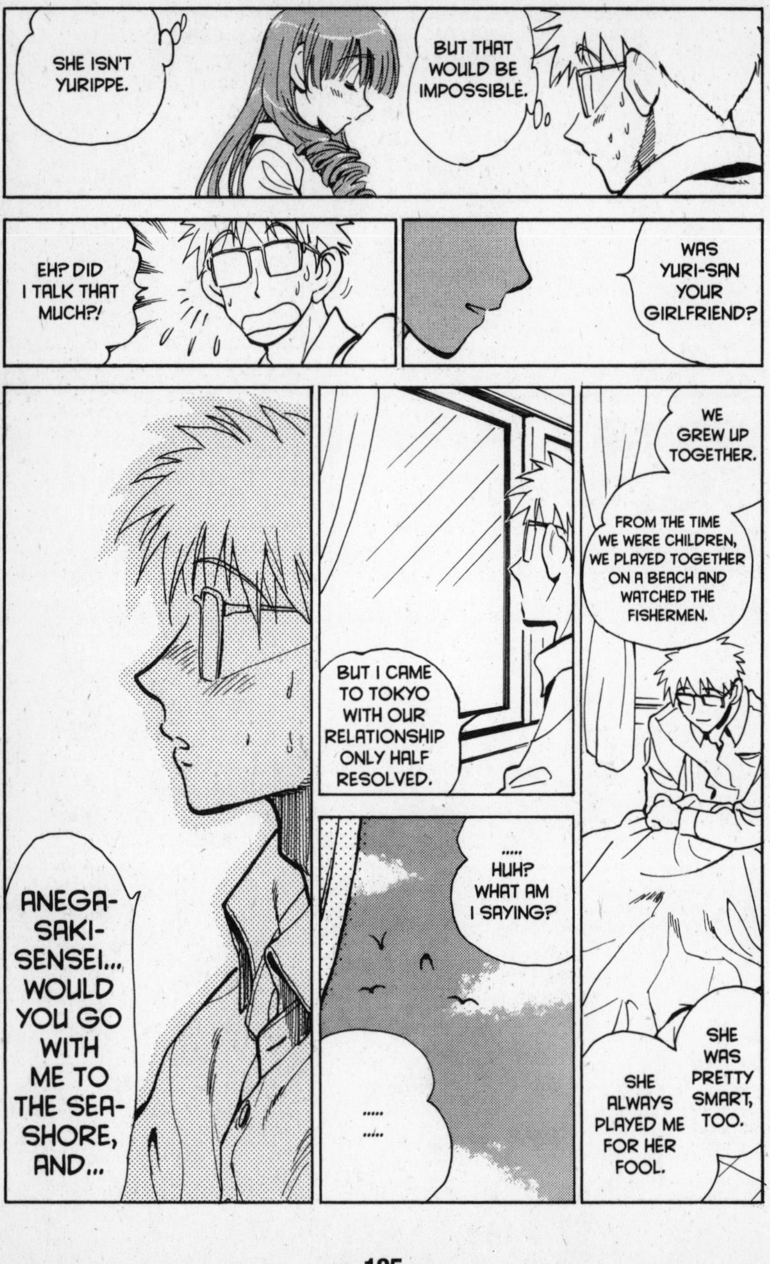
BUT THAT WOULD BE IMPOSSIBLE.
SHE ISN'T YURIPPE.
WAS YURI-SAN YOUR GIRLFRIEND?
EH? DID I TALK THAT MUCH?!
WE GREW UP TOGETHER.
FROM THE TIME WE WERE CHILDREN, WE PLAYED TOGETHER ON A BEACH AND WATCHED THE FISHERMEN.
SHE WAS PRETTY SMART, TOO.
SHE ALWAYS PLAYED ME FOR HER FOOL.
BUT I CAME TO TOKYO WITH OUR RELATIONSHIP ONLY HALF RESOLVED.
..... HUH? WHAT AM I SAYING?
....
ANEGA-SAKI-SENSEI... WOULD YOU GO WITH ME TO THE SEA-SHORE, AND...

Two People with a Little Ice Thrown on Their Fevers.

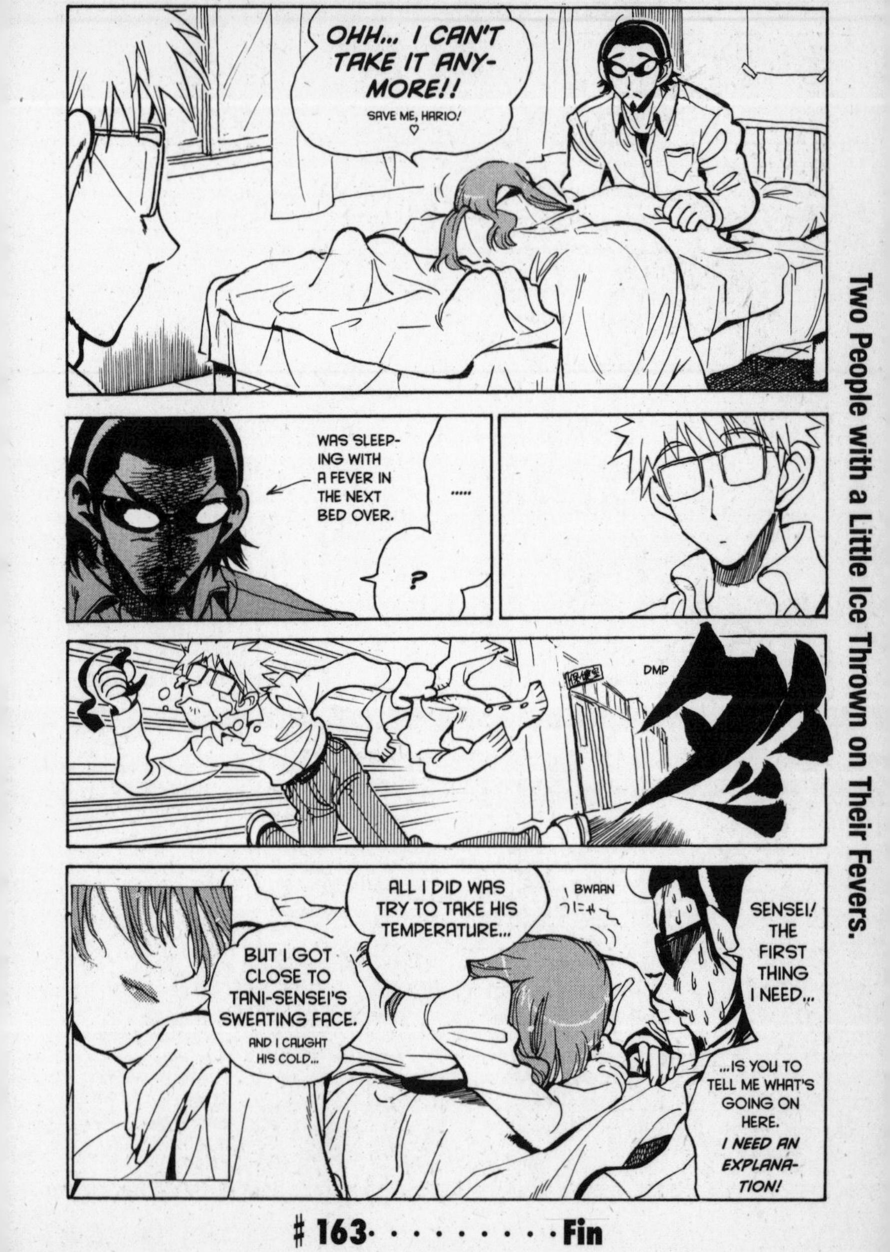
OHH... I CAN'T TAKE IT ANY-MORE!!
SAVE ME, HARIO! ♥
.....
WAS SLEEPING WITH A FEVER IN THE NEXT BED OVER.
?
DMP
SENSEI! THE FIRST THING I NEED...
BWAAN
ALL I DID WAS TRY TO TAKE HIS TEMPERATURE...
BUT I GOT CLOSE TO TANI-SENSEI'S SWEATING FACE.
AND I CAUGHT HIS COLD...
...IS YOU TO TELL ME WHAT'S GOING ON HERE.
I NEED AN EXPLANATION!

163· · · · · · · · ·Fin

#164 COCKTAIL

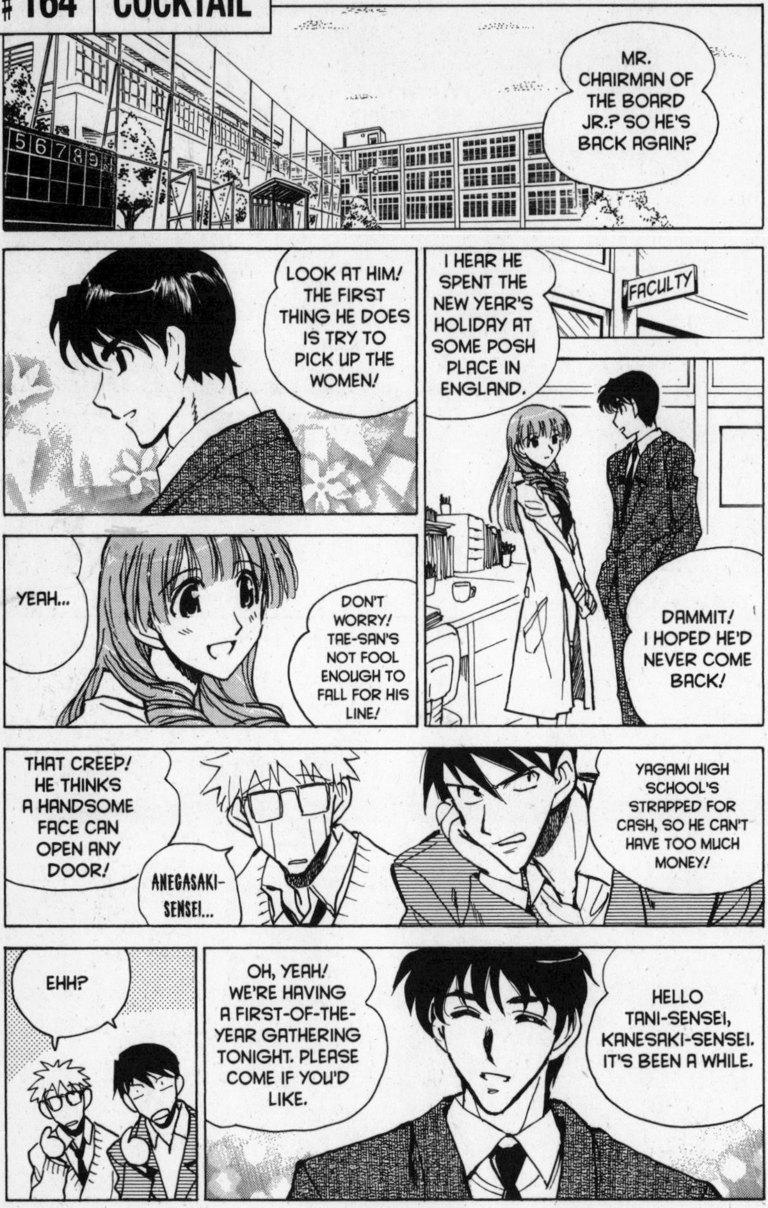

MR. CHAIRMAN OF THE BOARD JR.? SO HE'S BACK AGAIN?
FACULTY
I HEAR HE SPENT THE NEW YEAR'S HOLIDAY AT SOME POSH PLACE IN ENGLAND.
DAMMIT! I HOPED HE'D NEVER COME BACK!
LOOK AT HIM! THE FIRST THING HE DOES IS TRY TO PICK UP THE WOMEN!
DON'T WORRY! TAE-SAN'S NOT FOOL ENOUGH TO FALL FOR HIS LINE!
YEAH...
YAGAMI HIGH SCHOOL'S STRAPPED FOR CASH, SO HE CAN'T HAVE TOO MUCH MONEY!
THAT CREEP! HE THINKS A HANDSOME FACE CAN OPEN ANY DOOR!
ANEGASAKI-SENSEI...
HELLO TANI-SENSEI, KANESAKI-SENSEI. IT'S BEEN A WHILE.
OH, YEAH! WE'RE HAVING A FIRST-OF-THE-YEAR GATHERING TONIGHT. PLEASE COME IF YOU'D LIKE.
EHH?

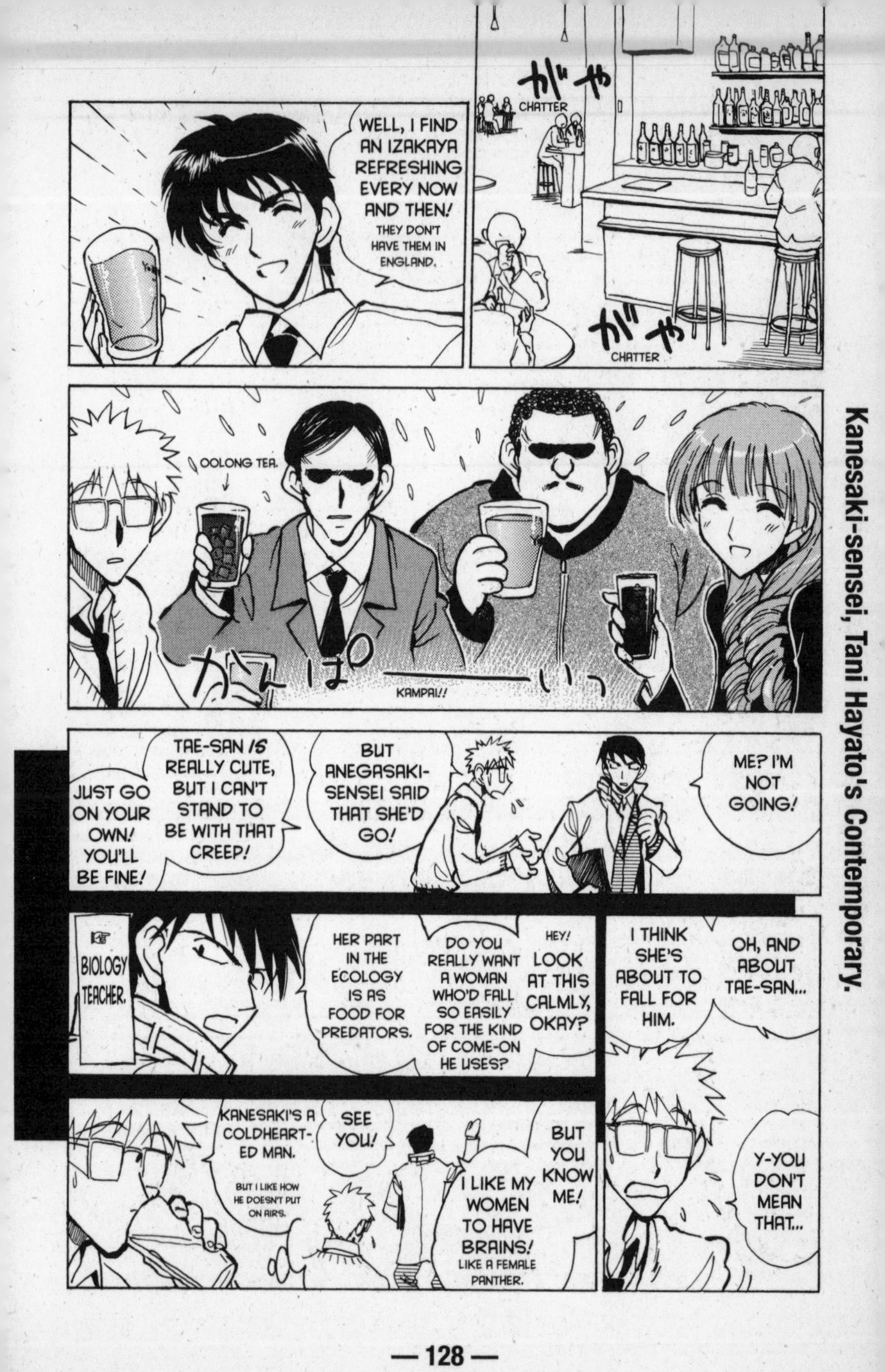

がや
CHATTER
がや
CHATTER
WELL, I FIND AN IZAKAYA REFRESHING EVERY NOW AND THEN!
THEY DON'T HAVE THEM IN ENGLAND.
OOLONG TEA.
かんぱーい
KAMPAI!!
ME? I'M NOT GOING!
BUT ANEGASAKI-SENSEI SAID THAT SHE'D GO!
TAE-SAN IS REALLY CUTE, BUT I CAN'T STAND TO BE WITH THAT CREEP!
JUST GO ON YOUR OWN! YOU'LL BE FINE!
OH, AND ABOUT TAE-SAN...
I THINK SHE'S ABOUT TO FALL FOR HIM.
HEY! LOOK AT THIS CALMLY, OKAY?
DO YOU REALLY WANT A WOMAN WHO'D FALL SO EASILY FOR THE KIND OF COME-ON HE USES?
HER PART IN THE ECOLOGY IS AS FOOD FOR PREDATORS.
BIOLOGY TEACHER.
Y-YOU DON'T MEAN THAT...
BUT YOU KNOW ME!
I LIKE MY WOMEN TO HAVE BRAINS!
LIKE A FEMALE PANTHER.
SEE YOU!
KANESAKI'S A COLDHEARTED MAN.
BUT I LIKE HOW HE DOESN'T PUT ON AIRS.

Kanesaki-sensei, Tani Hayato's Contemporary.

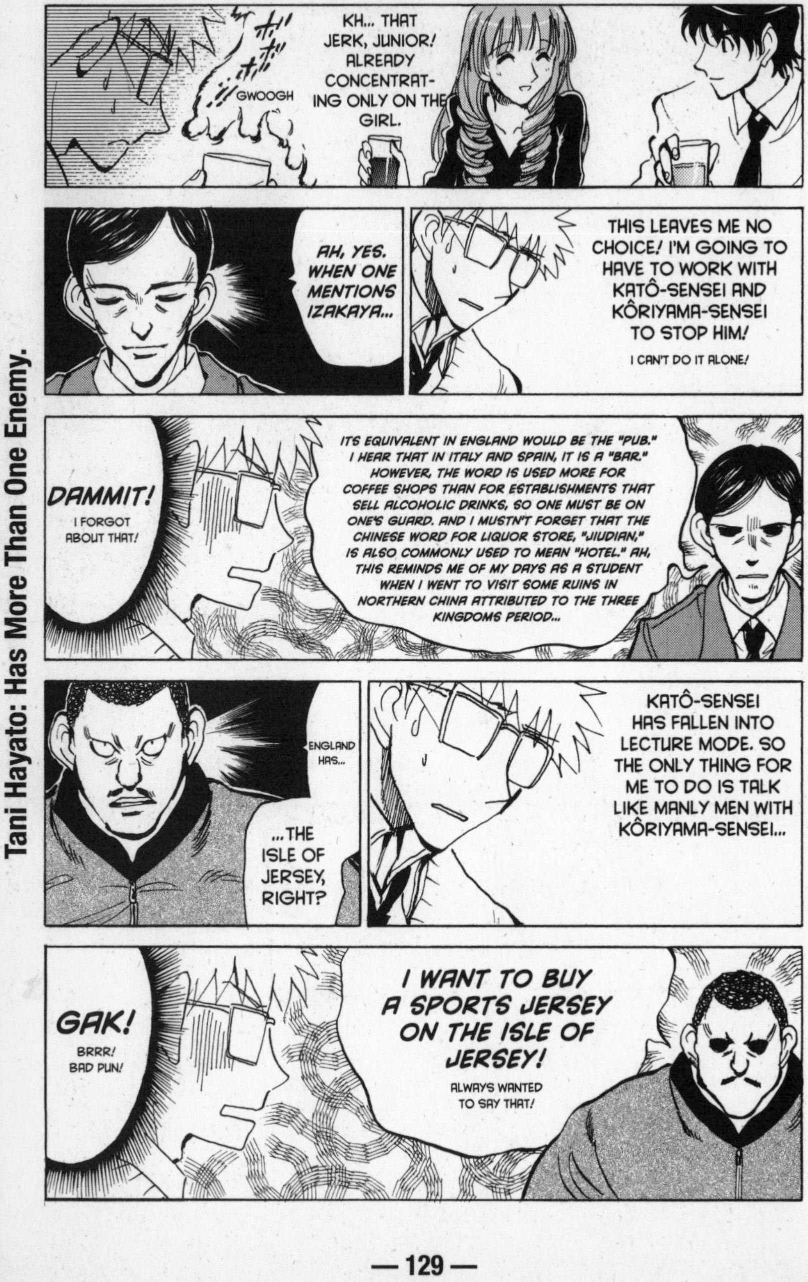
KH... THAT JERK, JUNIOR! ALREADY CONCENTRATING ONLY ON THE GIRL.
GWOOGH
THIS LEAVES ME NO CHOICE! I'M GOING TO HAVE TO WORK WITH KATÔ-SENSEI AND KÔRIYAMA-SENSEI TO STOP HIM!
I CAN'T DO IT ALONE!
AH, YES. WHEN ONE MENTIONS IZAKAYA...
ITS EQUIVALENT IN ENGLAND WOULD BE THE "PUB." I HEAR THAT IN ITALY AND SPAIN, IT IS A "BAR." HOWEVER, THE WORD IS USED MORE FOR COFFEE SHOPS THAN FOR ESTABLISHMENTS THAT SELL ALCOHOLIC DRINKS, SO ONE MUST BE ON ONE'S GUARD. AND I MUSTN'T FORGET THAT THE CHINESE WORD FOR LIQUOR STORE, "JIUDIAN," IS ALSO COMMONLY USED TO MEAN "HOTEL." AH, THIS REMINDS ME OF MY DAYS AS A STUDENT WHEN I WENT TO VISIT SOME RUINS IN NORTHERN CHINA ATTRIBUTED TO THE THREE KINGDOMS PERIOD...
DAMMIT!
I FORGOT ABOUT THAT!
KATÔ-SENSEI HAS FALLEN INTO LECTURE MODE. SO THE ONLY THING FOR ME TO DO IS TALK LIKE MANLY MEN WITH KÔRIYAMA-SENSEI...
ENGLAND HAS...
...THE ISLE OF JERSEY, RIGHT?
I WANT TO BUY A SPORTS JERSEY ON THE ISLE OF JERSEY!
ALWAYS WANTED TO SAY THAT!
GAK!
BRRR! BAD PUN!

I'LL HAVE TO DO SOMETHING ON MY OWN!

AHH! WHILE I'M DITHERING HERE, THE TWO OF THEM ARE GETTING CLOSER AND CLOSER...

EH? DO YOU MEAN IT?! I'VE NEVER BEEN...

TRULY! ENGLAND IS A WONDERFUL PLACE!

I'D LOVE TO SHOW YOU AROUND!

I KNOW! HOW ABOUT DURING SPRING VACATION?

ALREADY LOST THE SEATING BATTLE.

KATÔ   KÔRI

TANI   ANE

DEKI

BARTENDER

BUT TAE-SAN'S ON THE OTHER SIDE OF THE COUNTER...

Tani Hayato: Friendless and Isolated.

NO, WAIT A SECOND! IF I DON'T DO THIS JUST RIGHT, KATÔ-SENSEI WILL COME IN AND DOMINATE THE DISCUSSION!!

...SO I'VE GOT AN ENGLAND-RELATED TOPIC THAT JUNIOR DOESN'T EVEN KNOW ABOUT!

HERE I AM THE ENGLISH TEACHER, AND THE CLASS TRIP IS COMING UP...

WHICH VERSION OF ENGLISH DID YOU LEARN? THE QUEEN'S ENGLISH? AMERICAN?

OH YES! THERE'S ALSO AUSTRALIAN, ISN'T THERE?

COME TO THINK OF IT, TANI-SENSEI, YOU'RE THE ENGLISH TEACHER, RIGHT?

I-I GUESS I AM...

IT'S JUST NO GOOD... I CAN'T EVEN GET AN OPEN-ING!!

TINK

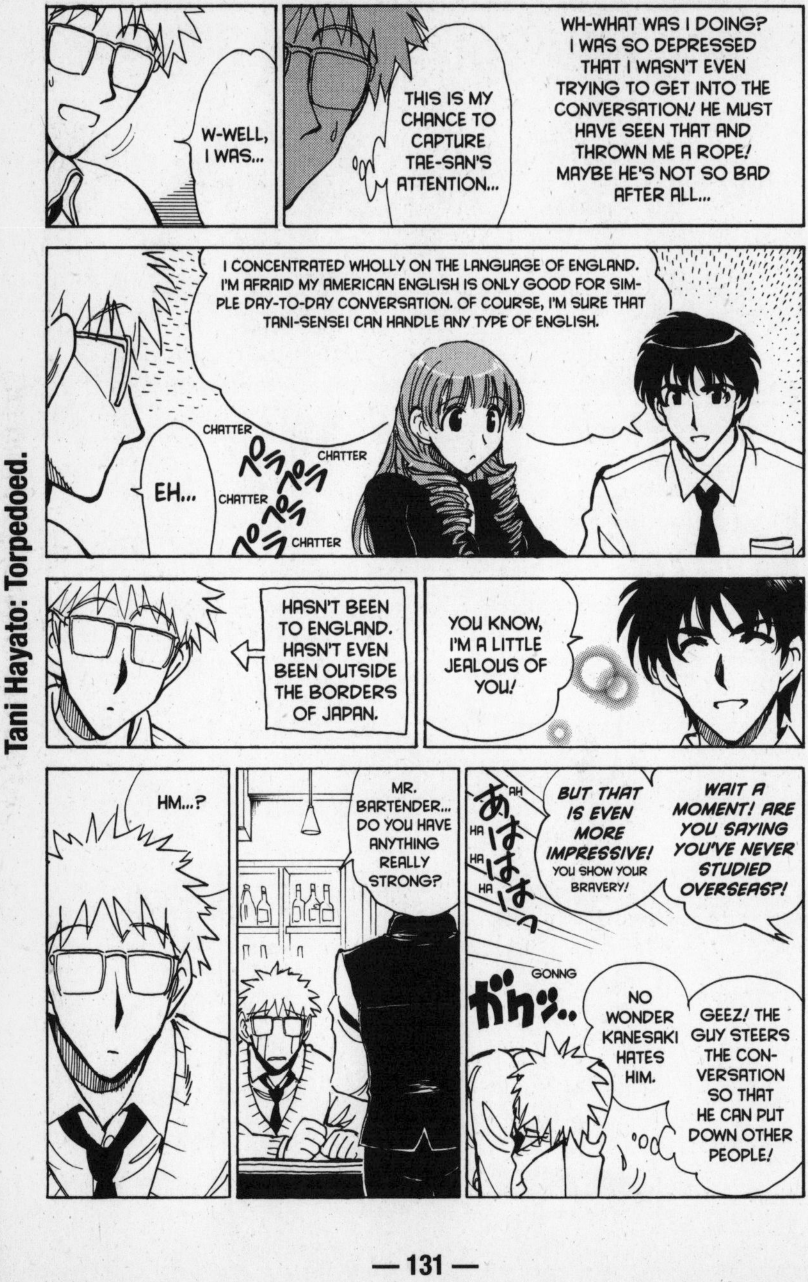
WH-WHAT WAS I DOING? I WAS SO DEPRESSED THAT I WASN'T EVEN TRYING TO GET INTO THE CONVERSATION! HE MUST HAVE SEEN THAT AND THROWN ME A ROPE! MAYBE HE'S NOT SO BAD AFTER ALL...
THIS IS MY CHANCE TO CAPTURE TAE-SAN'S ATTENTION...
W-WELL, I WAS...
I CONCENTRATED WHOLLY ON THE LANGUAGE OF ENGLAND. I'M AFRAID MY AMERICAN ENGLISH IS ONLY GOOD FOR SIMPLE DAY-TO-DAY CONVERSATION. OF COURSE, I'M SURE THAT TANI-SENSEI CAN HANDLE ANY TYPE OF ENGLISH.
CHATTER
CHATTER
CHATTER
CHATTER
EH...
YOU KNOW, I'M A LITTLE JEALOUS OF YOU!
HASN'T BEEN TO ENGLAND. HASN'T EVEN BEEN OUTSIDE THE BORDERS OF JAPAN.
WAIT A MOMENT! ARE YOU SAYING YOU'VE NEVER STUDIED OVERSEAS?!
BUT THAT IS EVEN MORE IMPRESSIVE! YOU SHOW YOUR BRAVERY!
AH HA HA HA
GONNG
GEEZ! THE GUY STEERS THE CONVERSATION SO THAT HE CAN PUT DOWN OTHER PEOPLE!
NO WONDER KANESAKI HATES HIM.
MR. BARTENDER... DO YOU HAVE ANYTHING REALLY STRONG?
HM...?

Tani Hayato: Torpedoed.

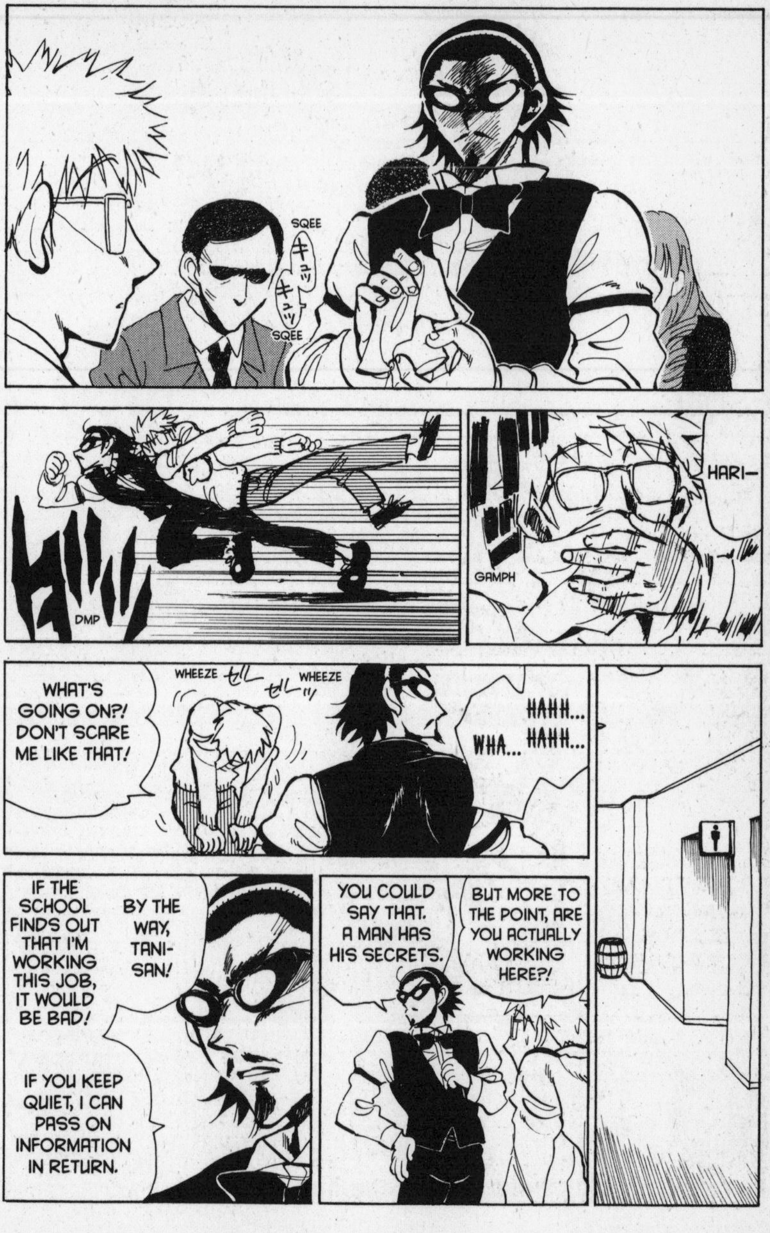
SQEE
キュッ
キュッ
SQEE
HARI—
GAMPH
DMP
HAHH... HAHH...
WHA...
WHEEZE
WHEEZE
WHAT'S GOING ON?! DON'T SCARE ME LIKE THAT!
BUT MORE TO THE POINT, ARE YOU ACTUALLY WORKING HERE?!
YOU COULD SAY THAT. A MAN HAS HIS SECRETS.
BY THE WAY, TANI-SAN!
IF THE SCHOOL FINDS OUT THAT I'M WORKING THIS JOB, IT WOULD BE BAD!
IF YOU KEEP QUIET, I CAN PASS ON INFORMATION IN RETURN.

Tani Hayato: Has Had a Date with Harima.

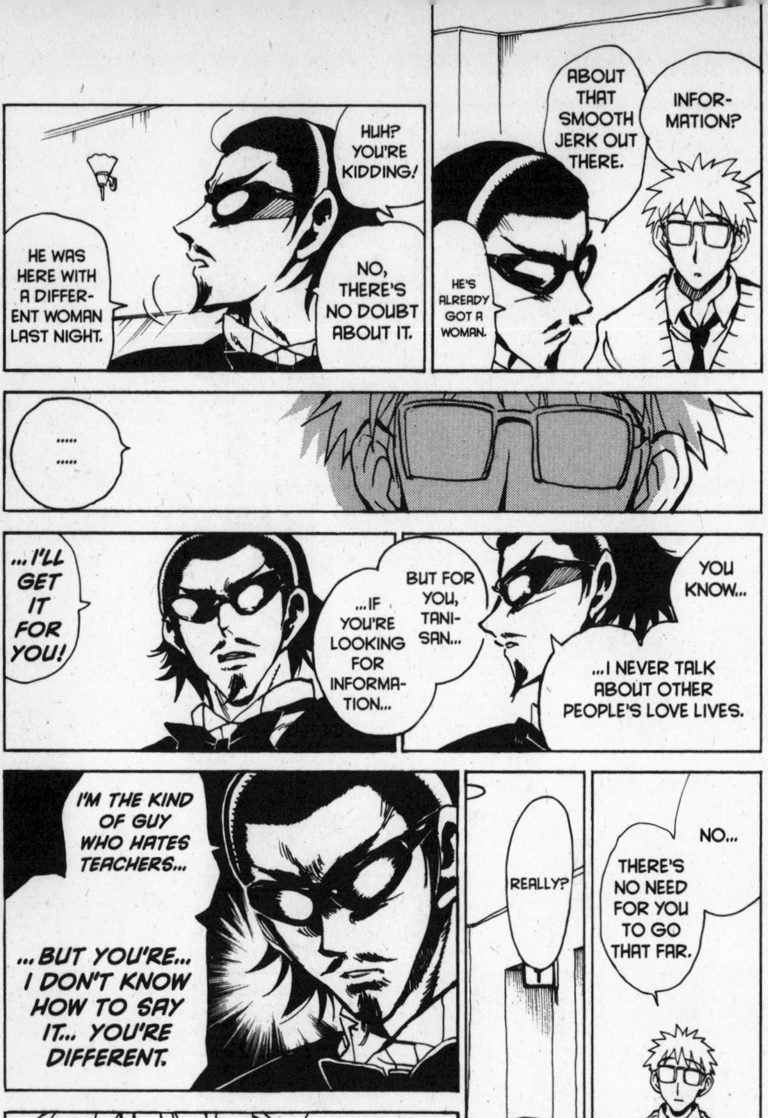
INFOR-MATION?
ABOUT THAT SMOOTH JERK OUT THERE.
HE'S ALREADY GOT A WOMAN.
HUH? YOU'RE KIDDING!
NO, THERE'S NO DOUBT ABOUT IT.
HE WAS HERE WITH A DIFFER-ENT WOMAN LAST NIGHT.
....
YOU KNOW...
...I NEVER TALK ABOUT OTHER PEOPLE'S LOVE LIVES.
BUT FOR YOU, TANI-SAN...
...IF YOU'RE LOOKING FOR INFORMA-TION...
...I'LL GET IT FOR YOU!
NO...
THERE'S NO NEED FOR YOU TO GO THAT FAR.
BUT THANKS FOR OFFERING.
REALLY?
I GUESS I BUTTED IN WHERE I'M NOT WANTED, HUH?
I'M THE KIND OF GUY WHO HATES TEACHERS...
...BUT YOU'RE... I DON'T KNOW HOW TO SAY IT... YOU'RE DIFFERENT.
I SEE... WELL, JUST DON'T OVERDO THE PART-TIME WORK. OKAY, HARI—

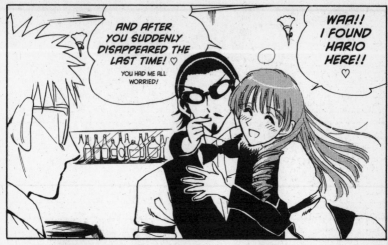

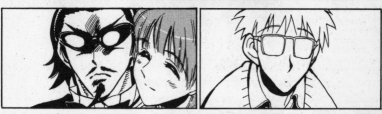

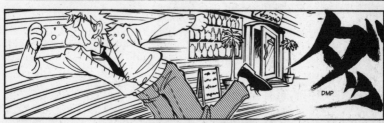

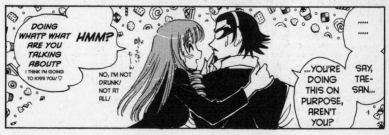

Master, Line Me Up with a Cocktail That'll Make Me Forget My Pain. (Tani)

WAA!! I FOUND HARIO HERE!! ♡
AND AFTER YOU SUDDENLY DISAPPEARED THE LAST TIME! ♡
YOU HAD ME ALL WORRIED!
DMP
.....
.....
SAY, TAE-SAN...
...YOU'RE DOING THIS ON PURPOSE, AREN'T YOU?
酔ってないも〜ん
NO, I'M NOT DRUNK! NOT AT ALL!
HMM?
DOING WHAT? WHAT ARE YOU TALKING ABOUT?
I THINK I'M GOING TO KISS YOU! ♡

164· · · · · · · ·Fin

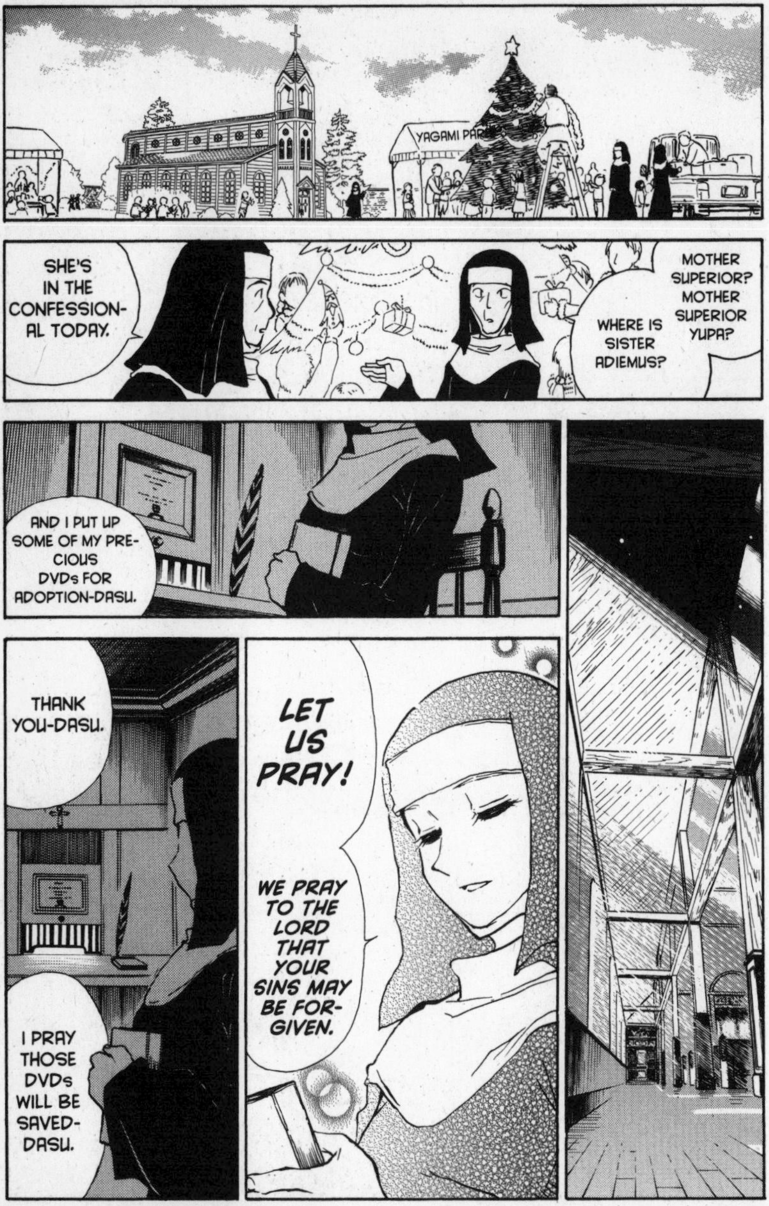
MOTHER SUPERIOR? MOTHER SUPERIOR YUPA?
WHERE IS SISTER ADIEMUS?
SHE'S IN THE CONFESSIONAL TODAY.
AND I PUT UP SOME OF MY PRECIOUS DVDs FOR ADOPTION-DASU.
LET US PRAY!
WE PRAY TO THE LORD THAT YOUR SINS MAY BE FORGIVEN.
THANK YOU-DASU.
I PRAY THOSE DVDs WILL BE SAVED-DASU.

♭ 34 SISTER ACT

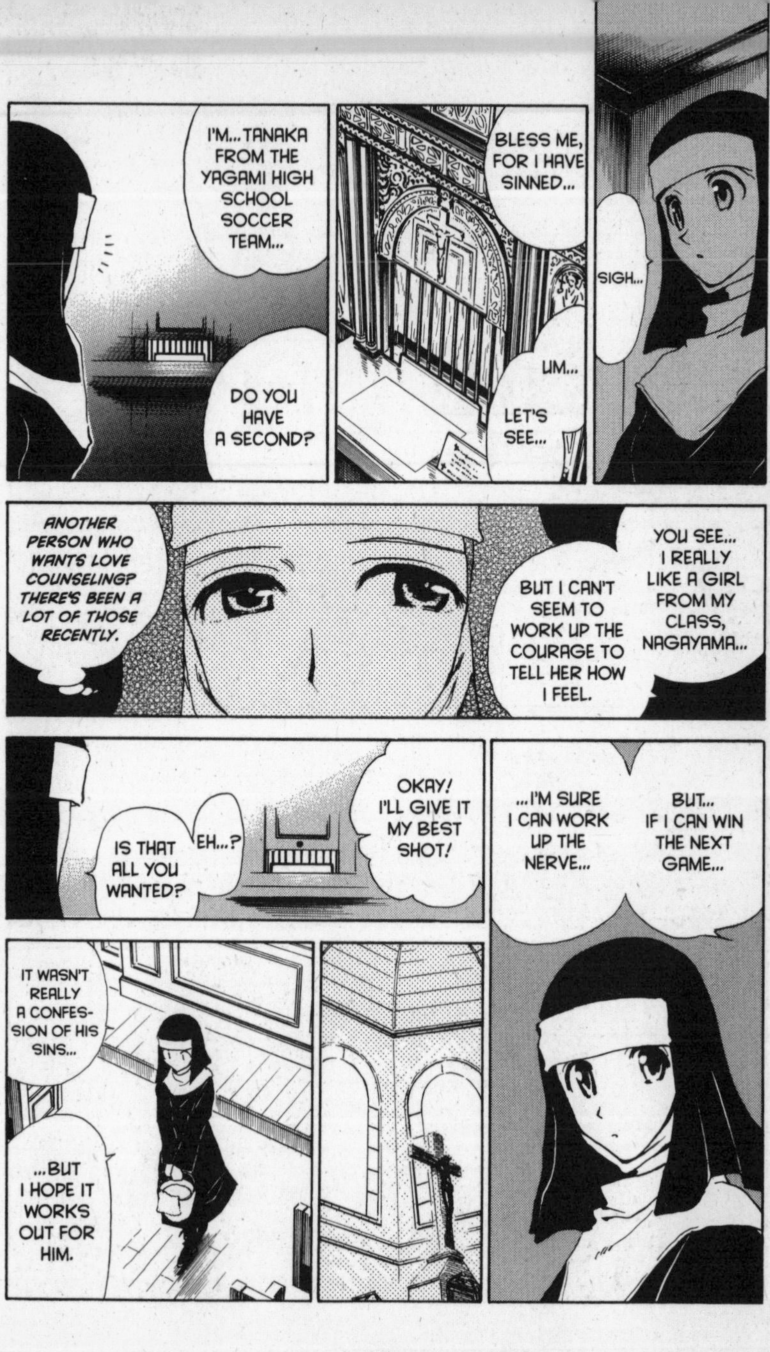
SIGH...
BLESS ME, FOR I HAVE SINNED...
UM...
LET'S SEE...
I'M...TANAKA FROM THE YAGAMI HIGH SCHOOL SOCCER TEAM...
DO YOU HAVE A SECOND?
YOU SEE... I REALLY LIKE A GIRL FROM MY CLASS, NAGAYAMA...
BUT I CAN'T SEEM TO WORK UP THE COURAGE TO TELL HER HOW I FEEL.
ANOTHER PERSON WHO WANTS LOVE COUNSELING? THERE'S BEEN A LOT OF THOSE RECENTLY.
BUT... IF I CAN WIN THE NEXT GAME...
...I'M SURE I CAN WORK UP THE NERVE...
OKAY! I'LL GIVE IT MY BEST SHOT!
EH...?
IS THAT ALL YOU WANTED?
IT WASN'T REALLY A CONFES-SION OF HIS SINS...
...BUT I HOPE IT WORKS OUT FOR HIM.

Takano: Wipe Your Mouth.

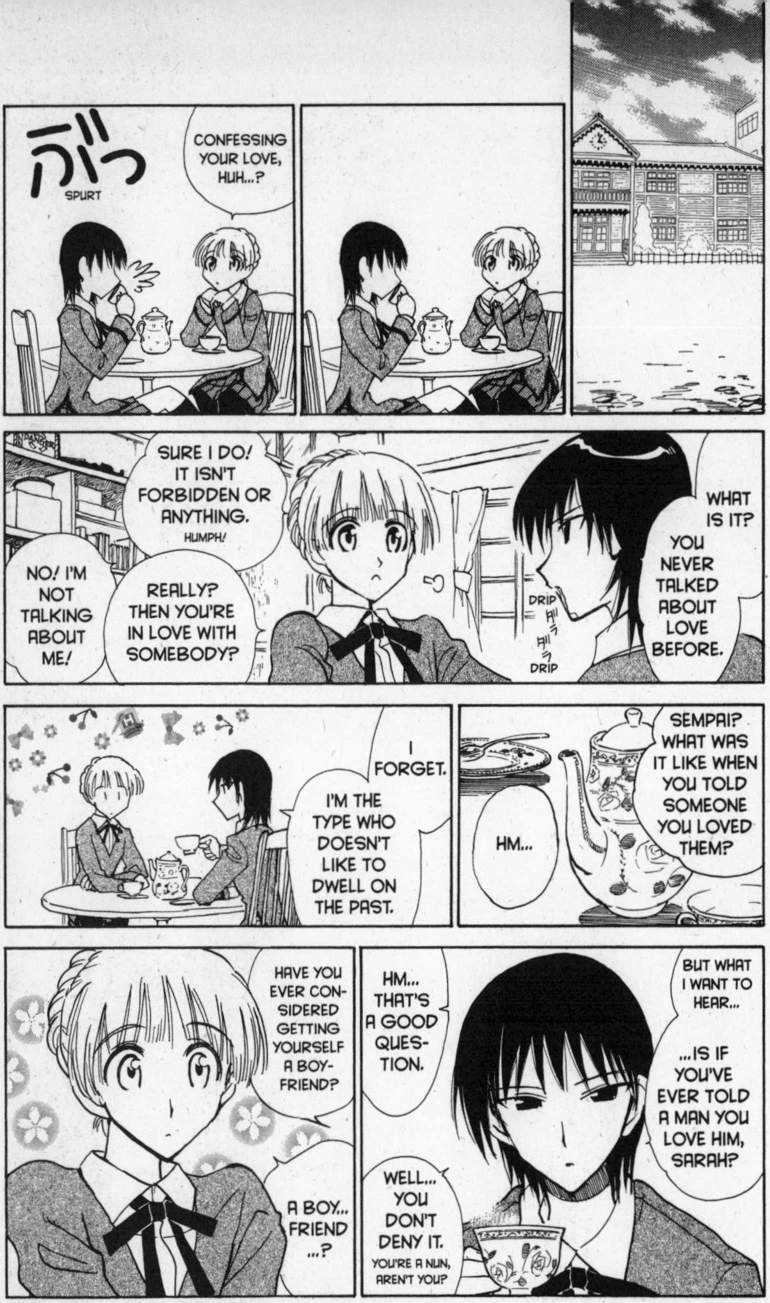

CONFESSING YOUR LOVE, HUH...?
ぶっ
SPURT
WHAT IS IT? YOU NEVER TALKED ABOUT LOVE BEFORE.
DRIP
DRIP
SURE I DO! IT ISN'T FORBIDDEN OR ANYTHING.
HUMPH!
REALLY? THEN YOU'RE IN LOVE WITH SOMEBODY?
NO! I'M NOT TALKING ABOUT ME!
SEMPAI? WHAT WAS IT LIKE WHEN YOU TOLD SOMEONE YOU LOVED THEM?
HM...
I FORGET.
I'M THE TYPE WHO DOESN'T LIKE TO DWELL ON THE PAST.
BUT WHAT I WANT TO HEAR...
...IS IF YOU'VE EVER TOLD A MAN YOU LOVE HIM, SARAH?
HM... THAT'S A GOOD QUESTION.
WELL... YOU DON'T DENY IT.
YOU'RE A NUN, AREN'T YOU?
HAVE YOU EVER CONSIDERED GETTING YOURSELF A BOY-FRIEND?
A BOY... FRIEND ...?

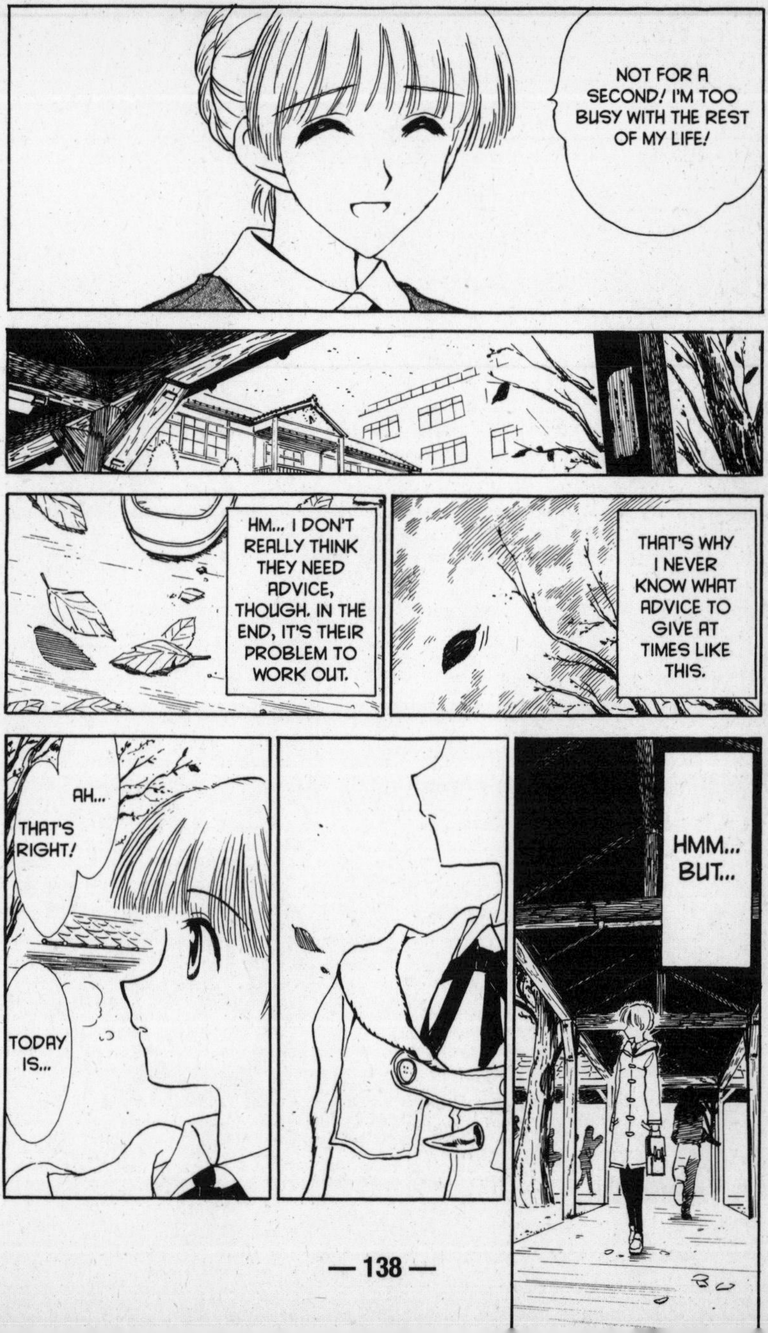
NOT FOR A SECOND! I'M TOO BUSY WITH THE REST OF MY LIFE!
THAT'S WHY I NEVER KNOW WHAT ADVICE TO GIVE AT TIMES LIKE THIS.
HM... I DON'T REALLY THINK THEY NEED ADVICE, THOUGH. IN THE END, IT'S THEIR PROBLEM TO WORK OUT.
HMM... BUT...
AH...
THAT'S RIGHT!
TODAY IS...

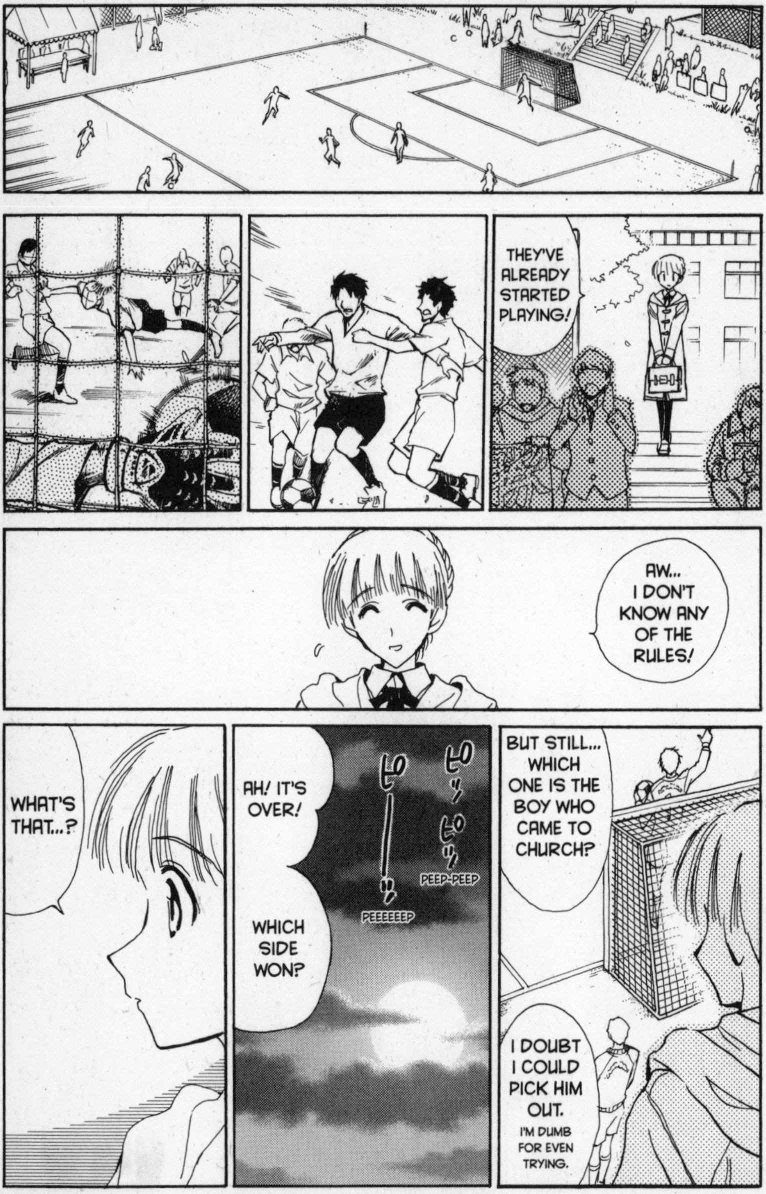
THEY'VE ALREADY STARTED PLAYING!
AW... I DON'T KNOW ANY OF THE RULES!
BUT STILL... WHICH ONE IS THE BOY WHO CAME TO CHURCH?
I DOUBT I COULD PICK HIM OUT.
I'M DUMB FOR EVEN TRYING.
ピッ ピッ
PEEP-PEEP
ピーーッ
PEEEEEEP
AH! IT'S OVER!
WHICH SIDE WON?
WHAT'S THAT...?

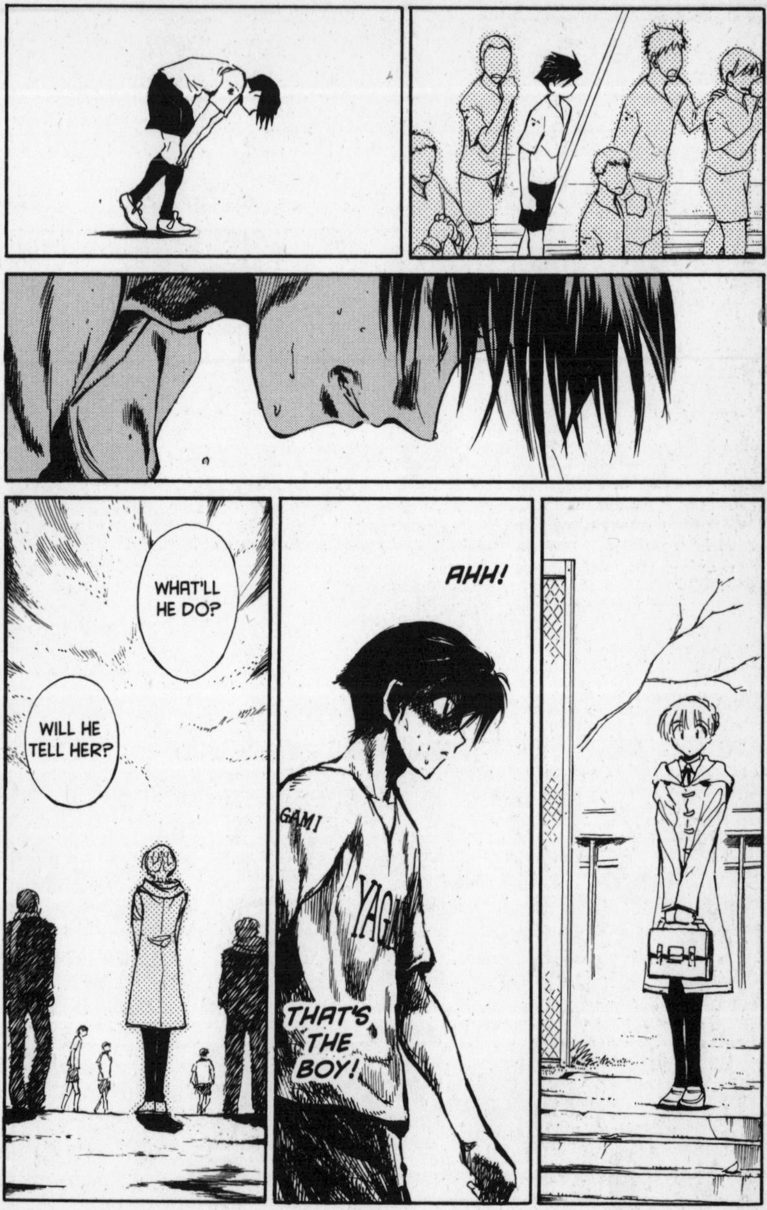
AHH!
THAT'S THE BOY!
WHAT'LL HE DO?
WILL HE TELL HER?

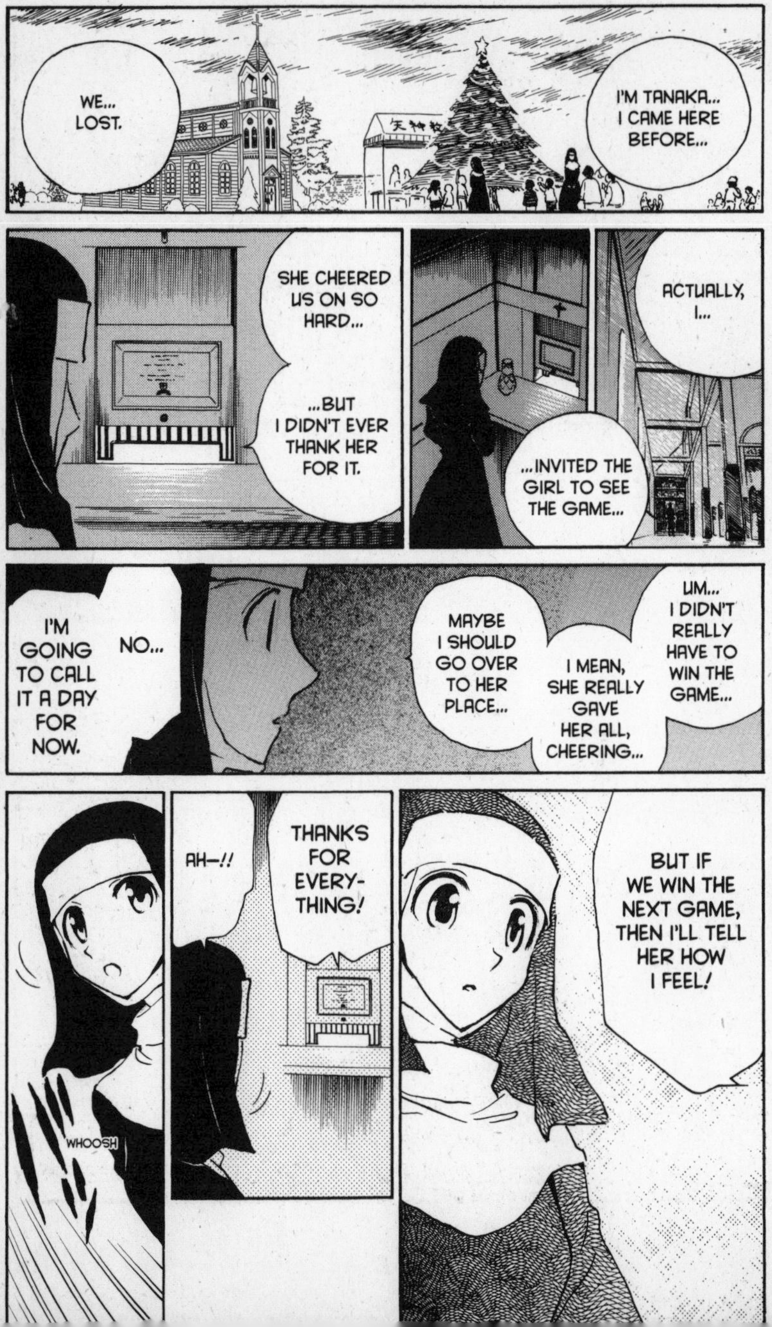
I'M TANAKA... I CAME HERE BEFORE...
WE... LOST.
ACTUALLY, I...
...INVITED THE GIRL TO SEE THE GAME...
SHE CHEERED US ON SO HARD...
...BUT I DIDN'T EVER THANK HER FOR IT.
UM... I DIDN'T REALLY HAVE TO WIN THE GAME...
I MEAN, SHE REALLY GAVE HER ALL, CHEERING...
MAYBE I SHOULD GO OVER TO HER PLACE...
NO...
I'M GOING TO CALL IT A DAY FOR NOW.
BUT IF WE WIN THE NEXT GAME, THEN I'LL TELL HER HOW I FEEL!
THANKS FOR EVERY-THING!
AH—!!
WHOOSH

See the Start of Tanaka and Nagayama's Relationship in Volume 8.

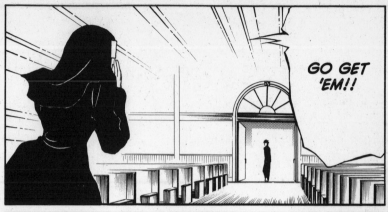

Sister Adiemus: Still Learning.

GO GET 'EM!!
I SAY! SISTER ADIEMUS!!
THIS IS A CHURCH!! SACRED GROUND!!
YOU SEEM TO BE IN HIGH SPIRITS.
DID SOMETHING GOOD HAPPEN TO YOU TODAY?
EH HEH HEH! IT'S CONFIDENTIAL INFORMATION.
HMM.
STILL, I CAN HANDLE THAT.

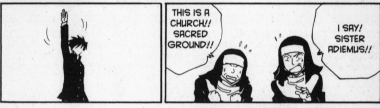

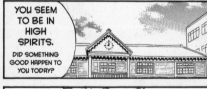

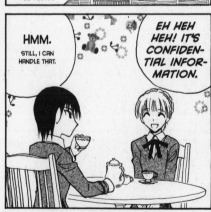

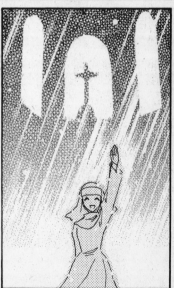

♭34 . . . . Fin

♭35 CONTE D'HIVER

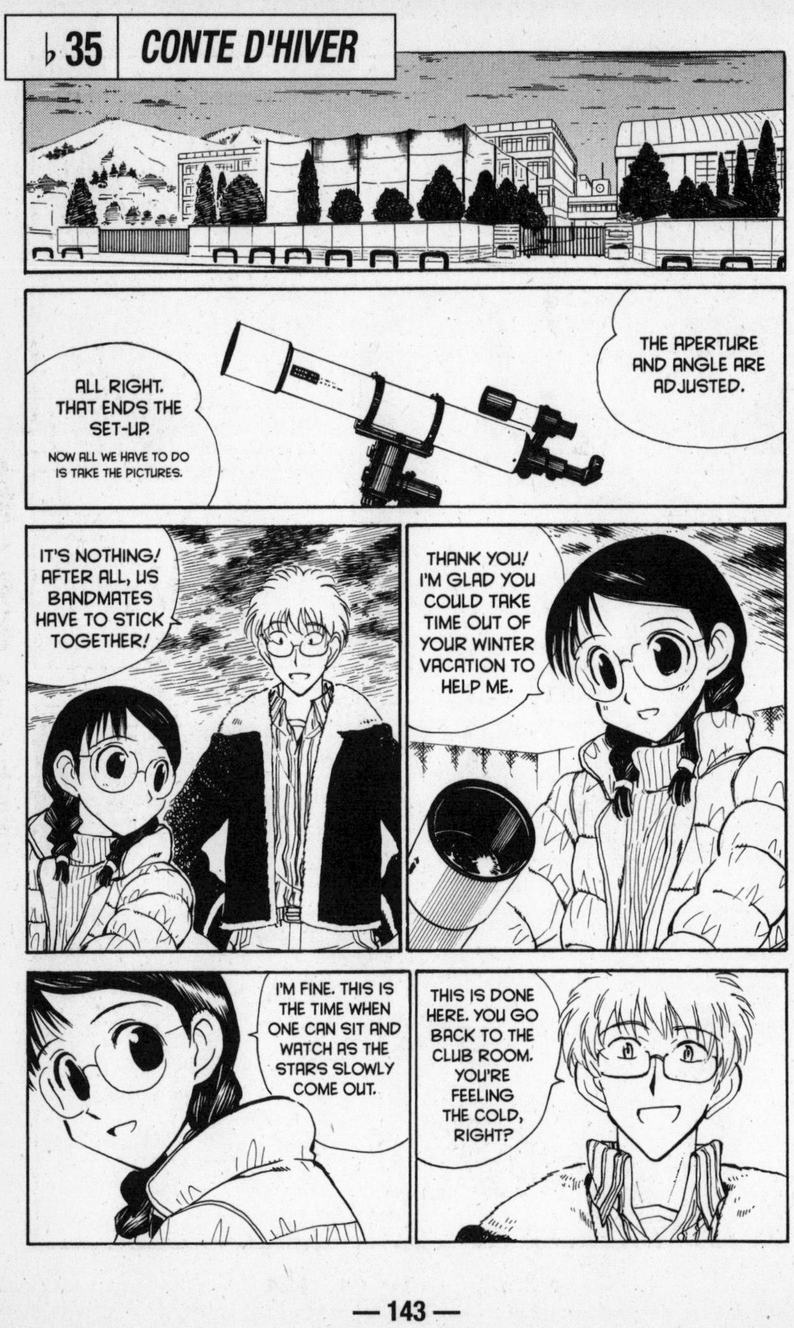
THE APERTURE AND ANGLE ARE ADJUSTED.
ALL RIGHT. THAT ENDS THE SET-UP. NOW ALL WE HAVE TO DO IS TAKE THE PICTURES.
THANK YOU! I'M GLAD YOU COULD TAKE TIME OUT OF YOUR WINTER VACATION TO HELP ME.
IT'S NOTHING! AFTER ALL, US BANDMATES HAVE TO STICK TOGETHER!
THIS IS DONE HERE. YOU GO BACK TO THE CLUB ROOM. YOU'RE FEELING THE COLD, RIGHT?
I'M FINE. THIS IS THE TIME WHEN ONE CAN SIT AND WATCH AS THE STARS SLOWLY COME OUT.

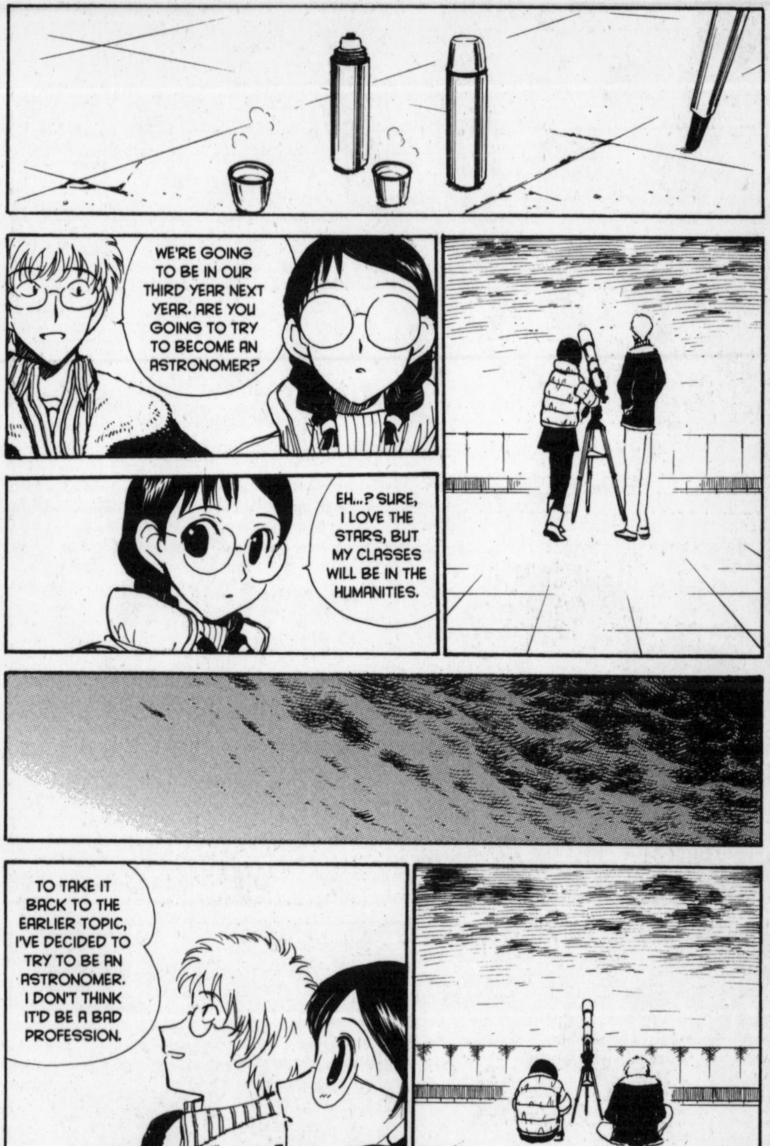
WE'RE GOING TO BE IN OUR THIRD YEAR NEXT YEAR. ARE YOU GOING TO TRY TO BECOME AN ASTRONOMER?
EH...? SURE, I LOVE THE STARS, BUT MY CLASSES WILL BE IN THE HUMANITIES.
TO TAKE IT BACK TO THE EARLIER TOPIC, I'VE DECIDED TO TRY TO BE AN ASTRONOMER. I DON'T THINK IT'D BE A BAD PROFESSION.

Yûki Tsumugi: A Member of the Astronomy Club.

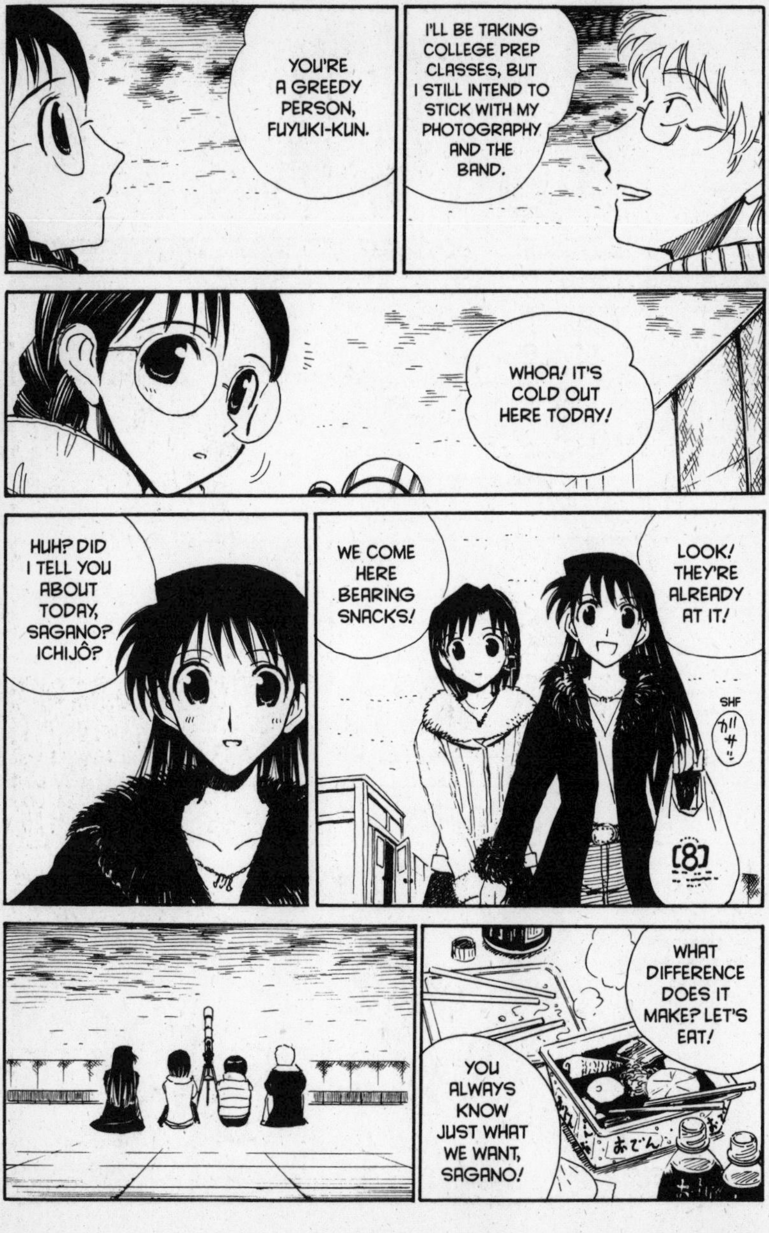
I'LL BE TAKING COLLEGE PREP CLASSES, BUT I STILL INTEND TO STICK WITH MY PHOTOGRAPHY AND THE BAND.
YOU'RE A GREEDY PERSON, FUYUKI-KUN.
WHOA! IT'S COLD OUT HERE TODAY!
LOOK! THEY'RE ALREADY AT IT!
WE COME HERE BEARING SNACKS!
SHF
HUH? DID I TELL YOU ABOUT TODAY, SAGANO? ICHIJÔ?
WHAT DIFFERENCE DOES IT MAKE? LET'S EAT!
YOU ALWAYS KNOW JUST WHAT WE WANT, SAGANO!
おでん

Fuyuki Takeichi: Class 2-C's Cameraman.

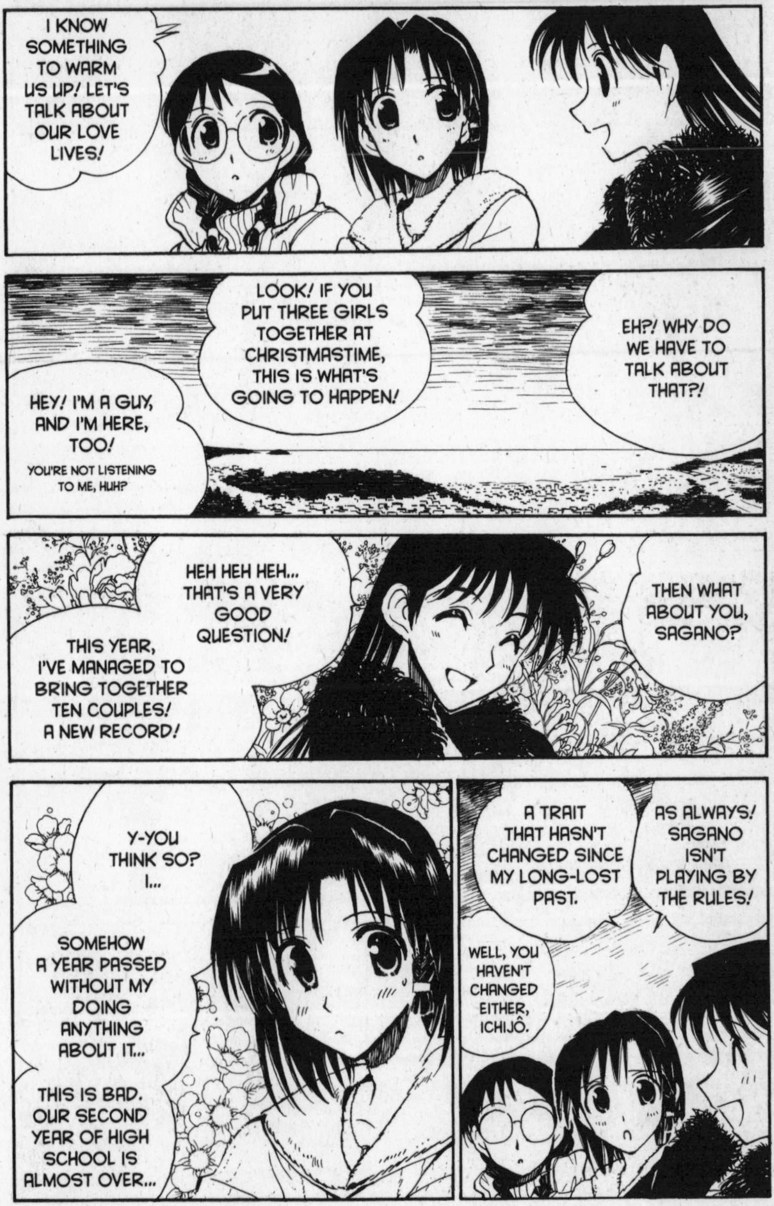
I KNOW SOMETHING TO WARM US UP! LET'S TALK ABOUT OUR LOVE LIVES!
EH?! WHY DO WE HAVE TO TALK ABOUT THAT?!
LOOK! IF YOU PUT THREE GIRLS TOGETHER AT CHRISTMASTIME, THIS IS WHAT'S GOING TO HAPPEN!
HEY! I'M A GUY, AND I'M HERE, TOO!
YOU'RE NOT LISTENING TO ME, HUH?
THEN WHAT ABOUT YOU, SAGANO?
HEH HEH HEH... THAT'S A VERY GOOD QUESTION!
THIS YEAR, I'VE MANAGED TO BRING TOGETHER TEN COUPLES! A NEW RECORD!
AS ALWAYS! SAGANO ISN'T PLAYING BY THE RULES!
A TRAIT THAT HASN'T CHANGED SINCE MY LONG-LOST PAST.
WELL, YOU HAVEN'T CHANGED EITHER, ICHIJÔ.
Y-YOU THINK SO? I...
SOMEHOW A YEAR PASSED WITHOUT MY DOING ANYTHING ABOUT IT...
THIS IS BAD. OUR SECOND YEAR OF HIGH SCHOOL IS ALMOST OVER...

And All Four Are in the Same Band. Just So You Know.

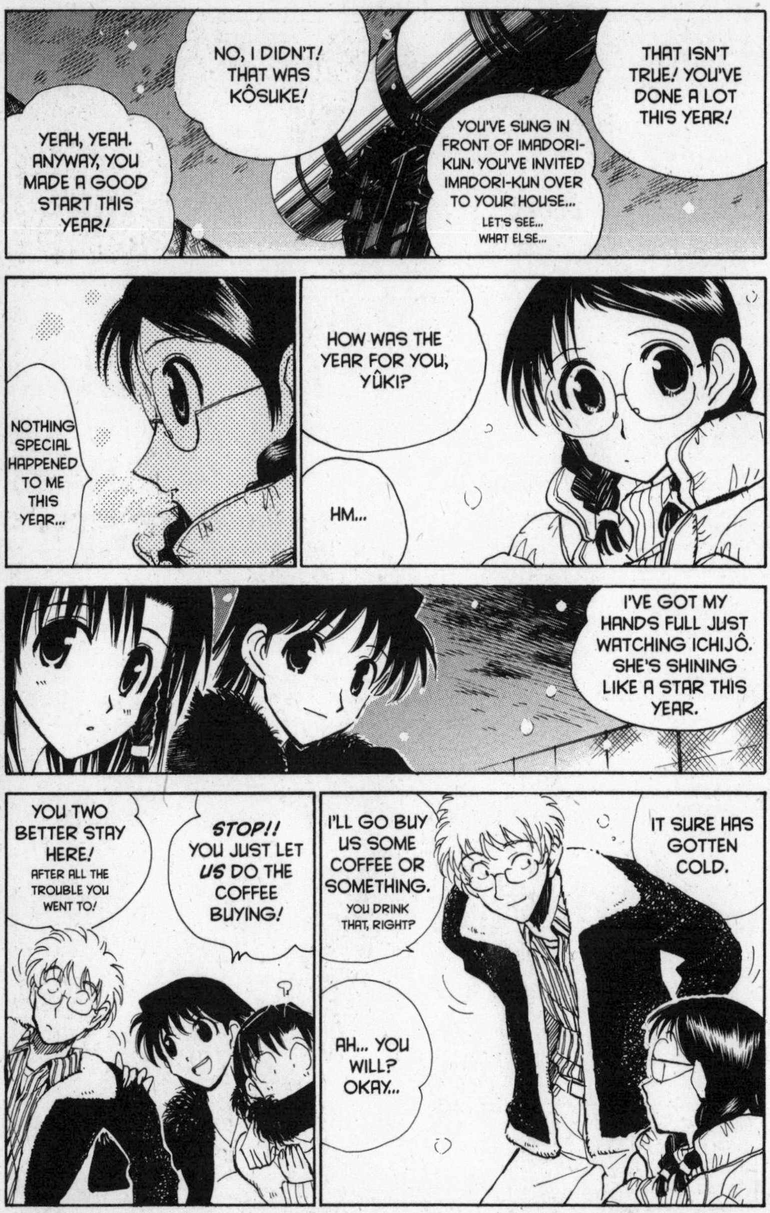
THAT ISN'T TRUE! YOU'VE DONE A LOT THIS YEAR!
YOU'VE SUNG IN FRONT OF IMADORI-KUN. YOU'VE INVITED IMADORI-KUN OVER TO YOUR HOUSE...
LET'S SEE... WHAT ELSE...
NO, I DIDN'T! THAT WAS KÔSUKE!
YEAH, YEAH. ANYWAY, YOU MADE A GOOD START THIS YEAR!
HOW WAS THE YEAR FOR YOU, YÛKI?
HM...
NOTHING SPECIAL HAPPENED TO ME THIS YEAR...
I'VE GOT MY HANDS FULL JUST WATCHING ICHIJÔ. SHE'S SHINING LIKE A STAR THIS YEAR.
IT SURE HAS GOTTEN COLD.
I'LL GO BUY US SOME COFFEE OR SOMETHING.
YOU DRINK THAT, RIGHT?
AH... YOU WILL? OKAY...
STOP!! YOU JUST LET US DO THE COFFEE BUYING!
YOU TWO BETTER STAY HERE!
AFTER ALL THE TROUBLE YOU WENT TO!

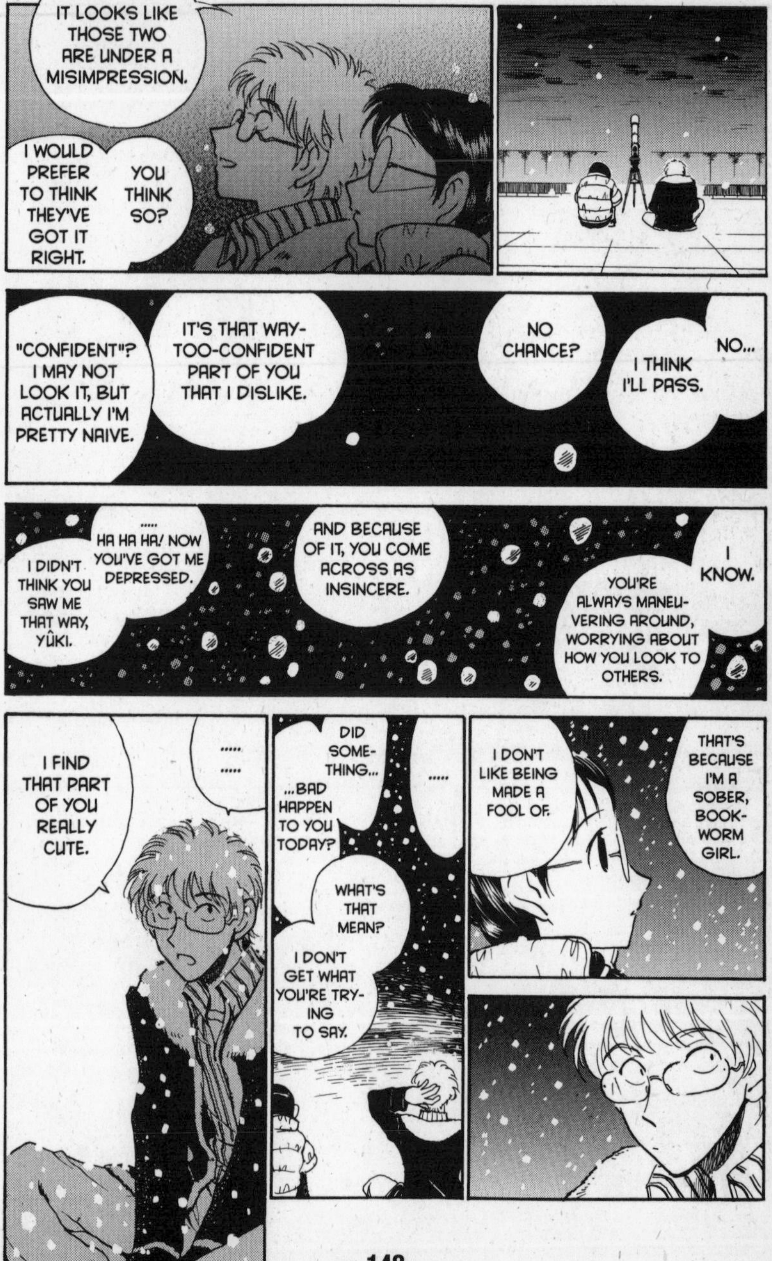
IT LOOKS LIKE THOSE TWO ARE UNDER A MISIMPRESSION.
YOU THINK SO?
I WOULD PREFER TO THINK THEY'VE GOT IT RIGHT.
NO...
I THINK I'LL PASS.
NO CHANCE?
IT'S THAT WAY-TOO-CONFIDENT PART OF YOU THAT I DISLIKE.
"CONFIDENT"? I MAY NOT LOOK IT, BUT ACTUALLY I'M PRETTY NAIVE.
I KNOW.
YOU'RE ALWAYS MANEUVERING AROUND, WORRYING ABOUT HOW YOU LOOK TO OTHERS.
AND BECAUSE OF IT, YOU COME ACROSS AS INSINCERE.
..... HA HA HA! NOW YOU'VE GOT ME DEPRESSED.
I DIDN'T THINK YOU SAW ME THAT WAY, YÛKI.
THAT'S BECAUSE I'M A SOBER, BOOKWORM GIRL.
I DON'T LIKE BEING MADE A FOOL OF.
.....
DID SOMETHING... ...BAD HAPPEN TO YOU TODAY?
WHAT'S THAT MEAN?
I DON'T GET WHAT YOU'RE TRYING TO SAY.
....
I FIND THAT PART OF YOU REALLY CUTE.

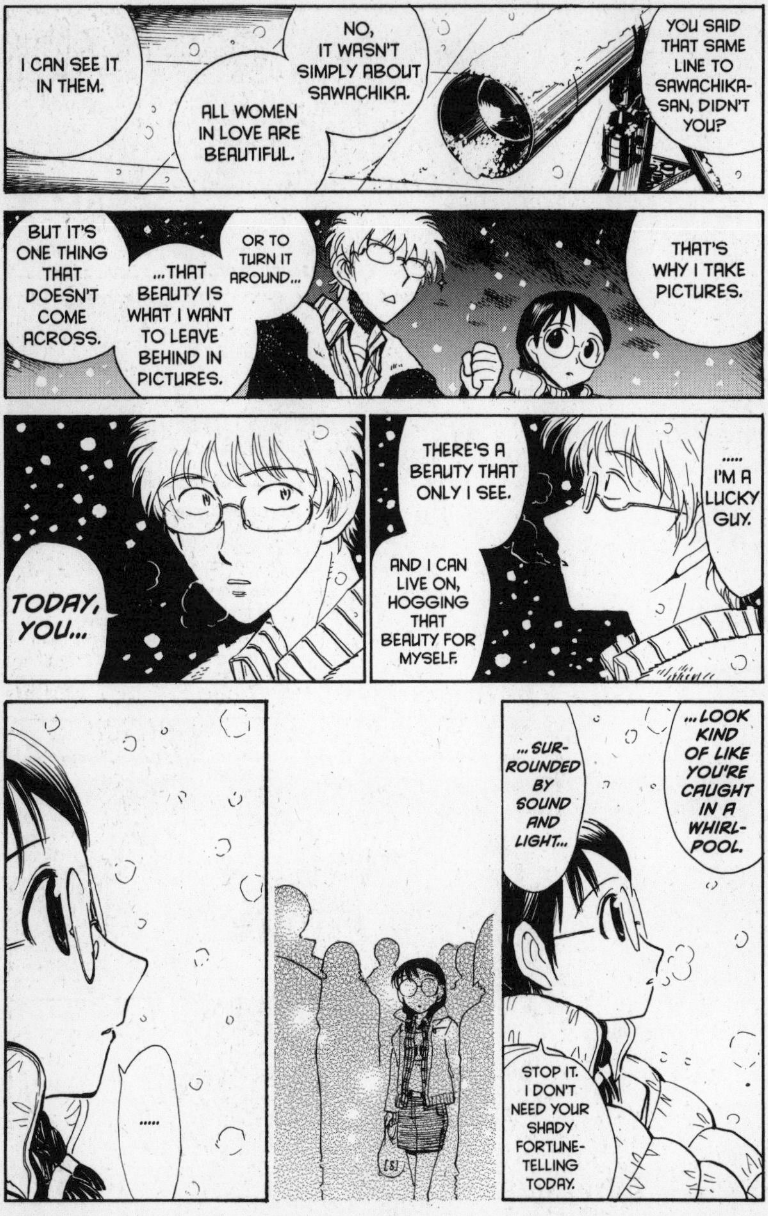
YOU SAID THAT SAME LINE TO SAWACHIKA-SAN, DIDN'T YOU?
NO, IT WASN'T SIMPLY ABOUT SAWACHIKA.
ALL WOMEN IN LOVE ARE BEAUTIFUL.
I CAN SEE IT IN THEM.
THAT'S WHY I TAKE PICTURES.
OR TO TURN IT AROUND...
...THAT BEAUTY IS WHAT I WANT TO LEAVE BEHIND IN PICTURES.
BUT IT'S ONE THING THAT DOESN'T COME ACROSS.
..... I'M A LUCKY GUY.
THERE'S A BEAUTY THAT ONLY I SEE.
AND I CAN LIVE ON, HOGGING THAT BEAUTY FOR MYSELF.
TODAY, YOU...
...LOOK KIND OF LIKE YOU'RE CAUGHT IN A WHIRLPOOL.
... SURROUNDED BY SOUND AND LIGHT...
STOP IT. I DON'T NEED YOUR SHADY FORTUNE-TELLING TODAY.
.....

It's Because She Saw Them from Far Off.

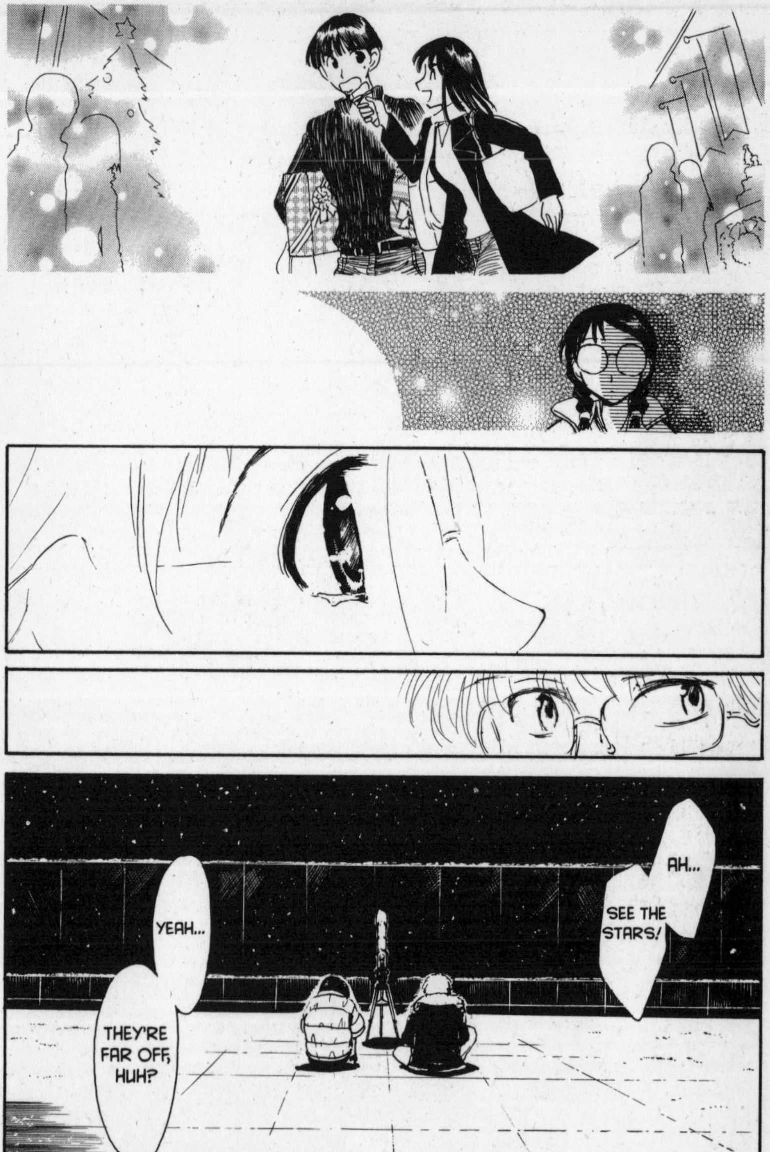
AH...
SEE THE STARS!
YEAH...
THEY'RE FAR OFF, HUH?

♭35· · · · · · · · · ·Fin

♭36 COLD HEAT

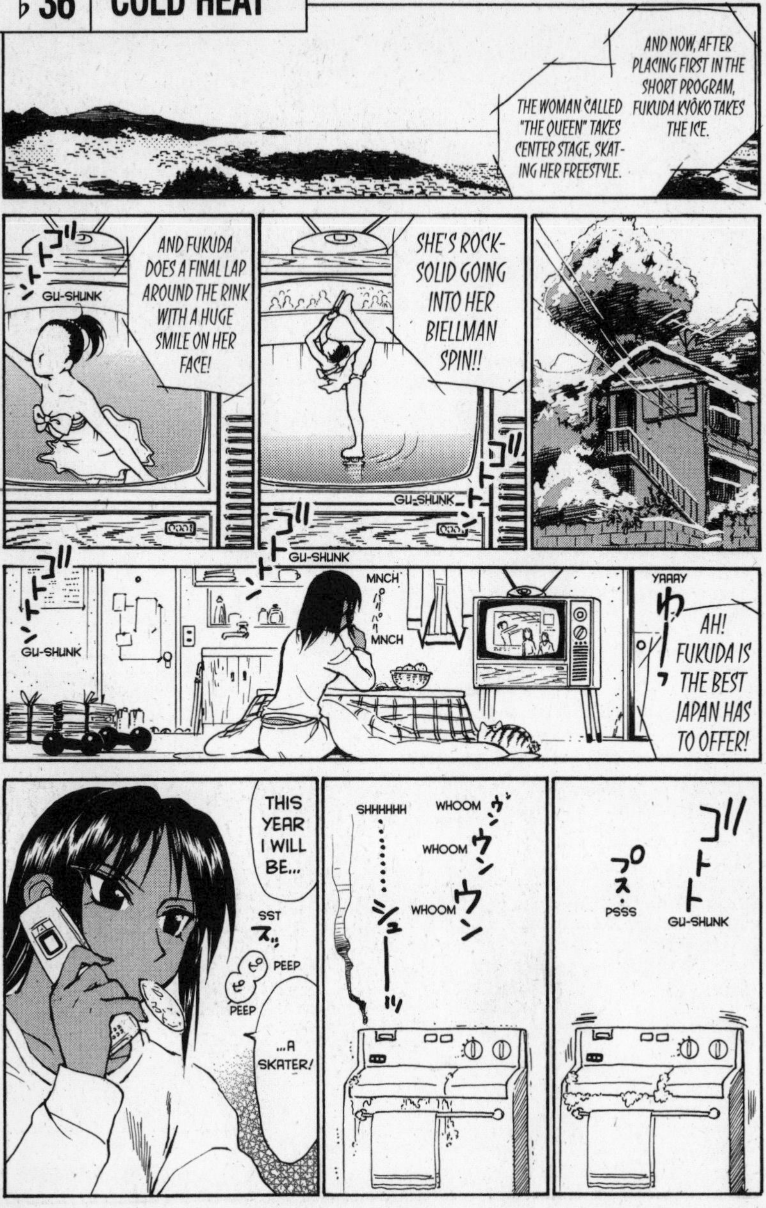
AND NOW, AFTER PLACING FIRST IN THE SHORT PROGRAM, FUKUDA KYÔKO TAKES THE ICE.
THE WOMAN CALLED "THE QUEEN" TAKES CENTER STAGE, SKATING HER FREESTYLE.
SHE'S ROCK-SOLID GOING INTO HER BIELLMAN SPIN!!
GU-SHUNK
AND FUKUDA DOES A FINAL LAP AROUND THE RINK WITH A HUGE SMILE ON HER FACE!
GU-SHUNK
GU-SHUNK
YAAAY
AH! FUKUDA IS THE BEST JAPAN HAS TO OFFER!
MNCH
MNCH
GU-SHUNK
GU-SHUNK
PSSS
WHOOM
WHOOM
WHOOM
SHHHHHH
THIS YEAR I WILL BE...
SST
PEEP
PEEP
...A SKATER!

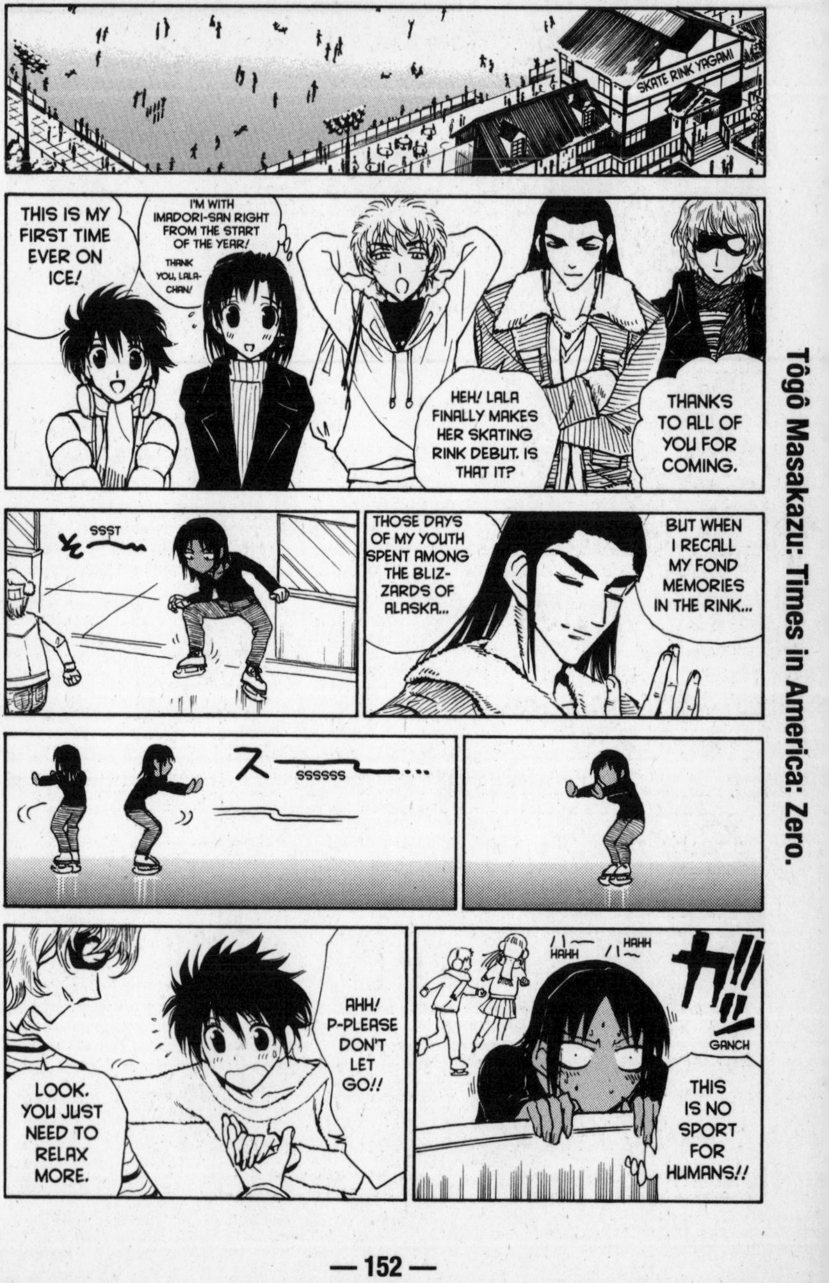
SKATE RINK YAGAMI
THANKS TO ALL OF YOU FOR COMING.
HEH! LALA FINALLY MAKES HER SKATING RINK DEBUT. IS THAT IT?
I'M WITH IMADORI-SAN RIGHT FROM THE START OF THE YEAR!
THANK YOU, LALA-CHAN!
THIS IS MY FIRST TIME EVER ON ICE!
BUT WHEN I RECALL MY FOND MEMORIES IN THE RINK...
THOSE DAYS OF MY YOUTH SPENT AMONG THE BLIZ-ZARDS OF ALASKA...
SSST
SSSSSS
HAHH
HAHH
GANCH
THIS IS NO SPORT FOR HUMANS!!
AHH! P-PLEASE DON'T LET GO!!
LOOK. YOU JUST NEED TO RELAX MORE.

Tôgô Masakazu: Times in America: Zero.

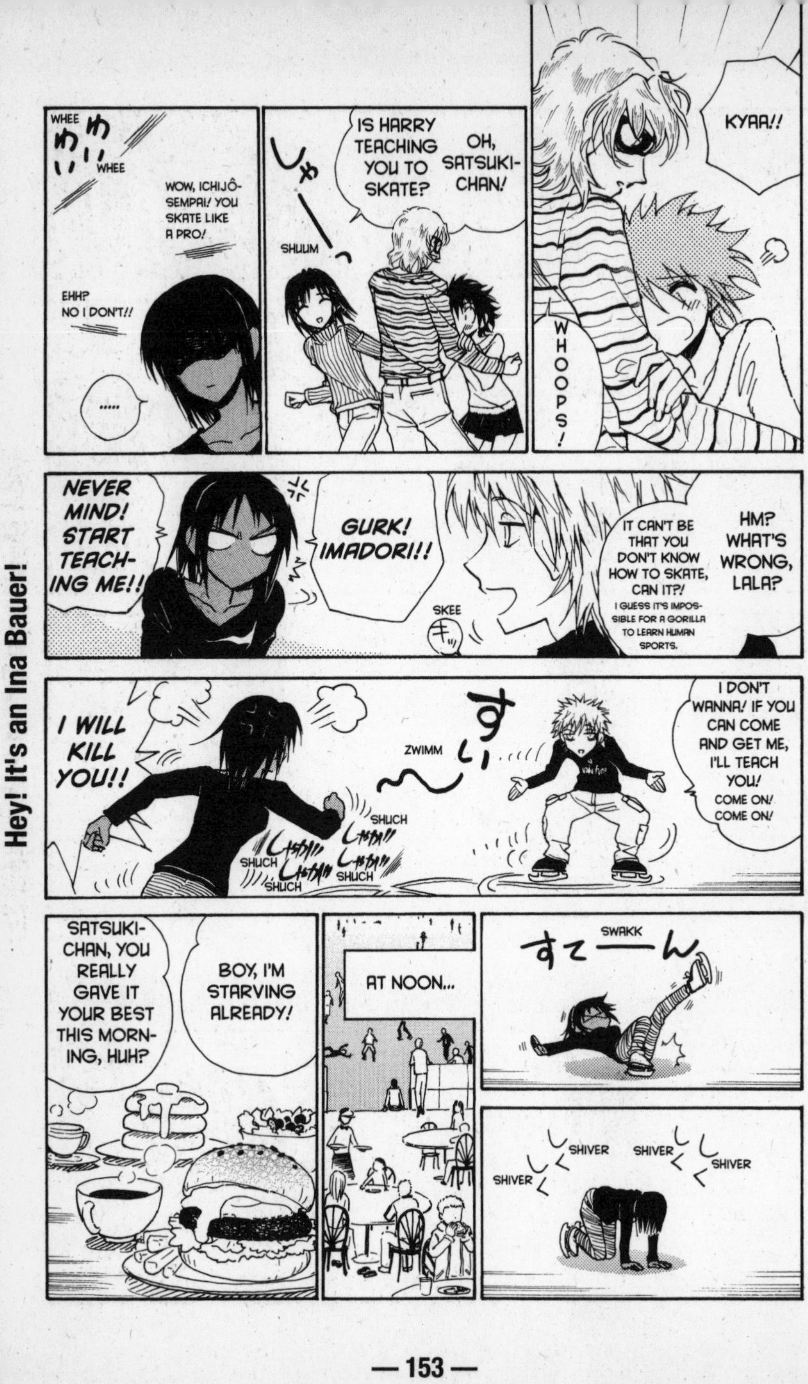
KYAA!!
WHOOPS!
OH, SATSUKI-CHAN!
IS HARRY TEACHING YOU TO SKATE?
SHUUM
WHEE
WHEE
WOW, ICHIJÔ-SEMPAI! YOU SKATE LIKE A PRO!
EHH? NO I DON'T!!
.....
HM? WHAT'S WRONG, LALA?
IT CAN'T BE THAT YOU DON'T KNOW HOW TO SKATE, CAN IT?!
I GUESS IT'S IMPOSSIBLE FOR A GORILLA TO LEARN HUMAN SPORTS.
SKEE
GURK! IMADORI!!
NEVER MIND! START TEACHING ME!!
I DON'T WANNA! IF YOU CAN COME AND GET ME, I'LL TEACH YOU!
COME ON! COME ON!
すい
ZWIMM
SHUCH
SHUCH
SHUCH
SHUCH
I WILL KILL YOU!!
すてーーん
SWAKK
SHIVER
SHIVER
SHIVER
SHIVER
AT NOON...
BOY, I'M STARVING ALREADY!
SATSUKI-CHAN, YOU REALLY GAVE IT YOUR BEST THIS MORNING, HUH?

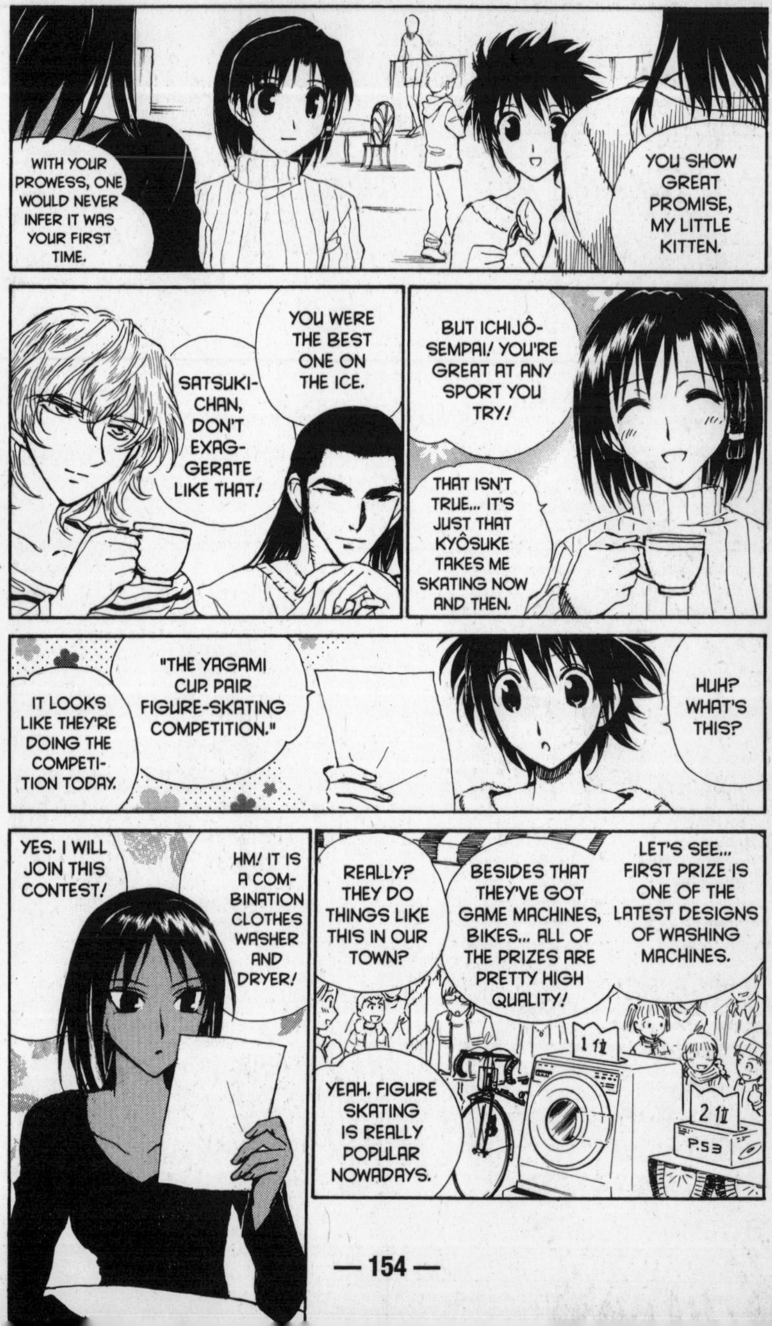
YOU SHOW GREAT PROMISE, MY LITTLE KITTEN.
WITH YOUR PROWESS, ONE WOULD NEVER INFER IT WAS YOUR FIRST TIME.
BUT ICHIJÔ-SEMPAI! YOU'RE GREAT AT ANY SPORT YOU TRY!
THAT ISN'T TRUE... IT'S JUST THAT KYÔSUKE TAKES ME SKATING NOW AND THEN.
YOU WERE THE BEST ONE ON THE ICE.
SATSUKI-CHAN, DON'T EXAG-GERATE LIKE THAT!
HUH? WHAT'S THIS?
"THE YAGAMI CUP. PAIR FIGURE-SKATING COMPETITION."
IT LOOKS LIKE THEY'RE DOING THE COMPETI-TION TODAY.
LET'S SEE... FIRST PRIZE IS ONE OF THE LATEST DESIGNS OF WASHING MACHINES.
BESIDES THAT THEY'VE GOT GAME MACHINES, BIKES... ALL OF THE PRIZES ARE PRETTY HIGH QUALITY!
REALLY? THEY DO THINGS LIKE THIS IN OUR TOWN?
YEAH. FIGURE SKATING IS REALLY POPULAR NOWADAYS.
HM! IT IS A COM-BINATION CLOTHES WASHER AND DRYER!
YES. I WILL JOIN THIS CONTEST!

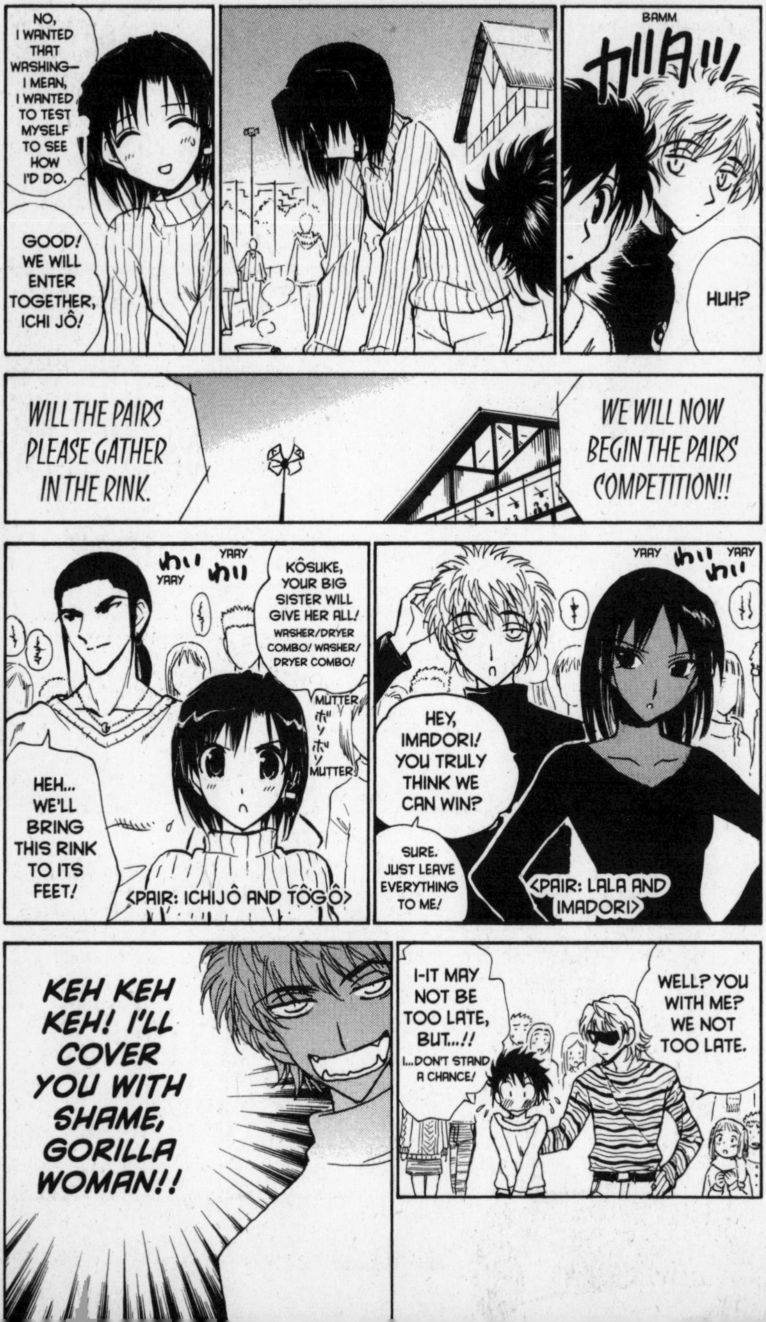
BAMM
HUH?
NO, I WANTED THAT WASHING— I MEAN, I WANTED TO TEST MYSELF TO SEE HOW I'D DO.
GOOD! WE WILL ENTER TOGETHER, ICHI JÔ!
WE WILL NOW BEGIN THE PAIRS COMPETITION!!
WILL THE PAIRS PLEASE GATHER IN THE RINK.
YAAY わい YAAY わい わい
HEY, IMADORI! YOU TRULY THINK WE CAN WIN?
SURE. JUST LEAVE EVERYTHING TO ME!
<PAIR: LALA AND IMADORI>
YAAY わい わい YAAY
KÔSUKE, YOUR BIG SISTER WILL GIVE HER ALL!
WASHER/DRYER COMBO! WASHER/DRYER COMBO!
MUTTER ボソ ボソ MUTTER
HEH... WE'LL BRING THIS RINK TO ITS FEET!
<PAIR: ICHIJÔ AND TÔGÔ>
WELL? YOU WITH ME? WE NOT TOO LATE.
I-IT MAY NOT BE TOO LATE, BUT...!!
I...DON'T STAND A CHANCE!
KEH KEH KEH! I'LL COVER YOU WITH SHAME, GORILLA WOMAN!!

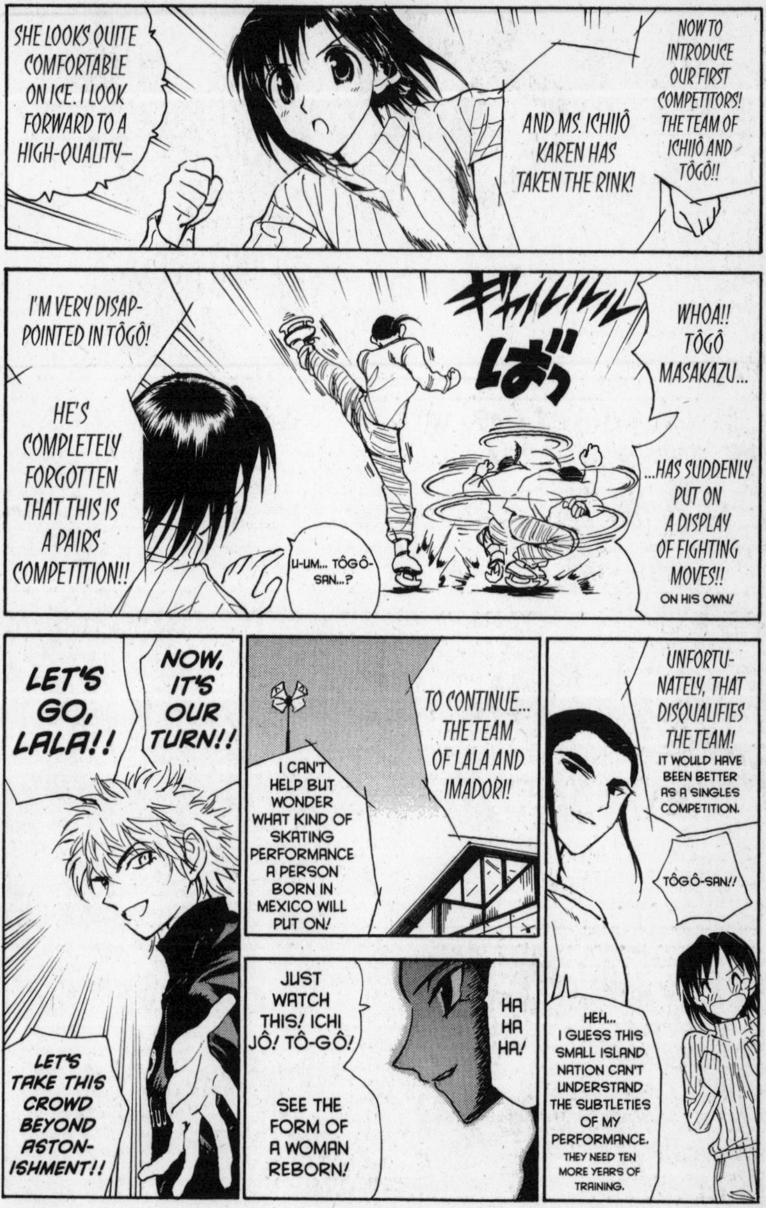
NOW TO INTRODUCE OUR FIRST COMPETITORS! THE TEAM OF ICHIJÔ AND TÔGÔ!!
AND MS. ICHIJÔ KAREN HAS TAKEN THE RINK!
SHE LOOKS QUITE COMFORTABLE ON ICE. I LOOK FORWARD TO A HIGH-QUALITY—
WHOA!! TÔGÔ MASAKAZU...
I'M VERY DISAP-POINTED IN TÔGÔ!
...HAS SUDDENLY PUT ON A DISPLAY OF FIGHTING MOVES!! ON HIS OWN!
HE'S COMPLETELY FORGOTTEN THAT THIS IS A PAIRS COMPETITION!!
U-UM... TÔGÔ-SAN...?
UNFORTU-NATELY, THAT DISQUALIFIES THE TEAM! IT WOULD HAVE BEEN BETTER AS A SINGLES COMPETITION.
TÔGÔ-SAN!!
HEH... I GUESS THIS SMALL ISLAND NATION CAN'T UNDERSTAND THE SUBTLETIES OF MY PERFORMANCE. THEY NEED TEN MORE YEARS OF TRAINING.
TO CONTINUE... THE TEAM OF LALA AND IMADORI!
I CAN'T HELP BUT WONDER WHAT KIND OF SKATING PERFORMANCE A PERSON BORN IN MEXICO WILL PUT ON!
HA HA HA!
JUST WATCH THIS! ICHI JÔ! TÔ-GÔ!
SEE THE FORM OF A WOMAN REBORN!
NOW, IT'S OUR TURN!!
LET'S GO, LALA!!
LET'S TAKE THIS CROWD BEYOND ASTON-ISHMENT!!

Often Said of Tôgô: Lone Wolf.

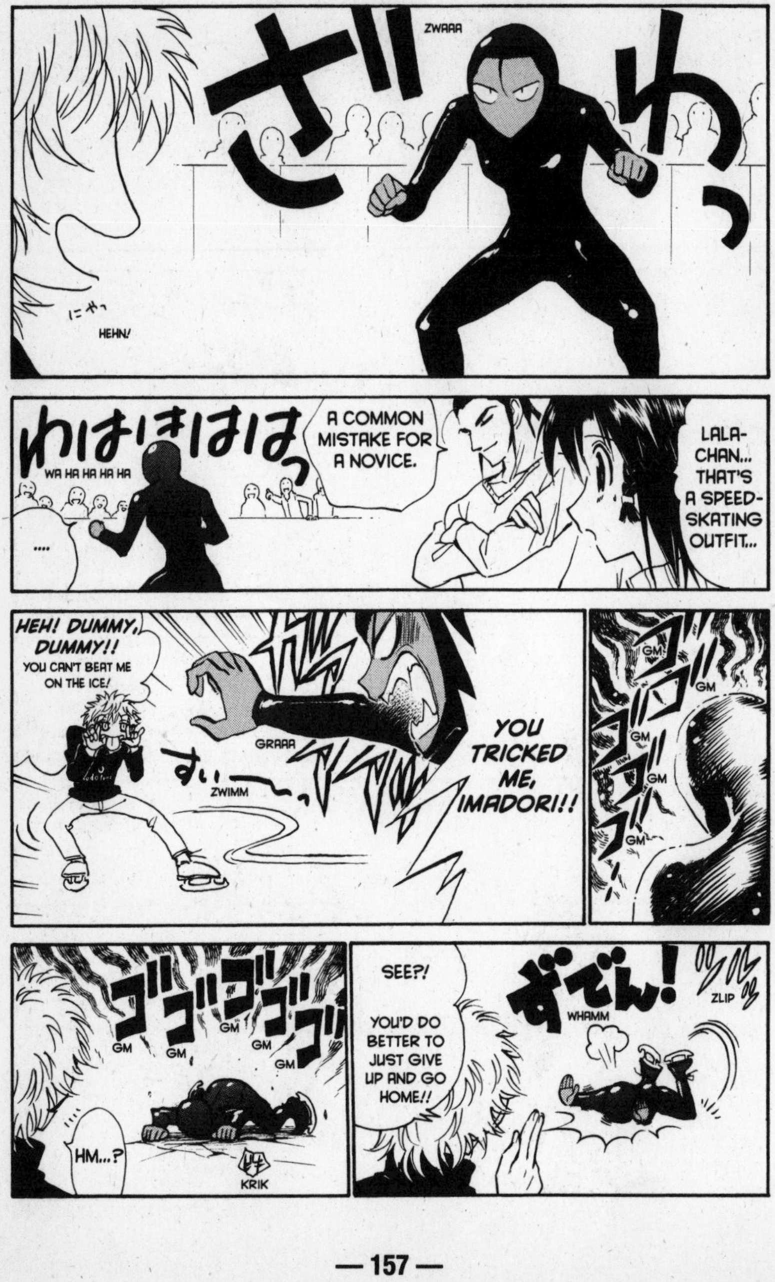
ざりゅっ
ZWAAA
にやっ
HEHN!
LALA-CHAN... THAT'S A SPEED-SKATING OUTFIT...
A COMMON MISTAKE FOR A NOVICE.
わはははは
WA HA HA HA HA
....
ゴゴゴゴ
GM GM GM GM GM
HEH! DUMMY, DUMMY!!
YOU CAN'T BEAT ME ON THE ICE!
GRAAA
YOU TRICKED ME, IMADORI!!
すいーっ
ZWIMM
ZLIP
ずでん!
WHAMM
SEE?!
YOU'D DO BETTER TO JUST GIVE UP AND GO HOME!!
ゴゴゴゴゴ
GM GM GM GM GM
HM...?
KRIK

And He Goes Round and Round as if He Were in a Washing Machine.

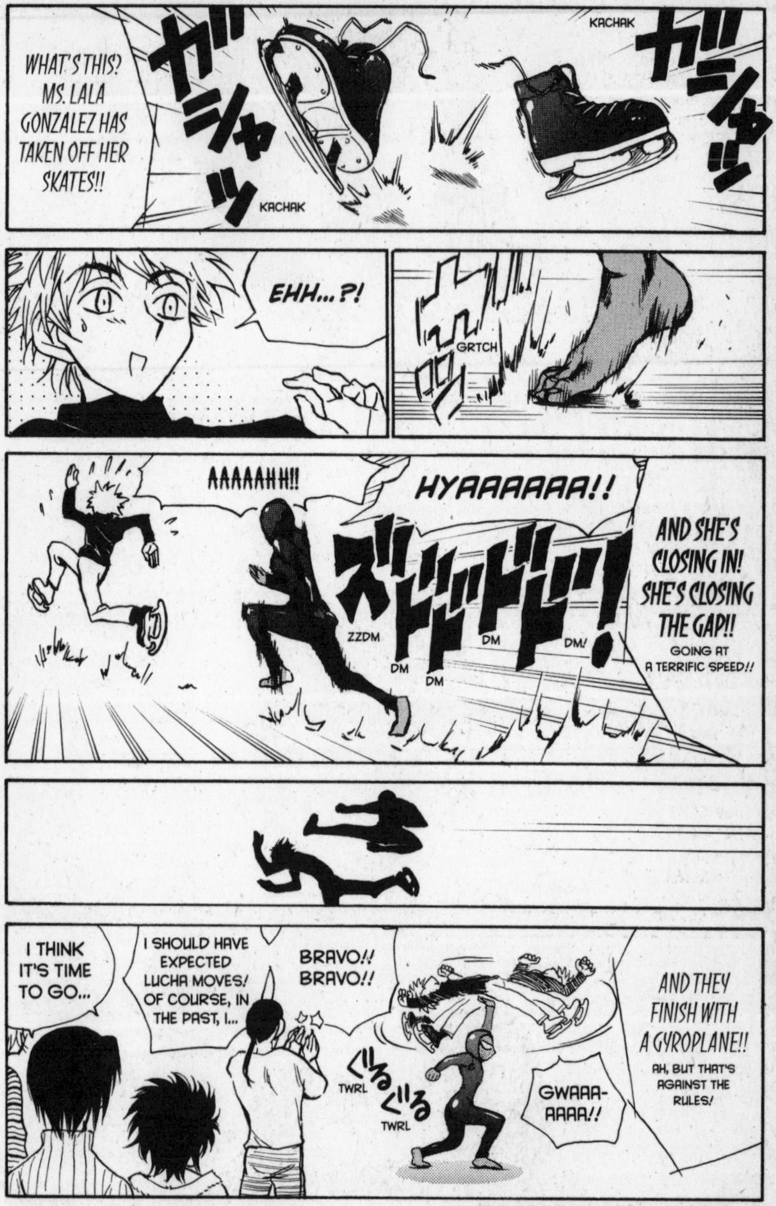
KACHAK
ガシャッ
WHAT'S THIS? MS. LALA GONZALEZ HAS TAKEN OFF HER SKATES!!
ガシャッ
KACHAK
GRTCH
EHH...?!
AND SHE'S CLOSING IN! SHE'S CLOSING THE GAP!!
GOING AT A TERRIFIC SPEED!!
HYAAAAAAA!!
ズドドドド!
DM!
DM
DM
DM
ZZDM
AAAAAHH!!
AND THEY FINISH WITH A GYROPLANE!!
AH, BUT THAT'S AGAINST THE RULES!
GWAAA-AAAA!!
ぐるぐる
TWRL
TWRL
BRAVO!! BRAVO!!
I SHOULD HAVE EXPECTED LUCHA MOVES! OF COURSE, IN THE PAST, I...
I THINK IT'S TIME TO GO...

[TO BE CONTINUED IN VOLUME 14]

BONUS RUMBLE

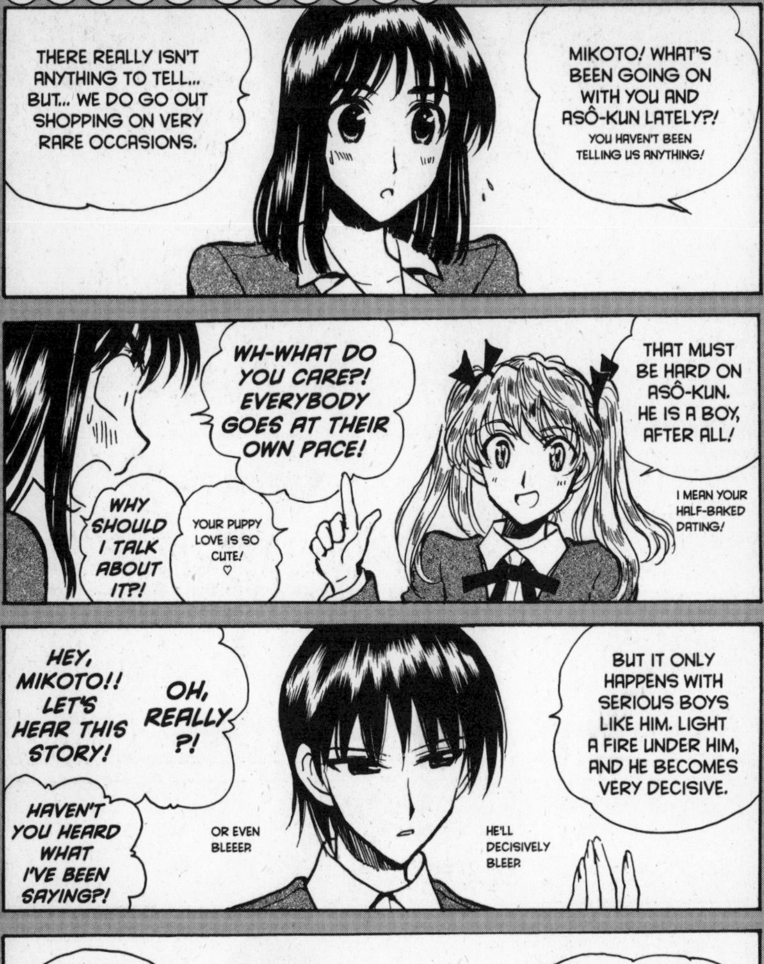
MIKOTO! WHAT'S BEEN GOING ON WITH YOU AND ASÔ-KUN LATELY?! YOU HAVEN'T BEEN TELLING US ANYTHING!
THERE REALLY ISN'T ANYTHING TO TELL... BUT... WE DO GO OUT SHOPPING ON VERY RARE OCCASIONS.
THAT MUST BE HARD ON ASÔ-KUN. HE IS A BOY, AFTER ALL!
I MEAN YOUR HALF-BAKED DATING!
WH-WHAT DO YOU CARE?! EVERYBODY GOES AT THEIR OWN PACE!
YOUR PUPPY LOVE IS SO CUTE! ♡
WHY SHOULD I TALK ABOUT IT?!
BUT IT ONLY HAPPENS WITH SERIOUS BOYS LIKE HIM. LIGHT A FIRE UNDER HIM, AND HE BECOMES VERY DECISIVE.
HE'LL DECISIVELY BLEER
OR EVEN BLEEER
OH, REALLY?!
HEY, MIKOTO!! LET'S HEAR THIS STORY!
HAVEN'T YOU HEARD WHAT I'VE BEEN SAYING?!
YOU KNOW ASÔ-KUN! HE'LL NEVER SHOW YOU THE DIRTY THOUGHTS HE'S THINKING.
....
I'M BEGINNING TO FEEL PRETTY SORRY FOR ASÔ-KUN.

SPECIALLY DRAWN FOR THIS VOLUME.

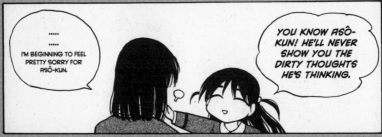

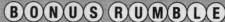

BONUS RUMBLE

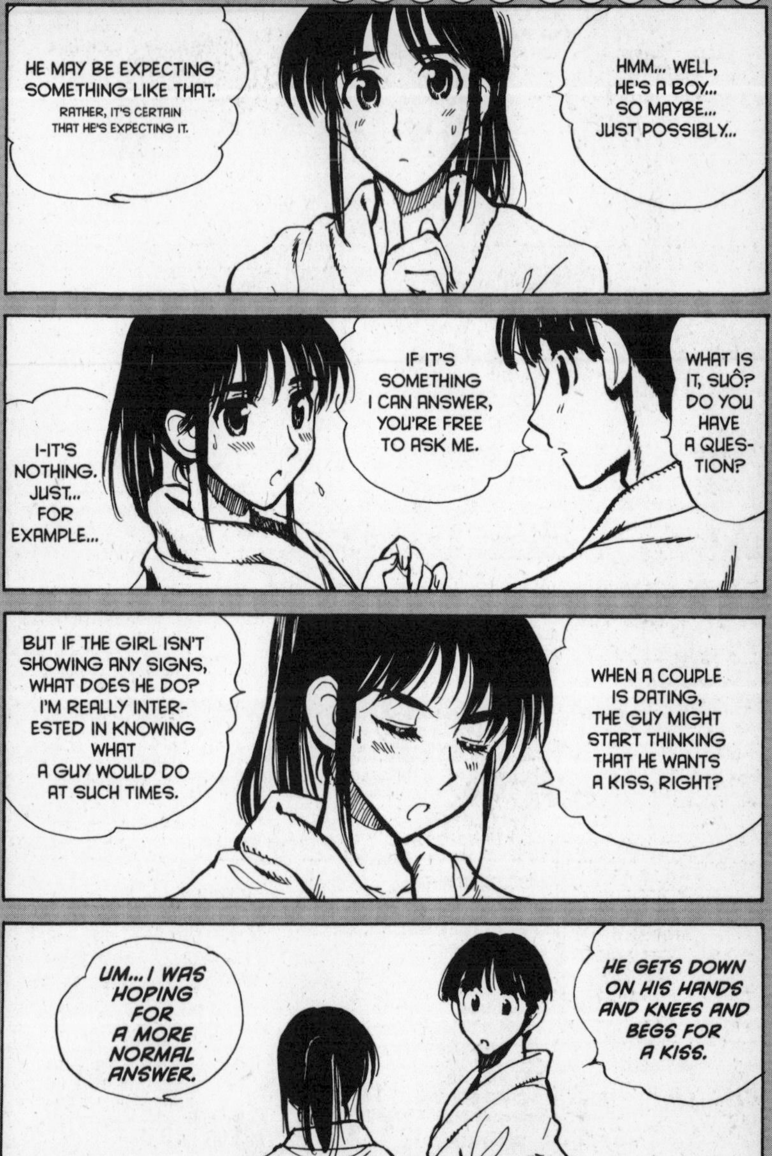
HMM... WELL, HE'S A BOY... SO MAYBE... JUST POSSIBLY...
HE MAY BE EXPECTING SOMETHING LIKE THAT.
RATHER, IT'S CERTAIN THAT HE'S EXPECTING IT.
WHAT IS IT, SUÔ? DO YOU HAVE A QUES-TION?
IF IT'S SOMETHING I CAN ANSWER, YOU'RE FREE TO ASK ME.
I-IT'S NOTHING. JUST... FOR EXAMPLE...
WHEN A COUPLE IS DATING, THE GUY MIGHT START THINKING THAT HE WANTS A KISS, RIGHT?
BUT IF THE GIRL ISN'T SHOWING ANY SIGNS, WHAT DOES HE DO? I'M REALLY INTER-ESTED IN KNOWING WHAT A GUY WOULD DO AT SUCH TIMES.
HE GETS DOWN ON HIS HANDS AND KNEES AND BEGS FOR A KISS.
UM... I WAS HOPING FOR A MORE NORMAL ANSWER.

BONUS RUMBLE

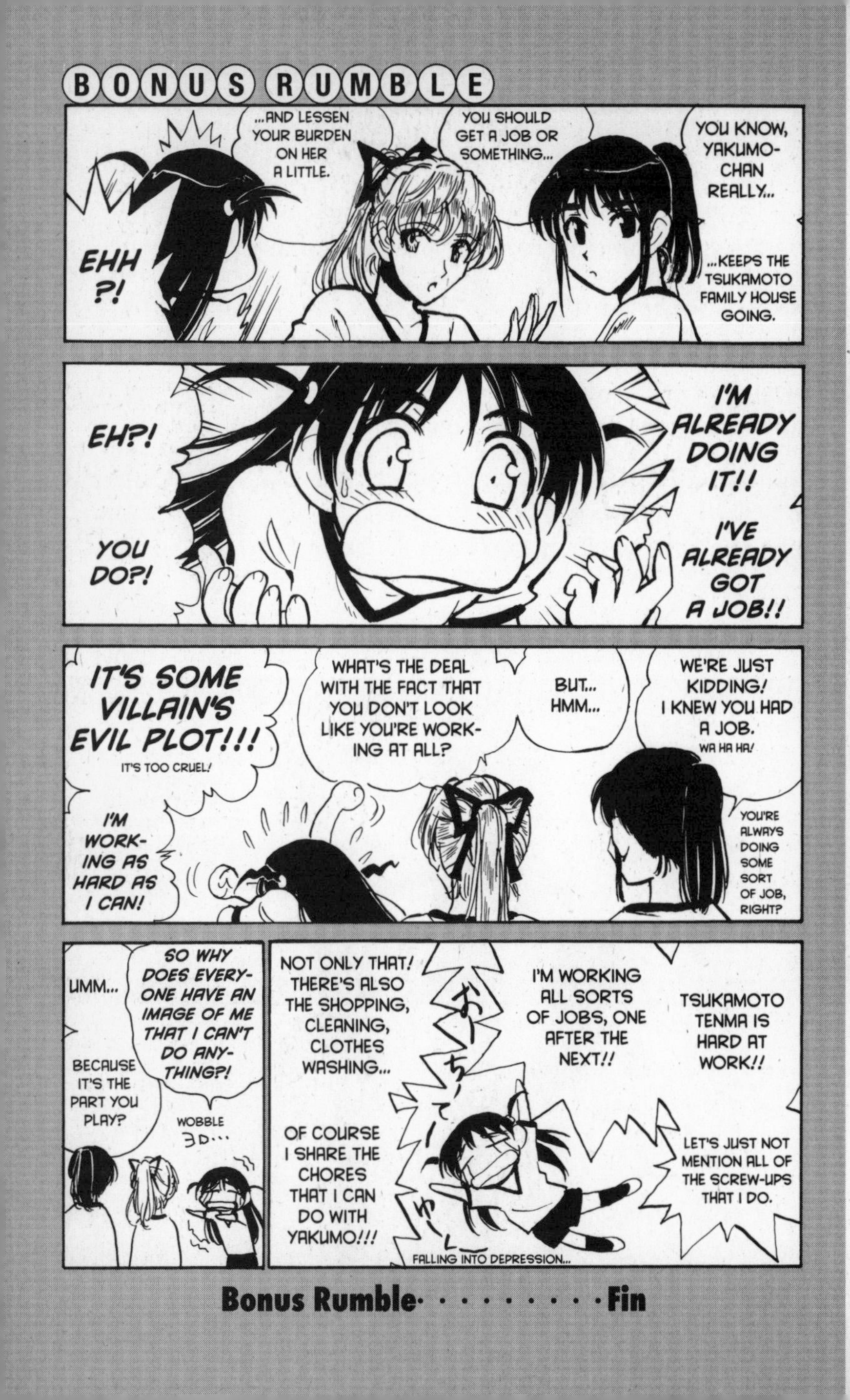

YOU KNOW, YAKUMO-CHAN REALLY...
...KEEPS THE TSUKAMOTO FAMILY HOUSE GOING.
YOU SHOULD GET A JOB OR SOMETHING...
...AND LESSEN YOUR BURDEN ON HER A LITTLE.
EHH ?!
I'M ALREADY DOING IT!!
I'VE ALREADY GOT A JOB!!
EH?!
YOU DO?!
WE'RE JUST KIDDING! I KNEW YOU HAD A JOB.
WA HA HA!
YOU'RE ALWAYS DOING SOME SORT OF JOB, RIGHT?
BUT... HMM...
WHAT'S THE DEAL WITH THE FACT THAT YOU DON'T LOOK LIKE YOU'RE WORKING AT ALL?
IT'S SOME VILLAIN'S EVIL PLOT!!!
IT'S TOO CRUEL!
I'M WORKING AS HARD AS I CAN!
TSUKAMOTO TENMA IS HARD AT WORK!!
I'M WORKING ALL SORTS OF JOBS, ONE AFTER THE NEXT!!
NOT ONLY THAT! THERE'S ALSO THE SHOPPING, CLEANING, CLOTHES WASHING...
LET'S JUST NOT MENTION ALL OF THE SCREW-UPS THAT I DO.
OF COURSE I SHARE THE CHORES THAT I CAN DO WITH YAKUMO!!!
FALLING INTO DEPRESSION...
SO WHY DOES EVERYONE HAVE AN IMAGE OF ME THAT I CAN'T DO ANYTHING?!
UMM...
BECAUSE IT'S THE PART YOU PLAY?
WOBBLE
ヨロ…

Bonus Rumble· · · · · · · · ·Fin

About the Creator

Jin Kobayashi was born in Tokyo. *School Rumble* is his first manga series. He has answered these questions from his fans:

What is your hobby?
Basketball

Which manga inspired you to become a creator?
Dragon Ball

Which character in your manga do you like best?
Kenji Harima

What type of manga do you want to create in the future?
Action

Name one book, piece of music, or movie you like.
The Indiana Jones series

Translation Notes

Japanese is a tricky language for most Westerners, and translation is often more art than science. For your edification and reading pleasure, here are notes on some of the places where we could have gone in a different direction in our translation of the work, or where a Japanese cultural reference is used.

Omiai marriage meeting, page 3

Although love marriages have been making great strides in popularity, arranged marriages are still a large part of Japanese culture. The two prospective candidates meet each other, usually surrounded by family and go-betweens, and have a short conversation regarding such topics as school and work history and hobbies. Either candidate has the option to refuse. Arranged marriages are considered "safer" than love marriages—less prone to divorce—since both families are invested in making sure the marriage works.

Kagemusha, page 3

As fans of Kurosawa movies know, a *kagemusha* is a look-alike for a feudal lord and a decoy for assassins.

What are your hobbies? page 3

As mentioned above, this is one of the standard questions asked during an *omiai*. Asking about one's hobbies is so routine, it is almost a cliché.

Eri-san, page 6

Although in most families parents drop the honorifics to show intimacy, there are all sorts of familial relationships in Japan, and all sorts of ways honorifics can be used within a family. Rich or traditionally high-born families may have different rules for the use of honorifics when addressing one another.

Phimosis, page 28

Um...it's a man thing. This is a family-friendly manga, okay? If you really need to know, then look it up. Sure, one survey reportedly put the percentage of phimosis at 50 percent of Japanese men. But Yoshidayama wasn't talking about it anyway. Forget it. Ahem.

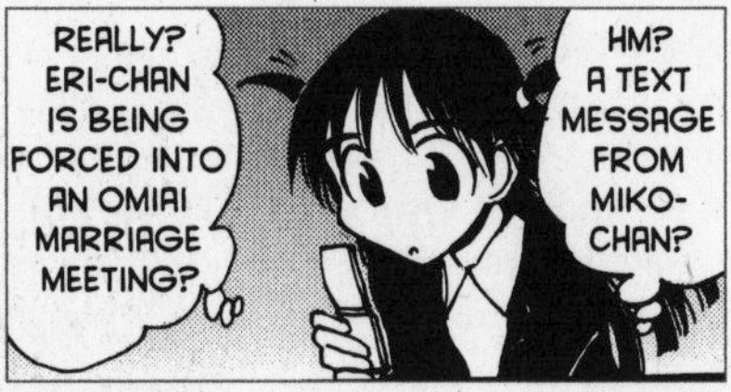
HM? A TEXT MESSAGE FROM MIKO-CHAN?
REALLY? ERI-CHAN IS BEING FORCED INTO AN OMIAI MARRIAGE MEETING?

Dasu, page 31

Many types of sentence-ending words or sounds can illustrate one's character. Nishimoto Ganji's "-dasu" is just one of those sounds. It has no particular meaning.

Bambinas, page 36

Yes, he said "bambinas" in the Japanese version, too.

Emperor Penguins, page 43

Takano is talking, of course, about the sixty five-day brooding period during which male emperor penguins stand on the frozen ice-pack, keeping their eggs warm and eating nothing while the female is off in the sea finding food. The female then brings back the food to regurgitate for the newly hatched chicks.

Young Gama, Pin-up Idols, page 62

There is a type of *seinen* (young men's) manga magazine called "Young," such as *Young Magazine* and *Young Sunday*. These run more risqué *seinen* manga and feature photo collections of pin-up idols in various stages of undress.

Jingle Bells, White Christmas, page 73

These Western holiday traditions are also familiar to the Japanese.

First Dream of the Year, page 87

One's first dream of the new year is said to be prophetic. The three best things to dream about are (in order) Mt. Fuji, a hawk, and an eggplant. Any of these symbols are said to bring good fortune for the year.

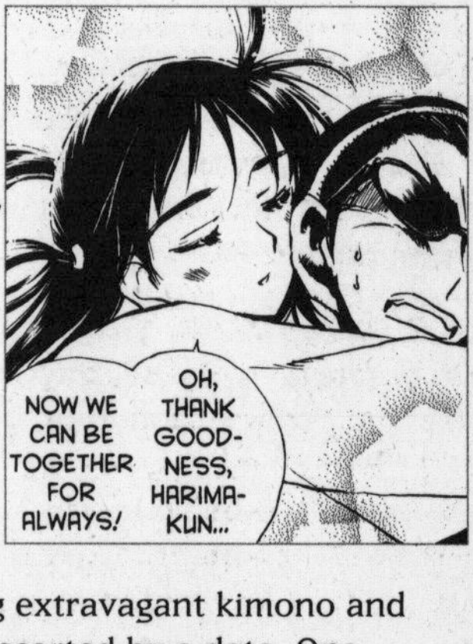
OH, THANK GOOD- NESS, HARIMA- KUN...
NOW WE CAN BE TOGETHER FOR ALWAYS!

New Year's Observances, page 87

One of the few widely followed religious observances in Japan is a New Year's visit to a temple or shrine (usually several of each). Some make an event of it, wearing extravagant kimono and arriving at the tolling of the midnight bell escorted by a date. One throws a coin into the offering box, makes a quick prayer that may include a wish, and then goes on to other New Year's festivities.

Congratulations, page 87

The standard greeting on the new year is *akemashite omedetô gozaimasu*, or "Congratulations on seeing in the New Year." This is said when one first meets someone after the clock strikes midnight on New Year's Eve. The phrase is usually followed by *kotoshi mo yoroshiku onegaishimasu*, "Please look well on me this year, too." I translated the follow-up phrase as, "Let's make the best of this year, too," which is a little closer to the intent. (Before the clock strikes midnight on New Year's, the greeting is *yoi o-toshi o*, which means "Have a good year.")

Shishi-mai, page 91

The Shishi-mai Lion Dance is an ancient Chinese import, but like most imports has been adapted to Japanese tastes. Originally a prayer for household safety and good harvest, it is now performed as a good-luck charm as a part of the New Year's festivities. The dance varies, depending on the region. Variations include one- and two-man lions, and dances with more than one lion.

Clothing Stores on New Year's, page 95

There are especially extravagant holiday sales at most department stores, so the first days of the new year are big shopping days.

New Year's Kite Flying, page 99

New Year's doesn't seem to be the ideal time for kite flying, but Japan has not always used the Western calendar for New Year's. The original Japanese calendar was a lunar calendar, and the new year fell at the start of springtime (when flying kites would be more appropriate). But kite flying has remained a New Year's tradition throughout the centuries. Kites are thought to have come to Japan toward the end of the seventh century, and in Buddhism they symbolize a way of giving thanks.

Battling Kites, page 100

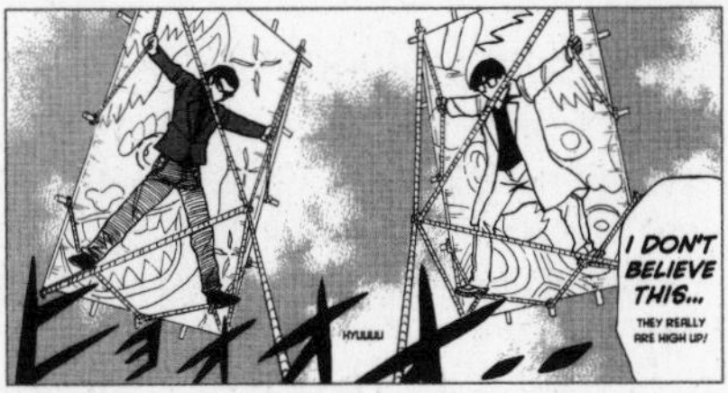
I DON'T BELIEVE THIS...
THEY REALLY ARE HIGH UP!
HYUUUU

Battle kites are of a strikingly different construction than other Japanese kites, so they are thought to be an import. The most prominent theory is that they are derived from the Indian fighter kite introduced to the Japanese by foreigners at Nagasaki, the only port open to foreign visitors during the Edo period.

Hundred Verses Collection, page 103

Also called *karute* ("carte" or "cards"), this is a popular indoor game played on New Year's. Each of the cards contains a poem from the *Hyakunin-isshu* (Hundred Verses Collection), a famous collection of *waka* poems. It is played pretty much as Ichijô describes it, except not usually as a contact sport.

The Priest Ne Yoshi Tada Poem, page 103

This is said to be a tenth-century poem that compares the course of true love with the perils of boatmen on a stormy sea.

Hagoita (Battledore and Shuttlecock), page 104

Another rite of the spring new year (see the kite flying note above) that was kept even after the New Year's date was moved to coincide with the Western calendar. Actually Hagoita, as a game, isn't all that popular, but the paddles with their elaborately decorated backs have become a popular collector's item. They have become a traditional gift on the birth of a baby girl.

The Beatles, page 109

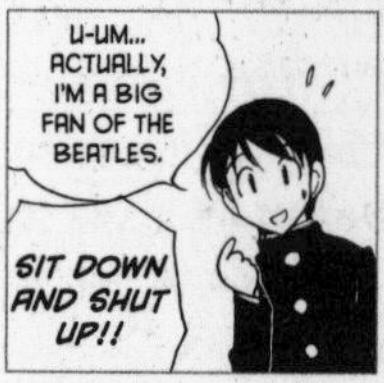
U-UM... ACTUALLY, I'M A BIG FAN OF THE BEATLES.
SIT DOWN AND SHUT UP!!

The Beatles were nearly as popular in Japan as they were in English-speaking nations. Most karaoke establishments will have very few English-language songs, but their repertoire will include the more popular Beatles tunes.

Warring-States period, Oda Nobunaga, page 114

During the warring-states period of Japanese history (1467-1573), many charismatic leaders vied to become the shogun of all Japan. The Ashikaga shoguns fell to their own internal divisions, leaving the country open to any warrior who could take it. The one who finally did was Oda Nobunaga. Although he forcibly brought Japan under his rule, thus ending the warring-states period, he never gained full control of all parts of the nation as Tokugawa did some twenty years later.

Takeda, page 114

Takeda Shingen was one of Oda Nobunaga's rivals during the warring-states period. He was a fierce warrior of ruthless ambition but also a good administrator, who, unlike many other lords of the period, had the support of the working classes in his home area.

Guan Xing, page 114

This is a play on words. *Kankô* is the word for "tourism," but a soundalike name, also pronounced *kankô*, is the Japanese pronunciation of Guan Xing, an officer and warrior for the Kingdom of Shu in the Chinese epic, *The Romance of the Three Kingdoms*. I tried to keep the pun related as closely to Guan Xing as possible.

Saitô Dôsan, Serpent, page 115

Dôsan was reported to have "stolen a state" to become head of the Saitô clan during the warring-states period. He married his daughter to Oda Nobunaga to cement an alliance, but he was defeated and killed by his own son, Saitô Yoshiatsu, in 1556. He was known as the "Serpent of Mino" because of his ruthlessness.

Toyotomi Hideyoshi, Date Masamune, page 115

Toyotomi Hideyoshi ruled Japan in the aftermath of Oda Nobunaga's death. He consolidated power to such an extent that he went on to invade Korea. He fell ill and died in 1599, leaving a son too young to take power and succeed him. One of his field commanders was Date Masamune, who had ambitions of his own before Hideyoshi took him into service. Date Masamune went on to a high rank in Tokugawa's power structure at the beginning of the Edo period.

Uesugi, page 115

Uesugi Kenshin, the "Dragon of Echigo," was a rival of Oda Nobunaga and Takeda Shingen. Many of his followers believed he was Bishamonten, the Japanese god of war.

Asai, page 116

Asai Nagamasa married the sister of Oda Nobunaga, but when Nobunaga broke his word and invaded the region of Echizen, Asai allied himself with the Asakura clan of Echizen, fought Nobunaga, and was defeated. He tried to ally himself with Takeda Shingen but again was defeated, and he ended up taking his own life.

Isenokami Hidetsuna, Ittôsai, page 118

Aside from founding the Shin-Kage-Ryû school of fencing, Hidetsuna also declined an offer to become Takeda Shingen's vassal. He did, however, change his name from Hidetsuna to Nobutsuna to honor Shingen (whose original name was Harunobu). Ittôsai Ito was a swordmaster of the late warring-states period. He formed the Ittô-Ryû one-cut school of swordsmanship, and is said to have survived thirty-three individual combats in his travels throughout Japan without losing once.

Going to Tokyo, page 119

If one wants to get ahead in life, one must move from the rural areas to an urban center, the biggest of which is Tokyo. Going from the boondocks to the big city is a common theme throughout the world, but it has reached new heights of cliché in Japan.

Aomori, page 120

The prefecture at the northernmost tip of the main island of Honshu, Aomori is known for being a faraway, rural province.

Grew up together, page 125

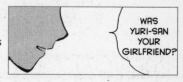

WAS YURI-SAN YOUR GIRLFRIEND?

Being *osananajimi*, or "childhood friends," is a very romantic notion. It is often assumed that close male/female friends will marry someday.

Izakaya, page 128

Izakaya are a cross between a restaurant and a pub. As the *zaka* part of the word—the same kanji used for sake ("rice wine")—indicates, they serve all kinds of spirits, but they also provide a wide variety of snacks and meals. *Izakaya* tend to be lively, noisy places.

Conte D'hiver (A Tale of Winter), page 143

The second of director Eric Rohmer's Four Seasons cycle of movies, which includes *Conte de Printemps (A Tale of Springtime)* in 1990, *Conte D'hiver (A Tale of Winter)* in 1992, *Conte D'été (Summer's Tale)* in 1996, and *Conte D'automne (Autumn Tale)* in 1998.

Ina Bauer, page 153

After the 2006 Winter Olympics, the Ina Bauer became the most famous figure-skating move in Japan. The Japanese had high hopes for medals that year, but until the figure skating finals, Japan had not achieved even one gold. In the women's finals, Shizuka Arakawa was in third place after the short program, behind Sasha Cohen and Irena Slutskaya. In the freestyle, Cohen and Slutskaya both fell, but Arakawa performed a clean program. Her jumps were not outstanding, but her layback Ina Bauer became the signature element that won her Japan's only gold medal of the Turin Olympics. Afterwards, the term "Ina Bauer" was very much in vogue with the Japanese media.